Bruno Sammartino

THE AUTOBIOGRAPHY OF WRESTLING'S LIVING LEGEND

BY

BRUNO SAMMARTINO

WITH

Sal Anthony Corrente

Edited by Colin Bowman

The brutal WWWF match up between Bruno Sammartino and Baron Mikel Scicluna from March 11, 1966 at Madison Square Garden was captured by LeRoy Neiman

© Copyright 2019 Bruno Sammartino.

All rights reserved. Except for use in a review, the reproduction or utilization of this work in any form or by an electronic, mechanical or other means, now known or hereafter invented, including xerography, photocopying and recording, and in any information storage and retrieval system, is forbidden without written permission.

Printed in the United States

Wrestler
WRESTLING PROGRAM
CIVIC ARENA - FRI. JULY 24, 8:30 P.M.
Promoted by Spectator Sports, Inc.
WRESTLING PROGRAM
CIVIC ARENA - FRI. APR. 17 8:30 P.M.
Promoted by Spectator Sports, Inc.
WRESTLING PROGRAM
CIVIC ARENA - FRI. SEPT. 12, 8:30 P.M.
Promoted by Spectator Sports, Inc.
3 LUCKY NUMBERS ON PROGRAMS WIN 2 RING-SIDE TICKETS FOR THE NEXT ALL STAR WRESTLING CARD AT THE CIVIC ARENA FRI. OCT. 10th
Price 25c
The
BRUNO
COURSE
of
BODYBUILDING
by
BRUNO SAMMARTINO
World's Mightiest Developed Man and Strongest Athlete
WRESTLING PROGRAM
CIVIC ARENA - FRI. FEB. 12, 8:30 P.M.
Promoted by Spectator Sports, Inc.
WRESTLING PROGRAM
CIVIC ARENA - FRI. OCT. 10, 8:30 P.M.
Promoted by Spectator Sports, Inc.
IVAN KOLOFF
BRUNO SAMMARTINO
3 LUCKY NUMBERS ON PROGRAMS WIN 2 RING-SIDE TICKETS FOR THE NEXT ALL STAR WRESTLING CARD AT THE CIVIC ARENA FRI. NOV. 14th
3 LUCKY NUMBERS ON PROGRAMS WIN 2 RING-SIDE TICKETS FOR THE NEXT ALL STAR WRESTLING CARD AT THE CIVIC ARENA FRI. JULY 24th

Contents

A Message from Sal Corrente ix
About Sal Corrente.. xvii
About the Editor xix
Dedication xxiii
Acknowledgments xxv
Foreword.. xxvii
Welcome xxxiii

My Early Years in Italy... 37
Coming to America.. 49
Earning a Living.. 63
My Professional Career Begins... 89
Unraveling the Mystery 97
The Match of my Life 113
Going Back Home 127
Remembering the Great Ones 139
Losing, Winning, and Learning.. 159
The Beat Goes On 185
Life After Wrestling 203
The Winds of Change 221
Looking Back 229
Final Thoughts, Final Shots... 255

Photo Gallery 279

Retirement ... Again 397

Tributes 417
Man. Icon. Legend. Friend by Bill Apter. 419
Sal Corrente 423
Davey O'Hannon..435
Larry Zbyszko 439
Tito Santana..447
Honky Tonk Man 451
Mick Foley 455
Jimmy Hart..459
Larry Richert..463
James J. Dillon 475
Michael Bochicchio 479
Blackjack Brown...483
Stan Hansen 487
Dominic DeNucci...491
Gary Michael Cappetta 495
Afa "The Wild Samoan #1" Anoai 497
Remembering Bruno by Dr. Mike Lano 499

Obituary 504
Final Farewells...506

Away from the Spotlight by Mike Migut 515
Darryl Sammartino 533
Bruno and Carol Sammartino Foundation 536
Carol Sammartino..539

BRUNO! BRUNO! BRUNO! 541

The Ten-Bell Salute 567

"Throughout my career I wanted people to have a positive image of the World Wrestling Champion. Now when I hear the wonderful comments and positive things people say about me, it makes me feel good that I never did anything negative."

BRUNO SAMMARTINO
Wrestling's Living Legend

*This book was completed before Bruno passed away.
We were never in a rush to publish the book, because
if I am honest, I thought that we had forever.
I am comfortable telling these stories because Bruno
was finally comfortable with them being told.
It won't be the same without him. It hasn't been the same
without him, but here are many of the stories that people
who read the original book have been asking for. ~Sal*

A Message from Sal Corrente

My earliest memories of Bruno Sammartino were of him being attacked.

Nikolai Volkoff and his manager, "Classy" Freddie Blassie, were double-teaming Bruno on a World Wrestling Federation (WWF) TV show. It was the late '70s and Bruno was a broadcaster alongside Vince McMahon, Jr. while Blassie, a longtime Bruno opponent, was managing some of the most hated men in wrestling.

Bruno Sammartino and Sal Corrente

Blassie had claimed over and over that Volkoff was stronger than Sammartino. After countless boasts by Blassie, Sammartino couldn't take it anymore—he challenged Volkoff to an arm wrestling match right then and there.

I was thrilled to finally see the "Living Legend" in a competition of some kind. I had read and heard many stories about Bruno, but because I had gotten such a late start as a wrestling fan, never had the opportunity to see him wrestle.

As Bruno started to take off his jacket, Blassie and Volkoff's demeanor quickly shifted from smug bravado to genuine concern. However, as Sammartino took off his jacket, the ever wily Blassie hit him in the face with his trademark cane.

Having gained the upper hand, Blassie and Volkoff then laid a beating on Sammartino, resulting in a match being signed shortly after. I vividly remember wanting to go to Madison Square Garden to see him get his hands on Volkoff, but I didn't get the chance.

Thank goodness for sportscaster Warner Wolf, who used to give pro wrestling results on WCBS-TV news. That night, I even got to see a film clip, in addition to learning that Bruno had taken care of Volkoff. I found out years later why this series of matches had taken place. In a discussion with Vince McMahon, Sr. Vince took the position that Nikolai Volkoff was no longer main event material. It was Bruno who knew that Nikolai could still be a viable opponent. He told Vince that he would "shoot a small angle" with Volkoff and Blassie on television. Once again Bruno was proven right as they sold out all the big clubs. In knowing Bruno, I am sure he was happy to help his long time friend prove he was still a monster heel that the fans would turn out to see get beaten up by their hero.

As time progressed and my love of the sport grew, I got to see Bruno wrestle at both Madison Square Garden and Shea Stadium. I also went to the Westchester County Center in White Plains, New York, to see him destroy Larry Zbyszko. Their feud had been legendary and it was another rabid packed house hoping to see their hero annihilate the arrogant Zbyszko. Recalling that night to Bruno, I told him that I had no idea how I could have gotten out of that building if a riot broke out. They must have broken every fire code in that building.

In the late '80s, I was lucky enough to get to know Bruno through phone conversations thanks to my friend Blackjack Brown. Before too long I met Bruno personally, and we've gotten along very well ever since. I speak to him often and have had the chance to travel and work with him. Bruno is a man of his word, highly credible—not only in life, but also the wrestling business, where that level of integrity is rare. For all his fame and achievements, Bruno Sammartino is a very humble man and someone whose handshake means more than most men's signature.

I am constantly amazed when people who don't know Bruno meet him for the first time, whether they've heard of him or not.

Sal Corrente, Bruno, and Jimmy Hart

One occasion I can recall was with my old tag team partner, "Carolina's Own" David Isley. Growing up in Charlotte, North Carolina, David was a huge wrestling fan—but as Bruno never wrestled in the Carolinas, he didn't have a chance to watch him live in the ring.

For years, David had looked forward to meeting Bruno someday. They always say never meet your heroes, but after David finally met the man who had accomplished so much in the business David loves, his opinion was that he had met a very classy and humble man (there isn't an ounce of arrogance in Bruno). David also stated that Bruno is to wrestling what the iconic Dallas Cowboys coach Tom Landry is to football.

Another friend of mine, longtime wrestling fan Paul Schaller, who was born in Michigan and raised in North Carolina but now lives in Arkansas, where he is the CEO of ABC Financial Services, got his chance to meet Bruno at the second "WrestleReunion" event that took place in Valley Forge, Pennsylvania. I've heard him say on many occasions since, that you can really feel the level of respect that people have for Bruno. He is revered like no other. I find that to be absolutely true. When you're with Bruno, you can tell you're in the presence of a special person.

Former AWA Vice President and co-founder (with Wally Karbo) of IWA Championship Wrestling, Rob Russen, born in Pennsylvania and currently residing in the Philippines, had this to say: "My feeling has always been that the closer you get to any star, the less it shines. But my theory does not hold true when it comes to Bruno Sammartino. He is every bit as much the star as a human being as he was as the 'Living Legend' in pro wrestling."

Bruno's journey, personality, and presence transcends the wrestling business. Cindy Morgan, the actress who famously played Lacey Underall in *Caddyshack*, got the chance to meet Bruno at a couple of autograph shows. I first let Cindy see a DVD interview that Bruno did for "WrestleReunion" where he talks about his life. Cindy is someone who had never heard of Bruno Sammartino, but she couldn't stop watching the DVD because she felt his story—part of which you will experience in this book—was so compelling. She really looked forward to meeting this man who had been through and achieved so much. I bet that other than myself and my longtime friend Mick Foley (a big fan of Cindy's), the only other wrestler she can and does consider a friend is Bruno.

These separate opinions from different types of people are echoed many times throughout the country and around the world. If you had the opportunity to meet Bruno at a public appearance, it will be one of those moments you will hold on to for a lifetime. He never wanted a fan to feel like it wasn't worth their time or money to meet him.

I have heard many fans give their recollections of Bruno and talk about the impact he had on their lives. It is fascinating, but not very surprising. To be in the presence of Bruno Sammartino is to be in the presence of a unique and special individual who came from nothing and rose to the top of his profession.

All of which is why I felt it was so necessary to get his book back into print and available to the world.

BRUNO SAMMARTINO
"Muscles"

Steak is his favorite dish,
And to be a wrestler is his wish.

Bruno's yearbook photo, Schenley Class of 1955

Bruno's autobiography is far more than the story of a wrestler. It is a story of a young boy who grew into a man and the adversity he faced along the way. It's a story that should inspire everyone who reads this book to feel that their dreams are achievable.

In the pages of this book you will hear about the support of a mother who sacrificed everything for her family and the strength of a wife who was true to her man and raised a family while having to share that man with the world.

This book will tell you about a family that went through many trials and tribulations, frequently facing financial adversity while trying to live the American dream. You'll meet a young boy who finally escaped to the land he thought had streets paved in gold—a boy who epitomized the skinny weakling in the Charles Atlas bodybuilding ads who got sand kicked in his face.

You'll have the chance to think about how you would have reacted to learning a new language in a strange place while being regularly attacked by your schoolmates. You'll discover the steps that Bruno took to overcome the barriers presented to him—and the challenge of adjusting to a life with a father he waited 14 years to meet.

Bruno at the 2012 Professional Wrestling Hall of Fame banquet. He had been inducted in 2002

This is the story of a young adult who grew into a man who worked hard to become a hero to the Italian people (he was known as the "Italian Superman"). You'll read how he sacrificed every day of his adult life and professional career to entertain fans—earning the name given to him by the fans, "The Living Legend" while remaining humble every step of the way.

You'll follow the journey from when Frank Tunney gave Bruno the opportunity to save a company and to make his own name, and discover how Bruno got the opportunity to become World Wide

Wrestling Federation (WWWF) champion, after being run out of the company the first time, and why he had to come back and win the title again. Just as Yankee Stadium was known as the House that Ruth Built, the WWWF (predecessor to the WWE) should be known as the Company that Sammartino Saved.

Bruno headlined arenas around the world for many years, constantly in demand by promoters outside of the WWWF. He's a man who has earned his rightful place alongside such '60s sports greats as Mickey Mantle and Willie Mays.

Many wrestling books have been written in the years since this book was first published, but again: This is not a wrestling book. This is a story of a family that truly lived through hell—and survived with the weakest of the bunch making his mark in the world by becoming the most successful pro wrestler of his era and the single greatest live attraction month after month, year after year.

Remember, in Bruno's day there were no pay-per-view broadcasts, souvenir T-shirts, or the plethora of merchandise that would help a wrestler make money. There was just one thing: screaming, cheering fans, packing buildings to chant his name—"Bruno! Bruno! Bruno!"

Hollywood writers get paid a lot of money to create a story like this, but this story has no one punching up the script, only real people living a real-life drama.

I suggest that you read the book when you have some time to devote to it, because it will be hard for you to put it down and even harder for you to forget after you read it. It will leave you sure of one thing though: that all things are possible no matter who you are or where you come from.

You'll realize that we all have some type of hero and "Living Legend" inside of us and that dreams are yours to follow.

It has been many years since this book was first released. Much has happened in Bruno Sammartino's life since 1990 and it is my pleasure to publish this updated version. I hope you enjoy this book and I look forward to your feedback.

Sal "The Big Cheese" Corrente
SammartinoBook@aol.com

TRI - STATE WRESTLING

HOLDER OF WORLD-WIDE

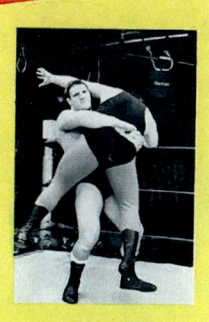

WRESTLING FEDERATION CHAMPIONSHIP

CHAMPION BRUNO SAMMARTINO

Bruno and Sal: November 2008

About Sal Corrente

Born and raised in Yonkers, New York, "The Big Cheese" Sal Corrente started his quest to become a part of the wrestling business in 1981. His break came thanks to an opportunity given to him by Anthony Attanasio, Mike D'Avanzo, Dominick Marcello, and three-time WWF World Tag Team Champions: Afa "The Wild Samoan #1" Anoai and his brother Sika "The Wild Samoan #2".

Sal Corrente

Over the years, Sal has worn many hats: promoter; referee; manager; and finally he became a wrestler (he has yet to hang up his stripes or boots). He met Bruno Sammartino almost 20 years ago and has forged a close friendship with the "Living Legend."

Sal has worked with Bruno at a consulting level and as a booking agent. He considers it an honor to work with Bruno and a necessity to bring this book back into print. He has always considered Bruno Sammartino to be the Babe Ruth of professional wrestling.

Sal currently resides in South Florida.

Colin Bowman with Bruno at WrestleReunion

About the Editor

A lifelong wrestling fan, Colin Bowman achieved his dream of publishing *World Championship Wrestling Magazine* in 1994.

Having grown up in the UK watching Mick McManus, Jackie Pallo, and Kendo Nagasaki to name a few, he discovered American wrestling when his favorite, "Exotic" Adrian Street moved to the states in the 80s and he followed his career through imported wrestling magazines. This expanded wrestling universe intensified his interest in the sport. He started a wrestling merchandise company, and began distributing *Pro Wrestling Illustrated Weekly* in the UK, which eventually led him to become a UK correspondent and photographer, working on the first WCW tour in 1991. Several tours and events were covered for WCW, PWI, and several European publications. Before WCW Magazine, he was the Editor of *Wrestling Big Shots* and co-founder of *Power Slam Magazine.*

In 1996, he met Bruno for the first time while covering WCW's live tour of the North East. Bruno was the special referee for a series of matches between Randy Savage and Ric Flair.

Following WCW, Colin teamed up with his longtime mentor Jimmy Hart at the XWF, Wrestlicious, and WWL. Colin met Sal Corrente during the production of the *6:05—The Reunion* PPV, and although Colin couldn't turn back time and book a match up between former NWA Champion Dory Funk, Jr and the Living Legend Bruno Sammartino, he did bring them together in a match for the first time ever with Bruno managing Dory and his partner Mike Graham. A fitting tribute to wrestlers from the pre-Attitude era of wrestling who built the sport into the behemoth it is today.

From 2006 onwards, Colin worked with Sal on all the WrestleReunion events as well as the Hulk Hogan vs. The Giant match in Memphis, TN.

Of all the superstars Colin has worked with and met, Bruno Sammartino is the standout. A true gentleman, who exuded modesty, patience, and integrity, with nothing ever being too much trouble when it came to the fans.

When asked about Bruno, Colin says, "We will never see his like again. To quote the final frame from the 6:05 PPV 'Championship belts are won and lost, but Legends are forever'."

Colin currently resides in Orlando, Florida.

Dory Funk, Jr held the NWA World Championship from 1969-1973 while Bruno was WWWF Champion from 1963-1971 and 1973-1987. They appeared together on the WWL PPV 6:05-The Reunion in 2006

Bruno, "Exotic" Adrian Street, and "Cowboy" Bill Watts

Emilia Sammartino

Dedication

This book is dedicated with all of my love to my mom

Bruno Sammartino with his mother Emilia Sammartino

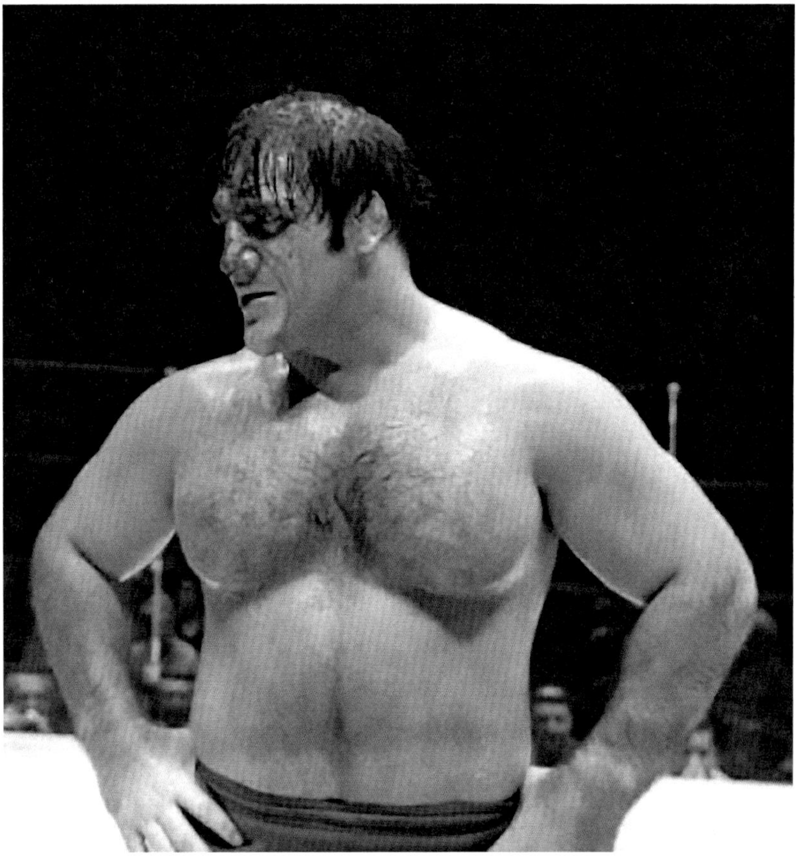

Acknowledgments

The author and publisher gratefully acknowledge the following individuals and companies for their assistance.

Frank Amato, Don Antal, Margie Antal, Bill Apter, Colin Bowman, Eric Caiden, Bill Cardille, Debra Ciarelli, Christine Coons, Civic Arena Corporation, Bob Conley, Mike D'Avanzo, Frank Diaz, Lynne Dyer, Rita Eisenstein, Anthony Fratantoni, Getty Images, Highspots.com, Hollywood Book & Poster, Hollywood Collectibles Group, Pat Jefferies, Ken "Lord Zoltan" Jugan, Kappa Publishing Group, Joe Katrencik, Mike Lano, Phil Levine, Stu Leviton, Pete Lederberg, Georgiann Makropoulos, Dominick Marcello, Paul McCollough, Bob Michelucci, Diana Michelucci, Lenny Mitchel, Brad Morris, Bob Mulrenin, George Napolitano, National Wrestling Alliance (NWA), Bill Otten, Craig Peters, Pro Wrestling Illustrated, Pittsburgh Post-Gazette, Tom Rooney, Stu Saks, Carol Sammartino and the Sammartino Family, Pete Schappert, Jim Shafer, Brian Thompson, Time Magazine, World Wrestling Entertainment (WWE).

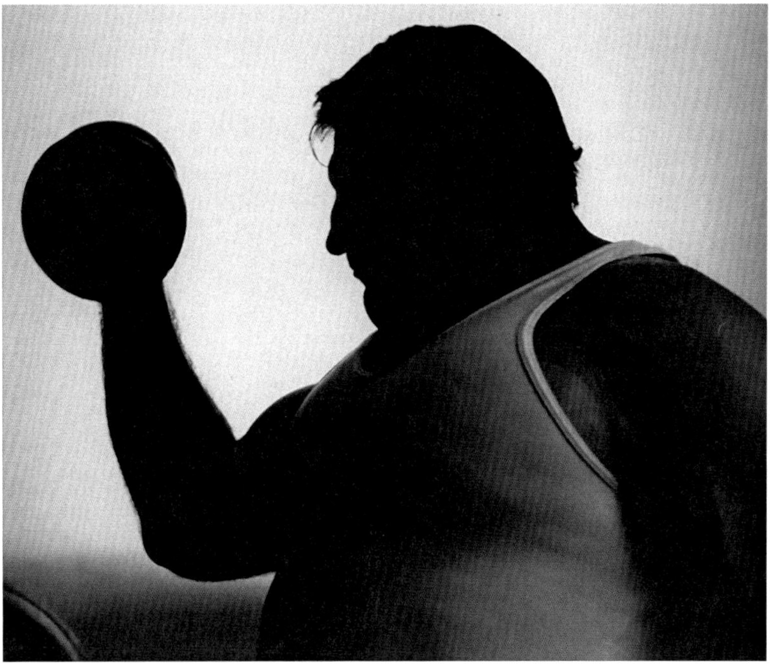

Foreword

I first met Bruno Sammartino in the early '60s. I was a fan attending college with the dream of becoming a professional wrestler. I wasn't in MSG the night Bruno defeated Buddy

Bruno battling a true "strongman" Ken Patera in the Boston Garden on February 9, 1980

Rogers in record time to become World Champion, but I was seated in the Garden the night Bruno hoisted 600+ pound Haystacks Calhoun up in the air, off his feet, just as Bruno had promised he could and would do. The fan reaction was such that I remember you could actually feel the building vibrate.

I attended college in Reading, PA, and every Wednesday evening I would go to the taping of the wrestling show at the NBC studio in Philly. One week a blizzard hit, and though enough wrestlers made it to the studio, no PA Athletic Commission referee ever showed up. As a familiar face I was asked if I could referee. I did the entire one-hour show and suddenly I was added to the PA referee roster, and later to NJ as well. I had the privilege of being the third man in the ring for many sold-out events in Philly and Boston where Bruno had title matches with Killer Kowalski, Gorilla Monsoon, Baron Scicluna, George "The Animal" Steele, The (Original) Sheik, and Ivan Koloff among others. I graduated from college and taught school, among other things, while continuing to referee on a part-time basis.

Bruno had a brutal series of matches against Superstar Billy Graham

I was the referee at the Boston Garden for the third in a series of three matches between Bruno and Kowalski. It was a "Texas Death Match" where there had to be a winner. I got hit with a chair and knocked out in a bloody mess. The dressing rooms emptied and Sammartino and Kowalski were pulled apart and police escorted them back to their dressing rooms. I was attended to by paramedics and carried out on a stretcher. No decision was rendered. (There was a fourth sold-out match in Boston with Bruno and Killer, and one of the former boxing champions was brought in as "special referee" to guarantee there would be a definitive winner). I saw Bruno about a week later and he thanked me for a job well done, and asked if I was taken care of. I told Bruno that I had been given my standard referee compensation in Boston, but nothing more was said. I admitted that I was a little disappointed, but I never said anything. Bruno told me that he was glad that I didn't say anything and that he would handle it from there.

A week later there was an outdoor show at the ballpark in Reading. I wasn't assigned to referee, but I went to watch. The main

Bruno was often a special referee after he retired

event was Bill Watts and Dr. Bill Miller (Bruno wasn't there). Phil Zacko was the promoter and when he saw me he called me off around a corner. He reached in his pocket and pulled out a wad of cash and counted out several hundred and handed it to me. It was another week until I saw Bruno again and he asked if anyone had seen me since our conversation. I gave him a nod. He asked if I was satisfied. Bruno already knew the answer by the big grin that covered my face, and of course I thanked him. That was over forty years ago. It was a lot of money then, but to me it was more than the money. Here was Bruno Sammartino one of the greatest champions in the history of the business, and he went to bat for me at a time when certainly I wasn't in a position to do anything for him. My story is one of many

I have heard over the years involving Bruno. They all speak to the character of Bruno Sammartino the man.

Thanks to The Sheik, I eventually got to put on the tights for the first time. I moved to Detroit, but there wasn't a full-time spot open. Sheik was honest and told me to keep my job until business picked up, and meanwhile he would book me as much as he could. He was true to his word, and I even worked the big shows at Cobo Hall and Joe Louis Arena. Before Sheik's business picked up, my company transferred me to Warren, Ohio. I found myself at the far end of The Sheik's territory and not in a position to expect much in the way of bookings. I remember looking at a map and realizing that I was less than ninety miles from Pittsburgh. I wrote to Bruno and went to the next big show at Pittsburgh's Civic Arena. I was greeted warmly by Bruno and he looked at Ace Freeman (the matchmaker) and told Ace that he wanted me booked every weekend (which was the only time they ran), starting that next weekend, even if it meant adding a match to the card. I stayed there over a year and got invaluable ring experience with some of the best talent in the business.

I met Jim Grabmire and he took my picture when he left for a summer in Charlotte. Jim called me and told me that Jim Crockett, Sr. would book me on Jim's word. I quit my job and drove to Charlotte in one day. The year was 1971, just months before I turned twenty-nine, I was finally a full-time professional wrestler and got to live my dream.

There are many people that have helped me along my journey. However, if Bruno had not been there for me (just as he had been after Boston), and gave me the chance to work steady every weekend, well, I hesitate to think where I might be today. If I had to pick out only one person that most impacted my career it would have to be Bruno Sammartino. Fifty years later, I am proud to call Bruno my friend and I don't have the words to properly express the respect and admiration that I have for him.

Thank you Bruno!!!
James J. Dillon
PWHF 2013, WWE Hall of Fame 2012

's Edition

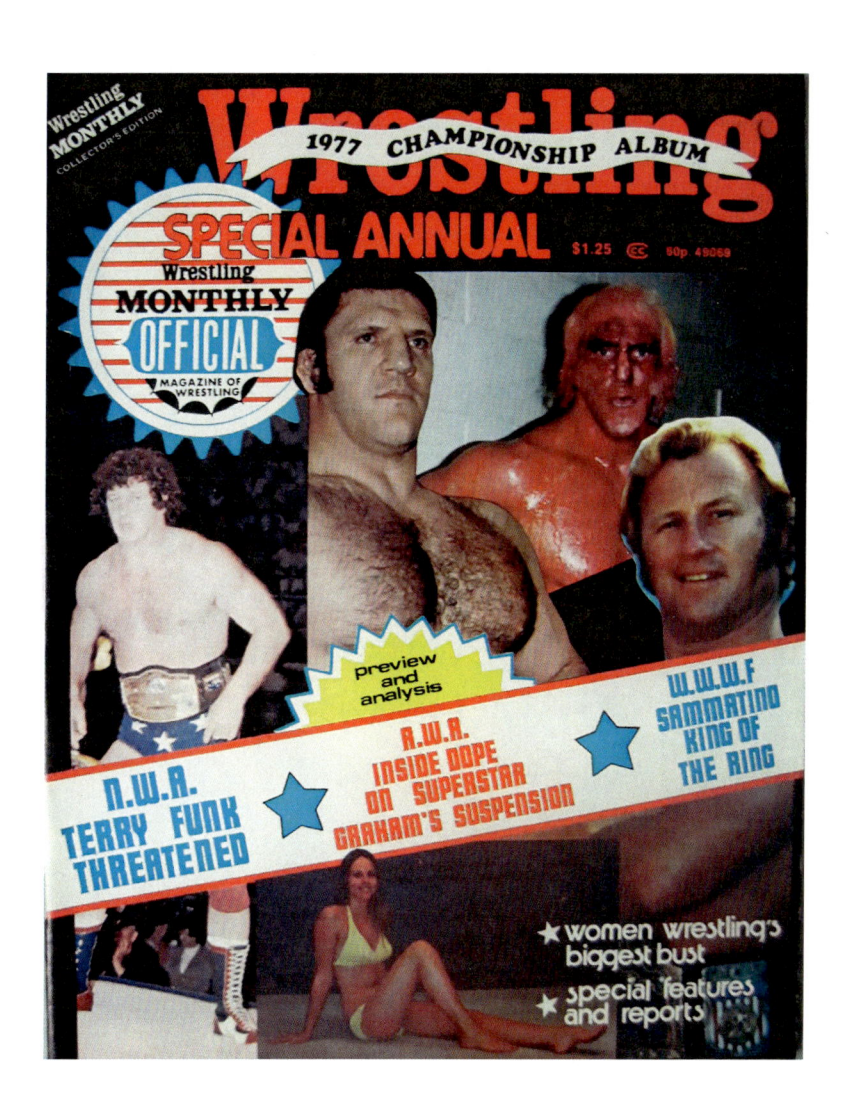

Wrestling

1977 CHAMPIONSHIP ALBUM

SPECIAL ANNUAL $1.25 50p 49069

Wrestling MONTHLY OFFICIAL MAGAZINE OF WRESTLING

preview and analysis

N.W.A. TERRY FUNK THREATENED

A.W.A. INSIDE DOPE ON SUPERSTAR GRAHAM'S SUSPENSION

W.W.W.F SAMMARTINO KING OF THE RING

★ women wrestling's biggest bust
★ special features and reports

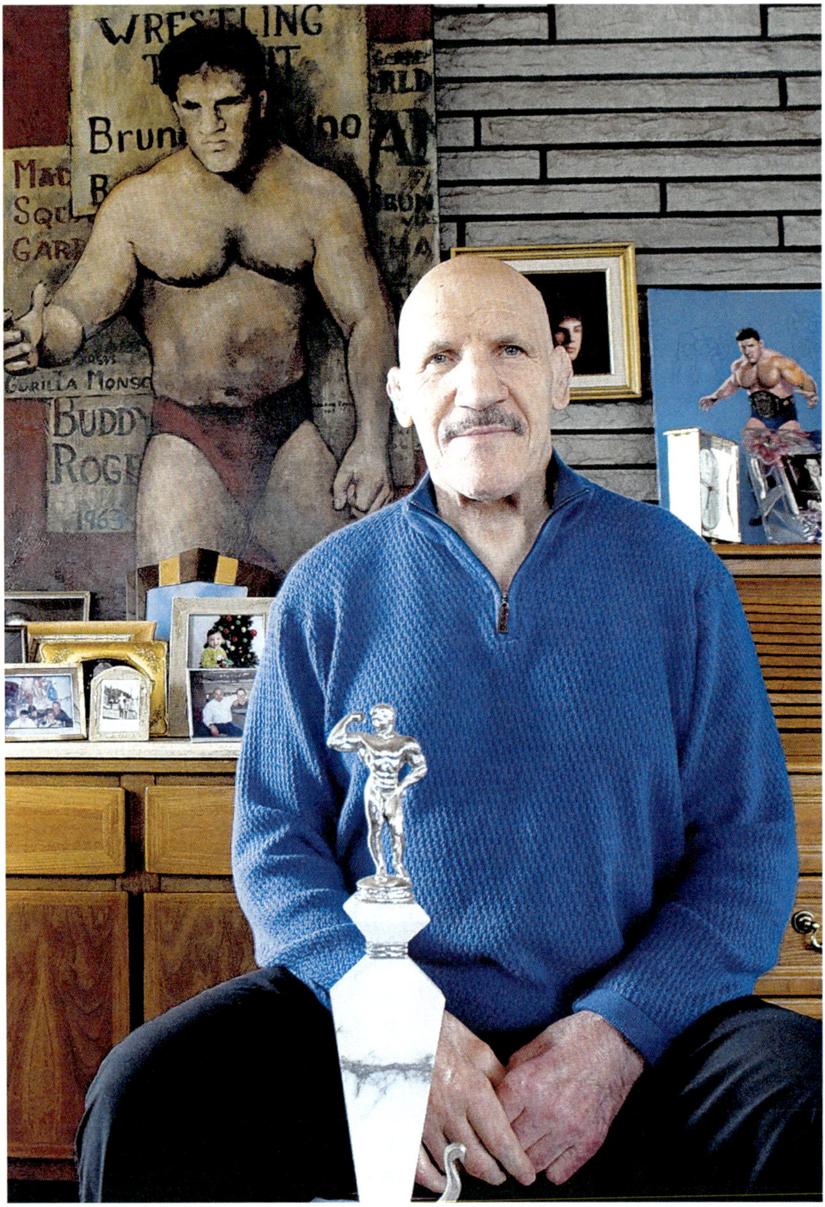
WRESTLING
1963

Welcome

When I was a very young kid growing up in Italy, I used to hear stories about people who had been to America. They said that the streets were paved with gold and, as a child, I took that literally. I really thought you could reach down and scoop up handfuls of the stuff.

Of course, when I came to the United States at age 14 I saw that the streets *weren't* paved with gold, but I began to understand what those who had come before me had meant: America is the land of golden opportunity.

For me, a boy from another country, what did it mean coming to America? Chances are that I would not have stayed in the town where I was born. Many like me left to go into the world because the war had devastated my village. Years later, as a professional wrestler in places like Australia, South America and all over, I met people from my hometown. All of us had to leave that town to go and find work and to make a life for ourselves. We just couldn't do that anymore in Italy.

I feel that I was so lucky to come to this great country, America, where I had the freedom to do what I wanted to do—learning to be a carpenter at the place where I got a job working construction, and joining the YMCA to train. I had the opportunity to practice with college wrestling teams so I could gain experience in what I loved best, and then to become a professional wrestler. I felt lucky even just getting the chance to cut the grass.

As the old saying goes, "Only in America." I believe that America gave me the opportunity to live my dream, which was to be a champion. I was able to give my family a much better life than I ever experienced as a youngster. Today, even though I'm retired, I still sometimes wake up and I'm afraid somebody's going to pinch me and tell me it was all a dream, that I'm not in America, but back in the mountains, starving and hiding from the German troops.

Even with all of the traveling that I've done (and I've visited countries with great beauty and tremendous histories), I can honestly say that I've never been anywhere in the world that could come within a mile of the United States of America. This is truly the greatest country in the world. I thank God and I thank my dad every day of my life for giving me the chance to live in this land. For me it is a privilege to be an American.

Bruno Sammartino
HOF 2013

Bruno Sammartino

BRUNOSAMMARTINOFOUNDATION.COM

I am never too busy for our wonderful first responders

LIVING LEGEND

BRUNO SAMMARTINO

PROGRAMMA

ORE 16.00 — RITROVO IN PIAZZA SAN ROCCO, E INCONTRO CON LA CITTADINANZA E I FANS; A SEGUIRE SIGNING EVENT

ORE 17.00 — VILLETTA COMUNALE, CERIMONIA DI GEMELLAGGIO PIZZOFERRATO - PITTSBURG; SVELAMENTO STATUA DEDICATA A BRUNO SAMMARTINO

ORE 18.00 — SALA CONSILIARE, PROIEZIONE DOCUFILM SULLA VITA DI BRUNO SAMMARTINO; A SEGUIRE L'ABRUZZO E LO SPORT NEL TEMPO E NEL MONDO

ORE 19.45 — PIAZZA SAN ROCCO, A SEGUIRE APERITIVO;

5 AGOSTO PIZZOFERRATO

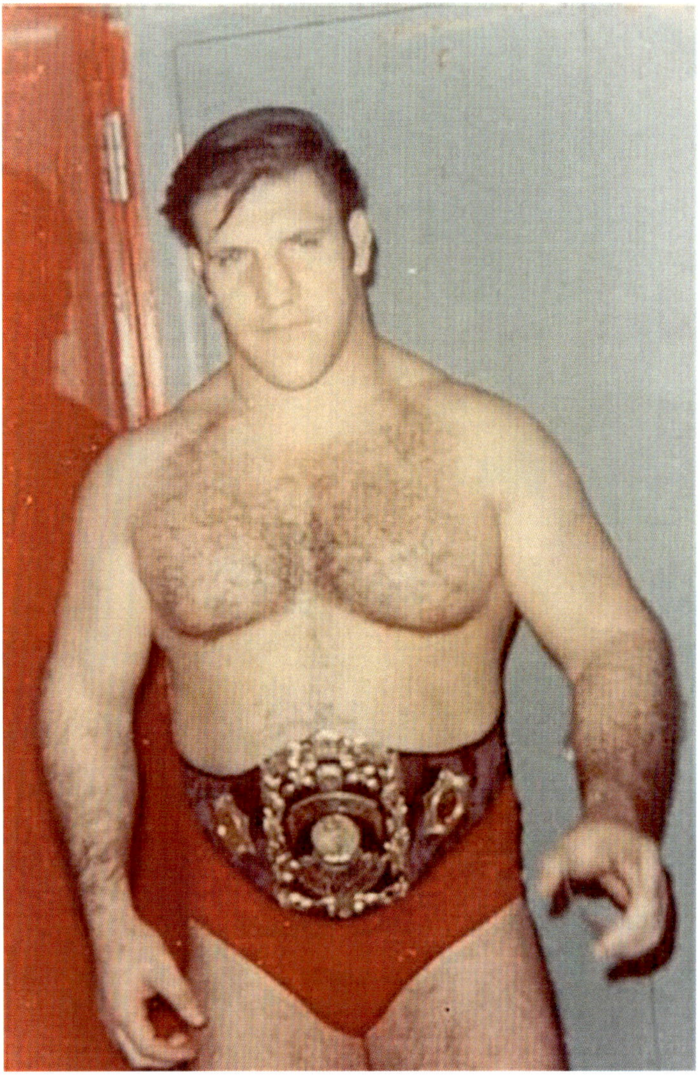

My Early Years in Italy

I was born October 6, 1935, in a little Italian mountain town called Pizzoferrato. The youngest in my family, I was also the biggest, weighing more than 11 pounds at birth.

My dad, Alfonso, was a blacksmith by trade. In January 1936, when I was only three months old, he left Italy for America. He went there to work and earn enough money to buy land on which he could build a home for his wife and family.

Concerta was my dad's older sister. She and her husband had earlier immigrated to the Pittsburgh area, so my dad went to live with her in an area they called Little Italy. Now it's known as Panther Hollow.

My dad was born in January 1891, so he would have been 45 when he came to America. He used to tell me that in those days it was easy to find work. Workers were needed everywhere. He said that eight or nine men from the same town might come over and board with Italian families who were already here. They might only have a mattress on the floor, but they would eat well, have a place to stay, and still be able to send money back home.

Dad told me that blacksmiths were used in construction back then. He would use his skills to fix shovels, picks, and other equipment that got broken. After doing that for a time, he went to work in the steel mills. He worked very hard, trying to save every dime he could.

A couple of times before 1936, my dad had traveled to the United States. He would work for a while, then return to Italy to be with his family. But in 1936, the War had started and travel routes were closed. We were stuck in Italy and Dad was stuck in America. For long periods of time, there could be no communication whatsoever. I think my dad went through every bit as much hell as we did—not knowing anything, hearing about fighting going on and learning about casualties.

So in Italy it was my mother Emilia who kept the family together while my dad was away. I lived there in our stone house with my older brother Paul and my older sister Mary.

To show you how things were when I was young: There were no doctors in Pizzoferrato and many children and adults got sick—and often died—from nothing more than things like the flu virus. Simple medications could have saved lives back then, but none were available, so many people perished at an early age.

I lost my sister, Annita, when she was 13 and my brother, Sandrino, when he was only two. My mother had also borne twins but, sadly, they passed away shortly after birth.

We had a field where we grew nearly all of our food. Just about everything we ate—wheat, corn, and potatoes—we raised right there.

Because we were very high up in the mountains, we used to get an enormous amount of snow in the winter. We would be literally snowed in for months due to these severe snowstorms, so we had to make provisions for this in the early fall.

Pizzoferrato, Italy—where I was born

The basement of our house was divided into sections, and that's where we kept our potatoes, wheat, flour, corn or whatever. Then, when the snows did come, we were just stuck in the house. We had our food and fire and just waited for the storms to stop.

The doors to our house opened to the inside, not like they do here. The reason for this was that you would have to dig yourself a tunnel to get to the street because the wind would drift the snow higher than the door.

There was no work to be done in winter, since everything was paralyzed by the snow, so when we could get out, we went skiing.

This life was very normal for me as a child. I played with the other children when I could and I worked when I had to, which was a great deal of the time in the spring, summer, and fall. I would go with my brother and sister to the fields where we would help our mother with the crops. That was my childhood through late-1943 and early-1944.

The War started out rather simply for us. When the first Germans came to our town, they came in small groups. They were from the regular German army and were merely scouting the area for good military positions. They didn't bother us or show us any hostility, so we thought little of it.

A few would appear occasionally to check out different areas in our mountains. You see, Pizzoferrato had only a population of 900 or so, but from its position you could see many other villages just like mine. We used to walk from one to the other or go by horse and buggy, but for the Germans the important thing was rapid mobility. They needed to know all about our roads and our resources.

Several weeks later, after the first contact with the Germans, we were awakened one night by what sounded like the whole town coming apart—unbelievable roaring noises. Dozens, maybe hundreds, of armored cars and jeeps rolled through our town.

We were completely dumbfounded. We had never even seen as much as an automobile before this happened (although, before the war, I do recall seeing a small truck having a difficult time winding its way around the narrow and tricky roads). The Germans came like a storm, sweeping aside everything in their path.

Along with all their noise came a fierce pounding on our door. It was Uncle Camillo, who was married to my mother's sister. He was one of the kindest human beings I have ever known. He was just like a father to us kids, a gentle man. This night he had come to warn us that the SS, the storm troopers themselves, had moved into our area.

We realized that the SS was quite unlike the first soldiers who had occupied our town. The SS wanted the town only for themselves and they wanted the townspeople out. These troops became extremely violent when their wishes weren't met immediately, and many of our people perished under their jackboot. We fled with just the clothes on our backs.

One of my mom's brothers, also named Alfonso like my dad, owned a little cabin out in the fields. One of my strong memories is heading toward that cabin, running like crazy and being as scared as anyone can be. Fortunately, we made it to Uncle Alfonso's without incident, but my mother began to feel uncomfortable there.

You see, Uncle Camillo had joined with the partisans. His group and others like it linked up with the Allies to help direct them through the mountainous terrain.

And the war crept closer to us each day.

English soldiers, in another nearby town to us called Castell, were bombing the area with cannons. Because the English weren't sure of the German positions, at times we ended up in the line of fire. My mother said to us, "My God, if one of those bombs hits this little shack here, we'll all be killed!"

So she decided that we would head toward the big mountain

A bird's eye view shows the rugged terrain of Pizzoferrato

called Valla Rocca. She had gotten word that many of our friends and relatives from Pizzoferrato who had escaped the SS were hiding there. They felt it was a safe place that the Germans wouldn't dare bother with, because it was such a difficult and treacherous climb.

My aunt, Alfonso's wife, wanted no part of Valla Rocca. She was determined that she and her children were going to stay in that little cabin and rely on God's will to survive. My mother, on the other hand, believed that the Lord helps those who help themselves.

As the artillery fire continued to draw closer, we began to experience bombings from the air. Finally, my mother grabbed me, my brother, and sister and said, "Enough. We're heading toward the big mountain…Valla Rocca."

I've often been asked how I can remember this so vividly since I was so young when it occurred. All I can tell you is that nine years old is old enough to remember the feelings that you had when such fantastic things happen to you. You couldn't forget them if you tried.

As we were racing to the mountain, my mother would try her best to keep us all together. Every so often bombs would hit close by and actually raise us up off the ground. We seemed to be running first in one direction, then in another. I can remember one incident that I suppose I can look back on and laugh about it, but it sure wasn't funny at the time.

As I said, it seemed as if the bombs were exploding all around us when, in reality, they were probably much further away. In any case, a huge chunk of dirt flew through the air and hit my sister, Mary, square in the back, knocking her down. She began to scream hysterically that the bomb hit her. She thought that a piece of shrapnel had ripped into her. Of course, it had been just a hunk of dirt.

My mother just grabbed her and hollered at me and Paul to stay together. "Hold hands," she told us, and "stay close together." So we kept running.

We knew we weren't going to make it to the top of the mountain in one day, so we stayed at the bottom all night, hiding. We had no food, no lights, nothing. My mother, poor Mama, stayed awake, watching over us, worrying about the Germans, wolves, and other animals that might harm us.

As soon as dawn broke, we started to make the climb. It seemed to take forever to reach the top of that mountain. We were all so very hungry and tired, but we kept going until finally we made it.

I remember seeing paths cut into the woods by those who had arrived before us. They had constructed shelters that resembled Indian teepees or, maybe more accurately, like the log cabins that you have seen in the history books. The men had taken small trees and made logs from them, using the logs to erect the shelters. At the top was a hole for the smoke of the fire to rise through and there would be just one entrance. It was almost a barracks with the cracks sealed with mud and stones.

One of our neighbors, who had already built some of these shelters for his own family, was aware that my dad was far away in America. He realized that this poor woman, Emilia, and her three children were desperately in need of a place to stay, so he allowed us stay in one of these cabins.

The inside of these buildings were partitioned. Logs would be used as dividers to section off areas for separate families, and believe me, there were many people crammed into that small area. My mother, brother, sister, and I shared a tiny living space that barely allowed us room to lie down and sleep. I remember that the fall had brought the chilly air so a fire would be burning in the middle of the cabin to keep us all warm. We didn't have a lot of blankets to go around and we were always cold. I would watch the smoke rise from the fire and escape through the hole in the roof. We were stuck there, just waiting.

As far as food and clothing went, everybody was on their own. There was no such thing as being neighborly. Most of the people there weren't concerned with helping one another; they were just trying to figure out ways for them and their families to survive.

At night, my mother would often hike down Valla Rocca to make her way back to our house, which was now occupied by German troops who lived and slept there. She would sneak into our house through the back door using the key she still had in her possession. Then she would creep into the basement where we kept the food and fill her sack with our own provisions.

She took whatever she could as quickly as she could. Sometimes it was potatoes or corn. Other times it may have been flour. She would hurry back with this food for us kids to eat.

My mother at this time was 48 years old, and making so many of these trips up and down that mountain was not easy for her. But our food situation was desperate. That's why she went by herself: It was less dangerous than going with one or two others.

Of course, my mother wasn't the only adult who made these trips back into Pizzoferrato. Still, everybody who went on them was on their own.

When my mother would go down the mountain, she would always time it so that she would get into town late at night when the Germans were sleeping. There were guards, of course, but she knew the town inside and out, so she could avoid them fairly easily. She risked her life for us like this about once a week.

One time she was captured and put onto a truck with other prisoners. The back of that truck was rimmed with barbed wire, but that didn't stop my mom. She actually dove through it and was shot at, but she ran like the devil and hid in the dense woods that she was so familiar with. The Germans couldn't find her and she returned to us alive and well.

Another time as she was leaving town, a German soldier spotted her and he shot her, hitting her in the shoulder. She ran and dodged and got away from the soldier. She was a woman possessed. She knew she had those three children waiting for her on top of that mountain, and that their survival depended solely on her. Nothing would stop her from returning—nothing.

I remember those times when Mom would leave us. We'd hear the bombs exploding below. We weren't even sure where the shells were hitting, since there were many, many towns all over the area that were occupied and involved in the fighting.

We would be petrified when she left, worrying about whether she would return or not. Her trips would usually take two or three days, sometimes longer. While she was away, me, Paul, and Mary would sit on the edge of the mountain where we could look down to see someone returning. We just stared. No matter how hungry we were or how miserable the weather was, none of it mattered when we would spot our mom coming back up. I remember this as though it were yesterday. Oh, my God, what a feeling that was—to see her coming back!

From high atop the mountain, one could see the rooftops of the homes

That's how we would survive. If my mom had stolen some potatoes, she would put them on the fire and each of us would eat one potato. Another time, we would have a single ear of corn. If she got some flour, she would take water and make dough, and even though we had none of the other ingredients to go with it, there would be bread. Everything was rationed out so it would last.

There were times when we didn't get to eat at all, sometimes for days. Because there was so much fighting going on in the villages, my mom would have to stay away. When there was no food, we would fill our bellies with snow. I remember stuffing myself with snow many times. When the weather started to warm up, we would eat the spring dandelions and whatever other greens we could find. So many of the older people who were with us died off because there was nothing to eat but these things.

While we were hiding on Valla Rocca, the countryside still echoed from the bombings and we knew that many fierce battles were being fought. The Germans were being driven back and kept moving closer to us. In fact, the Germans did an exceptional job in holding on to our towns. It seemed that every time the British would try to advance, they would be beaten back. The Germans had the positioning advantage because of the terrain.

The Germans had also dug holes that were nearly the size of a room in the roads, then covered them up so cleverly that, as the Allied soldiers would try to advance, they would plunge into them and then the Germans would just machine-gun them down. The number of people killed was unbelievable. Eventually many of our people, especially the men, were able to help the British maneuver through our rough mountain roads.

The Germans, of course, were interested in finding out where we and others like us were hiding. They wanted to put a stop to any efforts to help the British.

Once, three German soldiers did discover our sanctuary. They came on horseback as far as they could, then climbed up the rest of the way on foot. That day, all the men (what few were still there with us) were out hunting for food. We were defenseless.

As I look back on that moment, I realize that my mom was the bravest woman I've ever known. She was totally aware of what was happening. I'm not sure to this day if we kids fully understood what the Germans were about to do.

Mom had my brother and sister on one side of her and me, the youngest, on the other side. She had her arms around all of us. She had no fear for herself. Her compassion was completely for us and she talked softly while the SS men were readying the machine gun to kill us.

She said, "Don't be afraid my children, because soon we'll be in Heaven and there will be no more cold, no more hunger, no more suffering. We'll all be together and we will be happy. It's going to be Paradise."

Luckily for us all, a couple of the hunters returned just in time. They saw what was happening and somehow managed to get behind the Germans without alerting them. On a silent signal, they rushed the three SS men and with knives, killed them and saved our camp.

We were able to take possession of the machine gun and all of the ammunition that the Germans had brought up the mountain. This gun was to be our defense in case more like them would find us. As it turned out, others did spot us, but they would be on horseback, see that the climb was too steep and would turn around and go back down just forgetting about those people who lived so high in the clouds.

Sometime during all these hardships I caught pneumonia. I guess starvation and the war had taken their toll on me. It was clear that I was dying.

My mother was so worried about me. She had already lost four children and did not want to lose a fifth. When my brother and sister had died, there had been a doctor who would visit once a month from Villa Santa Maria. That was all the medical help that was available in our village back then. But now, on top of Valla Rocca, there were no doctors at all—not even once a month.

Some people laugh at the remedies the old-timers talk about, but— tall tale or not—my mother took steps to save my life using those long- ago methods. She wrapped me up in whatever blankets she could find, then she boiled water in a borrowed pot and placed dampened blankets around me, which created a steam bath effect. After a good steaming, she uncovered me and placed leeches all over my back. (The theory was that these leeches would suck all of the poisoned blood from my system.)

You may call this a lot of bologna, but all I know is that, as sick as I was, I should have died…but I didn't.

We lived on the mountaintop for nearly 14 months. When we got word that the Germans had finally moved out of our town, we were elated. They left not because they had been whipped, but because they had been completely cut off from their supplies, so they had to retreat to the north.

Many people in our camp had died during this time from sickness and starvation. I remember the hell that it was for my own family. My brother Paul and my sister Mary were certainly not in the best of health after all we had gone through.

Because I was still too weak to walk on my own, my mom had to carry me all the way down the mountain. We were all suffering from the effects of our long exile, but she got us back home with the same determination she had shown in keeping us alive all those months.

When we reached Pizzoferrato, we were devastated to see the destruction from the bombings. Everything lay in ruins and there were bodies everywhere.

I remember seeing so many corpses of our own people, of the Germans, English and some Polish, and all those dead bodies didn't really make an impression on me. I know it sounds hard to believe, but it's the God's honest truth. We had lived through so much hell that nothing else seemed to make an impact.

So the townspeople who had survived and returned began to clean up the village, starting first with the removal of all the dead to a burial site. Later, I began to think about the soldiers who had died in my town. Nobody knew who they were. They became just faceless people buried in unmarked graves all over the hillsides. What of their families?

We found out quickly that we could return to our own house and live in it, even though parts of it had been blown apart. Even though the fighting had moved away, problems brought on by the war continued. Practically everything had to be rebuilt. The Germans had ransacked our village, taking everything they could when they left.

There were still no doctors and many kinds of sicknesses erupted, most likely the result of the decaying bodies harboring germs. Ammunition had been left all over the streets and people were being killed from accidentally stepping on hidden land mines. Children were getting maimed (and worse) from picking up live grenades.

It took time, but the townspeople cleaned up Pizzoferrato and began to rebuild. We started to plant new crops, too. I slowly regained my health, thanks to being back in our home and with my mother taking such good care of me in every way she could, scraping up a little bit of food here and there for us to eat, watching over me with her love. It took months but I got better—thanks to her.

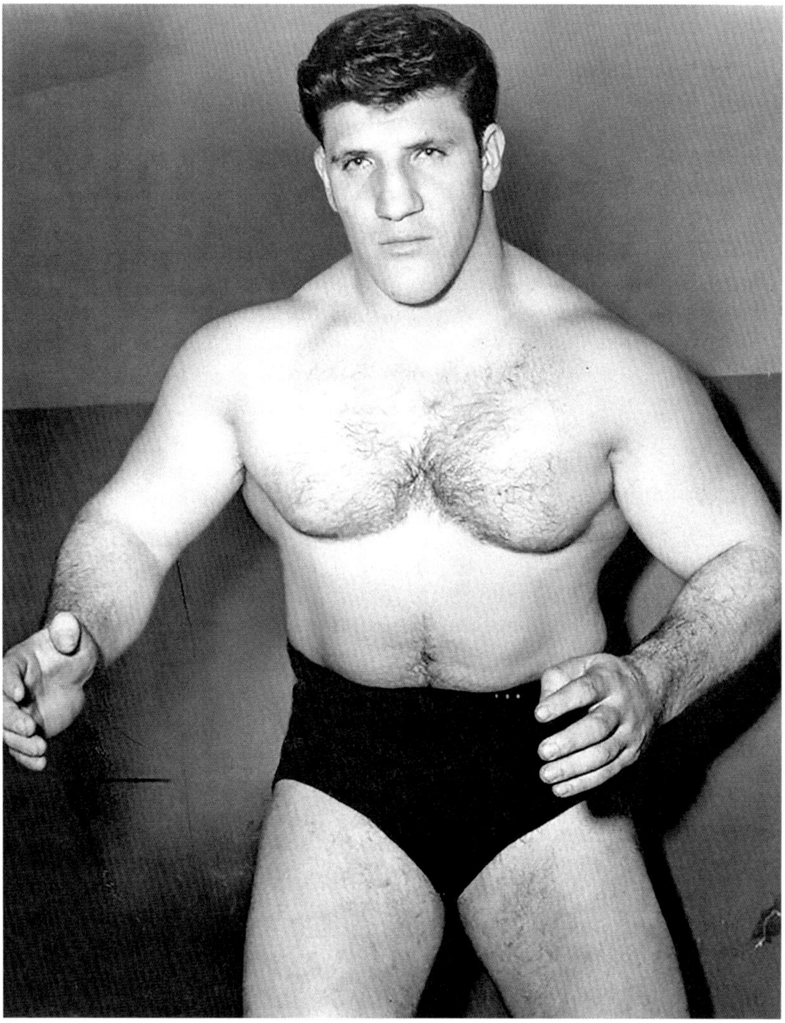

Coming to America

It was quite some time before we were able to communicate with my dad again. I never knew what my dad looked like because I had never seen a picture of him (he had gone to America within three months of my birth). In my part of the world, we didn't have cameras.

It wasn't until the war was over that my mom finally got word through to him. He found out that we were all well and alive, and in his return messages to us he described the hell he had gone through not knowing the fate of his family. He said he had tried to get news through the Italian newspapers and radio programs, but that all he heard about was the bombings and how the Germans had overrun our town. As we suffered in hiding, he never knew where we were—or even if we were still alive.

My mom tells me that she discussed with my dad whether or not he should return to Italy and care for us. She told him flatly that the only thing left in the Old Country was misery, and that we would all be better off in America.

I remember hearing the stories of America: streets paved with gold, a country full of mansions and of people who were filthy-rich. So when my mother told us that we were going to the United States to be with our father, we were all elated.

It wasn't until 1948 that we got our chance to leave.

At that time, all passage had to be arranged according to a quota system. I didn't pass the physical that was required, so we had to wait until our number came up again.

While we waited, my health improved. Our chance came around again in 1950, I was given a clean bill of health and we were on our way to America at last.

First we had to travel to Naples, where we would catch a ship to the United States. I was 14 years old and it was the first time I had ever left Pizzoferrato with its population of 900. When we arrived in Naples, I was stunned by the size and magnificence of this awesome city.

The first thing we did was hurry to look at the ship that would carry us across the Atlantic. There were two ocean liners that were docked in Naples. They were twin ships, the Saturnia and the Locania, and we heard that they had served in battle in the Middle East.

When we first saw our ship, the Saturnia, I didn't even realize that it was a ship. It looked so big to me—I thought I was looking at another city! My mother assured me that it was indeed going to take us to our dad in America.

Finally, after several days of waiting, we boarded on February 15, 1950, and steamed out of Naples.

I don't know much about ships, but I sure know that the Saturnia was no luxury liner. I couldn't decide which was worse: this voyage or the war. It took us 14 days to reach New York; they were 14 horrible days.

For those two weeks, we lived at the very bottom of the darn thing. It was one big open floor divided by curtains. We all slept in bunks and there was this large piece of canvas you would take and circle around your bed. My brother was on the bottom bunk and I was on the top, while my sister had the bottom of the other bunk with my mom sleeping above her.

Paul, Mary, and Bruno

Although not quite as bad, the arrangement reminded me of the small space we had shared during the war up on the mountain. I guess that this was the most economical way that my dad could afford to bring us to the States.

When we went up on deck, we would climb up flights of stairs to get there. Looking back I'm sure there were different levels of accommodation, where people with more money were traveling a little better than we were. Being young though, I didn't know that, so I accepted our quarters as just being the way you traveled on the high seas.

On our first day or two out, we were able to move about the ship whenever we wanted. Then the sea became so choppy that everyone in our section was confined below. Ironically, even though I was the sickly one, my brother Paul was hit the worst with sea sickness, although my sister Mary came in a close second.

Because my mother and I weren't quite as affected, we had to play nursemaids to Paul and Mary. They felt so ill, they couldn't even go to the bathroom—and, of course, they couldn't walk up the flights of stairs to where the meals were served.

Mom and I would walk up those narrow stairs and we would find somewhere to sit down and eat. The tables had little boards all around the edges to keep the food and dishes from falling off as the ship pitched and rolled. After we ate, we would take something back to my brother and sister so they could have some nourishment.

We were stuck in our area most of the time because the seas were so rough, but I remember seas calming as we approached land coming through the Mediterranean and past Gibraltar. A member of the crew yelled down to us to come above quickly and get some fresh air.

My brother and sister were still very ill (as we many others), and even though my mom and I weren't feeling very well, we made our way up to the deck. We sat down on crates and my mom kept repeating to me, "Take deep breaths, Bruno. The ocean air is fresh and good for the lungs."

The terrific sea air actually began to make me feel nauseated. The seas soon got rough again, and we were sent back down to our area. It seemed as though we spent the rest of the trip there resting, thinking about our new life, rolling and tossing in the high seas. What kept me going, of course, was the excitement about meeting my dad.

When we finally began to approach the United States, the seas calmed and once again we were permitted on deck. Even my brother and sister started to feel better as we neared New York.

A big disappointment to us was that we missed seeing the Statue of Liberty. We arrived at night and, for some reason, we were confined to our quarters and not allowed above until the next morning, long after we had passed Lady Liberty.

The next day, mass confusion reigned. All our fellow passengers were rushing to get off the ship and meet their loved ones. It had been a long and difficult journey for us and we were all glad it was over.

After we disembarked, we all headed to a nearby section of the docks where huge letters of the alphabet were posted. We were directed to stand under the letter that corresponded with the first letter of our last name, so we dragged our bags (and whatever else we had with us) and waited under the big "S" for Sammartino.

We stood there for what seemed like an eternity. My mother, sister and brother all looked one way and I faced the other. Even though I had no idea what my father looked like, I pictured him as a tall, husky guy. I knew that he was no longer a young man (he was close to 59 years old in 1950).

I saw what looked to me to be a very old man shuffling toward us. He wore a tattered hat and eyeglasses. I never looked at my mother to ask if this man was our father, I just stood there staring as he walked closer and closer to us.

While the others were peering off into the opposite direction, this old man came up to us and softly called out my mother's name, "Emilia?"

She whirled around and screamed, "Alfonso! Alfonso!" and that's how I realized that there was my dad, in the flesh.

He seemed overjoyed to see us. Still, he seemed more like a stranger than a father. I couldn't believe it. I knew it was going to take quite a bit of adjustment to get used to him.

Later that day, we took a train to Philadelphia. My dad's sister, her husband and family lived there, so we stopped briefly before heading to Pittsburgh. Of course, it was my first train ride.

One of our first family portraits taken in America

As we pulled into the Philadelphia train station, we heard the sirens of fire engines. It sounded almost like the war, the sirens blowing madly to tell us the bombs were coming. It shook me up, but my dad explained to me that in America when a fire starts, these special trucks rush to it and put out the flames with water. The explanation sounded good, but the noise of the sirens still scared me.

We stayed in Philadelphia for one day, visiting and sightseeing. My aunt and uncle drove us all around, proud of showing off the city. I looked everywhere for the streets of gold and the castles and was disappointed when I didn't see any.

The next day, we boarded the train to Pittsburgh. As I watched the countryside whisk by, I couldn't wait for the miles to pass, anxious to reach our new home. Maybe Pittsburgh was the place for mansions and golden highways!

As it turned out, my dad had purchased an old house in the Oakland section of town on Cato Street, perched on a hill, right above the smokestacks of the steel mills. He had agreed to pay $6,000 for the property, taking out a long-term mortgage.

In those days, Pittsburgh's reputation as a dirty, smoky city was no exaggeration. We lived right in the thick of it. I didn't regret coming to America, but it sure wasn't what I had envisioned.

Our home back in Italy may have been damaged by the war, but it was well constructed out of heavy stone. Of course, it didn't have inside toilets or running water or many of the luxuries of an American home, but at least where we lived there was clean air and sunshine.

When we walked into our new home on Cato Street, what I saw was falling plaster and peeling wallpaper. Instead of mountain stones, we had brick and wood. I wondered what we had gotten ourselves into.

Our new home on Cato St. in Pittsburgh

We were one of the first Italian families to move into this section of Pittsburgh, which was predominately inhabited by Polish, Irish and Jewish people. When we arrived, the Jews were just starting to move out and relocate in Squirrel Hill. Most of the other Italians were living in a place called Panther Hollow, or "Little Italy."

For the first few days, many of my dad's friends and relatives came over to meet us and it was wonderful to see them all. After things settled down, my brother, sister and I were enrolled in school because my dad wanted us to learn English right away. We attended Schenley High School, which was about a two-and-a-half mile walk from our house.

School was where, for the first time in my life I experienced prejudice.

As we walked to our classes, we would be continually taunted and called names like "dago" and "wop." We would even be beaten up because of our heritage. In the Old Country, this kind of behavior didn't exist. We were all Italians. If you argued with one another, there were no ethnic slurs tossed at you.

It was different in America. We didn't understand what these names meant, but we knew they weren't respectful. We were so grateful for having come to America—we had gone through a war and worried every minute about getting killed—but at the same time we were getting our noses bloodied just for being ourselves and having accents. But we would survive. We always did.

My brother Paul and I have always been extremely close. We knew how near to death we both were during the war, and that created a tight bond between us. We never really fought the way young boys are known to fight, we just liked each other an awful lot.

As we grew up, Paul became the responsible one. He always seemed to be older and wiser than his years. If my mother wanted us to go to the fields and bring some vegetables in for the supper table, Paul would be the one in charge even though he was only seven or eight. My mom could always trust him to do the things that I wasn't quite old enough or mature enough to do.

Paul and I at Christmas

When we had hard times in the beginning of our new life in Pittsburgh, Paul always played the big brother. I certainly got beaten up more than he did, and since he was a little huskier, he would stand up for me—even though he was nearly as undernourished as I was when we first came over.

Before long, our life began to settle into its routine and we learned our English. To my dad, this was the key to success for us: to be able to speak the language of the land.

Summer quickly rolled around. My mother talked with a landscape contractor by the name of Angelo Pasquerelli. He was able to line me up with a job while my brother worked for another contractor named Max.

Since my brother and I were both pretty frail boys, we wanted to do something about it. Maurice Simon, a Jewish kid we had met at school, saw the shabby treatment we were getting from the others and felt sorry for us. He wanted

My brother and I have always been close

55

to help and suggested that we join the YMHA— the Young Men's Hebrew Association. He promised that if we did, he would show us how to exercise with weights and how to train to become stronger and healthier.

Using weights was something we had never heard of before, and it cost money to join the Y—money we just didn't have.

When we both started working, we would turn our paychecks over to our parents because they were really struggling. The mortgage payment on the house was a significant monthly burden to my dad. His own mother was still alive, and he was trying to support her, too. He also had his own brothers and sisters who needed help. As a result, my brother and I rarely kept any money for ourselves.

Until we could find the money to join the YMHA, Paul and I managed to scrape together enough money to send for the Charles Atlas strength-building course we read about in all the magazines. I think it cost $5.

When we weren't working at our jobs, we would spend our days helping Dad knock down old plaster and re-plaster the walls. In the evenings, Paul and I would sneak into the basement and put our Charles Atlas course to use. We were learning all about "dynamic tension" and doing push-ups by the hour.

We were hiding from our parents because we were sure they would think we were silly, but finally I approached my mother about joining the Y. The Charles Atlas course was fine as far as it went, but I wanted to get more serious about bodybuilding. I explained to her that here was a club in town which Paul and I could join that would make us husky, strong and healthy. Mom, without knowing anything more about it, thought that it was a good idea.

I told her that the membership fee was something like $11 for each of us. She said perhaps we could keep a little bit of money from our paychecks for the membership; that's exactly what we did.

I always felt more comfortable talking to my mother than to my dad. He certainly wasn't an unreasonable man, but he still seemed more like a stranger than a father to me.

So my brother and I began to train. It was a revelation to me and I became addicted to it. There was no other feeling in the world to compare with working out. I felt in my gut that this was something for which I was destined and that someday, somehow, it would do something in return for me.

My brother and I at the dinner table with mom and dad.

At the same time, I began to develop an intense interest in wrestling, too. I guess I never wanted to let myself again be the malnourished, skinny kid I was back during the war. I quickly realized I had wrestling in my blood. I swear to you—I must have been born with it.

At Schenley High, I would always try to get other guys to work out with me on the mat. At that time, in the early 1950s, there were no wrestling programs in the city schools, so the guys I would wrestle with would be people I could pull in from my gym classes or from the football team after practice.

The football coach, Mister Gross, was my gym teacher. He knew Rex Peery, who was the wrestling coach at the University of Pittsburgh. He told Peery about this kid from the Old Country who simply loved to wrestle. Gross asked Peery if it would be all right to send him to work out with the college wrestling team.

Peery gave his okay and I started as soon as I could. After school, I would walk from Schenley High to the Pitt Field House way up on top of what the local residents call "Cardiac Hill."

Schenley High School in Pittsburgh's Oakland Section

I didn't realize at the time that Pitt had one of the finest wrestling teams in the country. They had Hugh Peery, Rex's son, who wrestled in the 1952 Olympic Games in Helsinki and would later be inducted into the National Wresting Hall of Fame. Another son, Ed Peery, was a three-time NCAA champion and was an alternate on the 1956 Olympic team. A guy named Joe Solomon became an unseeded national champion in 1954 (Pitt's second-ever) Ed DeWitt won two Pennsylvania state titles in high school and won an EIWA (Eastern Intercollegiate Wrestling Association) championship in 1956.

These guys were great.

Then there was me, suddenly going from working out in a gym with high school boys to wrestling nationally ranked college athletes. Talk about getting an inferiority complex!

No Pitt wrestler ever took me under his wing, but I don't mean this in a negative sense. These guys had academic responsibilities in addition to training. Many of them were on wrestling scholarships and they had to keep up with their grades as well as their wrestling. I remember that some of them would stumble into practice with bloodshot eyes because they had to stay up the whole night before studying for a test. There was just no time to take a special interest in some kid from high school.

But that didn't discourage me, it only made me more determined to work that much harder.

When I first started, I thought Coach Peery was going to tell me, "Get the heck out of there!" He didn't. We went all through the wrestling season with me working out with the team. And when I couldn't practice at Pitt (for example, if the team was on an out-of-town trip), I'd be pumping iron at the Y.

I remember some of my buddies teasing me about all the time I spent in training. While I was wrestling or pumping iron, my friends would be doing normal things like going swimming or taking a girl to the movies. It wasn't that I didn't have the desire to date, but I was a very bashful kid. And I had such a tremendous drive for what I was doing in the gym that I wasn't going to skip a session for anything. I was possessed—every hour I spent in training convinced me more than ever that this was my future.

As I progressed in my training, people started to look at me and take notice. I was growing larger and stronger. When I first arrived in America, I weighed slightly less than 90 pounds. When I graduated from Schenley in 1955, I weighed 225 pounds—that's how well my hard work was paying off.

At one point, I was offered a scholarship to wrestle for Pitt. The deal was to be a year-to-year agreement, and I only had to do two things annually for the scholarship to carry into the next year: I had to prove myself worthy as a wrestler and worthy as a student. If I didn't do well with either, I would be out.

But the arrangement never panned out and I never went to college.

My dad had been talking to Carmen Tropea, an Italian contractor in the building trades in the Pittsburgh area. Some years earlier, Dad had worked for Carmen as a laborer. He asked Carmen if he could get his son Bruno into the union as a carpenter. (My brother Paul had already gone out on his own and was working as a cabinet maker.)

Since my dad felt that joining the union was best for me, I followed his wishes. I didn't want to disappoint my parents, since opportunities for jobs were hard to come by. And I wasn't sure I could make the grade in college, so I turned down the wrestling scholarship. I would learn carpentry.

I really didn't have much confidence in myself with academics. I'm sure it had to do with the feeling I had first coming to America and not being able to speak a word of English (not to mention all the time and effort it took to master the language). Often when I would read books, there were many words I couldn't understand. It was a big handicap all through school.

My brother Paul would later join the service and, after his hitch was up, he went to college in the evenings under the G.I. Bill.

He was an extremely bright student. While I was struggling to graduate with a "C" average, Paul sailed through with an "A" average all the way. He was always walking to the library to do research and to study. I was never jealous of my brother. I truly admired his accomplishments and I used to brag about how bright he was.

I kept training, of course—nothing was going to stand in the way of that! When there was no wrestling at Pitt, there was the Y, where we had a wrestling ring set up. I used to coerce the guys who were wrestling at Pitt to come over and work out with me there.

Then I started to compete with the weights ... and I started winning contests. I began with the novice state meets, advanced to the junior, then on to the senior, winning all of them. I even went into a national meet with my power lifting.

Paul got to be pretty good with the weights, too. He topped the scales at about 215 and competed with me in many of the same meets. It was great to have him along at these competitions, encouraging me to push myself even harder.

So even though I wasn't going on to college and even though my father had a future as a carpenter set up for me, my dream stayed alive: One way or another, I would make something of myself with my strength and my dedication to training.

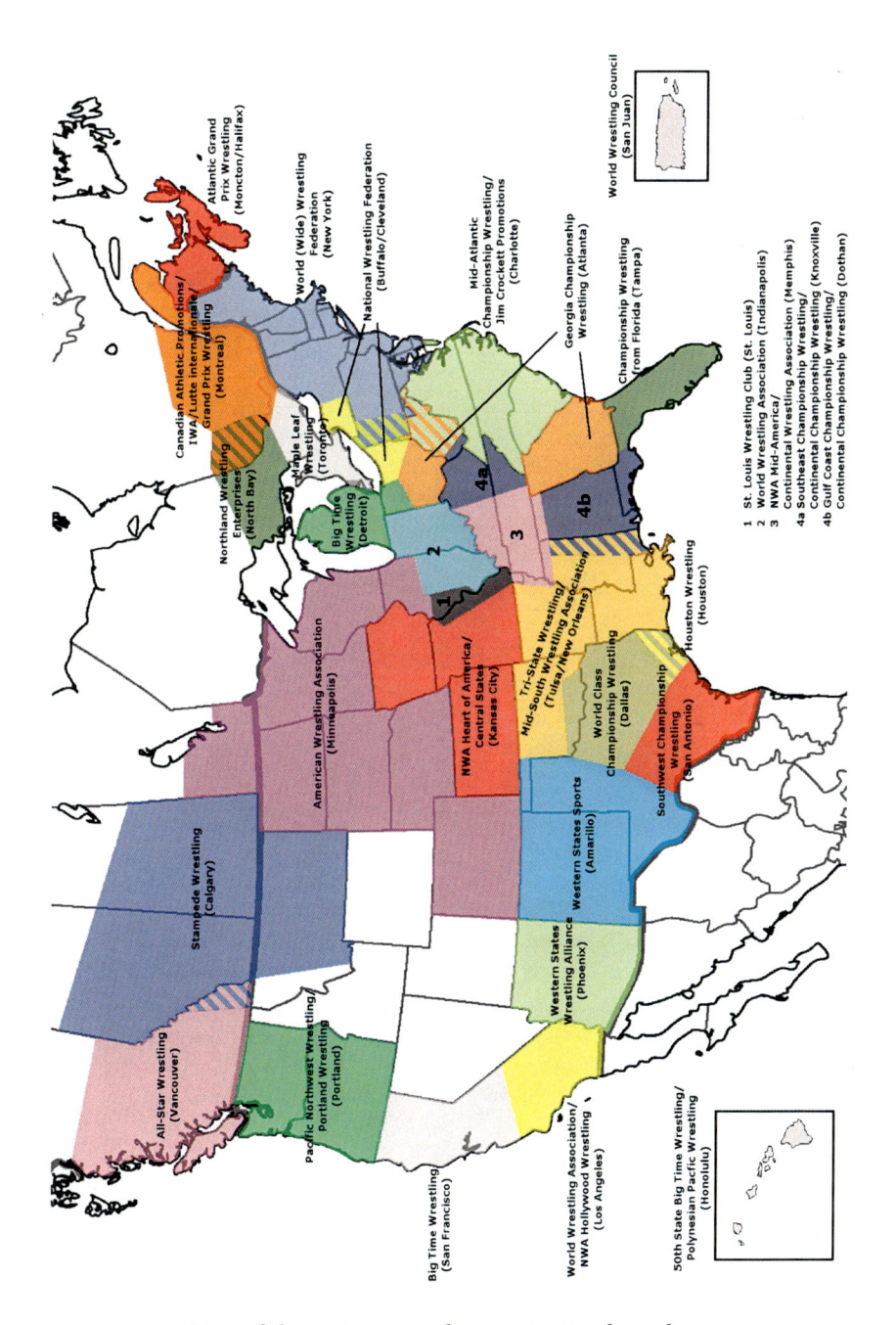

Map of the various wrestling territories throughout North America. The travel schedule could be brutal

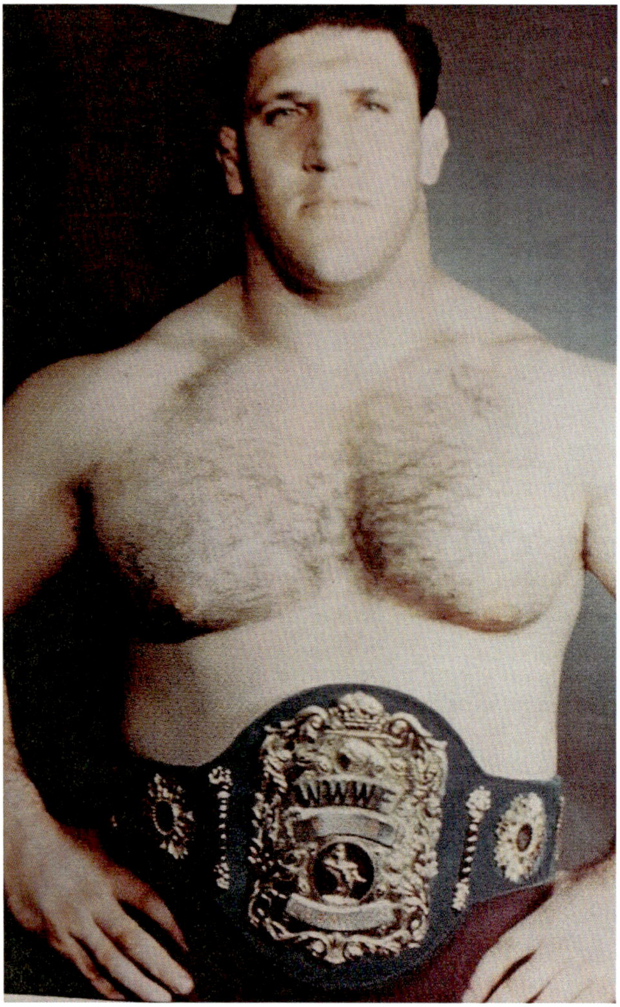
WWWF

Earning a Living

Thanks to my father's initiative, I started working soon after graduating from Schenley High School in June of 1955 as a union apprentice carpenter for Mr. Carmen Tropea. From the beginning I really didn't learn that much about carpentry. Since I was such a strong lad, the union crews were using me to load and unload trucks, to dig, pick, lift and carry. I did anything and everything but carpentry work.

Actually, I never complained. I was getting paid okay and I felt good about that. And no matter how many hours I worked during the day, even if I worked overtime, I'd rush home to Cato Street, grab something to eat, and then hurry off to the Y, which was that two-and-a-half mile walk.

I know kids today laugh when you tell them that you had to walk to school so many miles, but it was true. From my house to Schenley High School was two-and-a-half miles, then the Y was right down the street from that. And I would walk back and forth, in rain, sleet, snow or sunshine, regardless of how hard I had worked that day at the building site. I vowed never to miss a workout under any circumstances.

In early July, my mom came to me with some surprise news. She said that she had been actually saving money from the paychecks that my brother Paul and I had been handing over to her for the past few years. Now, she thought, there might be enough money to buy a car for me.

Mom was incredible. Here she was, putting away a dollar here and a dollar there until there was a nice-sized nest egg. And as luck would have it, our tenant, an auto mechanic named Jimmy who rented a room on the second floor in my parents' house, knew of a car for sale at the garage where he worked.

I went with him to look at it and it seemed fine. It was a 1952 Chevy which I bought for $715. Little did I know how important that car was going to turn out to be.

I had a training partner named Alex Philin. He was a tremendous weightlifter and really should have gone to the Olympics, but he got pushed around a little bit by politics. In the Olympic Games, if two competitors tie in the amount of weight lifted, then the rules say the person who is of lighter body weight gets selected. Alex had done exactly that—had tied another American lifter and was in line for Olympic selection because he was the lighter of the two—but the other athlete was picked. You figure it out.

At any rate, in the summer of 1955, Alex was going steady with a girl named Lola who went to Oliver High School across town. He didn't have a car, which made visiting his sweetheart difficult. When he discovered that his good buddy Bruno had just bought a 1952 Chevy, he seemed very happy for me. Why? Well, now I had the chance to bring these two lovebirds together.

So one early evening after we had just worked out and shortly after I had purchased my car, Alex asked me if I could drive him over to see his girlfriend. I said sure and off we went. I dropped Alex off at Lola's and headed back to Cato Street.

A few days later, Alex asked me again if I could give him a ride to Lola's. I was beginning to wonder if I had started Bruno's taxi service.

We cruised over to Lola's and this time she had one of her girlfriends visiting her. I asked Alex, "Who is that girl with Lola?"

Alex leaned over and told me that the girlfriend's name was Carol. As soon as I had seen her, standing there on the porch, something wonderful happened. I just knew that I had to get to know Carol better. When I drove home that evening, my heart was pounding.

The first chance I had, I asked Alex if he could arrange for me to meet Carol. He teased me a little but agreed to do it. So the next time I ferried Alex over to Lola's, I parked the car and went inside with him.

I was introduced to Carol. She seemed even more beautiful than when I had first caught sight of her. It turned out that she was just 16 and was still attending high school.

Before I left later on that evening, I asked Carol if she would like to go to a movie with me, Alex and Lola. As it was in those days, Carol had to ask her parents for permission.

In short order, arrangements were made for me to meet her parents. They looked me over top to bottom and gave their approval. Yes, I could go out with their daughter.

After that, Carol and I and Alex and Lola were like the Four Musketeers, double-dating like crazy. Of course, Alex was completely in favor of the arrangement since he still didn't have a car and needed transportation.

As I had grown up in the Old Country, I had my own ideas about what sort of woman I would want to marry someday. Immediately, I believed that Carol was that person. I just liked the way she behaved, the way she did things, everything about her.

After a lot of double dates, I successfully ditched Alex and Lola one evening so I could take Carol out and talk to her alone. A little time had gone by since we had first met because she had just turned 17. When the opportunity came to tell her how I felt, I took full advantage of it.

In Old County style, I confessed to her that I hadn't been going out with very many girls because I had such a ridiculous training schedule. Every day I was wrestling and weightlifting on top of working a full- time job. I told her that I really liked her and that I would like to go steady with her.

Now for me, going steady meant more than just seeing someone exclusively for a few months then moving on to another girlfriend. What it meant to me was that I wouldn't be seeing anyone else nor would she date other guys. The intent would be that when we could, we would get married. Carol liked the idea and so we started to go steady.

Throughout that summer of 1955, I continued working for Mr. Tropea, saw Carol when I could and worked hard at my training. I started to gain some recognition for my weightlifting, even setting some records. My local reputation got a boost when I began to appear on a local sports show in Pittsburgh hosted by the great Bob Prince, the "Voice of the Pittsburgh Pirates" after Rosey Rosewell retired.

These sports shows went out over KDKA-TV. Bob had me demonstrate weightlifting on live television. Since I had competed in both Olympic and power lifting, I was able to show the audience a range of lifting styles. If you had watched me from show to show, you would have seen me getting a little tougher each time I appeared.

Then summer turned to winter and in December of 1955, Mr. Tropea had to lay me off along with a lot of other guys. There just wasn't enough work to go around. So when I wasn't helping out at home, I spent more and more hours in the gym and waited for Carmen to bring us back.

We didn't get called for months, not until early spring of 1956 when Mr. Tropea needed us to work on a Greek church on the Boulevard of the Allies. The site was actually just a short distance from our house on Cato Street.

For as long as it lasted, it was good, steady income. Then the axe fell again and by mid-summer, I was laid off once more.

It was right around this time that my close friend and training partner decided we would go to "the weightlifters picnic" regardless of the fact that we were both broke.

My best buddy was Freddy DeLuca and he was just a great weightlifter who competed in the 148-pound class. Like me, he usually worked a tough day and then trained all night. In his class he set all kinds of city and state records.

That particular time, late summer of 1956, Freddy and I were both out of work and really pinching pennies. Despite that, we both wanted to go to York, Pennsylvania, for "the weightlifters picnic." York was where Bob Opfman, the coach of all the Olympic weightlifters, owned the York Barbell Club. Each summer he would invite weightlifters from around the country to come and compete at his club. It was a lot of fun and it gave everyone a chance to see athletes from all over the nation go head-to-head.

Freddy and I had gone to York a couple of previous summers, but now we were ready for anything. We felt that both of us had gotten a lot stronger and we wanted to take on all comers. Unfortunately, we had a distinct cash-flow problem.

At first, we had an arrangement where four other guys would come with us to share the expenses but, at the last minute, everybody backed down. It was just Freddy, me and Freddy's gas hog of an Oldsmobile.

So we schemed about how we were going to pull this caper off. We planned a budget for everything down to the last cent. We figured how much gas it would take to get there and back. We made sure we had enough money to eat a meal or two and we allowed ourselves $4 to find the cheapest motel room possible.

Posing on our front steps at Cato St with a couple of buddies

Off we went, driving straight through to York in one long day, pulling into town the night before the competition, searching for the cheapest room. After swinging past quite a few motels, we found one that charged only $2.50 for the night, but that was just for one person. We couldn't afford the room for two. Naturally Freddy checked in as a single while I hung around outside, making myself inconspicuous.

When we finally made it to the room, we both couldn't believe it. Even for $2.50 it was robbery. The room was smaller than most phone booths. The sheets looked like they hadn't been changed since last summer. The top half of one window was busted out.

I told Freddy that despite everything, I needed to get some sleep for the competition in the morning. I grabbed the blanket and slept on the floor and Freddy tried to fall asleep, lying on the broken mattress.

As we both lay there, trying to doze off, we kept hearing a very irritating noise that sounded like somebody chewing. Finally, Freddy couldn't take it anymore and switched the lamp back on. He looked down at the floor where he had put his shoes and there we saw we had a visitor. It was a huge rat, gnawing at Freddy's leather shoes.

I jumped up and the rat scurried off to his hole. I gathered up my clothes and said to Freddy that there was no way I was going to spend the night in that room. Freddy scrambled for his belongings and we climbed back in the car, having spent probably less than two hours in our room.

We headed for York Park where everything was happening the next morning and we slept in the grass that night. And we sure didn't get the greatest snooze, let me tell you.

When we woke up the next morning, people were already pouring into the park. We were both hungry so we went scouting for the cheapest food that we could find. That

Holding one of my many awards

turned out to be hot dogs. We downed a couple of them apiece and headed for the competition.

Guess what? We both did great! I remember doing a bench press of 475 pounds, which back then was an extraordinary lift. Freddy did very well for himself, too.

When the day was over and we were headed back to Pittsburgh in Freddy's Oldsmobile, we didn't even have enough money left for a victory hot dog. But I was so elated by my performance that I really didn't feel the hunger or the tiredness. I had such a good showing and had impressed so many of my fellow athletes that I felt like a celebrity, at least for the day.

On the way home, Freddy felt like he couldn't drive anymore so we switched. Soon after I started driving, I fell asleep at the wheel. The next thing I knew, I'd crossed over into the opposite lane of traffic. Freddy woke up just in time and started screaming and that woke me up real fast. My head jerked up and I saw cars coming straight at us. Freddy and I lurched for the wheel and we swerved back into our own lane. Believe me, that kept us awake for the rest of the trip.

In early fall, just when it looked like I was going to be cooling my heels all winter with no work, I got hired by the Henry Busey Construction Company. I had hoped that Carmen Tropea would get busy again but that hadn't happened. So I signed on with Busey, helping to build another church. I got a few months out of it and was laid off once more in November of 1956.

My life as an apprentice carpenter was certainly having its ups and downs. I spent Christmas and New Year's unemployed, and then in early February, I got a call to go work for the Johns Mansville Company. That lasted nearly three months until early May of 1957 before being laid off yet again.

By now my friend Freddy DeLuca had joined the Air National Guard. From the moment he went in, he kept bugging me, saying, "Bruno, you ought to join the Guard. It's great, man."

"What's so great about it?" I asked him.

Freddy explained it to me. "Bruno, you know that the draft is going to get you if you just sit back and let it. Sooner or later you're going to get drafted into the service. That means two full years with no time off. You do that, you're going to miss the weightlifting training. You're going to miss the wrestling you're so crazy about. And what about the apprenticeship you're serving. You can kiss that all goodbye if you get drafted."

I shook my head and said, "So how can I not get drafted? It's inevitable. Like you say, sooner or later."

"Bruno, the Guard's the answer. You go away for basic training for four months, but then you get to come back home. After basic, you just go away two days a month till your hitch is up. What do you say?" Freddy grinned at me.

How could I knock down his logic? It all made sense. I drove out to the 112th Division, talked to the recruiting officer there and signed up. For basic training, I was assigned to Lackland Air Force

Base, which is about 12 miles outside San Antonio, Texas. The Guard gives you a choice of what to specialize in, so since Freddy was in the medics, I said, "That sounds great. Put me in the medics." And I had a fine time in the medics, learning how to take blood pressures, how to draw blood, how to tell what blood type one has and how to give shots.

Then one day, a colonel came around and he saw me conducting business very properly as a medic and said, "What the hell is this man doing as a medic?"

What he was reacting to was my build. I was 265 pounds, big and muscular and breaking records as a power lifter. The colonel threw a fit because this strongman was being wasted as a medic. He immediately went to the sergeant in charge of the air police and demanded that I be placed there. Quicker than you could say it, I was out of the medics and into the air police.

Freddy was right. Going into the Guard was a very good move.

About six weeks after I came back from basic training in Texas, in early November 1957, I got very lucky and landed a job with Turner Construction.

Basic training at Lackland AFB in Texas

Its big project was the building of the Hilton Hotel in downtown Pittsburgh. A union agent had me placed there. The Hilton was really the best site going at the time.

Once I got settled in and got to know the men on the crews, I felt right at home. The guys used to kid me about how strong I was and how much food I ate. It's certainly true that I had an enormous appetite. I used to go to work with a shopping bag filled with just my lunch. My mom will tell you that she used to fix 14 or 15 sandwiches on homemade bread which she would cram into that shopping bag.

I probably drank seven quarts of milk a day. And when I came home at night my mom would make loads of pasta for us. I'd almost

An early photo of me training

never eat meat because we couldn't afford it. On rare occasions, we might eat chicken and then I could put away two whole chickens by myself. I guess my appetite was so large because I worked and trained hard and I was still growing. Those calories just burned up like nothing.

Well, the Pittsburgh Press somehow heard about the construction worker who was incredibly strong and who had this enormous appetite. One day when we weren't working, a Press reporter came over to my home and watched my mom fix me breakfast. She made me scrambled eggs and I also ate a loaf of bread, a box of cereal and two quarts of milk. The reporter was astounded!

Then he tagged along with me to the gym. I did all kinds of lifting just to show him my strength. He went back and did a piece on me that appeared in the Sunday Roto section which everybody read. The article generated a lot of good publicity for me.

Let me tell you about one experience I had while working at the Hilton Hotel. I was assigned to help out a Swedish fellow named John Miller who was my partner that day. We were stripping a beam that had just received a concrete pour. I was down below the beam, prying with a crowbar. John crawled up on top of the beam and he started to hit it with a sledge hammer. I couldn't see him because those beams were two and a half feet wide, but I sure could hear him overhead, banging away with his hammer.

Before I could yell up to him, "Hey, what are you doing?" the beam came loose all of a sudden, hitting me solidly and knocking me down an elevator shaft. Talk about Laurel and Hardy. I fell two stories into some plywood planking that the elevator workers had just positioned and I came to a crashing halt on that. If those boys hadn't

BRUNO SAMMARTINO

Here's What Happened After An Oakland Boy With Malnutrition Started Exercising

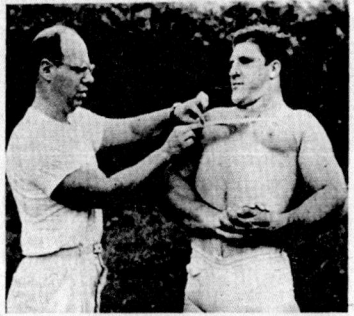

Sanford Kapner, a noted weight lifter, assists Bruno in developing his powerful body. The young giant's chest measures whopping 58 inches.

Pittsburgh

Seven boys form a human pyramid on the powerful frame of Bruno Sammartino, one of the world's most powerful men.

"ARE YOU a skinny, run-down weakling? In just minutes a day YOU too can add powerful pounds and vital, dynamic muscles . . . the envy of your friends . . ."

Glowing promises of "get strong" advertisements have no appeal to Bruno Sammartino of Oakland. There is no danger that anybody will think he is a skinny, run-down weakling. At 23 years of age, he is rated as one of the world's strongest men for his height of five feet, 10 inches and weight of 250 pounds. At present, the young giant—an apprentice carpenter working on the Hilton Hotel—hopes to add another 25 pounds in time for a weight-lifting contest this fall.

But just 12 years ago, Bruno was a skinny, run-down weakling. He was then almost starving in a small village in Italy after the war. Three members of his family had died of malnutrition before the survivors were permitted to migrate to America to be reunited with the father. At the age of 13 years, Bruno weighed 60 pounds, was placed on a special diet and was "always doctoring."

"I watched other boys play baseball and other games, but I was too sickly to join in the fun," he explains.

Bruno gradually put on weight and two years later weighed 115 pounds. But he was still too delicate to participate in athletics at Schenley High School. Sensing this frustration, Maurice Simon, a school companion, said, "Why don't you exercise up at the YMHA. They got weights and stuff up there."

Bruno took the advice, applied himself seriously to body building exercises and weight lifting. The pounds he added were muscle, and later he became a weight lifting instructor at the YM&WHA. After being graduated from high school, Bruno was offered a tentative scholarship by the University of Pittsburgh. At the same time he was offered a carpenter's apprenticeship, which he decided to accept. In the meantime he wrestled with the Pitt

40   The Pittsburgh Press, Sunday, September 7, 1958

The first article about me in
The Pittsburgh Press

THE AUTOBIOGRAPHY OF WRESTLING'S LIVING LEGEND

A dramatic example of Bruno's strength is his ability to perform pushups with four adults riding on his back.

Hercules

By William Faust
Press Fashion Writer

team and did a little boxing to continue his body-building routine. One offer the Pittsburgh Hercules was reluctant to turn down was a five-year contract of $15,000 a year to become a professional wrestler. Bruno prizes his amateur standing as a weight lifter, but there is a possibility he may some time accept the wrestling contract.

Maintaining his tremendous strength strains the purse strings of the young giant. He drinks seven quarts of milk a day. For breakfast he eats one dozen eggs, a loaf of bread and two quarts of milk. A two-pound steak is just a snack. Bruno hesitates to accept dinner invitations, for his terrific appetite can be embarrassing.

"I'm generally hungry when I leave the table," he says.

Apprentice wages, plus his appetite has prevented Bruno from marrying. But in seven months he will be a journeyman carpenter, and he intends to marry Carol Teyssier, a North Side girl he met at the wedding of a friend.

Bruno will attend the Weight Lifters' Picnic in York, Pa., this fall, and participate in the Eastern National Weight-Lifting Contest in October in the East Liberty YMCA. He is also tentatively scheduled to appear with Paul Anderson, the world's strongest man, on a new TV show, "Brawn vs. Brains."

Bruno's breakfast is 12 eggs, two quarts of milk and a loaf of bread.

The Pittsburgh Press, Sunday, September 7, 1958

September 7, 1958

been working there and laid that plywood, I would have plunged 19 stories down the shaft. Even so, I got shaken up pretty good and that set me back with my training.

Another time a foreman named Sal Williams came up to me to tell me about a business opportunity. He was well aware that I was the strongest man on the job site and he had seen me take on all comers at lunchtime in arm-wrestling. He wanted to know if I'd like to make an easy $50. When you're an apprentice carpenter making about $20 a day, then $50 sounds real good. I asked him what I had to do.

Apparently Sal had visited a carnival that was in Irwin just for the week. Irwin is a town just east of Pittsburgh. There he had seen a wrestling tent that featured a monkey who took on all challengers. The man who ran the exhibit bragged that nobody could last with his monkey for five minutes. Sal told the carnival operator that he knew a young fellow at work who definitely could last that long and more. So the two agreed to put up a $50 bet. It would be the monkey against me.

Sal told me that if I won, I could keep the $50. He just wanted to see me whip this monkey. I asked Sal how big the monkey was. He said he hadn't stuck around to watch a match so he hadn't actually seen it, but he didn't think it was very big.

Sal really had a lot of confidence in me, betting so much money on my behalf against an opponent he hadn't even seen. But he added, that night we could catch the monkey on television. He had heard it was going to be featured on a local news show called "Pitt Parade," which aired around 6 p.m. I told Sal I'd watch the show to size up this beast.

That night before I went to the gym, I flipped on KDKA for the news about the carnival. The camera showed a cage with this little shivering monkey in it, only about 18 inches high. That poor monkey looked like somebody's neglected pet. When I saw that, I said to myself you've got to be kidding. Who couldn't beat that chimp?

The next day I went up to Sal and I told him not to worry. I asked him how he could have any doubt that I wouldn't beat the monkey. I pledged to him that, "Not only will I last five minutes, but I'll whip that monkey with both hands tied behind my back." So the match was on for Friday evening after work.

Some of the guys at the site started kidding me, saying, "Bruno, don't you know those monkeys have sharp claws?"

I laughed, saying "I don't care. When I get my hands on that monkey, I will show you all what will happen to those claws."

Since I was so full of confidence, everybody began to feel sorry for the monkey. The fellows told me to go easy on the poor little animal. After all, it wasn't the monkey who made the bet.

Finally, Friday rolled around and a huge group from work all climbed into their pickup trucks and cars and headed to the carnival in a caravan. When we arrived, Sal escorted me over to the tent and a heavy-set man met us, handing me a release to sign that stated the carnival was not responsible for anything that might happen to me and that I was entering into this match of my own free will.

As I was signing the paper, I noticed that the heavy guy's right hand only had a thumb on it. The other four fingers were missing. Not being a real man of the world at age 20, I asked him what had happened.

He laughed and told me to be careful when I grabbed the monkey around the head. Even though the monkey had a muzzle on, the strap that held the device in place had a tendency to come loose … especially if I fooled with it in the wrong way.

The heavy guy kept hinting that the monkey had chewed off his fingers. I thought to myself, "Boy, that little animal must have some powerful jaws and teeth."

As I continued to talk with the heavy guy, I noticed there was a large cage, covered with canvas that was swaying back and forth. I asked him, "What on earth is making all the ruckus in that cage?"

He chuckled and snorted, "That's your opponent, son." I couldn't believe it. "My opponent?" I thought, "How could that little monkey make that big cage rattle and shake?"

The heavy guy just looked at me and laughed. Soon the time came for me to enter the cage. All of my buddies from work packed the tent and were shouting encouragement to me as I waited. Then the canvas was drawn up and the monkey was unveiled. Nobody could believe it at first, especially me. The animal was a huge and ugly orangutan! I stared at it for a second then shouted at the heavy guy over the crowd, "Hey, that's not the same monkey that was on TV!"

He rubbed his nose with his solitary thumb and snorted, "Who said you was gonna wrestle that monkey?" I took a deep breath and thought, "Oh, my God! What have I got myself into?" As I climbed inside and took my place at the opposite corner, I took a long look at the sucker. I almost froze because up close, the beast seemed even bigger, like King Kong or Mighty Joe Young. This was one ambitious looking animal, even with his muzzle on. I stretched a bit, working my neck and shoulders loose, kicking at the straw on the cage floor. I was wearing a sweat suit and had on a pair of tights over that. I still wore my construction boots over sweat socks. Remembering those warnings about the monkey claws, I had come prepared for combat. All the guys from work were screaming now. "Go get him, Bruno! Stomp that sucker!" That pumped me up and I started thinking that the match was going to be great!

We got the signal to go and the battle was on. At first the orangutan just stood in his corner, hanging onto the bars and staring at me. I got the idea that he thought I was afraid since I wasn't making any moves toward him. All of a sudden, like lightning, he swung at me, his claws aiming for my face. Faster than I could imagine, he attacked, his feet like two pistons, pounding into me. He hung onto me with his arms and then, boom, boom, boom with his feet into my sides. When I tried to duck, he was so swift and powerful that even when I tried to block his blows, he connected. Then as quick as he attacked, he darted away, taking up a position opposite me. He frowned at me, bewildered that I hadn't tumbled to the cage floor.

After that first flurry of blows, I had lost all fear of him because now I was angry and humiliated. I started to picture in my mind my amateur wrestling techniques. If only I could get behind him and force him to the floor, then I might have a chance to influence him. It was a good theory but as long as he continued to hang on the bars, I couldn't do anything.

I rushed him once, twice, three times with no luck. He darted away, leaving me grasping air. Then, on the fourth try I got behind him and was able to hook my arms around his chest. The crowd was going wild at this point.

At that time, I weighed around 265 pounds and was very strong, but when I moved to yank him down from the bars, he acted like he had a flea on his back. He swung around the cage with me hanging onto him for dear life. He always made sure to swing close to the bars so my back would scrape hard against the steel. After he circled the cage five or six times, I had to release my hold. I crashed to the floor, thinking my back was breaking.

The match went on, minute after minute and no matter what I would try, it was hopeless. The orangutan fought off all my best moves, then when I didn't expect it, he would let go of the cage with one paw and swing into me, sweeping me against the bars. I'd never wrestled anybody or anything as powerful as he was.

Fifteen minutes into the bout, I started to lose my vision. My eyes puffed up from the animal's steady pounding. I wasn't doing very well at all. We both took a couple of steps back and glared at each other. As he hung from his perch, I noticed that he was breathing heavily. Maybe I had started to wear him down.

I saw that his belly moved in and out as he sucked in air. It looked soft and I thought then that if I could connect with one hard shot to his midsection, maybe I might have a chance to end this struggle before I went blind.

I rushed him and punched at his belly but I only half-connected. As soon as I did that, the carnival man who owned the orangutan stopped the fight, screaming that I was disqualified. He shouted that I cheated because I had thrown a punch in a wrestling match.

So even though that big, hairy beast could do everything he wanted, I had to play by the rules. At any rate we did win Sal William's $50 bet. I had lasted well more than five minutes in the cage with this carnival Kong. And my buddies from work had something to talk about for quite a long time afterwards.

By the way, when I climbed down from the cage, all I had left on my body was my tights and my boots. The orangutan had shredded the rest of my clothes right off and I had blood all over my back and shoulders. My eyes were nearly shut from his attacks. As I headed out of the tent into the fresh air, I hoped that would be the last time anybody would make a monkey out of me!

I worked with Turner Construction at the Hilton Hotel job site for nearly two years, from November of 1957 to late October of 1959. Throughout all that time, I continued with my weightlifting career.

In the summer of 1959, I won another important contest—a state power lifting championship—and in the early part of fall that year, Bob Prince asked me to come back on his show to talk about it. Bob remembered me from my days as a novice lifter and wanted to follow up with my latest accomplishments.

So in mid-October, I went on his show and he was very kind to me, giving me a big build up. We chatted about how I had always loved wrestling, ever since I was a little boy in Italy and about how my childhood idol was the great Primo Carnera, the Italian boxing king. I had dreamed about growing up to become as strong and capable a man as Primo Carnera. Then Bob and I talked about how I went back and forth to Pitt and the Y to work out and how my life's ambition was to become a professional wrestler one day.

Little did I know that a man who was watching me on KDKA's Bob Prince Show that day was to have an enormous impact on my life. His name was Rudy Miller and he was the local promoter, representing Capitol Wrestling in the eastern region. (Incidentally, Capitol Wrestling eventually evolved into the WWF.) As Capitol's agent, Rudy handled all its shows in the Pittsburgh area, which included a

A dream come true was having my childhood idol Primo Carnera pose with me and Mom in our house

television studio wrestling program that aired on Channel 11.

The next day, Rudy was at the Channel 11 station and he happened to be jawing with a couple of friends of mine from high school—the Kartonis brothers. I was also in the Pennsylvania Air National Guard with these guys, so they knew me pretty well.

The Kartonis brothers used to work the studio wrestling shows there, taking the jackets from the wrestlers in their corners before the matches would begin. Rudy asked them if they knew this young kid from Pittsburgh, named "Bruno something," who had been on the Bob Prince Show the day before. He couldn't remember my last name.

They both knew who he was referring to right away and they chimed in that Rudy had seen Bruno Sammartino, a great guy and a tremendously strong wrestler. Rudy asked the brothers to get in touch with me and see if I would be willing to meet with him at the Channel 11 studios.

Rudy Miller, who I credit with discovering my wrestling talents

So the Kartonis brothers contacted me to say that Rudy Miller, a professional wrestling promoter, was interested in meeting me. Of course, this was what I had been waiting for, a chance to meet somebody in the wrestling profession, an industry where I knew absolutely nobody.

The following week I drove over to Channel 11 and made my way into the studio where live wrestling was broadcast. I saw the Kartonis brothers and walked over to join them. Then they introduced me to Rudy Miller and left the two of us alone.

Rudy started firing questions at me. "How much wrestling have you done in your life?"

I told him that what I said on the Bob Prince Show was true. I've loved wrestling ever since I was a little kid. Then I told him about my dedication to training and how I had walked every night after school to go and train at Pitt, wrestling with the college team. I mentioned how I continued to train at the Y, never letting up a minute.

He asked me to take off my jacket and shirt because he wanted to see what I looked like. Of course, thanks to my hard work and constant training, my physique did impress him.

Then he asked me a question that at the time I didn't quite understand. He said, "You say your name is Sammartino? You're Italian, right?"

"That's right," I said.

"But you were born in America?" he asked. I shook my head, "No, I was born in Italy."

Rudy's eyes opened a little wider. "Really? Do you speak Italian?" I laughed, "Of course. I was born and raised there."

He clapped his hands together and said, "That's great!"

I didn't understand why he thought that was so "great." I'm proud of my Italian heritage and I love to speak the language, but I just didn't get the connection.

In any case, Rudy asked me if I would like to travel to Washington, D.C., with him to meet a couple of other promoters, his partners Toots Mondt and Vince McMahon, Sr. That made me stop and think for a second.

As I said before, this was in the fall of 1959. I had just gotten married to my wife Carol on Sept. 12, after having gone together for nearly four years. As much as I wanted to say to Miller, "Yes, I'll go with you to Washington," I knew I couldn't do that immediately. I'd have to clear it with my foreman at work because I sure couldn't afford to lose my job just to go on an interview. And I knew I'd have to talk it over with my wife.

Carol and I had started out living with my parents on the second floor of their house and we really didn't have much of our own yet. Even though Carol had a job with Travelers Insurance as a typist, we still had to count on my salary as an apprentice carpenter to go with hers in order to make ends meet.

Rudy said to tell my foreman that I'd only be gone a couple of days and that this trip could be a very important step in my life. He said he doubted that I'd have any trouble and just get back to him when I got the okay. So I agreed to ask my foreman for permission to leave the job site for a few days to go meet Mondt and McMahon.

Frankly, I was more than a little nervous about it since my foreman, Ralph Trapazano from Philadelphia, had been very good to me. Thanks to him, I had finally started to make a decent wage at the Hilton Hotel site after being on the job there for two straight years, Mr. Trapazano had seen to it that my job responsibilities had started to grow.

Early on, Mr. Trapazano had come to me and said, "I heard from the business agent that all people ever use you for is bull-work. To load, unload, dig, and carry? Is that right?"

I said that was true.

"Well, you're an apprentice carpenter, right?"

I said "Yeah, that's right. And I'm getting a little worried about my apprenticeship running out without ever being allowed to handle a hammer or a saw." I added, "How am I supposed to get work later when I don't know anything about carpentry?"

Mr. Trapazano shook his head and said, "Well, Bruno, just listen to me. You're going to be an apprentice carpenter over here in my crew and if anybody tells you to do something that you're not supposed to do, then tell me about it. You know the apprentice rules, don't you?"

I said, "Yes, sir!"

There were a lot of people working on the Hilton Hotel job. I couldn't believe that anybody there really cared about me like Mr. Trapazano did. In the past, if anybody needed bull-work, they'd say "Go get Bruno" and anytime they needed somebody to lift, they'd say "Go get Bruno." Mr. Trapazano changed all that so naturally I didn't want to do anything to offend him or to show him I wasn't appreciative of everything he had done for me.

The next day when I went back to work, I was leery about even asking him. Here he was, giving me all that overtime and now I wanted to take off for Washington, D.C.

Finally, I went over to him in the middle of the morning and said, "Mr. Trapazano, may I have a few words with you?"

He smiled and said, "Bruno, I've told you a hundred times to call me Ralph."

I said, "I'm sorry Mr. Trapazano, but that's the way I was raised. You're my boss and I owe you respect so that's why I call you Mr. Trapazano."

"Okay," he said, "What's on your mind, Bruno?" So I told him how ever since I came from Italy when I was 15, I had a dream. It was a dream that I never even told my parents about because I didn't want to be laughed at or thought to be crazy. My dream was someday to become a professional wrestler and it was to this goal that I had trained so hard all of my life.

I told Mr. Trapazano that in fact when I left work, I would go to the gym for four hours every night and work out, day in and day out, week after week, weightlifting, wrestling and waiting for my chance to fulfill my dream.

Then with a big lump in my throat, I said that I had met a promoter by the name of Rudy Miller who wanted me to go to Washington, D.C. for two days, so that two other promoters could take a close look at me. I said that if my absence would cause any problems on the job, I would tell Miller just to forget it.

Mr. Trapazano waited until I was finished, smiled again and said, "Bruno, if things work out for you and you aren't coming back, just let me know. As far as I'm concerned, you have my permission to go."

I was overjoyed. After work, I went back to the television station and luckily Rudy Miller was still there. I told him that my boss had agreed to let me go. Then I stopped dead. "I don't have any money for a plane ticket. Maybe I'll have to drive there."

Miller said, "Don't worry about that stuff." He reached into his pocket, pulled out a big wad of bills and peeled off five $100 bills for me. He said, "Use this to buy your plane tickets and use the rest for any other expenses you might have on the way. It should be plenty but don't worry. I'll be meeting you down there too and I can give you more if you run out of cash."

Five hundred dollars to me was a fortune, especially since I was making $20 a day as an apprentice carpenter.

When I went home and told my wife Carol that a wrestling promoter had given me $500 to go to Washington, she asked me, "Bruno, why can't you get wrestling out of your head? Why don't you just forget it? You're going to be a carpenter. With me working for Travelers, we'll have enough."

I said to her, "Honey, I can't go through my life without giving my dream a shot. I have to try."

Finally, she was very unhappy about it but knowing how much it meant to me, she said that I should go.

So in mid-November, I went to the address in D.C. that Rudy Miller had given to me. There I met Toots Mondt, an old-time wrestler who had become a promoter, and his partner, Vince McMahon, Sr. We all sat down in their office and they started to ask me about my wrestling.

When did I start? How much experience did I have? Am I really Italian?

Then they did something that threw me. McMahon picked up the phone and called someone they knew who spoke Italian and he asked me to speak to this man. I got on the phone and the man says to me, "Buongiorno" and he asked me several questions in Italian such as "How long have you been in this country?" and "How much do you like wrestling?" I answered all of his questions in Italian.

After we had spoken for a while, the mysterious man asked me if I would put McMahon back on the line. He then verified to the promoter that yes, Bruno Sammartino spoke fluent Italian.

What I didn't understand at the time, but realized later was that if you were a foreigner in wrestling, it was a tremendous drawing card. The promoters loved to pit different wrestlers from different backgrounds against each other.

With my Italian heritage confirmed, Mondt and McMahon had me stay overnight. They even took me out to dinner.

The next day, bright and early, I was taken to a gymnasium in the area where a ring was set up. A couple of pro wrestlers were working out when we arrived so the two promoters asked me to see what I could do with one of them.

I climbed into the ring with the first man and went into my amateur stance. When he came at me, I immediately tried to get behind him, but he blocked me easily. I tried to get behind him a second time and again he blocked my move. Then I faked the move

Toots Mondt and his partner Vince McMahon, Sr.

behind, went for his leg and I took him down, riding him onto the mat. We went at each other for a while and to be honest, I impressed him.

Then the promoters had the second pro come in and I worked out with him, too. He tried different professional moves on me and I countered very well. You know, despite what people think there are a number of professional moves that are unfamiliar and therefore tough for amateur wrestlers. That's because amateur wrestlers aren't taught about submission wrestling. That's certainly not the case in professional wrestling where there are many pros who have mastered the art of total dominance of an opponent.

What helped me get through this tryout, even though I was being thrown moves that I'd never seen before, was my power, my strength and my quickness. Either I wouldn't get caught in them in the first place or I'd just bull my way out if I did.

After the two workout sessions were over and I had showered and toweled off, the promoters came back to me and said that I had impressed them. They wanted me to stay for a month and train with pros like the ones I had just wrestled with before they turned me pro. At first I didn't know what to say.

I blurted out "I have to go back to Pittsburgh because I told my boss and my wife I'd only be gone two days." Then it hit me. I said, "But wait a minute. Does this mean you think I 'm good enough to compete professionally?"

Both Mondt and McMahon nodded and said, "Yes, Bruno. Absolutely!" Then McMahon added, "Bruno, go back to Pittsburgh and tell them you're quitting your job. You're going to be a professional wrestler. We'll have the contract waiting for you when you get back."

I said, "Okay. Fantastic! I'll go back and make the arrangements, talk to my boss and discuss it with my wife."

And so I went back home and told Carol about what had happened to me. But instead of us dancing for joy, she nearly couldn't hold back her tears. We'd gotten married less than two months earlier and here I was talking about quitting the job I'd held for nearly two years to become a professional wrestler. It just didn't make sense to her.

The next day when I returned to work, I immediately went to see Mr. Trapazano and I told him everything that had happened. It didn't take him long to give me an answer.

He said, "Bruno, you don't really belong here in construction. You're a big, strong guy with a lot of talent. I think everybody's here for a purpose and I don't think that yours was to be a carpenter. Go ahead and follow your dream. I'll be watching in the newspapers to see what happens to you."

Grateful for his understanding and his blessing, I thanked him for the two years of steady work he'd given me and then I left for home. I told my wife that I had quit my construction job and then I told her parents.

They were surprised by what I had done, especially since I had never spoken to them about my plans. I told them that I didn't want anybody to think I was crazy, but I had always had this dream. I told them that I had to go chase it now, otherwise I might never have another chance to see if I was good enough or not. And they understood. Then privately, my in-laws told me not to worry about Carol. They said that they would take care of her and help her to understand what her husband was doing.

When I told my own parents what I had decided to do, they were definitely not in favor. My mother was scared about what would happen to her son, leaving home and going into a profession where I could be hurt. My father didn't see wrestling as a respectable business for a family man. They both were disappointed with my choice, but to their great credit they didn't fight me on it.

Everyone knew that I had to find out if I could make it as a pro. And I knew that everything I'd ever worked for was at stake.

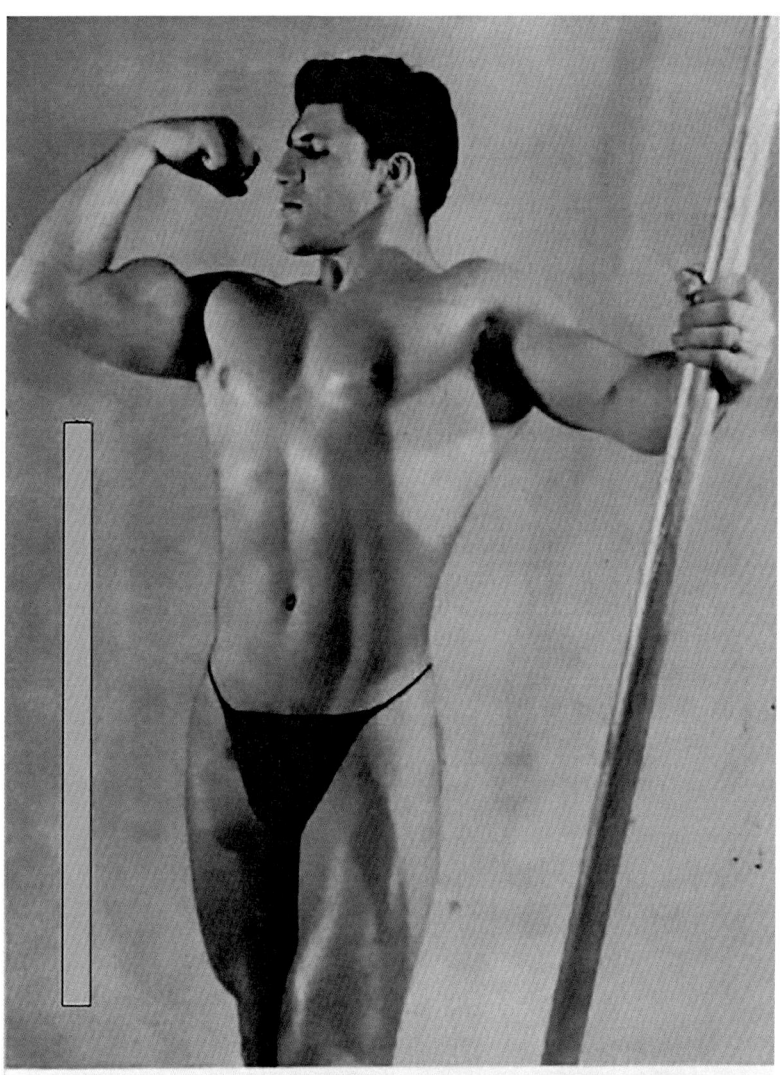

A BIG GUY is Bruno Sammartino of Pittsburgh, Pa. Bruno, who is 20, works out with Alex Pilin (see Page 14) and with good results, too. He's 5'10", weighs 215, has an 18¼" neck, and 17" arms, a 51" chest (!) which expands to 52½". All this top-side narrows down to a 33" waist. He bench presses 440 pounds. Photo is by Frank Collier.

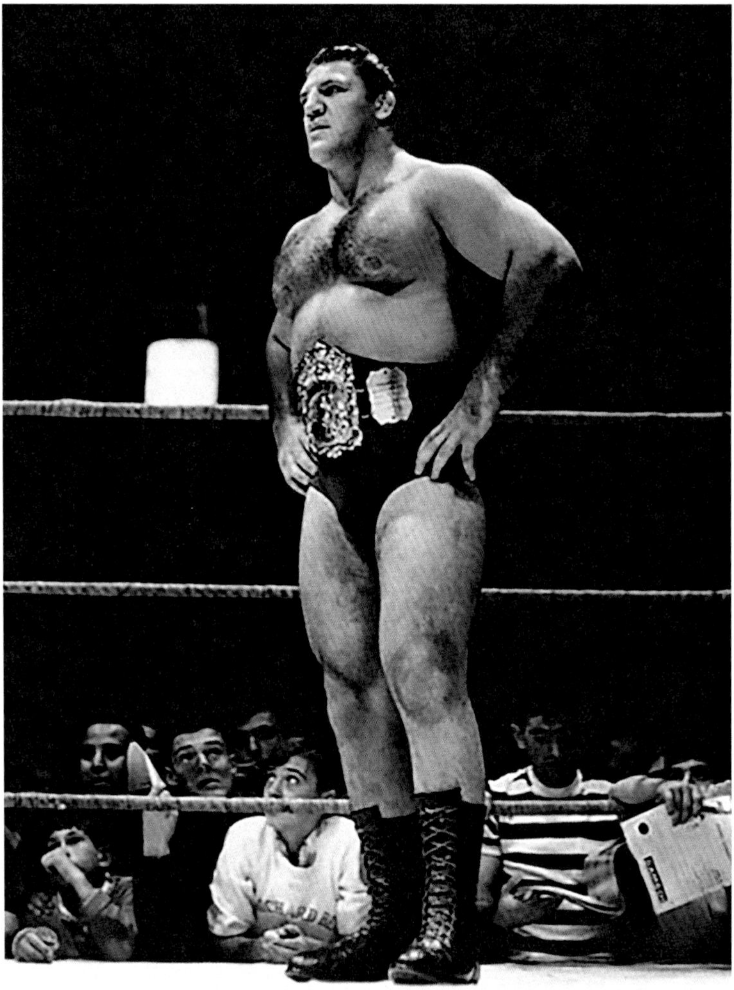

My Professional Career Begins

I left for Washington, D.C. as soon as I could make travel arrangements. When I got there I trained, and trained hard. Every morning I would work out with professional wrestlers who were signed on with the Capitol card, and then at night, when the pros would scatter to their scheduled bouts, I'd go to the local YMCA to pump iron.

I maintained that routine for a whole month and then it came time to turn pro. Mondt and McMahon handed me my contract and asked me to sign on the dotted line.

I had never seen a contract before and I didn't realize that I should have had an attorney look it over. At first glance, it seemed really simple to me. I was to be paid $250 a week salary and anything that I earned over that from box office proceeds would be split 50-50 with them.

Now, I'd never traveled much and not knowing how these things were handled, I asked them if the $250 that I was getting in salary was going to be enough to cover my expenses. I said that I didn't know what it would cost for hotels and meals or for transportation.

McMahon gave me his assurance that I would travel mostly by car and that there would always be someone driving with me to share costs. He told me that I'd be wrestling mainly between New York, New Jersey, Connecticut, and Pennsylvania.

"Okay," I said, "But really, I'm not so sure that $250 is going to be enough to live on and send money home to my wife."

McMahon told me, "Don't worry, Bruno. The $250 is only for your expenses. That's your guarantee. The bulk of your money is going to come from the 50-50 split."

What he said seemed to make sense. I felt good about it and

thought, "Okay, I'm 24-years-old. I can take care of myself." So I signed it.

When I called home to my wife and explained the deal to her, she said that she really didn't understand too much about it. It was obvious that she still didn't like the idea of me going off to become a professional wrestler. To her the money wasn't all that important. She just wanted to know when I'd be home and how often.

From the beginning, life was rough. For whatever reason, that $250 guarantee was all that I was getting. I never did get anymore than that $250. I can laugh about it now, years later, but believe me it was serious business at the time.

Yes, it was true that I was driving to all my matches but as it turned out, it was usually with one of Capitol's agents and he would still actually charge me transportation costs to make these trips. Then I was also paying for my hotel rooms, plus trying to curb my enormous appetite out of that $250.

So I was supposed to make my extra money from gate receipts everywhere I wrestled, right? After a while I was wrestling in Madison Square Garden and even then there weren't any gate receipts to split. That's what I was told, anyway.

The problem turned out to be that there had never been any predetermined amount specified as far as indicating what percentage of each match I would receive. The contract stated that I'd share in profits but not when the profits would begin.

Capitol just gave me whatever it felt like, whenever it felt like it. And it was never much.

I was quite a bashful person in those days and for a while I just kept quiet. I didn't want to stir things up. But after a while enough was enough and I finally went to Rudy Miller to ask him some tough questions.

"Rudy," I wanted to know, "When am I going to make some decent money?"

Rudy was patient with me. He said, "Bruno, you're new to this business. It's going to take a while to get yourself established. For now, you're going to have to manage your money carefully."

I said, "All I do with my money is pay bills. Sometimes after paying for my room, there's not even enough money left to buy food. And Rudy, I stay at the cheapest hotels I can find." What I didn't tell him was that with my penny pinching, I managed to send Carol about $75 of my guarantee every month.

He looked at me, smiled and said, "Bruno, you just got to be patient. Things will turn around for you real soon. You can depend on it."

Kola Kwariani

I was starting to have second thoughts about everything. Now I wanted to know exactly what was going on. I made a few inquiries and in a short time I found out that there was more to professional wrestling than meets the eye.

A New York promoter named Kola Kwariani kept coming up in conversation. It seemed that Kwariani had made a deal some time ago with Vince McMahon and Toots Mondt to combine the entire Northeast wrestling territory. Even though Kwariani was based in the Big Apple and McMahon and Mondt were based in Washington, D.C. they were actually partners in the running of the whole Northeast game.

Now, there was a feud going on, one that was shaking this partnership to pieces. The three promoters had decided to split the territory in half. Kola Kwariani was to receive New York, New Jersey, and parts of Connecticut. McMahon was going off on his own, taking Washington, Maryland, Pennsylvania and what was left of Connecticut.

Where did Rudy Miller and Toots Mondt fit in then? They sided with Kwariani in the feud. Wrestlers were caught in the middle of the fight. The promoters were playing a tug-of-war and each of the wrestlers had to decide which camp they would wrestle for from this point on.

I knew that I was under contract with Vince McMahon. I also knew that I was just barely scraping by on the money McMahon paid me. Miller and Mondt were pushing me to Kwariani, telling me that McMahon didn't have any real development plans for my career but Kwariani wanted me and Tony Rocca to join up as tag team partners.

I struggled with my decision, then finally agreed to go with Kola Kwariani. When I told Miller this, Rudy said that he and Toots would take care of telling McMahon the news. They said I was to report immediately to Kwariani's office at the Holland Hotel on 42nd Street in New York.

I flew up to meet the man. Kwariani, as it turned out, had been a powerful wrestler in his day. He wrestled as an amateur in his native Russia, then came to America to become a pro.

Now as an old man, he had become a promoter in the sport he loved. He spoke to me in a thick accent, almost too difficult to understand. "Bruno" he said, "You will wrestle for me and you will become a big star someday. All you have to do is just listen to me, Kola Kwariani, and do exactly what I say."

I answered quickly, "Yes, sir. Whatever you say." He impressed me as someone who knew the business and was an honorable man. So I began to wrestle for Kwariani in what turned out to be a very turbulent period in my career.

Shortly after I joined Kwariani's ranks, he got broadsided by the state athletic commission. This was the official wrestling association that had jurisdiction over him and it had just become very tough on violence. The association began to enforce restrictions on what may or may not appear on television and at live appearances in arenas. In other words, it took the bite out of what we could or couldn't do as wrestlers.

Down in Washington, D.C. it was a different story. McMahon had no commission to contend with so he was free to be as wild as he wanted to be. This translated into big box office. McMahon started to win the war for gate attendance as the fans flocked to the more exciting and exuberant matches he promoted.

Kwariani was in trouble. Other local promoters were abandoning the old Russian and calling for McMahon's services.

Finally, Kwariani brought me into his office and told me that if things continued the way they were, that I should try to find another promoter who could handle me better than he could. He just said that his hands were tied by the commission, and even though it was ruining his business, there was nothing he could do.

I went back to where I was staying and called Rudy Miller, telling him what was happening and asking him and Toots Mondt for their guidance. Where could I find another promoter who could take over for Kwariani?

Miller was blunt. He blamed Kwariani for all my problems. He told me that the best thing to do would be for him to talk to Vince McMahon to see if Vince would take me back. Miller said he wasn't so sure that this would work because he knew McMahon to be a man who held grudges.

Well, McMahon did agree to let me return to his fold but he certainly didn't have the noblest intentions. He conducted a war of nerves with me and he commanded the artillery.

Here's what he would do. Let's say he'd run two shows in his territory on one particular night. One show might be at the Civic Arena in Pittsburgh which is a large facility. The other show would be held in New Castle, a small town in Northeastern Pennsylvania. Guess who would end up going to New Castle to appear in the opening match?

As lightweight as those bookings were, McMahon would only give me one or two of them a week. The payoffs would be $20 or $25. I just couldn't survive on that kind of money, especially since my wife Carol had given birth to our first child, our son David, who was born on September 29, 1960. I now had even greater responsibilities to my family. I'd been a professional wrestler for close to a year and was just barely getting by. What was I to do?

I told Rudy Miller what was going on and he said there was nothing he and Toots could do for me. That's just the way McMahon operated. When you were on "McMahon's List," you stayed there.

Rudy suggested that I might be better off with another promoter in another territory. I told him I didn't know any other promoters.

Rudy volunteered to call around and see what he could dig up, promising not to let the word get around that I was looking for an escape route from McMahon.

Miller called Detroit promoter Johnny Doyle who said he could use an Italian name on his cards. I agreed to go with Doyle, thinking by now that anything which would take me out from under McMahon would be a good move.

I went to McMahon, told him that I was leaving after I finished my last two bookings and did just that. I wrestled two more matches then packed my bags for San Francisco.

That's right, San Francisco, not Detroit. While I was fulfilling my final obligations with McMahon, Johnny Doyle was already hard at work on my behalf. Doyle and a San Francisco promoter, Roy Shire, were collaborating with their first show at the Cow Palace. Because there were many Italians in the Bay Area, Doyle worked out a deal with Shire to have me booked there.

Once I arrived, I wrestled on the card, then stayed over to wrestle in some other local matches that Doyle had booked me for. While I was getting ready to do a TV match one night, a couple of guys from the state athletic commission cornered me before I went on. They told me that I couldn't wrestle that night because I had been suspended. I was astonished. "Suspended? What are you talking about?"

They were arrogant, smirking. One guy just said, "In plain English, Bruno, you can't wrestle. Suspended."

I stammered, "Why am I suspended? What have I done?"

"You mean you don't know what you've done? Or where you did it?" he said, turning away.

"I have no idea," I said. "That's too bad, Bruno. Just don't try crawling through the ropes tonight or any night. You're through."

The two men left me standing there, shaking my head. I rushed over to Doyle and cornered him, asking "Why had I been suspended? What had I done?"

Doyle shrugged, saying "Well, kid, I don't know what you did. I'll see if I can find out."

It took Doyle two days to get back to me. I was frantic and

upset, an innocent man accused of an unknown crime, and nobody was talking.

Doyle told me on the phone nothing that I didn't know already. He said, "All I know is that you're suspended. They won't let you wrestle in this territory anymore. I don't know what to tell you. Maybe you need to find yourself another place to go. There's a guy I know in Indianapolis, Jim Barnett. Let me give him a call. See if he can fit you in on a couple of matches."

After a few quick phone calls back and forth, I was on my way back east to Indianapolis. I had just enough money to get there and when I arrived, it was the same old song on the jukebox. Just as McMahon had done to me, Barnett was only giving me a $25 payroll for my matches. I got the small stuff and that was it. I couldn't even make enough money to feed myself or stay in a decent motel room, much less take care of my wife and baby boy.

Out of my $25 payoff, I would keep only $10 for myself and send $15 home to my wife. I wouldn't check into a hotel because where could you stay for $10? I'd go to a delicatessen, buy a loaf of bread and some cheap cold cuts, and I'd find a place to go and eat my meal, drinking gallons of water to wash it all down. Then instead of checking into a hotel, I'd go into the lobby of a nice place and sit in a sofa or chair, pretending to be waiting for someone. I'd spend as much time as I could in that chair or sofa until I was chased out.

I was becoming very despondent. So I tried to see the promoter, this Jim Barnett, to get him to tell me why I was only wrestling once or twice a week and why I was making such little money. I went to his office, but Barnett wouldn't see me. Nobody in his office could help me either.

I decided to make my way back home to Pittsburgh. That was it. I had no money and I was whipped. I couldn't figure out what the suspension had been all about. I had been judged and found guilty with my sentence being exile from the profession I loved so much.

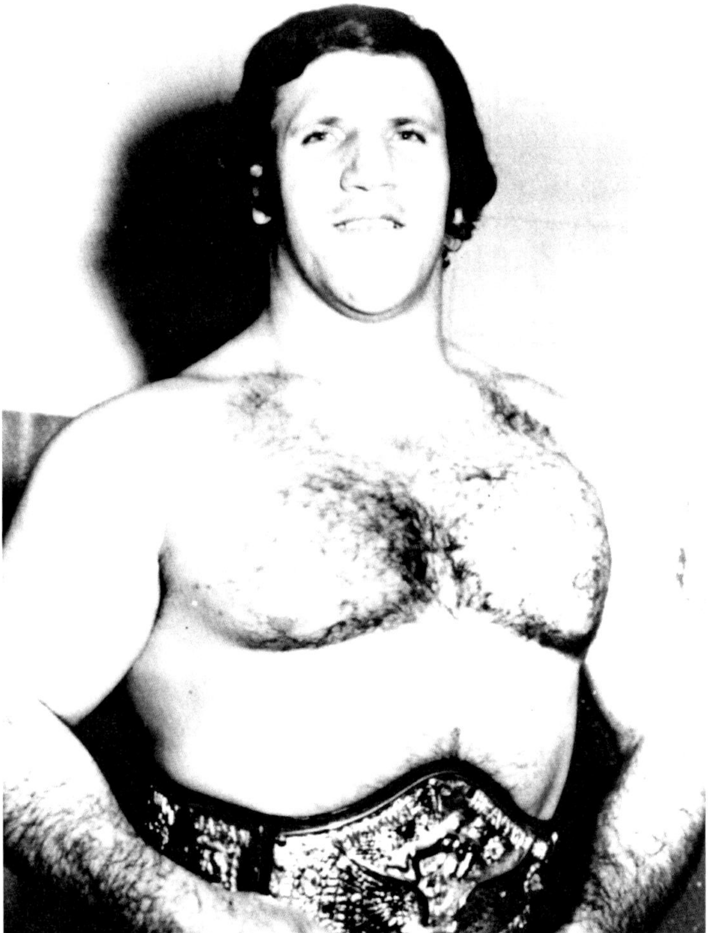

Unraveling the Mystery

I hitchhiked back to Pittsburgh. I had never hitchhiked in my life because I just was not that kind of person. I was very shy and bashful. But I had no money and no choice.

I made it home completely exhausted. I was depressed and confused. On the one hand, it was wonderful to be with my wife and family again, but how was I to support them now?

I called one of the local contractors who I had worked for several years ago, Mr. Henry Busey, and talked to him about returning to construction work. He agreed to hire me back as a laborer for a while.

While I had been gone, the wrestling game in Pittsburgh had taken on a different look. Toots Mondt had started promotions in Pittsburgh and had a guy named Ace Freeman was running the operation for him. But looks are deceiving at times because the Pittsburgh territory was still under Capitol Wrestling, and McMahon still held everyone on a short leash.

Here I am all smiles with McMahon, Mondt, and Bill Cardille

When Toots heard that I was back home working construction, he contacted me and asked if we could meet. When I went to see him, the first thing I wanted to know was if he knew anything about my suspension. I told him I hadn't been able to learn anything and because I had a wife and baby to support, I had to come home and find a job to feed my family.

Toots got straight to the point. "Look, I know this suspension has been rough on you but things can be worked out. First, let me ask you if you'd like to wrestle here in Pittsburgh?"

"Sure," I said, "But how much wrestling could there be here?"

Toots thought maybe three days a week minimum. I told him that I didn't think that I'd make enough money to take care of my family just wrestling three days a week.

Toots leaned back in his chair and said, "Bruno, let me tell you something. If you want me to, I can patch things up between you and McMahon. If that happens, then you'll be back on the full circuit."

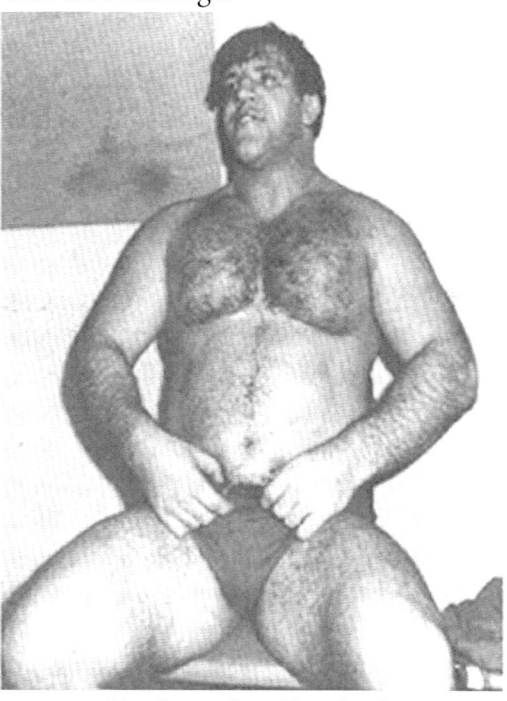

Tough match in New Castle, PA brings me only $11!

"What about the suspension?" I wanted to know.

"That can be taken care of too. All you've got to do is just give the word," said Toots.

Once more I went to the well. I told Toots that I'd take another chance on him if he could do all the things he said he could. And I knew that even though my dream had become tarnished, it was still alive in my heart.

So I started wrestling again for Toots and I found myself back in New Castle, PA, with an $11 payoff. Then I went to McKeesport and was paid $16. Another match I was paid $7.

I was getting very angry again. I went back to Mondt and laid it out for him.

"These matches just don't make it. You've got to do better for me." Toots told me to hold on. "I spoke to Vince earlier and we're going to get that suspension fixed for you. That means you can start wrestling all over the territory again."

"Does that mean that you know why I was suspended?" I asked. "And where my violation was supposed to have taken place?"

"It was in Baltimore, Maryland. You were scheduled for a match and you never showed up."

I cut in. "That's impossible. I've always made all my bookings, no matter what."

Toots just shook his head "Don't question it. The main thing is to get it cleared up. That's what counts." He reached into his wallet and handed me a wad of cash. "Here's money to fly to Baltimore. McMahon will meet you there and take you to the commission. Okay?"

Toots was right. Clearing up the suspension was what counted. I agreed to go as soon as possible.

I met McMahon in Baltimore and it was the first time I had talked to him since I had left him for Johnny Doyle. He told me that we would meet with the State Athletic Commission right away and that he wanted to make one thing clear. He'd do all the talking and I was to keep my mouth shut.

"Is that clear, Bruno?" McMahon asked me.

I nodded, "Sure, I understood. I won't say a word."

McMahon and I drove right over to the commission office and were ushered into a large room and all the commissioners and deputy commissioners were sitting at the table just staring at me. I just sat there like a dummy, keeping my mouth shut.

The head commissioner snapped at me, "For what you did, Sammartino, we should suspend you for life."

McMahon glared over at me, giving me the sign not to say

anything back to the head commissioner. I was still thinking to myself, "What is this guy talking about?"

The head commissioner went on, "Now because Vince McMahon has interceded on your behalf and has come to this commission personally, we are going to respect his request to lift your suspension. In addition, we are only going to fine you $500. As soon as the fine is paid, the suspension is no longer in effect."

McMahon motioned me not to speak again, then he said, "Thank you, Mr. Commissioner, for your consideration. We accept your decision."

"Let me tell you one more thing, Sammartino. If you ever do anything like this again," the commissioner added, "you will be banned from professional wrestling for life!"

After saying this, the head commissioner adjourned the meeting, a meeting in which I didn't say one word. Before we left their offices, McMahon had paid my $500 fine and then told me in the hall, "When you start working for me again, that $500 will be coming from your pay. Understand?"

"Alright. Fine. But still nobody said officially why I was suspended." I just wanted to know the truth.

McMahon glared at me. "Bruno, what's done is done. Just get your butt back to Pittsburgh and do your shows. Toots will tell you about your bookings from now on."

So I went back home and started wrestling again. What I quickly found out was that money was still as scarce as ever for me. Finally, when I worked Madison Square Garden and received a paltry $50 for my

An early studio pose. My ears still looked normal!

efforts, I made my mind up. I just couldn't go on with my life this way. Once again I became a very bitter guy. Very bitter!

Then I found out the story behind my suspension. I was enraged! Let me tell you what had happened.

As I have mentioned, McMahon held a grudge against me for leaving him and going with Kola Kwariani. When things didn't work out with Kwariani, McMahon had reluctantly agreed to put me back on his roster. The catch was that I only worked the curtain opener. He made me into the opening match against the worst of opponents and always in the smallest club. Then, even these miserable dates would be spread so far apart that I couldn't make a living.

That was when I went to Rudy Miller and appealed to him. Could he help me out with McMahon? And that was when Rudy contacted Johnny Doyle from Detroit and I ended up in San Francisco, wrestling for Doyle and Roy Shire.

It was at that point that McMahon decided that Capitol Wrestling was going to teach this "young wop" a lesson. Yes, that's how they referred to Italians in those days—"wop" or "guinea" or "dago."

What McMahon did was book me in Baltimore for a match and then just didn't tell me about it. When I finished my two remaining matches in Pittsburgh and left for the West Coast, to the best of my knowledge, I was through with Capitol.

Of course, I didn't show up in Baltimore. I didn't know about the match. McMahon then contacted the commission and asked them to take disciplinary action against this punk Sammartino.

I can just imagine McMahon on the phone to them saying, "I've had nothing but trouble with this kid. We've got to teach him a lesson. Who does he think he is, not showing up for a scheduled match?" Yes, I can just imagine. And I'm sure the commission listened well to what McMahon had to say, especially since they were being taken care of by the promoters.

I don't know what the commission members are like today but in those days, as far as I was concerned, they were corrupt, corrupt, corrupt. Look at my suspension. It was an illegal suspension. Before they can suspend you, you must be given a hearing where evidence is presented. You have to be given a chance to defend yourself against your accusers. You can't just be blackballed like I was. They had suspended me with no explanation and no reason. I never even received a notice, detailing the charges. I was never given the chance to appeal.

So why did McMahon tell me not to question the suspension? Because if I had, I would have found out that it was McMahon who had masterminded it all along.

What McMahon didn't count on was that this "young wop" did find out how he had been deceived. I began to look for an escape route once more, a way to pull myself loose from McMahon's web.

As things often happen, when you decide to make a move in a certain direction, events come together to allow you to do it. I found out that there was a promoter with a very good reputation who worked out of Toronto, Canada. His name was Frank Tunney and he was having trouble getting the crowds to come to his shows. The Pedro Martinez organization out of Buffalo, NY was running a show in Pittsburgh so I went down to see some of the guys and ran in to a friend Eric Holmback who wrestled as Yukon Eric. He is the one that told me about Frank Tunney and how business in Toronto was really down right now. He felt Toronto would be a good opportunity for me and that Frank Tunney was an honorable man.

I contacted Tunney early in 1961 and told him that I was an Italian wrestler who could speak the language fluently. I told him that I understood that there were more than 500,000 Italians living in Toronto and that if he would give me the opportunity, I could draw those people in to see me wrestle.

After thinking it over, Tunney quickly agreed. I asked him only one favor. I told him, "No one must know that I am coming to Canada. When I arrive I'll be happy to explain to you the reason for my secrecy but, until I do, you must not tell a soul."

Tunney said that was alright with him, then asked me when I could be in Toronto.

I explained to him that I still had a few dates left with Capitol which I had to fulfill. We figured out a starting date for me and that was that. I was on my way to Canada.

By now, I was growing up and getting a little smarter. I contacted

McMahon and verified all the dates for my bookings. Then I told him not to book me for any more matches. He wanted to know what the hell was going on.

I told him calmly that I was fulfilling all my obligations with him and that I was leaving Capitol. I wouldn't say where. That was my business. I didn't trust McMahon one tiny bit. To cover myself against anything like what had happened the last time, I sent certified letters to each and every State Athletic Commission office in the United States of America, saying that I was booked with Capitol Wrestling until a certain date. If I should be booked by them after this date, it would be done without my agreement or permission. I added that I would be employed by another company and that Capitol no longer represented me.

This time, I had all of those certified receipts in hand. No one was going to level me with false accusations, not again.

My decision to wrestle in Canada drew a lot of fire and generated considerable anger from Capitol. It didn't take long for McMahon and Mondt to find out that I was in Toronto and to apply the pressure once more, this time on Frank Tunney.

My first few months up north were as bad as back home. I wasn't making much money. But Tunney booked me six nights a week and I wrestled as much as I could. I would find cheap places to hole up in and then send as much money as I could back home to Carol.

I had to face facts. We were in deep debt and getting deeper. Medical bills were piling up, stemming from physical problems that Carol had to face after the birth of our son David. Her problems were so bad that our doctor told us we weren't to have any more children until Carol had recovered. In the meantime, the stack of bills rose higher and higher.

To make extra money I agreed to be booked for every possible appearance and I began a campaign to help my own situation. I became my own public relations man.

I contacted the Italian press in Toronto, told them where I was from and spoke to them in Italian. I told them that I could perform feats that not many in the world could accomplish and I invited the reporters to the gym to watch me train. They came and saw me doing a 570-pound bench press, a world record lift in those days. I squatted more than 700 pounds. As I was lifting these enormous weights, the photographers started to snap pictures like crazy. Soon they ran stories in their newspapers about me, calling me "The Italian Superman."

I found happier times in Toronto

I used the same tactic with Italian radio, informing stations about my background, then appearing on the air, talking about the Old Country. I told the audiences all about coming to the U.S. and about how happy I was to be wrestling in Toronto.

I was doing something that no one had ever done for me before ... promoting Bruno Sammartino. And it worked. The crowds started to come to see Bruno, one of Italy's "Favorite Sons."

A few months after I had started wrestling for Tunney and business was picking up, he invited me to dinner at a great Chinese restaurant in the heart of Toronto. Frank liked to have a few drinks now and again, and this night he told me things that if sober, he might not have said.

Frank was a man about 5'10" in his late '40s when I met him. He had grayish hair that he combed straight back with a parting in the side. He wore glasses, had a little pot belly, always had a cigar in his mouth, and a smile that wrapped around it.

That night he said, "Bruno, I'm very glad that I don't let people influence me very easily. I could have made a bad mistake about you, had I listened. And you wouldn't have deserved it. Now that I know you better I am so glad I took a chance on you."

I asked him what he was talking about. Frank told me, "When you first arrived here in Toronto, I got a phone call about you."

"A phone call? From who?"

"That's not important. What's important is that they told me you're nothing but a troublemaker and that I should let you go immediately."

"I think I can guess who made that call," I said.

"They told me I'd have nothing but problems with Sammartino and that you weren't worth the time of day. I told Vince that if he was correct in his judgment, then I'd just tell you to pack your bags and go back to Pittsburgh."

I nodded and said, "Vince McMahon. I see. What else did you say?"

Tunney took another sip of his drink. "You know, Bruno. I had to take a chance on you. Let's face it. Things hadn't been going well for me until you showed up. A half a million Italians can't be all wrong. The crowds are getting bigger thanks to you. I want you to know that I appreciate everything you're doing for me. If you want to make Toronto your home, you can stay with me as long as you want."

For the first time in I don't know how long, I felt good. Tunney's words picked me up. I felt like I had a shot, like I was going to get a decent chance.

I felt good not only for me but for my wife. You know, even as bad as life was for us at the time, she had never complained. I realized that I wasn't the provider for her that I wanted to be. Knowing that brought me very low, many times.

Because I had gone through such difficulty during the war and afterward, the last thing in the world I wanted to do was to bring somebody into my life, and instead of making life better, make it worse.

My father-in-law was an accountant so I guess you'd call Carol's family "middle-class." Not poor by any means. Although my father-in-law didn't make that much money, he did own his own home and drove his own car, which he traded in every two or three years. And the family used to go to Atlantic City or to Florida for vacation every year.

Carol had known a life that wasn't as bad as the one she was living with me. But never once did she chastise me. She'd never say, "See how things have worked out. I asked you not to try and do what you're doing. Now look what has happened to us."

After my dinner with Tunney, I telephoned Carol and told her that I thought I was about to get my shot. And that I had worked out an arrangement with Tunney so I could get home every two weeks for one day. This made her very happy, to know that we could be together. So right on schedule, I'd wrestle in Wellant, Ontario on Saturday, then rush to catch a bus to Buffalo, New York. I'd jump on the midnight bus from Buffalo and arrive in Pittsburgh by mid-morning on Sunday. It seemed like that bus stopped every other mile. Then I'd spend a day at home with my family, and early Monday morning I'd hurry out to Pittsburgh airport and catch a flight back to Buffalo. In Buffalo, I'd bus to wherever I was scheduled to wrestle that night, which was usually Hamilton. Tunney would always try to book me close to Buffalo on Monday nights to accommodate my trips back home.

I began to make a name for myself in Canada.

My career was starting to build momentum. All throughout Canada, the word was that Toronto was dead for wrestling until the powerful young Italian guy had come to town. All of a sudden, Frank Tunney was getting requests from Winnipeg and Vancouver from other promoters. Could we use Bruno for our show here? Could you spare him next week in Montreal?

Tunney would readily allow me to travel to Vancouver, to Calgary, and to Montreal to wrestle there for other promoters. Thanks to that, my name was getting recognition throughout Canada.

I can recall a situation that occurred just before a scheduled match that I was going to have against Lou Thesz in the Maple Leaf Gardens in Toronto. At the time, Thesz was the NWA Champion so they wanted to build me up very strong. I was going to wrestle a guy by the last name of Shumway, he was a really big guy. We were doing TV in Hamilton, Ontario where he was a local policeman. He had family in the crowd as well, but he had agreed to put me over in the match. Well, when we got in to the match he told me that he changed his mind, and he couldn't put me over, it would be too embarrassing for him. I didn't know what to do, I thought I am wrestling Lou Thesz soon, I can't let this happen. I shot him in to the ropes and when he came off I hit him as hard as I could with a closed fist and knocked him out. He was out cold. I pinned him and after

*I began to make a name for myself in Canada. Here
I am wrestling Dick "The Bulldog" Brower*

that day I never saw him again. I was given no choice, it was very important that we do well in the Maple Leaf Gardens, and if he had a problem with what he was asked to do, then he should have said so before the match, not during.

I have to say here that Frank was one of the most decent people I've known in my life. I don't really know if there are any other promoters who could compare with him. He was simply a nice man who was always willing to listen to the other guy and help out when he could. God rest his soul now. He died in 1983 at the age of 70. I'll certainly never forget him and what he did for me.

I remember going to Winnipeg one time to wrestle Gene Kiniski. The weather was so cold I didn't think that anyone would show up for the matches, but when I arrived at the arena the line to get in went around the building. I was preparing for my match when a guy named Rod Fenton, who was involved with the promotion, came in to the room and said, "You know why you're here right"? I was still young and naive so I said "I'm going to wrestle Gene Kiniski tonight" He replied, "Well he is going to beat you in two straight falls." At that point I was annoyed and I said, "I don't think Kiniski can beat me in two straight falls, as a matter of fact I may beat him in two straight falls." I got Fenton upset so Wally Karbo came in to the room to try to calm things down. I had never heard of Rod Fenton and while I always wanted to do what was best and what made sense, he had been very disrespectful, and I didn't appreciate it. Once Karbo came in we got things worked out and decided to split the first two falls. In the third fall I got counted out of the ring.

While all this was going on in Canada, back in New York, wrestling was in bad shape. Buddy Rogers was the World Champion and the crowds were going from bad to worse. When Capitol heard that Bruno Sammartino was having lots of success up north, they (Vince McMahon, Sr.) decided to try and lure me back.

Around the end of 1962, Ace Freeman, Capitol's man in charge in the Pittsburgh area, gave me a call while I was at home visiting my family. He said Vince McMahon wanted to talk to me.

I told Ace, "If Vince wants to talk to me, let him call me directly." I wasn't going to call him, not after everything that had happened between us.

I went back to Canada the next day, wrestled for two weeks straight and came back to Pittsburgh again. This time McMahon called me at home personally.

He said, "Bruno, I understand you're doing alright in Canada. Congratulations."

"Vince," I said, "I thank God that I have met a man who believes in me. Yes, I am doing well. I'm being treated well and I am very happy in Canada."

"But Bruno, you know and I know that New York is the big time. That's where all the action is."

I paused a second then said, "Vince, I understand that New York isn't doing too good right now. In fact, I hear it stinks."

Vince sputtered, "Yeah? Who told you that?"

"Oh, a couple of wrestlers that I met in Canada had come up there because they said they couldn't make a living in New York," I said.

"Look," Vince interrupted, "Maybe things were down a few

months ago, but right now it's different. Let me say three words to you … Madison Square Garden. If we do the right thing by you … you know, promote the hell out of you …"

That's where I stopped him. "Vince, I was there for you once before. Why wasn't the right thing done then?"

He jumped in again, "One thing you have to learn in this business is to bury the hatchet. Mistakes were made. Maybe I made some. Maybe you made some. You have to forget about the past and go with the future."

We argued back and forth. I had been in Canada now for about a year and a half. I told McMahon that I still didn't think that I was anywhere near wearing out my welcome there. I was doing well and I had a feeling that my good luck was going to continue.

"Vince, just listen to what has happened. I have offers from St. Louis. The National Wrestling Alliance (NWA) wants me to go there. I got calls from Minneapolis, from California. I got a trip lined up to go to Japan."

And we talked, on and on over a period of a couple weeks. McMahon kept hitting me with his logic. New York was the big time. Why wasn't I there, getting my share?

Finally, McMahon convinced me of one thing—if I was given the proper opportunity, I believed I could make it in New York. It wasn't about the money at that point. I was happy with the money I was making so even though Vince McMahon, Sr. offered me more. If I was going to make the move back to NY it had to be on my terms

In my 18 months in Canada, I had learned about success and about promotion. I knew that if I returned to Madison Square Garden that it would have to be for the biggest prize—the Heavyweight Championship. So I told McMahon that I would return to New York only if he put me in the ring with Buddy Rogers for the title. Buddy Rogers wasn't necessarily popular with the other wrestlers as he hurt many wrestlers in the ring on purpose, but for some reason he was popular with Vince McMahon, Sr. I can also tell you why I didn't like Buddy Rogers. When I was a young guy, and getting a fair amount of publicity for things like picking up Haystacks Calhoun, Buddy Rogers thought that it would be good for him to have a series of matches with me and beat me to build his own reputation up even more. Well, I was warned about Buddy by Angelo Savoldi and "The Golden Boy" Arnold Skaaland that I should be careful because Rogers had hurt a lot of guys intentionally. Well, one night in the ring in Steubenville, Ohio I was wrestling Buddy Rogers. He called a spot where I was to hit him with two tackles and when I went for the third tackle he was going to give me a scoop slam. He was purposely too close to the ropes and he threw me out of the ring in to the ringside chairs and on to the cement floor. Of course, just as Arnie and Angelo predicted, Buddy came over to me apologizing and saying that it was an accident. Well a few weeks later I was wrestling Buddy Rogers again in Washington, D.C. I made sure to create my own "accident". Of course, Rogers wasn't happy about it. I told him that I was sorry, it was an accident just like in Steubenville. Well from that point on neither Rogers or I had any use for each other.

I put Vince in a tough position. He was a big fan of Buddy Rogers, but at the same time his business was hurting, and a change needed to be made. The decision was made that I would come back to the territory and Buddy Rogers would be told that I had agreed to "put him over" in Madison Square Garden, in the middle of the ring. While Rogers didn't like me, he had no reason to not believe his biggest benefactor, Vince McMahon. He would have told him that I had been bought off for $3,000.00, a great deal of money at that time. The stage was set for my return. I had total faith in myself being able to beat Buddy Rogers, regardless. Keep in mind, he was going in to the match thinking that I going to put him over for a great one time payoff from Vince McMahon, Sr.

THE AUTOBIOGRAPHY OF WRESTLING'S LIVING LEGEND

Buddy Rogers and Bruno Sammartino, old enemies in the ring, and out of it as well, at a rare meeting between the two men in Fort Lauderdale, Florida, 1990

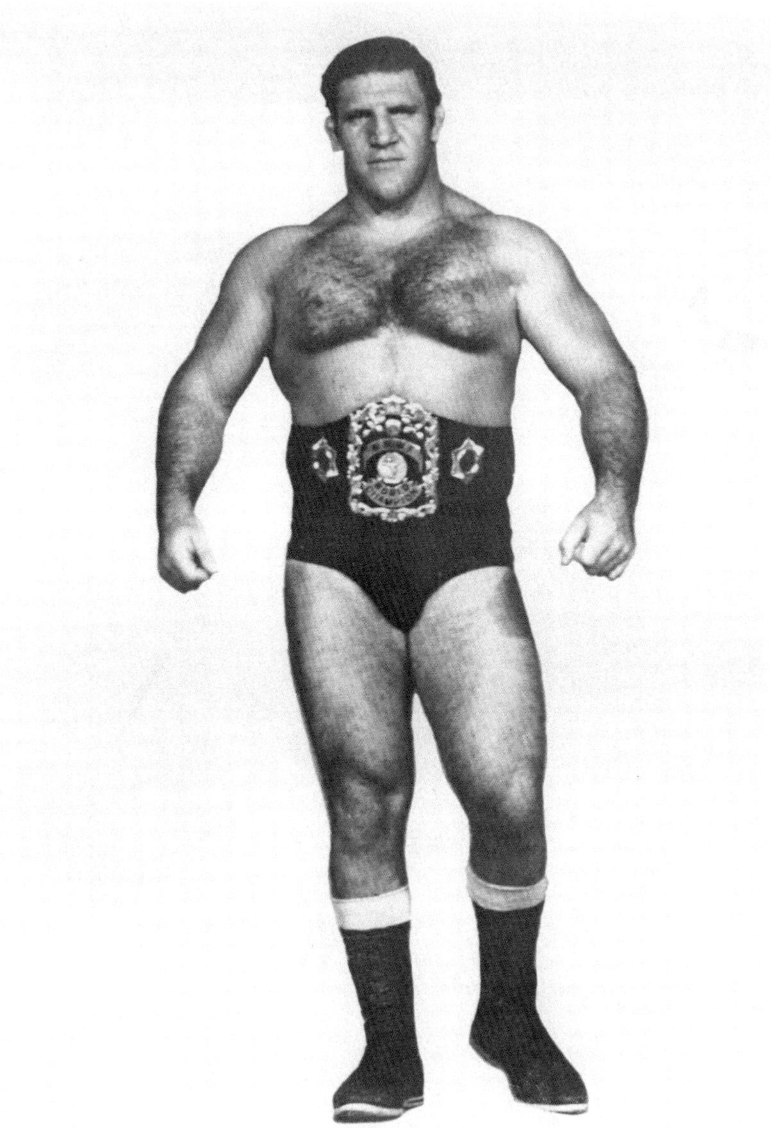

The Match of my Life

After getting McMahon's commitment for the title match, I sat down with Frank Tunney and explained everything to him. I was going to leave the final decision up to him. I owed him all the success that I had known up to that point. He had given me a chance to excel in my profession and nobody had ever done that before. I certainly didn't want to do anything that would hurt Frank in any way.

I told him all that McMahon had said, how Vince wanted me to come back to New York, and how he had agreed to put me in the ring with Buddy Rogers for the title.

Frank looked at me and smiled, "You're right of course. With that championship belt, you'd be a smash draw. I'll agree to release you, but can you do something for me?"

"What's that, Frank?" I wanted to know.

"Just come back up here every two weeks and wrestle for my big show. That's all I ask."

I shook his hand and gave him my personal guarantee. "This I will do for you, Frank. You can trust me on it."

He seemed genuinely happy for me and said, "Your word is good enough for me, Bruno. Good luck in New York."

With that, I called McMahon the next day and told him that I had made all the proper arrangements with Frank Tunney. In exchange for allowing me to return to the States, I had agreed to travel every second Sunday to the Maple Leaf Gardens in Toronto and wrestle on Frank's main card. McMahon quickly approved these terms.

Before I hung up, I asked him again, "Is my match against Rogers guaranteed?" McMahon assured me that it was.

But getting Rogers into the ring to wrestle me was harder than McMahon had anticipated. Rogers had as much dislike for me as I did for him. Buddy was not very anxious to wrestle me, never mind for the title in Madison Square Garden. Of course, once it was explained to him that I would be putting him over in the middle of the ring he was very agreeable. It's just that type of thing that would feed the ego of Buddy Rogers, especially since he didn't care for me anymore than I cared for him. The match was set for May 17, 1963, at the site of the old Madison Square Garden on 38th Street, right in the heart of New York. My attitude was simple. If I was going to meet a lion, I would defeat that lion.

In February 1963, I returned from Canada and began to wrestle again in my old territory. I vowed to take the next three months and sharpen my skills, work on my strength, and pump myself up mentally for the Rogers match.

It was shortly after I had gotten back that I ran into Buddy Rogers in Pittsburgh at the Civic Arena. I was appearing in a preliminary bout one night and just as I was about to go on, I saw Rogers enter the arena. He was dressed to the teeth, smoking a big cigar. He stepped out into the passageway and surveyed the crowd.

It was almost show time and the place was practically empty, maybe 2,000 fans in an arena that could hold nearly 10,000. What Rogers failed to understand was that he was the champion, and the man that was expected to bring in the crowds. I would have been embarrassed to take the approach that he did, it makes me angry every time that I think of it.

Rogers attitude was, "Who wants to wrestle for an empty house?" So he goes and tells the doctor on duty that he was having some chest pains and he wanted to excuse himself for the night. He thought that the doctor would say, "Don't wrestle tonight and see how you feel tomorrow."

The doctor did excuse Rogers that evening, but instead of forgetting about it, he went to Commissioner Solomon in Pittsburgh and told him about Rogers' chest pains. Commissioner Solomon was known as a tough, strict overseer, and when he heard this, he suspended Buddy Rogers' license until such time as Rogers could receive a medical examination and a clean bill of health. Solomon contacted all the other commissioners around the country and within 24 hours, Rogers was suspended. He had outfoxed himself.

McMahon was furious. Here was his star attraction, a so-called tough guy whose license had been lifted for medical reasons. McMahon herded Rogers into Georgetown Hospital in Washington, D.C. and ran him through a complete medical examination, which he passed with flying colors.

After that report came back from the hospital, Rogers was reinstated nationwide. He went back to wrestling his regular card, crushing his opponents, looking ahead to his match with me with growing concern.

At last, the night of the match arrived. For a while, waiting in my dressing room, I heard reports that Rogers wasn't going to show up. Since the championship bout was the last match scheduled for the evening, 1 had plenty of time to think about what had happened to me since I had turned pro in November 1959.

I thought about the struggles, the hardships, the suffering ... and I thought about my wife and child. My God, I remember thinking, this night is what it's all about. To get to this level still isn't enough. I've got to make it work. If I fail now, there'll be no second chances.

All these ideas were colliding with each other in my head as I waited for my match. Before that night, I was striving to do anything to get to this point and now I was saying to myself, "What if it doesn't work?"

By the time the trainer came and knocked on the dressing room door, I was pumped up higher than I'd ever been before.

When I got into the ring with Rogers, he was expecting the match to go his way. He had been told that I had agreed to get beat with the figure four leg lock for $3,000 ... a great deal of money at the time. No matter what a promoter might feel for a performer at some point, what the promoter believes is best for business is what has to be done. It was Vince McMahon's belief that Rogers wouldn't drop the title to me willingly, so they couldn't tell him the truth, he would have never gotten in the ring with me. After that it would be up to me. It was Toots Mondt who really suggested not telling Buddy what was really going on because he believed that Buddy wouldn't go for it, and would probably fake an injury and just not show up for the match. I looked him in the face and said "Buddy, don't believe the bullshit, do your best, because I am going to do my best." He had a puzzled look on his face. I couldn't wait for that bell to ring. I came in like a tank! That's the truth, like a tank! I grabbed for Rogers and his reaction confused me. He stood frozen, not moving.

Then I dove straight at him and scooped him up with every bit of strength that I had, throwing him onto my shoulder. I screamed at him over the roar of the crowd, "Give up or I'll break your back!" I never heard Buddy say a word all I know was that the referee told me to put him down and I knew he had given up.

He had submitted like a lamb to the slaughter, he gave up. Within 48 seconds, Buddy Rogers was defeated and Bruno Sammartino was the new champion!

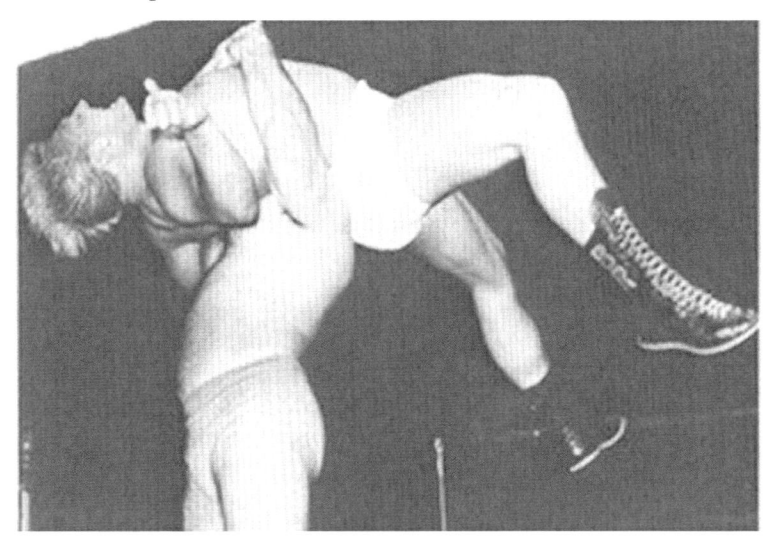

Madison Square Garden May 17, 1963
Bruno Sammartino defeated Buddy Rogers for the World Wide Wrestling Federation (WWWF) Championship before a capacity attendance of 19,639

I thought the roof was going to pop off the Garden. The crowd noise was incredible. When they put the belt around my waist, it was a great, great feeling. I was thrilled beyond belief because I had always known in my heart that this moment would happen.

For 10 or 15 minutes, I couldn't leave the ring to go back to my dressing room. My compatriots, my Italian fans, rushed in and raised me up on their shoulders, parading me around for the world to see. The police finally had to call for reinforcements to free me.

But while all this was happening, I suddenly got a chill, that same cold feeling that had visited me before as I waited for the match to begin. This was the top, but what if the fans forget me? What happens if I can't fill the arenas like I did in Canada?

When the police got me back in my dressing room at last, I closed the door behind me and just sank down into a chair. I sat there for a long time, thinking, letting everything soak in.

After a while, everybody in the Garden was gone except me.

A stunned Buddy Rogers remains on the mat as the new champion raises his arms to the crowd

I got up from my chair and went to take my shower. I muttered to myself, "This is what you wanted! Stop being so negative! Remember what you did in Toronto. If it worked there, it can work in New York."

I reminded myself of the huge Italian population in New York, the support that they would give me. How El Progresso, the Italian newspaper based in New York, would back me. I started getting that adrenaline pumping again, thinking about what lay ahead for me. I pushed the negative thoughts out of my mind.

I got dressed, packed my little duffel bag and walked out of the Garden. Now, the house was empty and most of the lights were off. The only sound was the echo of my footsteps.

I decided to walk back to my room on 42nd Street from where the Garden was on 38th. I was staying at a cheap hotel because I guess I still felt very insecure about my financial future

As I headed back, I tried to put everything into perspective. After all the suffering I had put myself and my family through, after those seven months of hell while I lived under the shame of an illegal suspension, after skirting around the country not having money to stay in a decent hotel or even to buy a meal, after all that, was the misery finally coming to an end?

As I passed a phone booth, I suddenly stopped and thought, "Oh, my God, I've got to call my family and tell them what's happened."

I dialed my mom and dad's number and let the phone ring for what seemed like a very long time. My wife and I didn't even have a phone at the time and whenever I called, I'd have to phone my parents and then they would run upstairs to our second floor apartment and tell Carol that I was on the line.

My sister Mary, who lived across the street, answered the phone. At first I thought I might have dialed her number by mistake since the two numbers were similar.

When she answered and heard my voice, she screamed, "Bruno! Oh, my God!" and I thought, "What the heck's wrong with her?"

She stammered, "My God, Bruno. They just said on the 11 o'clock news that you won the title in Madison Square Garden!"

I couldn't believe it. "They did! They announced it on TV?"

"Yes, Bruno. They said on the news that you beat Buddy Rogers in 48 seconds and now you're the new Heavyweight Champion of the World! Mom and Pop are here now. Bruno, they're so proud of you!"

I said, "So everybody knows already! I didn't think this was going to make the news in Pittsburgh."

My dad got on the phone next and said, "Son, we are all very proud of you. We are toasting you with a glass of wine right this minute."

Being the World's Heavyweight Champion still hadn't sunk in

Then my mom took the phone and she asked me in a tiny voice, "Bruno ... si fatemale? Did you get hurt or anything?" I laughed and told her, "No, Mom, I didn't get hurt." "Nothing hurts?" she wanted to know. "No, Mom, nothing hurts. It was a short match, only 48 seconds. He never did a thing to me, I did it all to him."

And I could hear her saying, "Oh, thank God! Thank God!" You have to remember at that time my entire family believed that wrestling was 100% legitimate so they worried about me getting hurt. In this case of course, that might have been the situation once I let Buddy Rogers know that he had been double crossed by McMahon, he could have chosen to fight, that's why I gave him no chance at all. At the time, I was one of the strongest men in the world. I can only believe that Buddy Rogers believed he had no chance to beat me legitimately.

After I hung up and continued walking back to my hotel, I thought, "Wow! That's great! They know all about it back in Pittsburgh."

Right around the corner from my hotel there was a small hole-in-the-wall deli where they sold fried chickens, prepared on a rotary spit. To celebrate, I went in and bought two birds, got a half gallon of orange juice and went up to my room with my feast. I sat there on the edge of the bed, ate my chickens, drank my orange juice, and watched the postage stamp sized television on the dresser. After I finished my victory meal, I felt very tired and I went right to sleep.

I got up pretty early the next morning. Champion or not, I had a match scheduled that evening at the Sunnyside Gardens and the bout was to be telecast. I went over to the gym that I frequented in New York, called the Mid City Gym. It was owned by Tommy Minichiello back in the day, and it would later be featured in the movie Pumping Iron. It is now owned by Vince Consalvo and is no longer at 48th and 8th its now located at 345 W 42nd St. I wanted to pump a little iron to keep myself fine-tuned. I really liked that gym and Tommy. Tommy has been retired for a while now and living in the Fort Myers, Florida area but we still keep in touch via phone. I guess winning the championship still hadn't sunk in. As I walked over to the club, I remember wondering if anybody else besides my family in Pittsburgh, and the fans at the Garden last night knew about my victory.

My question was answered as soon as I walked into the gym. All of the guys started screaming, "Congratulations!" I was just amazed. Everybody kept coming over and pounding me on the back. It took quite a while to get through my routine that morning.

After I left the gym, I took a shortcut back to the hotel. On my way back later that morning, people were now yelling at me, "Hey, Bruno! Congratulations, Bruno!" When I sat down to eat at a restaurant, all of a sudden I was getting recognition from everywhere. I just kept thinking to myself, "Wow!"

As I came out for my match that evening at Sunnyside Gardens, the crowd stood up and began chanting my name, "Bruno! Bruno!

Bruno!" I never had expected this kind of impact from winning the championship belt. Never! It had happened so quickly!

"Lady Luck" started to run with me. Before my victory over Buddy Rogers, Capitol had been near bankruptcy. The business had been sinking lower and lower into the ground.

Now thanks to the generous support of many fans, particularly the Italians, the wrestling turnstiles began to spin faster and faster. These were the fans who believed in me and what I was accomplishing. And they remembered me from before my suspension, a struggling young Italian kid who had hooked up with the giant Haystacks Calhoun one night, and lifted him off the mat.

The fans never forgot that. Even when I defeated Buddy Rogers, they still remembered me as the guy who picked up Haystacks Calhoun, and as the guy who did push-ups with two men sitting on his back.

Maybe I should say a word here about Haystacks. Haystacks weighed about 625lbs but I felt that I could lift him. In professional wrestling, to pull off a lot of the maneuvers we do, you need the cooperation of your opponent. In this particular case due to the sheer size of Haystacks Calhoun I told him not to help me at all. As long as he didn't fight me I had faith in my strength and lifted him off the mat when he had a side head lock on me. The crowd in the Garden was screaming at what they had just seen. No wrestler had been able to slam Haystacks Calhoun, but I did it.

Eventually I was booked to wrestler Killer Kowalski in Madison Square Garden. Killer got his nickname because of a match he had against another very powerful man, Eric Holmback, who was known

I thought that MSG was going to come apart when I lifted Haystacks Calhoun

in wrestling circles as Yukon Eric. Yukon Eric weighed around 300 pounds, but was only about 6'3" tall. Eric looked like a lumberjack, wearing those lumberjack shirts with the sleeves torn off. He always wore jeans and boots and, for him, that was no gimmick. That was Yukon Eric. If you recall from earlier in the book, Yukon Eric was the man that recommended that I go to Canada and work for Frank Tunney. It was that advice that not only changed the direction of my career but allowed me to build the life I always wanted to give my wife and children. I remember meeting Yukon Eric in Ontario. After he finished wrestling, he would rush out into the freezing night air, jump naked into a nearby lake, swim across the lake and back, then climb back into his jeans and shirt and go about his business. He was a real outdoorsman.

Eric also owned some very bad cauliflower ears, churned into that condition from years of wrestling. Killer Kowalski, in a match with Yukon Eric, actually ripped off Eric's right ear—pulled it clean away. After that Kowalski was known as the "Killer." In later years, if you ever saw Yukon Eric, you would have noticed that his dark blonde hair was longer on the right side of his face. He grew his hair that way to cover up his missing ear.

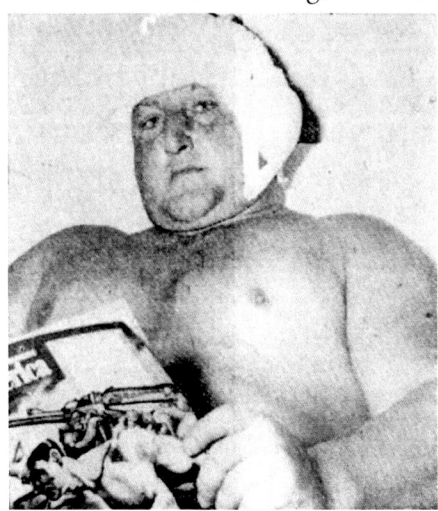

Yukon Eric recommended I go to Canada. He had lost his ear in a match against Kowalski in 1952

So here it was, September 1963, four months into my championship reign and my Madison Square Garden match with Kowalski was a sellout. At that time, Killer was one of wrestling's biggest draws. Yet even though my name was relatively brand new to many people, the fans were really rallying to my support. This particular bout which pitted the young champ against the established star seemed to catch the public's attention.

Our battle was a continuous blur of action. Kowalski's

Killer Kowalski and I do battle outside the ring

reputation as a human dynamo was well deserved. I remember many of the other wrestlers watching our match that night from the wings were wondering which of us was going to run out of steam first.

The fans erupted into cheers every time I laid a finger on Killer. I think the crowd really wanted to see me defend my title with a vengeance. Finally, after close to 40 minutes of non-stop wrestling, I pinned Kowalski for a count of three and walked away to the roar of the crowd. While professional wrestling had predetermined winners, I always went out to the ring with the goal of making it look like an actual athletic contest. I loved wrestling someone like Killer Kowalski who was in tremendous condition and was very believable. Over the years, I wrestled Walter "Killer" Kowalski more times than I can count.

As the days and months passed by, the fans filled the arenas to see me perform. That's when I told Vince McMahon that I wanted to cut down on the number of television appearances I was making.

I didn't think it was wise to have so much exposure on television. I was wrestling no-name guys, week-in and week-out, and I was showing up on the tube almost every weekend.

If the people wanted to see me wrestle, let them come to the arenas. That was the name of the game. Fill the arenas and let television serve as the promotional tool. And McMahon agreed. How could he argue with success?

So in 1963 and 1964, the same years that The Beatles got hot, my career caught fire. I started selling out Philadelphia's Convention Center, and Pittsburgh's Civic Arena, and Baltimore's Civic Center, or wherever I was going. It was fantastic!

Then I went to Japan and did phenomenal business there. In Australia, arenas were sold out every night for the entire month I was there. When the chance came for me to go to Australia I asked for—at the time what was a lot of money—$5,000.00 a week. I knew it was too much to ask for, but this was my chance to get even with Jim Barnett who had starved me out of the business in Indiana doing the bidding of Vince McMahon, Sr. I told Vince to tell Barnett I wouldn't go for anything less and eventually it was agreed to and I went on a very successful tour. I remember Jim Barnett saying "My boy, it cost a lot to get you here but it was well worth it." I then went to South America and was also well received.

I was wrestling every single night for months at a time, sometimes twice a day. It was absolutely one of the best periods in my life. "Success" became one of my favorite words.

Johnny Valentine, Bruno, Argentina Apollo

MADISON SQUARE GARDEN MAY 17, 1963
Bruno Sammartino Defeated Buddy Rogers For The World Wrestling Championship   Capacity Attendance 19,639

Going Back Home

The appearance schedule that I took on after I won the championship was starting to take its toll. Month in, month out, I wrestled almost daily. I was upset that I wasn't able to see my wife Carol and my son David very much. I began to think about taking a break from it all. The chance to do that came from an unlikely fan.

I'm talking about Monsignor Fusco from the Pittsburgh Diocese. He would come to the Civic Arena to see me wrestle, and eventually we met and became good friends.

The first time we had lunch together, Monsignor Fusco blew my mind. First, he said he had met Primo Carnera many years ago. And if that wasn't enough, he said that he understood that I was an opera lover, which I was. He went on to say that he had personally known the world-famous Italian tenor Enrico Caruso. To think that he had actually spoken to those two giants in their professions! Well, we had lunch together many times and I was always fascinated with the stories he would tell.

Monsignor Fusco was just one of the nicest men you could ever meet. He mentioned how he had gone back to Italy many times and I certainly envied him for that. Little did I realize how powerful a man he was in the Catholic Church, and that many of those trips were on church business to the Vatican.

One time he said to me, and this was in the early part of 1966, "Bruno, my boy." That was his favorite expression. "Have you ever gone back to Italy since you came over as a boy?"

I replied sadly, "No, Monsignor. I've not gone back." "Well, are you planning on going back" he asked.

I shrugged. "Yes, eventually. I very much would like to go back and see my family, but right now, it's so hectic. My schedule is so crazy."

Monsignor Fusco smiled broadly. "Well, Bruno, when you do, please let me know about your plans because I would like to arrange for you to meet the Pope."

I stared at him in disbelief. I thought to myself, "Come on." I know he's an influential man, but just like that?" I said, "Monsignor, are you telling me that if I went back to the Old Country that I could have a private audience with the Pope?"

"Absolutely," he said. "I can arrange it."

I blurted, "Monsignor, if you can arrange this, it would be the highest honor that I've ever known."

"No trouble, Bruno, my boy," said Monsignor Fusco. "Just find out when you can travel, and I'll take care of the rest."

The very first chance I could, I sat down with Vince McMahon in his office in Washington, D.C. I told him that my schedule was getting too ridiculous and that I wanted to take a break—just for one week—and fly back to Italy. I told him that this was the chance of a lifetime because I had somebody working for me to arrange to see the Pope. Besides that, it would give me the opportunity to return to my hometown and visit with my friends and relatives whom I hadn't seen since I was 14 years old.

Vince thought it over for a few seconds and said, "Okay, we'll work it out for you." He didn't go into specifics at the time, but later I found out that he definitely had ulterior motives.

At any rate, McMahon and I figured out the timing and once that was settled, I got in touch with the Monsignor. He told me that he had a good friend in Rome who would drive me wherever I wanted to go, and he mentioned that he'd arrange for a suite for me and my family at the Excelsior Hotel in Veno, Viento. All I could say was, "Great! That's great!"

After alerting my family in Pizzoferrato that I was coming back for a visit, my wife and I packed our bags and made all the necessary preparations to get ready for the trip. Even though our son David was only five and a half years old, we weren't going to let him miss out on the adventure.

We flew to Rome on March 25, 1966, and went straight to our hotel to unwind. After a good night's sleep, the very next day I had a call from a Vatican spokesman, acknowledging that Monsignor Fusco had been in touch with them. He went on to say that our Papal audience would be in three days and that they would get back to me for the final arrangements. After I hung up, I was elated. It really was going to happen … an audience with the Pope.

Then an hour or so later, the phone rang again. He said his name was John and that he was a friend of Monsignor Fusco. He turned out to be the man whom Monsignor Fusco had contacted to drive us around. Actually that was his business. John had a fleet of cars and he would take tourists all over the countryside for a fee of $25 a day, up to 10 hours a day. Today, for similar service in Italy, you'd have to cough up $500 to $600 per day—quite a difference.

The next morning John picked us up and began showing us all of the sights. He took us to some great restaurants for both lunch and dinner. We kicked around Rome for two whole days and the experience was just wonderful.

Then the big day arrived. John drove us to the Vatican. I remember that we waited in a small room with Monsignor Rocco, and my wife and I were getting more nervous by the minute. Finally, the time came and we were called in to see His Holiness, Pope Paul VI. Monsignor Rocco escorted us into an adjoining room where we waited for his entrance.

Both my wife and I had considered beforehand what we would say and do when we went in, but we were terribly nervous about it. I remember saying to John in the car on the way over, "I'm very nervous. What's appropriate and what's not appropriate to do when you meet the Pope?"

John laughed and said, "Just relax. When you go in, the first thing you do is bow. Then you kiss his ring and greet him." Then John added, "Don't be afraid because he will talk to you. He will ask questions. He will talk."

With John's advice in mind, I began rehearsing what I was going to say to the Pope. I thought I'd say, after I kissed his ring, "Holy Father, this is the experience of my life. Never did I ever think that I was going to have such a great honor. I was born here in Italy and then I went to America as a young boy and who would have ever thought that such a boy could grow up and meet with you, Holy Father."

Yes, that sounded good to me. I would give that speech exactly. Well, what happened didn't exactly go according to plan.

My wife Carol was sitting there with our son David in the meeting room and I stood right behind their chair. When Pope Paul entered, we did as we had been told by our driver, John. I kissed his ring after Carol did and then the strangest thing happened. My wife and I were both nearly paralyzed. We couldn't say anything.

A very young David strikes a wrestling pose

David, though, just looked at Pope Paul and said, "Hey, I remember you. I saw you on television!"

The Pope had made a visit to the United States about six months prior to our trip to Italy. Of course, the television coverage had been enormous. I thought to myself, "Oh, boy, David. Nice move!"

But the Pope laughed and then asked in Italian what our son's name was.

With a quavering voice, I answered, "Davida," then I added, "My wife's name is Carolina and I am Bruno Sammartino." At that point I managed to say what a great honor it was to meet him.

Carol never spoke a word. She was absolutely frozen. I began to tell him about the profession I was in and I got the feeling, though I'm not positive, that the Pope was not overly thrilled about me choosing such a violent way to earn a living.

As we talked, David kept interrupting asking, "What's this?"

and "What's that?" The Pope seemed to be such a saintly person and he took very kindly to our son. Once he asked David a question about his school. Just before we concluded our audience, we had our picture taken with Pope Paul. I had arranged for this to happen before our meeting. I had been told that they were not willing to allow photographs to be taken if the pictures were going to be used in any way for publicity or to advance my career.

I assured the Pope's people that I would never use them while I was a professional wrestler for any publicity, in any way, shape or form. I said that these pictures would be something that my family and I would cherish for the rest of our lives. With my guarantee not to benefit from their public use, permission was given and the photographs were taken. Our audience lasted perhaps only 10 or 15 minutes. When it did end, Carol kissed his ring. She had kissed his ring when we entered and kissed his ring when we left, and never opened her mouth in between—not one time.

When we walked out of the room, Carol and I were both trembling. It was a feeling that's very difficult to describe—kind of thrilled with what had happened yet disappointed in some ways. There was so much we had wanted to say and didn't.

The next day John picked us up at our hotel and we were off to visit Pizzoferrato, my old hometown. We had been joined by my uncle who had traveled into Rome from Pizzoferrato to greet us.

On the way we stopped in Casino, which was a village I remembered well.

During the war, it had been one of the most bombarded areas in all of Italy. During the battle for Monte Casino, thousands of men on both sides were killed.

When my mother, sister Mary, brother Paul, and I had passed through the village on our way to America, it was nothing but rubble. All we saw were stones, tossed by the bombs into an awful sculpture of destruction. In fact, the battle that had raged there left nothing standing. On our journey back though in 1966, Casino had become a beautiful city again. I was so impressed by the effort that it must have taken to resurrect the town.

We stopped in Casino for lunch and while we were eating, I

noticed that after my uncle had excused himself from our table, he had made a beeline for a telephone. In fact, he had been on the phone several other times that morning. I didn't know what he was up to. Being polite, of course, I didn't ask him.

After lunch, we climbed back in the car and began driving again. Finally, I spotted La Torra, the mountain in which our town was cradled. La Torra went straight up into the air. You had to climb it from the back because from the front, the mountain was one long plunge.

At one point, we passed the site where my father had been born. His little home was still there and the tiny church that my uncle, the priest Don Vincenzo Sammartino, had built with his own hands. It was also at this place during the war where a furious battle had been fought. Back then, we had found many, many bodies inside and outside the church.

We passed the church and pressed on, up and up into the mountains we drove, finally pulling in the town square, La Piazza. That's where I found out the reason that my uncle had been making all those phone calls. He was arranging my homecoming.

Waiting for us in the square were all of the townspeople. Everyone had taken the day off from work and they were all assembled in front of the town's new municipal building. Talk about getting goosebumps! I was overwhelmed by it all, speechless almost like I was with the Pope.

I stepped out of the car and started to recognize people who I remembered from so many years ago. Then out of the crowd came an old man who I didn't recognize immediately. He was thin weighing no more than 110 pounds, and his walk was unsteady.

He called out my name and then I realized that this was my precious Uncle Camillo. He had always been like a father to me. Certainly he was the kindest human being that I've ever met in my life. We embraced and as I hugged him, we both began to cry.

THE AUTOBIOGRAPHY OF WRESTLING'S LIVING LEGEND

*Our home in Pizzoferrato as it looked during
my return trip to the Old Country*

I found out later that the reason he had shriveled down to almost nothing, from the robust, handsome man he'd been was that he was a dying man. He had stomach cancer and the illness had nearly taken its toll completely. The man who I had loved so dearly had been brought low by this killing disease.

And then I saw my mother's sister Aunt Agnes there, too. And we all cried some more.

We went into the municipal building because the town officials wanted to formally greet me there. Speeches were made saying how proud everyone was of Bruno Sammartino's accomplishments as a champion and how much honor I had brought to them.

Everything was completely unexpected. I probably came across that first day as a big idiot because I was absolutely speechless. I was so overwhelmed that I just stood in my place and kept saying "Hello" to all the people.

We stayed for several days and as our stay lengthened, I began to meet everyone more informally. I wanted to share memories with my old friends and relatives, and I wanted to meet them all, their children and grandchildren. I definitely didn't want to leave my hometown behind with the impression that I was some kind of big shot. Everyone told me though that I was still the same kid that they remembered.

I went to all their homes to have a little coffee with everyone and talk. Of course, all of my relatives were fighting over who would have us for lunch and who would have us for dinner.

One memory that I had from when I was a little boy was how excited we were about anyone who had just come back from America. Whoever this person was, we imagined we knew him just by the way he walked, a special walk that spoke of worldly wisdom. We liked to follow him around town, probably hoping that some of the magic would rub off on us.

Often, I recall, the people whom we tagged along behind would throw us pennies so we could buy candy. There was a favorite local store in town where basic foods were sold, and where a jar of penny candy lay hidden under the counter. We would dash to the store to spend these special bits of cash.

All these memories came flooding back because as soon as I would leave the hotel where we were staying, little kids would be waiting for me on the street outside my door. The first day I gave five or six of them each a dollar from America. In 1966, a dollar was worth about 500 lira and 500 lira was fantastic to them. These kids looked at the money and felt like, my God, they were rich now.

The next day 15 kids showed up at the hotel to greet me so I gave each of them a dollar. I guess I started looking like the Pied Piper with all these children trailing behind me. My wife Carol was amazed by it all. I told her that by watching those kids she was watching me as a kid, too.

We left after spending nearly four days there, and it was a very tough feeling to handle. Again, the whole town had taken off from work and they all assembled once more in the town square to say goodbye.

It was so very painful too because I knew I'd never see my Uncle Camillo again. Most fathers were not as good as he was. I hugged him close to say goodbye. He was so choked up he couldn't speak, couldn't say goodbye. He just stood there, not moving.

We finished saying goodbye and giving our thanks to all the townspeople for being so gracious during our stay there. As our car pulled away, I looked back to see my Uncle Camillo, his eyes following us as we rounded the corner and headed back to Rome.

That was the last time I saw him. As I grew up, he had given me love and understanding. Uncle Camillo was just simply a special human being. I still miss him very much.

Rome always fascinated me. As a child, I loved to read about ancient history. During our visit, I had hoped to spend more time in the city, visiting the Colosseum, the Catacombs or Caesar's Forum. But because I had not been aware of how ill my uncle was, the last couple of days in Italy were very somber for me.

Finally, after a week that I'll never forget, my family and I returned to America. The very next day, I left on tour for Australia.

Before I left though, I checked in with Vince McMahon on the phone. He asked me how the trip went.

"Fantastic," I said.

Before I could go into detail, he butted in. "Did you get pictures of you and the Pope?" he wanted to know.

"Yes, they gave us permission to take some."

"Great," he said, "Now here's what I want you to do. Get a few dozen copies made and then mail them to …"

"Wait a second, Vince. Hold on! I'm not mailing those photos anywhere." I'm not back one hour and already McMahon's getting me steamed up.

"What do you mean, Bruno? Those pictures would be incredible publicity."

I just said no to him. "I gave my word that those pictures would never be used for promotion as long as I was a professional wrestler. I promised the Pope that I would not do that. Just forget it, Vince."

I hung up the phone, packed my suitcases for Australia and tried not to let McMahon get to me. After I returned from my trip, the pictures of our audience with the Pope were waiting for me. They were beautiful and clearly showed me, Carol and David with Pope Paul. I went out and had some 8 x 10 pictures made but under no circumstances was I going to give them to the media.

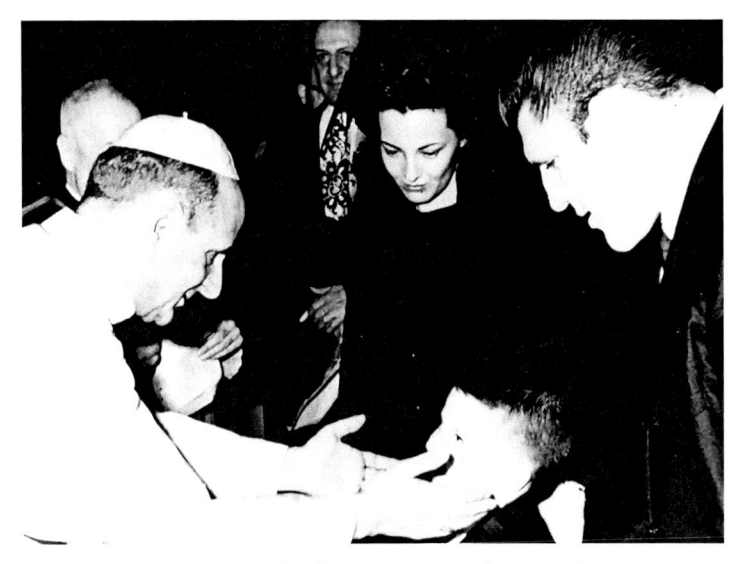

Now it can be shown—a rare photograph of our audience with Pope Paul VI

I found out that my Papal audience had been publicized anyway while I was gone when some newspaper man had asked me questions about it. I called up McMahon and asked him, "What's going on, Vince?"

McMahon answered, quick as you please, "Well, Bruno, you said you weren't allowed to use the pictures, but I'm sure the Pope didn't mean that you had to keep the whole meeting secret."

I could sense that Vince wasn't being sarcastic when he said that. I answered, "Well, you've got me there. Nobody said anything about that. But just realize, I am not going to have those pictures used for any reason."

Vince surprised me. He paused, and then said, "Well, if you made that promise and you feel that strongly, then I guess there's nothing I can do about it."

So we never did use them. And you know what? Holding to my promise caused me grief with the media. Newspaper reporters would come up to me and say sarcastically, "Hey, Bruno, I understand that you had an audience with the Pope when you were in Italy recently. And that you had pictures taken. How about letting us take a look at them?"

I told them of my promise. I was even afraid to just let them look at them for fear somehow a copy would be made. So these guys went away and wrote negative things about me, saying that I had claimed to meet with the Pope, and that I claimed to have pictures, and that I claimed to have made a promise not to show the pictures. Most of this nonsensical criticism came from New York writers. But even the writers in Pittsburgh, my hometown, leveled the same charges. I just had to take it because well, how can you break your promise to the Pope?

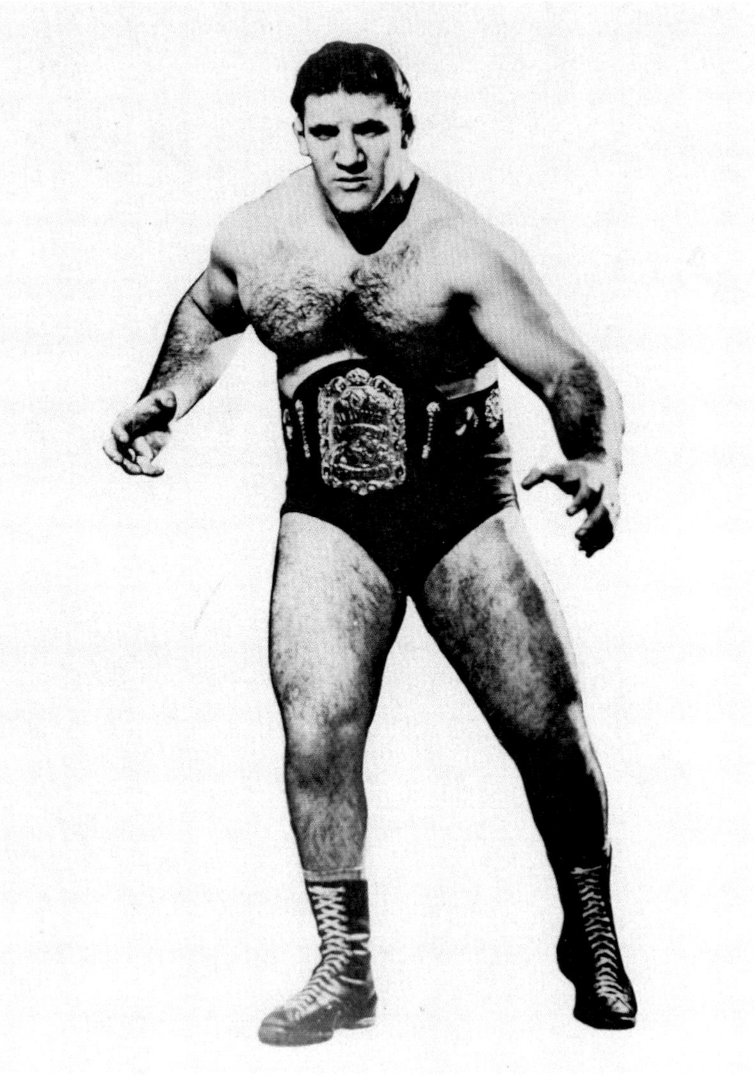

Remembering the Great Ones

As a child in Italy, my idol was Primo Carnera. The people would tell fantastic stories about this hulk of a man and I would listen to them all with the wide eyes of a young boy. If they would have told me that he was 20 feet tall, I would have believed it.

In reality, Carnera was about 6'7" tall and weighed 270 pounds, at the most. In today's wrestling world, Primo would be no giant. What made him stand out was his lean, big-boned physique. For somebody from Italy, there's never been anybody bigger. I always dreamed that I would be like him some day.

As I grew into my profession as a wrestler, besides Primo Carnera, there were a number of other competitors in the business who made their impact on me. When I was first coming up, Gorgeous George and Antonio Rocca seemed to me to represent the best in my sport.

An incident happened soon after I had turned pro that gave me a very different slant on the realities of wrestling. It occurred in December of 1959 after I had been in the professional ring no more than a month and a half.

McMahon had booked me into the Convention Center in Philadelphia against Gorgeous George. I was elated because here I was still wet behind the ears and now I was slated to take on someone of the stature of this man.

Well, what didn't immediately sink in for me was that Gorgeous George was no longer in his prime, even though I was aware that he was nearly 42 years old in late 1959. I do remember thinking that 42 seemed pretty old for a pro wrestler. I guess to a young kid like me anything older than 25 seemed ancient.

The bout turned out to be a painful experience. When I wrestled him, I was surprised to find out that the legendary Gorgeous George weighed no more than 215 pounds and was only 5'10" tall, if that.

He was a very capable wrestler, but a lot of his fair-weather fans didn't seem to think so anymore. Other fans were even more critical. When they looked at Gorgeous George all they saw was the gimmick, a guy dressed in fancy robes strutting around the ring, smelling perfume, and tossing back his curly blonde hair.

Gorgeous George had been a skillful wrestler

His real name was George Wagner and early in his wrestling career, he found himself getting nowhere, even though he had great skills. Then a friend of George's, a chef in a restaurant where he ate, said to him, "You know, George, if you did something that would bring attention to yourself, it might just help you become a hit."

George asked his friend if he had any suggestions and the chef said "I've got just the thing for you. You have a great head of hair. Why don't you let it grow longer, curl it, bleach it, then you put on this big, fancy robe."

As they say, the rest is history. George followed the chef's advice to the letter and he became a big drawing card for years. As time wore on, some fans began to get on his case for his so-called arrogance, yet most seemed to still respect his wrestling abilities.

As time marched on and other stars took the spotlight, George started to fade away into the shadows. So when I met him at the Philadelphia Convention Center, he was no longer on top—far from it. I hadn't realized that he no longer had a big name across the country.

To me, young Bruno Sammartino, who had read and heard about the man, meeting Gorgeous George in the ring was a thrill.

The painful thing was that when I was actually wrestling this legend, shooting back and forth on the canvas, I could hear catcalls coming out of the dark, yelling for me to be careful or I'd hurt the old man. And some fans hollered for me to "take care of that little dried-out so-and-so."

They used really nasty names that I don't care to repeat. It got to me and I remember thinking, "My God, is this what happens to you at the other end of the tunnel?"

As the younger and stronger man, I was booked to win the

Primo Carnera was my boyhood idol

match that night, but what happened that night with me and Gorgeous George would stay with me for the rest of my career.

After the match, I went back to my dressing room, knowing that George must have heard those remarks as well as I did. I wondered what it had done to him. I never found out because when I came out of my dressing room, he had already left the building.

A few months later, in 1960, I not only got the chance to meet my boyhood idol but actually became his tag team partner for a while. Of course, I'm talking about Primo Carnera.

McMahon dreamed up the team. Because Primo was still a big name, McMahon wanted to keep him in the ring. Everybody knew that Primo's appeal, especially with the Italians, hadn't diminished, even though his abilities had deteriorated to almost nothing.

So they put me, a young Italian guy just coming up, with Carnera in tag team matches. McMahon figured that Carnera would draw the crowds, and Sammartino would do the wrestling.

That was the way it was. Carnera was the showcase. He would make his entrance into the ring for 10 seconds or so,

Working with Carnera was the thrill of a lifetime

tag out and let Bruno do the wrestling. That was fine with me. I didn't even care if I had to wrestle the whole match by myself. To me it was just such an honor to be on the same team as Primo Carnera. I was so thrilled that even though I knew he was getting most of the money, it didn't bother me one bit. Even though my own personal situation was bad, I said, "Let Primo get the money. God bless him." He was my hero so all that didn't matter.

I'm sure I would have continued on the Carnera/Sammartino team longer, but again the remarks I heard brought me down. Fans would say, "Primo … Primo. You're too old to wrestle. Why don't you retire instead of hiring this young guy to wrestle for you?"

Hearing those insults aimed at Primo was like putting a knife through my own heart. It bothered me most of all that Primo would hear the same words.

My experiences with Gorgeous George and with Primo Carnera reinforced one important principle in me though. I vowed to myself that I would never let happen to me what I had seen happen to those two wrestling greats. I made a solemn promise to get out of wrestling while I was still at the top of my game.

Another legendary character that I met in my rookie year was Antonino Rocca. Rocca was born in Italy, but his family left there when he was 16 and moved to Buenos Aires, Argentina. There he worked as a tailor in a shop with his father.

Rocca was an excellent athlete, playing soccer and wrestling professionally in Argentina. He came to the United States as a wrestler in 1947 and became an immediate sensation.

His manager was Kola Kwariani, the man who had discovered him in South America. As I mentioned earlier, I was to have my own personal dealings with Kwariani, but that was later down the road.

Kwariani was this burly Russian who had also immigrated to America to cash in on his own wrestling prowess. He actually had been touring Argentina when, by chance, he caught Rocca on the same card as he was appearing.

A few years later when Kwariani was getting too old to wrestle, Kola decided to pursue promotion and managing, and he remembered Rocca as somebody with extra special talents. Kola worked things out and brought Rocca to the states where he began to personally manage Rocca's career.

I was quite excited about meeting Rocca when the chance came. I idolized him much like I did Primo Camera but, for an Italian, he was a bit of a typical Latino.

I was even his tag team partner a few times. I'll say this: Rocca was always in great condition and always gave his matches all that he had. It was his wrestling skills that I questioned, frankly. By no means was he a poor wrestler. I mean to say he was more of an acrobat, an aerialist. In this, he could pull off phenomenal stunts that nobody else could.

A chance to team up with another wrestling great ... Antonino Rocca

    The only negative thing that I will say about Rocca was that I sensed as the years went on, he was the kind of guy who didn't like to share the spotlight with anybody. He certainly didn't want to see a young wrestler like me become a threat to his throne. When I found this out later, his attitude disappointed me.

    Rocca went on to have a great career until he aged to the point where he could no longer do those incredible aerialist feats. Because of that, he was forced to retire.

    Sadly, I later found out that the deal he had with his promoters was not a very good one. They actually took two-thirds of his income so that when he retired, his financial condition was poor indeed. That shocked me, because I thought wrestling would have made him a wealthy man. After all, the name "Antonino Rocca" had been a top draw for a long time.

    The saddest part of the story came a few years after his retirement when he tragically died at the age of 47. The cause was listed as uremic poisoning.

As I think about these greats from my early career, I recall courageous men who have given their all to a profession they loved. In some cases, they continued to wrestle long past their prime because I suppose they couldn't imagine a life without the sport. Mostly, I remember them for their dedication to the fans and to the business of professional wrestling.

With that said its time to address the media and their criticism of professional wrestling. A lot of comments and criticisms were in regards to the blood in wrestling. In my day we worked very tight so that we gave the people a very believable product. Of course, that meant that we bled many times without it being planned, along with those times when it was. So many of the members of the media wanted to find out the secrets behind bleeding in wrestling. In truth there were times when bleeding would be a part of the storyline and through various ways we would cut our heads with razor blades. In this day and age things like this don't really take place anymore. The WWE at the current time doesn't want blood as a part of their product at all. Of course back in our day we didn't have to worry about things like AIDS, or the concerns that TV stations would have with blood on television. I will also add that in trying to uncover secrets in regards to how things went in professional wrestling, people would create their own reality, like saying we used blood capsules. I have never seen a blood capsule. If such a thing exists, it never made its way in to any match of mine. If you saw blood in any of my matches, it was my blood, no matter how I got opened up.

Another criticism of professional wrestling that I've heard leveled is this: the way wrestling works is that a wrestler wins here in Pittsburgh one night and then loses tomorrow in New York City. That's the way the game goes, the critics say.

Of course, to anybody who has ever said that I say, "Sheer nonsense!" If anybody looks at the records of wrestlers like Antonino Rocca, Lou Thesz, Verne Gagne, Don Leo Jonathan, Big Bill Miller or Gorilla Monsoon, you'll see a win/loss ratio that's fantastic. In these athletes' careers, you'll see that they lost very few matches.

I would point to my own professional record, too. As far as pins or submissions, I never submitted once in my life. If I've ever been pinned, it was only three or four times total during my entire 23-year-long career.

Big Bill Miller was a tough competitor

Miller stays on the mat after one of our bouts

In reality, promoters "pushed" who they wanted to and with a big enough push almost anyone can "get over" with the fans, at least in the short term, providing the wrestler is booked properly. It didn't always have to do with talent, some of the most talented performers didn't have the charisma to work "on top", they either became what we referred to in those days as a "jobber", in today's politically correct world, they are more commonly known as enhancement talent, someone paid to lose but also to make his opponent look great in the ring. In reality, many of those guys were more talented them some of the stars, but talent without star quality doesn't always work out. In some cases, if you had the right look but maybe couldn't do interviews they would give the wrestler a manager to speak on their behalf, and help create interest in the upcoming match.

After I won the championship in May of 1963 it was the end of one journey and the beginning of another. If you recall I was very happy in Toronto working for Frank Tunney and it took a lot of convincing for Vince McMahon to get me to come back to the

WWWF and take another chance on a company that had let me down twice. I am sure that McMahon would have never called me at all or met any of my conditions to come back unless he was really in a tight spot. At the time the business wasn't doing well with Buddy Rogers as the champion. It was likely more about Buddy Rogers attitude towards the business, than it was his appearance, showmanship, and skills. He tended to come in to a territory and do what we called "hot-shotting". His approach was to do things that were outside of the normal to get crowds to come to the arena, but for the long term health of the territory it just never works. What would usually happen is that Buddy Rogers would leave a territory just as it started to go bad and leave it up to someone else to try and rebuild.

    I came to the realization quickly that one of the things that I could do to help things out was to adapt my style to my opponents' style. I was the guy that would be staying in the area and be at the same clubs month after month. I would be wrestling guys that were billed as strongmen, like Hans Mortier and Killer Kowalski, but they wouldn't all be strongmen types. You would also have guys that were good high spot guys, like Mike Scicluna, who I wrestled many times, you could go through a good series of moves with them at a fast pace off the mat. In many territories, the challenger adapted their style to the champions. I felt like this was a mistake and didn't want to repeat it in the WWWF.

    As business started to pick up I was given an opportunity to bring in some of my own opponents, guys that I felt that we could make big money with, and since I was becoming successful Vince gave me a chance to pick some of my challengers.

    One of the first guys that I wanted to bring in was a gentleman by the name of Robert Morella, who wrestled as Gorilla Monsoon. I had been with Gorilla in Toronto for a year and felt like we could really do some good business. I got in touch with "Gino" as he was called by friends and told him that I had "the belt" now—which is how we described being the champion—and that he should come to NY because I felt he would get a real opportunity to make some money. He was very hesitant because he had heard things weren't going very well in NY, but because of our relationship he believed me and he agreed to come. It ended up being a great move for Gino, he was with the company basically for the rest of his life as a wrestler, and eventually became part owner of the company. When the company was sold to Vince McMahon, Jr. he became an agent and commentator.

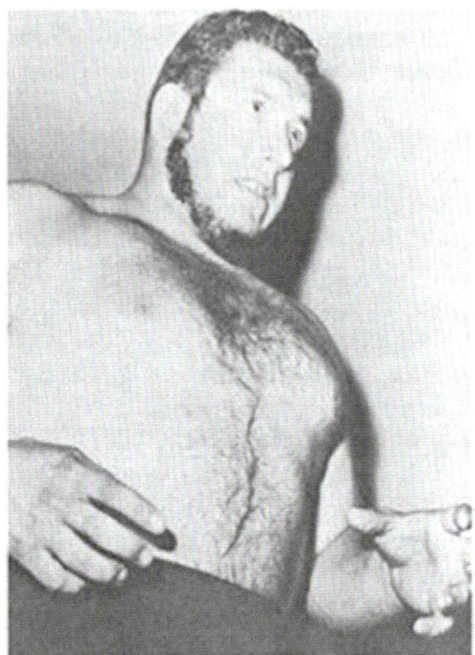

I met another guy in Australia named Toru Tanaka, his real name was Charles Kalani. I told Vince McMahon that I wanted to bring him in and he gave his permission right away.

Gorilla Monsoon

I did have a problem one time getting a guy named Big Bill Miller into the territory. He had a reputation of being somewhat of a troublemaker and had been in involved in an incident with Buddy Rogers that Vince was aware of. He didn't want to take a chance on him. I told Vince that because of the way I knew many guys felt about Buddy Rogers that I was willing to ignore the stories. I also made it clear he had no reason to be concerned as I was the guy that would be working with him. I eventually got him to agree to bring in Big Bill Miller.

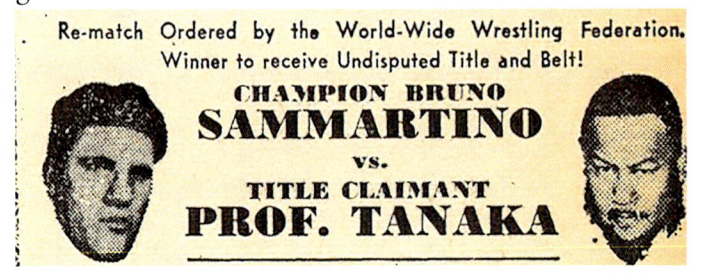

I believed that having the proper opponents would be a major part of what would make us successful, and all of the men above became some of my favorite opponents ... and we made money with all of them.

One of the important things about your opponents was determining how many times you would wrestle them in the same arena before you moved on to the next opponent. You wanted to keep things interesting and work for return matches with the right opponents. We did very well with that and we seemed to have a winning formula for success.

At times, Vince McMahon wanted to do a favor for his promoter friends around the country who wanted to get one of their performers in to Madison Square Garden, and around the NY territory for a while. They wanted me to wrestle guys that I didn't believe were qualified for main event status, but Vince pushed very hard when these chances came up. I used it to my advantage by agreeing to wrestle these guys, but we wouldn't work any return, we would just have a match and I would beat them right in the middle of the ring. It was good that the fans saw me from time to time as Champion just beat someone, and not always working for a return match. After a while that would seem predictable and repetitive.

George Steele was always tough

Vince McMahon also owned the Pittsburgh territory which was doing very poorly. I had been watching what was going on there the local guy running things for McMahon was Ace Freeman. At some point Vince McMahon approached me about buying the territory. In the back of my mind I felt that Vince wanted me to buy it since it was losing money and it would put me in a position where I needed him more. We agreed to a price of $20,000.00, plus I would give him 10% of the net proceeds from the Civic Arena show in Pittsburgh. It wasn't a full time territory. It was only running on Friday and Saturday nights in western PA, Ohio, and West Virgina. I took the deal because I was very confident that I knew exactly what the problems were in the territory, and believed that I could fix it and make it successful.

The first thing that I did was contact Ace Freeman and tell him that I would keep him on if he wanted to stay, but that things were going to change. I felt that the number one problem is there were too many Champions they even had a Hungarian Champion. The people weren't buying it, so in turn they didn't support the territory. I told Ace if he wanted to stay on he would have to follow my specific directions and the first one was that all the title belts had to go away, except that I was recognized as the World Champion, since I was the WWWF Champion. The Kangaroos would also remain as the World Tag Team Champions. At first he didn't like the idea, he felt that I shouldn't make the changes. I explained that the territory was losing money and he could only stay if he did exactly as directed. At that point Ace Freeman decided that he wanted his job more than he wanted to defend how the business had previously been run.

It wasn't long after that I was contacted by the man that discovered me, Rudy Miller. At the time he needed work so he asked if I could use him. I told him yes that I could. I made it clear to him that he should be a part of all the phone meetings that I had with Ace Freeman where I would lay out how I wanted things to go. He knew that he was to report to me if my directions weren't followed to the letter.

One other move that I made was to have my father-in-law who was an accountant by trade, and currently retired, handle all

Don Leo Jonathan was a great opponent. He passed away on October 12th 2018

the money. I felt like my interests were well protected. I used some local talent from around Pittsburgh and brought in talent from around the country as well. Of course, I had Vince McMahon as a source of talent as well. When I needed the loan of someone, he wasn't in any position to tell me no, and don't forget he still had a financial interest in the territory doing well. It took about a year, but the people finally started turning out again. We had a weekly wrestling program that aired live called Studio Wrestling. At the time we didn't film it and retain the film, which is too bad, because it would have been worth a lot of money today to the WWE Network.

I held on to the company for about 6 years making money for five of those years and eventually selling the company for double what I paid for it. It was tough to be wrestling full time and run the company, plus I had heard that eventually the local TV station would be getting a new station manager and that manager didn't want wrestling anymore. I sold the company to Newton Tattrie, who wrestled as Geeto Mongol, he was one half of a successful tag team with Bepo Mongol—who went on to much more success later as Nikolai

Volkoff—and later on teamed with Bolo Mongol (Bill Eadie)— who went on to further success first as The Masked Superstar and then as part of another tag team called Demolition. He just recently retired from active competition in the ring.

I had warned Newton before he bought the territory about the situation at the TV station but he didn't believe me and wanted to proceed with the sale. Of course, eventually he did lose TV, and no wrestling company is going to survive without television.

During my championship reign, as I just mentioned, there was a sister organization to the World Wide Wrestling Federation (WWWF) called the National Wrestling Alliance. The NWA held its own matches in its own territories and crowned its own champion.

In the late 1960s, the NWA champ was the great Lou Thesz, a man who was just an incredible technician in the ring. Of course, I was still the WWWF champion. Talks started to be generated concerning the unification of the two federations in April 1969, first informally over the telephone, then in formal meetings in a number of different cities. Sam Muchnick, the president of the NWA, and Willie Gilzenberg, the president of the WWWF, along with Vince McMahon and Toots Mondt, initiated unification discussions. Typically enough, these meetings never involved me or Thesz, who were the two reigning champions. We didn't know what was going on, what rules were being discussed, and if a unification title

Lou Thesz in his prime

THE AUTOBIOGRAPHY OF WRESTLING'S LIVING LEGEND

I never really enjoyed wrestling The Sheik

match was being cooked up. Finally, I was bold enough to ask Gilzenberg a direct question. I said, "Willie, you guys have met in St. Louis. You've met in Chicago. You've met in New York. What's holding everything up? I'm just as much a part of this as anyone else and I want to know what's happening. What are the problems here?" Gilzenberg answered that all parties had come to an agreement that unification was going to take place. The one problem that remained was with the title match to be scheduled between Thesz and me. It had already been determined that I would be the one to win the match and unify the title. McMahon had stated that he needed me at least 17 days out of the month in order to fill the arenas he controlled, Sam Muchnick said that the NWA needed me at least 16 days a month to make ends meet. When I heard this kind of drivel had brought negotiations to a standstill, I called for a meeting of my own. I asked Willie Gilzenberg, Phil Zacko who was also with the WWWF office, Vince McMahon, and Kola Kwariani to meet with me in Washington, D.C. When the date was set, I hopped a plane from whatever part of the country I found myself in and came to the meeting. I opened by saying, "You guys have been at all these meetings with the National Wrestling Alliance, talking non-stop about unification. I said to the men at the meeting, and particularly to Vince McMahon, "You people are discussing who gets

Bruno 16 days and who gets Bruno 15 days. And what it all means, is from the time this unification happens, I'll be wrestling seven days a week, 52 weeks out of the year. Let me tell you gentlemen, if you can't get your heads together and work out a way where you'll wrestle me 25 or 26 days a month, then I won't be a part of it. I need time off, not only for health reasons, but for family purposes, too. I don't get a chance to see my family at all right now, and the schedule you're suggesting is going to be even worse. So let me caution you that as you continue to have your unification meetings, don't argue about who gets Bruno for 16 days and who gets Bruno for 15 days. Argue instead about who's going to get Bruno for 12 days and who's going to get Bruno for 11 days, because I will not accept a title match if you men make any other arrangement." Then I concluded my remarks, thanked them all for coming and left.

vs. Baron Von Raschke

I found out later that the WWWF contingent had one more meeting of its own. Somebody, and to this day I don't know who, got up and said "Why bother with unification at all? We got Bruno and he's such a star attraction that he's filling all of our arenas anyway. Unification means only one thing. We're going to have less of him to go around and how is that going to benefit the WWWF?"

That was the argument that carried the day. They decided not to unify and they called me once again. They told me that they took into consideration everything that I had to say and that they had decided to scrap plans for the unification with the NWA. And that was that.

Before I close this chapter, let me tell you about one man who I wanted to wrestle, but never got the opportunity. That was Andre the Giant. Now I'm talking about a young Andre, when he was such a force in the late 1960s and early 1970s.

In those days, Andre stood more than 7' tall and weighed around 450 pounds. He could really move and do fantastic things in the ring. After that though, he just became a shadow of his former self in the latter part of his career.

When I first saw Andre perform, I said I wanted to take him on. So I went to Vince McMahon and told him, "Vince, since I'm world champion, I think it's important to work toward a match between me and Andre the Giant. He's making quite a name for himself and he deserves it. I just don't think it looks good for me not to defend my title against such a strong opponent.

"Besides," I went on, "it's a match made in heaven. It'll be a great box office draw. What's also important is to show the world that anybody who deserves a crack at the title will get it."

McMahon was shaking his head all the while I was talking. He said finally, "This whole thing's been brought up to me before. I've thought about it but it's a no go. Here's why: Andre the Giant is unique because of his size. What that means is that you can't keep him tied down to one territory. You've got to keep moving him around the country because believe me, once people see a guy like that in the same arena time after time, the novelty wears off fast. And one thing more, Bruno, whether you won the match or Andre wins the match, the WWWF loses either way."

I didn't follow his logic. "Explain that one to me, Vince."

"Simple," McMahon answered. "If you beat him, then that's the end of Andre. He'll no longer be the eighth wonder of the world. We've been promoting him by saying he's unbeatable. You beat him and that kills him off right there. And if Andre beats you, as champion he'll not draw. There just aren't that many opponents who could stand up to him that the fans would pay to see. And you'd be hurt by it because in the eyes of the fans you're no longer the best because Andre the Giant had conquered you."

McMahon said that he would think it over, but he never went through with the match. Since McMahon held Andre's contract and since Andre himself never showed any interest in wrestling with me, the match never materialized.

Bruno vs Andre was a match everyone wanted to see

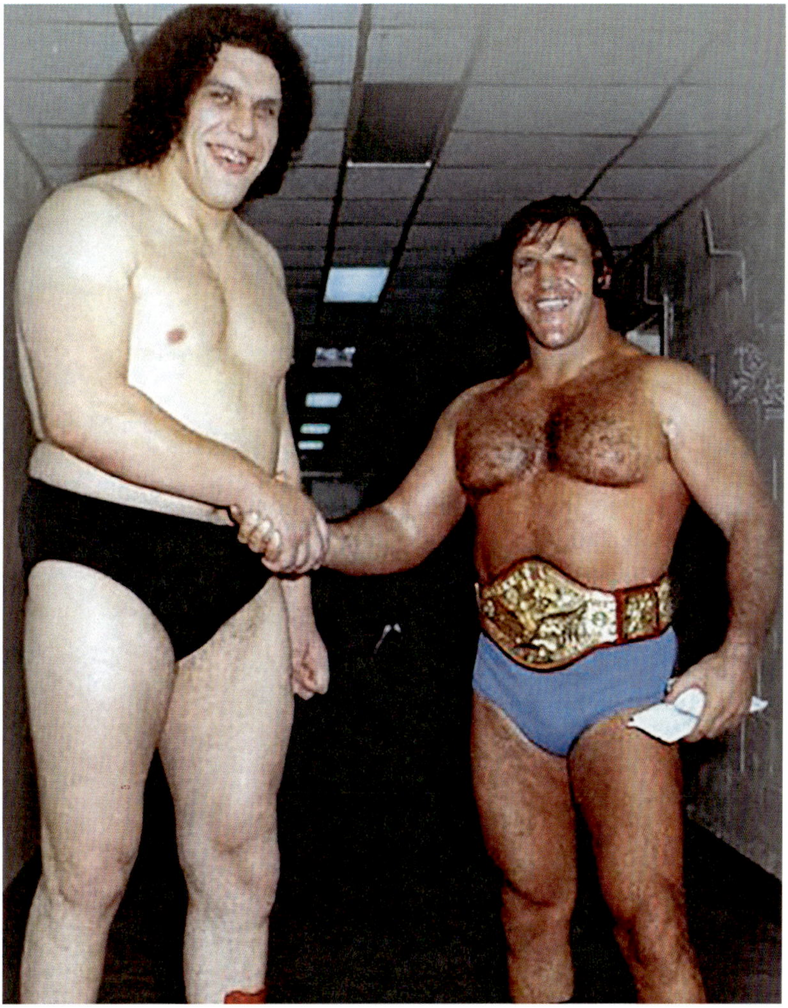

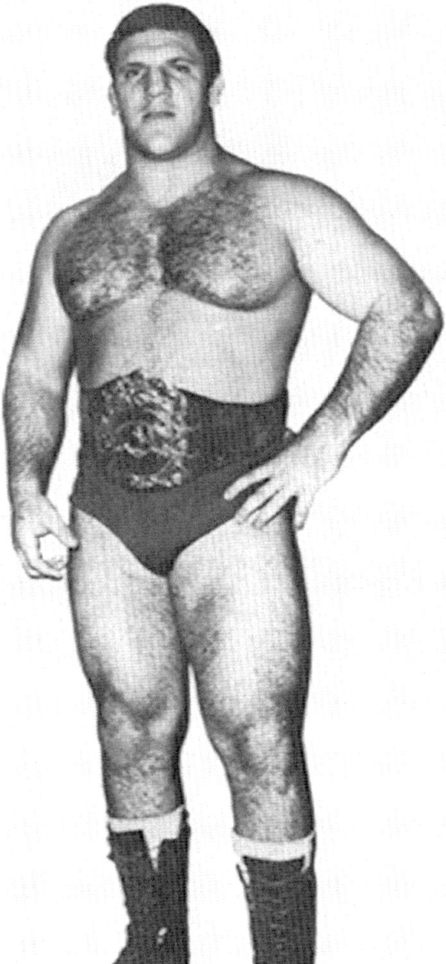

Losing, Winning, and Learning

On January 8, 1968, our twin sons were born. Their names are Danny and Darryl. Because of the hardships that Carol had to undergo during her first delivery of David, we were so happy that everything went well this time. When they were born, I had promised myself that I wouldn't be away as much and as often as I had been with David. It wasn't until 1971 that I got the chance to really keep that promise.

The circumstances that brought about my opportunity to spend more time at home certainly didn't come about by desire or intention on my part. Let me tell you what happened.

By the end of 1970, and into the early weeks of 1971, I had been champion for more than seven-and-a-half years. My schedule had been grueling because I'd been on a six or seven-day work week for all of that period. And I'd had injuries all along the way—the elbows, the ribs, fingers, knees, and back. You name it and I had it—cuts, scrapes, contusions, sprains, strains, and breaks. In my day, we wrestled in boxing rings with every little or no give, there was no padding outside the ring. In todays wrestling world the rings have a lot of give. I feel like they are almost a trampoline. That's not to say that the body is made for this kind of abuse, even with the spring in todays rings, but in my day taking slams and backdrops onto a floor with no give to it certainly took its toll. Not to mention being thrown out of the ring onto hard floors many times made out of concrete with no padding. At the time, I was booked every night possible even in "B" or Secondary clubs which likely could have sold out with the rest of the talent in the territory. If I could have had some of that time off, there is a good chance that I would have been able to go on longer, but at the time the concern was selling out every building, not my health or longevity. In an unprecedented move, I told Vince McMahon that I wanted to drop the belt to someone and take time off. I gave them a chance to find someone but they were in no hurry to do so. I eventually gave them a drop dead date and recommended that I lose the title to "The Russian Bear" Ivan Koloff who was managed by Capt. Lou Albano, my very good friend in real life, but my mortal enemy in the wrestling world.

Koloff drove his knee into my chest before pinning me

I wrestled Koloff many times over the years. I had discovered him, He was actually a Canadian named Oreal Donald Perras that began wrestling as Red McNulty. In those days, he was about 6ft and 300lbs, but could move like a cat. Later on in his career he slimmed down to about 240lbs. It was agreed, and on January 18th 1971 the match would take place. I was not happy to find out that although they were going to give the title to Ivan Koloff, he was just going to be a transitional champion to pass the title along to Pedro Morales in about 30 days time. If I had known what the plans were I would have never recommended Koloff. I wouldn't have expected him to hold the belt for seven years like I did, but I did think he had a great chance of keep the territory strong and healthy. We had packed the fans into Madison Square Garden. It had been a complete sell-out with thousands of people turned away at the gate and the fans inside were going to get their money's worth. They would be seeing something that they had never seen before. In speaking to Vince McMahon he wanted the match to be booked so that Koloff would cheat to win. I had no desire to participate in that type of a "finish." I felt that for seven-and-a-half years I had beaten everyone cleanly at some point, and it was now my turn to lose cleanly in the middle. So we worked something else out. I had Koloff catch me with a knee that cut me on the side of my head. Koloff rushed at me, scooped me up and gave me a powerful body slam, and then punctuated that with a knee drop across my throat. As I "sold" the move, Koloff scrambled up onto the top rope and hurled himself down into me, driving another knee across my chest.

As quick as a flash of dynamite, he covered me. I listened as the referee slammed his palm into the canvas three times. After seven-and-a-half years of being champion, the torch had been properly passed to a very deserving man, Ivan Koloff.

I pulled myself up off the mat and for a second it wasn't clear to me what had happened. I thought at first that something was wrong with my ears.

Here I was in the middle of Madison Square Garden with 21,500 fans looking on and I couldn't hear a thing. I actually thought

I passed the torch to Ivan Koloff

that something happened to me and I was deaf, but then my manager Arnold Skaaland came in to the ring to "check on me" and I could hear what he was saying. Then I realized what had happened. The people were just sitting there in a state of shock! No one could believe that Bruno Sammartino had lost the match. The whole Garden was as quiet as a tomb.

Then I started hearing little cries, whimpers. Talk about emotional moments, this was one that really got to me.

I heard sobbing. I heard cries. Someone called out, "Bruno, you're still the best! We love you, Bruno!"

As I stepped out of the ring and walked back to my dressing room, fans reached out to pat me on the back, or to touch my robe. I heard someone say, "You'll be back, Bruno! Don't worry. We all love you!" I got very choked up about what the fans were saying to me as I left the floor of the Garden. They had given me such great support all through the years, and even though I had lost my title that night, they stood by me. In the dressing room, many different people came around to console me—promoters, other wrestlers. Of course, the media came asking questions. How did I feel now that I had lost? What were my plans now? Was I going to retire?

Eventually the dressing room cleared and I was left to my own thoughts. I remembered being in this same dressing room nearly eight years earlier, when I had just won the title and how strong my sense of pride had been. How great my feelings of responsibility to my fans had been. This night though, I felt a great sadness. Perhaps I had let them all down—the fans, my family, the promoters.

Then a new feeling came over me. I actually started to feel good about my possibilities. I had put in my time, and my financial situation was certainly not the same as it had been in those early days. I had my home, my financial security, and my family.

I started to think, "Hey, maybe this whole thing is going to be okay because now I can go home and spend time with my family. Now I can allow the aches and pains from all the nights of pounding start to heal."

I began to accept my decision to have them take the belt off of me. I began to see positive things coming out of my loss.

I enjoyed my free time away from the ring

The next day I had no place to go but home. All the dates that I had been signed for were for the new champion to fill. It was now up to Ivan Koloff to defend he WWWF title. I caught a plane and went home. When I arrived, Carol and the rest of my family thought I would be devastated. Instead, they saw a happy, almost jubilant guy come home. And I know that deep down inside, they too were happy when they realized that I would be with my family from now on.

I really just wanted to heal. For about a month, I didn't do anything. I decided to be good to myself and I quit training so as not to put any type of stress on any part of my body. After a while, I started feeling much better.

After those four weeks, I went back to training. Guess I couldn't live without it.

Carol and I at a gala

Then to my surprise, offers started coming in from promoters all over the country. Now that I was free from having to defend my title, dates started opening up for me.

I thought, "Look at this, I'm no longer the champion and still everybody is calling me."

I said to myself, "Okay, I'll take all the additional time I need to heal up properly, train hard, then go from there."

I scheduled bouts at my own pace, far enough apart so that in a week I would only wrestle perhaps twice. That was certainly a far cry

I always kept in touch with my family while on the road

from the old days where sometimes a week equaled seven work days. I started traveling to places like St. Louis for a match, then I'd go off to California, or I'd bounce over to Tennessee, Florida, and New York.

Vince McMahon, Sr. still booked me too, on behalf of the WWWF, and he'd have me appearing in Philadelphia, and even at Madison Square Garden once in a blue moon. Then the promoters in Japan would call me and I'd say I couldn't commit for three weeks but I'd agree to one week. And then I'd book myself for two weeks of relaxation after I'd get back from the Far East. All in all I was really enjoying my life immensely at that point, because I got to spend much more time at home.

This lifestyle lasted nearly two years, from January 1971 to December 1973. Then just when I least expected it, "Lady Luck" had other things in mind for me. I received a call from Vince McMahon. He wanted to meet with me so I said OK. We scheduled a meeting in Pittsburgh Airport, so he flew to Pittsburgh with his son Vince McMahon, Jr. I was asked to come back and take the belt for a year only, but I had no real motivation to do it. I was working as much as I wanted to and making good money. In the negotiations, Vince, Sr. said that I would only have to work 3-4 days a week, and only at the large clubs. I eventually thought there was no reason not to do this, so I agreed.

I had agreed to travel to Japan for 10 days, starting the last week in November 1973. So in the meantime another transitional champion was put in place, when Stan "The Man" Stasiak beat Pedro Morales for the title. It was just like the Koloff situation where in a few weeks I would be back from Japan and face Stan Stasiak in Madison Square Garden for the title on December 10th 1973.

So I was the champion again which meant that I would likely make more money, but I gave up a good bit of my freedom and independence at the same time. It was my job to get the territory back on its feet. I felt comfortable in my abilities to get things back to where they were, but I had gotten very used to my freedom.

I have to say Vince McMahon was true to his word, I only was booked in the bigger clubs while the rest of the talent took care of the secondary clubs, and business was good.

I wanted to be sure to mention a man that didn't get anywhere near as much recognition as he should have, his name is Cowboy Bobby Duncum. While I was the champion I still continued to go to Japan as often as I could. On one of my tours I saw this young guy wrestling, he was a big strong boy, but he had only been in the business a few years. I thought to myself that we could do good business with him if I got him to NY, so I asked him if he would be interested in coming. He was extremely appreciative of me asking him, so I got his number and told him that he would be hearing from Vince McMahon sometime after I got back to the States.

When I told Vince about Bobby he said, "Bruno I never heard of the guy." I told him, "Vince, don't worry about it, he will be great for us." So Vince called and got him up to NY. In the WWWF things worked differently than they did in other areas. In NY when you wrestled a guy on television, if you were a guy that the territory was pushing, you would dominate your opponent and they would get very little or no offense at all, especially if they were a jobber. If you worked in other areas the matches would be more competitive, so I had to tell Bobby to be sure and be the aggressor, don't give the other guy anything and make sure the match wasn't competitive. You have to keep in mind, no matter what Cowboy Bobby Duncum had done in other areas, or around the world, no one in NY had ever heard of him and soon he would be headlining the greatest sports arena in the world challenging for the WWWF title. We had to be sure that the people believe that he had a chance to beat me.

As I expected, we did good business with Bobby, and I loved wrestling him. He went on to have a long career in the business, working in numerous territories and even coming back to the WWF during the title reign of Bob Backlund, challenging him for the title. I didn't believe that they handled Bobby right his second time and so the fans didn't consider him as a great challenge to Backlund's title. He had a son who eventually became a wrestler Bobby Duncum, Jr. but he died early in life, and from what I understand Bobby drifted away and has never appeared at any of the wrestling conventions or autograph shows that I have appeared at over the last 30 years or so. He is someone I would like to see again.

Another opponent that I had was Bruiser Brody. He was a big guy who hadn't yet made a huge name for himself, but I enjoyed wrestling him. I remember that I was going to wrestle him in Madison Square Garden, but I don't remember what we were originally going to do in the match. He requested that we do something different, something that would protect him more than me just beating him in the middle of the ring. It was important to him because he hoped to come back and wrestle for the WWWF again. He went on to a great career around the world, even becoming tag team partners with Stan "The Lariat" Hansen in Japan.

Waiting for my opponent

Enjoying the fruits of my labor

    Over in Japan there was Giant Baba. He was my friend and also the promoter for All Japan Pro Wrestling. He is the man that I chose to go to Japan for, even though Vince McMahon had a working relationship with Antonio Inoki. I had never gotten along with Inoki and I had no intention of going to work for him. At one point I was contacted by a representative from All Japan who said that Giant Baba wanted to promote Stan Hansen as the man that broke my neck. I told them that it was fine with me. It was that boost that helped skyrocket Stan Hansen to worldwide fame and success and to become a major star in Japan. He also formed that great tag team in

THE AUTOBIOGRAPHY OF WRESTLING'S LIVING LEGEND

The time off meant I could heal and enjoy my family

Japan with Bruiser Brody. In a sad turn of events, Bruiser Brody was killed in an incident in Puerto Rico in 1988. I know that he was going to soon be coming back to the WWF, and likely would have had a great run and major recognition if his life hadn't been cut short in a senseless tragedy.

The fans never forgot me and I tried to sign autographs for them whenever I could

The one guy that I certainly remember most vividly was Stan Hansen, not for his wrestling skills particularly, but for what happened in the ring with him. It would change both of our lives forever. He broke my neck!

There have been all kinds of ridiculous stories written about how Hansen broke my neck with a lariat. That's all those stories are, just nonsense.

Hansen was a big man, 6'4" or so, weighing in around 310 pounds. And he was green, a real rookie. People might say that I didn't take him seriously, but that's not the case.

I always took everyone seriously and was always on my guard.

On this night, April 25, 1976, we were going at a pretty furious pace for nearly 15 minutes. I'm looking at Hansen and thinking, "Boy, this guy is out of gas already!"

It was obvious he was tired. The fact was that Hansen, a young man in his 20s, just didn't have the stamina that I still had in my 30s.

I started coming off the ropes and catching him with tackles. Then it happened. He tried to scoop me up for a body slam and he didn't have the strength left in his arms to execute it properly. He got me up in the air, but couldn't handle my weight to slam me onto my back. Instead, Hansen dropped me—dropped me right on top of my head—and my neck broke.

It was like I had taken a bolt of lightning through my body. I nearly blacked out and yet the match continued. Nobody knew that my neck had snapped and we kept wrestling for a few more minutes. I was operating on pure instinct alone. Then, Hansen made an attempt at a second body slam and got caught using an illegal hold while he was trying to pull it off. The referee charged in and disqualified Hansen and only then was the match halted. From that point on, all I remembered were flashing red lights and an ambulance siren. The pain had put me out.

After the match, I was rushed by ambulance to a hospital in New York. Ringside people suspected that something very serious was wrong. I heard later that the state athletic commissioner himself had attended the match, and when I was dropped on my head, he turned to his companion and said, "My God, that man's been seriously hurt."

I had absolutely no feeling on one side. The rest of me was in excruciating pain.

I was always asked when I was coming back

Bernard Spiegle, a friend of mine who's also my tax attorney in New York, would always come to the Garden and watch me whenever I was in town. Usually after the show, Bernie and I would go to my favorite Italian restaurant in the city, Delsomme, which some dear friends of mine from Sicily, the Cardinale Brothers, had opened. There was no Old Country cuisine the night I broke my neck though.

Bernie rode with me in the ambulance. As I fought through the waves of pain, I kept thinking about my wife. I knew how frightened she was going to be when she heard about my injury.

And I worried about my parents. They were both in their 80s then and I mumbled to Bernie, "My God, if my parents hear that their son is in a New York City hospital with a serious injury, there will be two heart attacks in Pittsburgh."

After we arrived at the hospital and I was examined, the doctors told me that I was to stay put. They didn't want me to move another inch until they could figure out what they wanted to do with me.

Being in a hospital was the last place I wanted to be, I needed to be back among my friends, family, and fans

I tried to talk to Bernie, tried to make sense of it. "Bernie, I know why they don't want me to leave the hospital. They just don't want to be responsible for what might happen to me. Tell them that I have to take that risk. I've got to get back home. Tell them to get a release from my doctor in Pittsburgh."

Then the fog rolled in on me. Somebody, probably Bernie, dialed my wife for me. I got on the phone and I tried not to scare her.

I told her that I got hurt in the match tonight, that I was at a New York hospital, but I was going to come home as soon as I could get a consent release from my own personal doctor. She sounded shaken up by my news, but she said she'd take care of it.

Carol then called Dr. Louis Civitarese, my physician for many, many years. I had met Doc Civitarese in Pittsburgh at ringside because he was the state athletic commission doctor. He attended all the matches in that capacity. I found out that he was a surgeon at Divine Providence Hospital and had gotten involved with wrestling as a hobby. He loved athletics. I trusted him completely and he always took wonderful care of me.

In a short while, Doc Civitarese was on the line, asking me what had happened. After I told him, he said that he was willing to fly to New York to attend to me. I told him no. I said that I had to come back to Pittsburgh so as not to upset my parents and that he had to tell the doctors here that it was okay for me to do that.

Finally, Doc Civitarese agreed after I assured him that I could travel and would be alright. He talked to the New York doctors and I was released into his hands. Bernie took me to the airport and saw me onto the plane.

I cannot even begin to describe what my flight was like from New York to Pittsburgh. The pain continued to explode in me. Any movement just made everything worse. Bar none, it was the most uncomfortable journey I think I ever made.

I remember when I arrived at Divine Providence in Pittsburgh, Doc Civitarese took one look at me and his face flushed. He was extremely angry with me and he proceeded to chew me out in no uncertain terms. He said, "Bruno, don't you understand what kind of injury you have?" I had no idea.

"Don't you understand that the slightest little bump or jerk or movement and the broken bone in your neck will cut into your spinal cord? And when that happens, you're either dead or paralyzed from the neck down!"

After getting over his initial shock at seeing me, Doc gathered his troops together, talking to his top neurosurgeon, and then his top orthopedic man. Through it all, it was clear that Doc Civitarese was totally in charge.

The next morning my sister Mary came to the hospital with my folks. I had asked my sister to bring them there as soon as she could before they overheard all sorts of wild stories on the news. She had briefed them as gently as possible that I had had an accident while wrestling in New York, and that I was now resting comfortably in the hospital in Pittsburgh.

Actually, reports of my injury were all over the television stations the night I came back. Fortunately, my parents went to bed before the 11 o'clock news so they had missed all the reports, thank God.

Both my brother and sister were worried that all the paisans would have heard the news and start to call my parents' home early in the morning asking, "How's Bruno? My God, how is he?" Of course, they would think that Mom and Dad would already have known. Fortunately, that didn't happen either.

When they first walked into my hospital room and saw the doctor there

At home with my twins

with all of his assistants, my parents started to get all shook up. My mom was really scared that I'd been badly hurt. But we all played it as though what had happened to me wasn't all that significant. That was the way I wanted it.

You know, after they went home later, they did start to get calls from friends and relatives from all over. They told everyone that their son was going to be okay, that it was alright. I'm not sure that Mom and Dad ever were really aware of the seriousness of my injury—and that's good. I found out later that the media bombarded the hospital with requests to get an interview with me, but it was no dice. Doctor Civitarese laid down the law, "No interviews! Not in his condition!"

Doc Civitarese adjusts my Miami Brace

Later in the day after my parents were gone, one of the specialists, the neurosurgeon, told me straight, "Bruno, I'm afraid that you will never be able to go back to wrestling. You've had your career and now that's over. You're finished with wrestling."

Then Dr. Best, who had been an orthopedic surgeon for the Pittsburgh Steelers, came to my room and sang a different tune. He said, "Athletes are strange birds, Bruno. What might be a crippling injury for an ordinary person is not necessarily the same for an athlete. I've seen athletes come back from some extremely serious injuries … injuries that have amazed me."

Best leveled with me. "Yours is a very serious injury. I don't know if you are interested in returning to wrestling, but I'm not going to rule it out for you. I'm not going to give you the gloom and doom approach like the others you've been hearing. Recovery may take time, but it is a possibility."

Even though the neurosurgeon had said I was through, here

was another expert telling me I had a chance. As for Doc Civitarese, he wasn't committing himself one way or the other. He knew how serious my condition was, and he also knew how I had recuperated from other injuries before. His approach was one of wait and see.

I posed with McMahon, Sr. and Pedro Morales before I left for Japan

I really hadn't expected to be wrestling for the title

While I was flat on my back in the hospital, the world of professional wrestling kept churning. International promoters were putting together a match between Muhammad Ali and the great Japanese wrestler Antonio Inoki. Yes, that's right. They were setting up a fighter versus wrestler bout.

In fact, Vince McMahon had attempted to get Ali and me into a similar match prior to the Ali/Inoki pairing. McMahon couldn't come up with the $6 million that Ali wanted, so my shot at Ali went by the boards.

But Vince's idea intrigued the Inoki backers in Japan, and the promoters there were able to get the Ali/Inoki match off the ground. It was to be fought in Japan, and shown simultaneously all over the world on closed circuit television.

McMahon still wanted a piece of this action so he went into

partnership with Bob Arum, who was doing the major promotion for it. McMahon committed himself for a large amount of money to obtain the closed circuit rights throughout the Northeastern region.

But the bout just wasn't moving. It was kind of eerie because there was no reaction to it from the fans. Nothing.

McMahon got very worried that if the match didn't go ahead, then it was curtains for him since he had a ton of money on the line. He would be facing bankruptcy, pure and simple.

So, while I'm lying there in the hospital bed, with tubes running this way and that, and with all these instruments hooked up, Vince called me. Since I couldn't hold the phone, the nurse held the receiver up to my ear.

He went straight to the point. "Bruno, I'm going to be dead, finished. This Ali and Inoki match isn't drawing flies. I need you to bail me out. Let me make a match between you and Stan Hansen. We'll have it at Shea Stadium and put it on closed circuit along with the Ali bout. Your match will be the one the fans pay to see and that'll save my butt."

All I could say to him was, "Vince, I don't know. I'm so banged up I can hardly talk let alone walk. Nobody knows what I'm going to be like in a couple of months."

But Vince kept pestering me, calling me day after day, and trying to talk me into agreeing to a match, all the while I was hospitalized with a broken neck. You had to know Vince to realize what the man was capable of.

When Doc Civitarese got wind that Vince McMahon was calling me constantly about a possible match, he got really ticked off about it. Everybody did, even my wife Carol.

She said, "Bruno, you better not even think about it. Vince isn't concerned about you at all. He's only out for himself."

That was true to a degree. What Vince was telling me was that his business was in deep trouble and he needed a miracle to salvage a serious situation.

Once, Doc Civitarese came in during one of Vince's calls. He grabbed the phone from the nurse who was holding it for me and he screamed into the receiver. "Is this Mister McMahon? Well,

Mister McMahon, I'm Doctor Louis Civitarese and I'm taking care of Bruno. I just want you to get one thing clear. Bruno is suffering from a broken neck. He is extremely lucky to be alive and, in fact, he came within a millimeter of being paralyzed from the neck down. As far as Bruno being able to wrestle again, that's to be determined way down the road. Now, Mister McMahon, before I hang up, let me ask you never to call Bruno again." And Doc slammed the phone down on Vince's ear.

But even that kind of treatment didn't influence McMahon to back off. The next time he called, the first thing he said to me was, "Don't ever put that last guy on the phone again. I don't want to talk to him."

So Vince kept calling and we kept talking. Finally, Vince came up with another scheme. "Look, Bruno. If we can at least make the announcement about your match with Hansen, say six weeks before it's scheduled, that would save me."

I answered quickly, "I don't want you to make an announcement and then I can't do it. That would make it even worse for you in the long run."

McMahon shot back, "I'm not worried about you not making it. Let's face the facts here. We can book a finish that protects you. We wont take any crazy risks. Believe me, we're not going to take any chances with your health. But again, we need you in that match to save the organization, or otherwise we're in deep, deep trouble."

I took a deep breath and said, "Okay, Vince. Go ahead and make your announcement."

Of course, when my family and Doc Civitarese heard what I had done, they were all furious with me. They couldn't believe that I would risk such a match. But I told them that it was something I had to do. There was too much at stake not to risk it.

Finally after about a month, I was released from Divine Providence.

Then for another month after that, I had to wear this ridiculous device that the therapists had rigged up called the Miami Brace. It was a steel contraption that fastened like a belt at the waist. It also had support bars that ran out from the waistband. One came up under my chin and the other one ran around back to support my neck. There were knobs that you could tighten or loosen to make the brace more or less comfortable. I was supposed to keep this thing on at all times. Well, at least I wore it all the way home.

Then shortly after I got home, Vince told me that he had lined up a television interview for me on Channel 11 and that now was the perfect time to make the announcement about my match. I made the trip to the station and got on the air and said that I was out to make things right between me and the guy who inflicted this injury on me. And that was that. The match was officially on.

I started doing some light training at home, and I do mean light. I really didn't want to put any kind of stress on my neck. I worked to tighten up muscles that had gone flat from laying around in the hospital.

When the date drew closer for the match with Hansen, the state athletic commission stepped in and said that they weren't going to allow it until they examined me and certified me fit. This worried me a little bit because I thought they might turn me down.

I flew to New York for the examination. Doc Civitarese was still angry with me for moving ahead with the match. He wanted to come to New York to be there when I was examined but, as it turned out, another one of his patients became seriously ill. He had to perform emergency surgery and couldn't come. It's ironic the way things happen.

Well, I passed my physical and Commissioner Foy himself gave his approval for the match to proceed. I do know that Commissioner Foy was a strict man with the rules and that if the commission's doctor had said no, then it would have been no.

As it happened, the match between Muhammad Ali and Antonio Inoki was a complete bomb, a total disaster. I don't even think Inoki's mother watched it. On the other hand, wherever my match with Stan Hansen went out on closed circuit, fans flocked to see it and paid good money to do so.

Our match was piggy-backed with the Ali/Inoki debacle and it also took place on that same evening.

In reality, I had no business being in the ring this night. I had

Stan Hansen and Freddie Blassie

signed myself out of the hospital and planned on heading right back to the hospital the next day. In today's wrestling, many times everyone dresses in areas where they get together and discuss their match. In those days that didn't happen often, and it certainly didn't happen in Shea Stadium. I couldn't take any chances with Stan Hansen that night. I went in the ring and took over the match and didn't give Hansen any chance to hurt me accidentally. I was in far too fragile a position at this point, lets face it the fans were only there for one reason, to see me rip his head off. It wasn't a match that went very long, only about 10 minutes, but the fans went home happy. There wasn't a clear winner, since Stan Hansen was counted out of the ring, but it all worked out. The next day I headed back to the hospital.

I didn't see Stan Hansen for a few months, but when I did I apologized for not giving him anything in the match, and although I didn't feel like he was paid fairly for what we accomplished—in

Program from Ali vs. Inoki, and me vs. Hansen

basically saving the company from bankruptcy—he didn't want to create any problems, because up to that point it was the biggest payoff that he had ever had.

I had my own concerns with my pay off since the deal that I made with McMahon was for a percentage of the closed circuit dollars. Who knows if McMahon even had the authority to offer it to me at the time, but a desperate man will say almost anything when backed in to a corner as McMahon was. The Ali/Inoki match, which had numerous political problems between the two camps, had nothing do with why there was little to no fan interest, but it did have a lot to do with the snooze fest that the match turned out to be.

McMahon ended up only paying me out of the receipts from the Shea Stadium gate. I had no contract, only a gentleman's agreement. Consequently, I didn't get a dime from any of the closed circuit revenues.

When I confronted McMahon about that, I said, "Vince, I came back with a broken neck to bail you out of your misery and now you're telling me there's no money from the closed circuit telecast!" McMahon said, "There's not much I can do for you, Bruno. I can't really give you anything from the closed circuit because I don't have the say on that. That part of the deal is controlled by the other promoters. Sorry."

So I was paid 10 percent from the Shea Stadium receipts and McMahon stayed in business. Would it be an understatement to say that I felt cheated?

One of my matches with Pedro Morales

With Mexican luchador Mil Máscaras

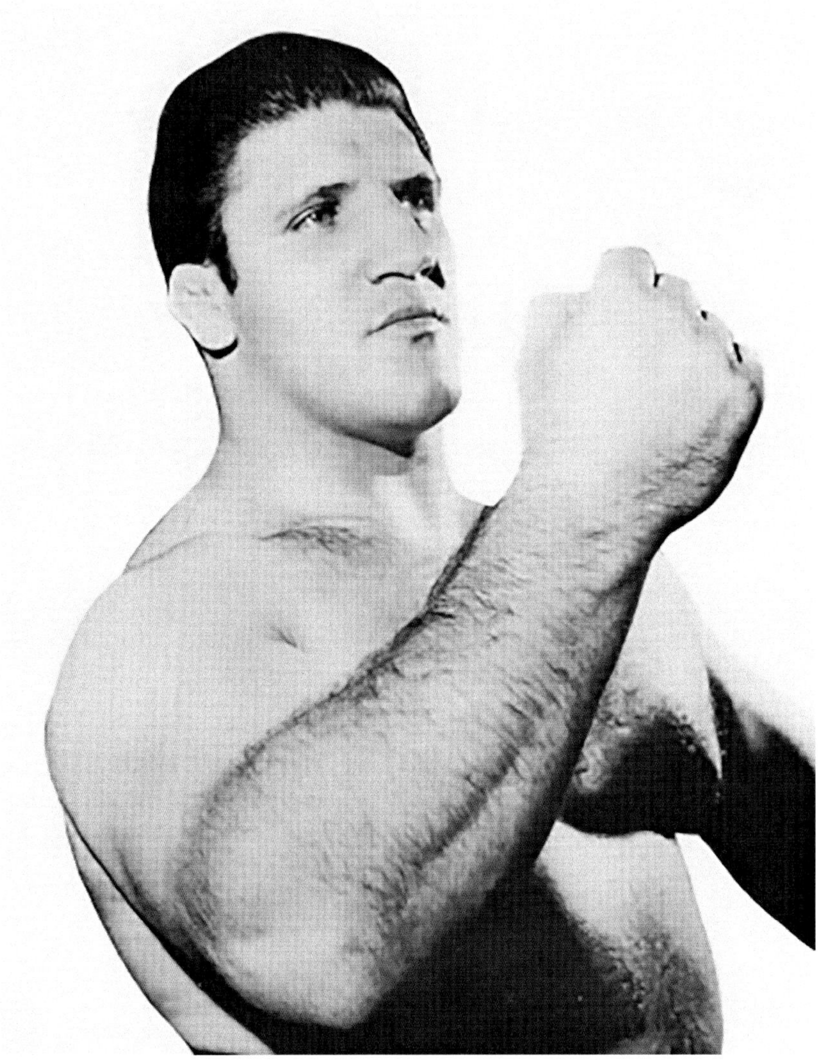

The Beat Goes On

The year 1977 rolled around, and by that time I was down to around 245 pounds. Even though I no longer carried the 275 pounds that I weighed throughout most of my career, I still felt I was as strong, if not stronger than most wrestlers out there.

Even so, by now I had started to talk about retirement, but it seemed like I was always talked out of it. The promoters kept telling me, "Why should you retire, Bruno? You're still in great shape, still one of the best in the business."

And other wrestlers would say to me, "Why retire? You're still at the top of your game and your injuries are healed."

What nobody knew was that every time I climbed into the ring, my neck would bother me. And other injuries to my back that I'd suffered over the years were starting to have a cumulative effect. Then there were some shoulder and leg problems that were now getting my attention.

What worried me the most was the nagging feeling of not quite being

Being introduced before one of my many matches

able to execute the great wrestling moves for which I was so well known throughout the 1960s. There was no question in my mind that these injuries were taking their toll.

I was getting a little self-conscious about myself and my abilities. I realized too, that new fans were always popping up and I didn't want them to see a guy who had been the best in the world in the 1960s, now not performing up to that level. I was very conscious of the fans' demand for excellence, so I pushed all the harder. If you recall, when I met with Vince McMahon, Sr. and Jr. the deal would be that I would come back for one year, but I let them talk me in to staying longer since I was making good money, and they were true to their word in regards to how often I had to wrestle. I finally let them know that I was done and for the second time. I demanded that they take the belt from me or I would quit as Champion. The office made the decision to have me pass the torch to a man named Wayne Coleman who was professionally known as Superstar Billy Graham.

Superstar Billy Graham had one of the finest physiques in professional wrestling. As with Koloff, I had wrestled and defeated Graham many times. When I dropped the title to Koloff, Vince McMahon, Sr. had wanted me to do some sort of finish to the match where Koloff cheated to win. I was very much opposed to that and finally won the argument. This time Vince McMahon came to me and said Bruno the last time we did it your way now we need to do it my way. We worked out a finish where Billy Graham would have his legs on the ropes as he pinned me. It was important to Vince McMahon that I looked strong and the people still believed in me. He was going to want to bring me in for appearances if he needed it, and he didn't want my drawing power to be hurt. If you are following, you have seen that when a villain won the title they didn't hold on to it very long. Then the title was passed along to a babyface. In this situation, Vince McMahon didn't have anyone that he wanted to pass the belt to, so he gave Superstar Billy Graham 9 months with the title. You have to realize, that although in comparison to my title reigns that doesn't sound like much, the two previous villains that were champions, Ivan Koloff and Stan Stasiak, combined I don't believe had the title for two full months

THE AUTOBIOGRAPHY OF WRESTLING'S LIVING LEGEND

Superstar Billy Graham would be the next champion

Eventually with no clear standout to give the title to the promoter and wrestling star of Championship Wrestling of Florida, Eddie Graham recommended Bob Backlund. He was a young All-American looking wrestler with a great amateur background who was in tremendous condition. In fact, as fate would have it, Billy Graham lost his title under virtually the same circumstances. They had booked a finish where Graham would throw his leg over the bottom rope, but the referee didn't see it, so Backlund became World Champion. He would hold that title for five-and-a-half years until he lost it to The Iron Sheik. He was the transitional champion who would pass the title along to Hulk Hogan.

After I lost the title to Graham, I again began seriously considering retirement. By now, I had proven my point to everybody. I could come back and wrestle again, even from a broken neck.

Before the Graham bout, I had my reasons to continue. I certainly didn't want to hear for the rest of my life on television and in all the wrestling magazines that Stan Hansen was the man who retired Bruno Sammartino. I wanted to come back and kill that story, so I wrestled for a good long while after my recovery, giving 100 percent at all times for the fans.

So now it's post-Graham and once more I was faced with the retirement question. And again, the promoters and my fellow pros argued with me. Why quit when you still have the skills to keep winning?

McMahon said, "Bruno, just go for a few more years. You're still young … I mean young for your years."

What his backhanded compliment meant, was that he still considered me in good shape, and here I was, in my early 40s. Actually, I had trimmed down a little bit more. My neck still was giving me problems, but I would never admit that to anyone.

So after the Graham bout, I thought I might as well keep going until I got a chance to think about everything more seriously. I cut down again on the number of matches I would accept, traveling occasionally to places like Los Angeles, St. Louis, and Boston. And you know what? I was very happy working at that pace and I continued that way for nearly three more years.

One interesting side-note to my career happened in 1978 when Vince suggested that I take up the role of television color commentator. That challenge intrigued me, so I agreed to do it.

I would sit at the announcer's table to comment on the other matches on the card, or sometimes I would do programs where my only function was to add my two cents worth to the proceedings. For a while I had a blast doing that, but finally after two years I gave up the microphone.

In February 1980, the decision to retire finally came to me. I had been on a tour of Texas, going to cities like Dallas, Houston, Amarillo, and Lubbock, along with a side excursion to Albuquerque, New Mexico. I can't say where or when it hit me, but I knew that it was time to call it quits professionally. I'm sure I could have gone on even longer, but the point was, why not retire? Maybe I started to think a little about Primo Camera and Gorgeous George's last days in the ring, and I sure knew I didn't want to go out that way.

When I came back after concluding that tour, McMahon had slated me for a TV appearance.

In 1980, while out on tour, I decided to retire

I had made up my mind that I was going to tell McMahon about my wishes. I was going to name the specific date when my retirement would begin, and I thought that the TV appearance would be the perfect forum for my announcement. Once again, fate stepped in to change my plans.

It was the early 1970s when I broke a young wrestler into the business by the name of Larry Zbyszko. Larry was a Pittsburgher who was a fantastic amateur wrestler. I first met him in 1970 when he was wrestling for North Allegheny High School. He compiled a tremendous record and wanted to turn pro right out of high school.

I suggested that it would be best for his career if he'd go earn a college degree first, and keep developing his wrestling skills at the college level. I told him if he did that, then I would help him become a pro. But I would not help him if he tried to turn pro after graduating from high school. I had talked to his parents about this and they definitely agreed with me. They also wanted Larry to go on to college.

Larry did his four years at college, and he came back to me and said, "Look, you had promised to help me get into professional wrestling if I went to college. Well, I did. Now I'm ready to turn pro. How about showing me what it takes?"

So I began working out with Larry quite a bit. I would bring in other wrestlers who I knew to give him all sorts of different competition. There was no question that Larry Zbyszko was an extremely talented athlete.

Finally, I felt he was good enough to hit the road. I called up a couple of promoters who I knew and they booked him right away. Larry went off to wrestle in Vancouver, British Columbia, where he stayed for quite some time. Then the promoters moved him back to the States after he had picked up considerable experience and he went to places in Florida, Georgia … all over the South actually.

Of course, I kept in touch with Larry as much as I could. A few times he was booked in Pittsburgh. I went to see him work and believe me, I was even more impressed. I talked to McMahon about checking Larry out. I told Vince that this new kid, Larry Zbyszko, was sensational and that he should consider booking Larry into New York. And when McMahon saw Larry, he agreed right away. He also thought Larry was a terrific new talent.

Even while we watched Larry in action, McMahon was working all the angles. He said that when Zbyszko hit New York, they'd introduce him as Bruno Sammartino's protégé. Vince thought that people would sit up and take notice of a guy who had trained with me.

When I spoke to Larry about the plans, I explained to him that he'd be starting at the bottom of the ladder, but it was a ladder that went from the basement of the big time all the way up to the penthouse. I told him that the best way to climb that ladder was slowly and with patience. I told him that in time I was sure he could be a tremendous headliner.

At one point Vince McMahon, Sr. put him in a tag team with

Tony Garea who was from New Zealand. He was another youngster but a few years older than Zbyszko. Garea ultimately stayed with the WWWF organization for almost his whole career in the ring and his longtime work for the company continued backstage as an agent/producer. On November 21, 1978 they won the tag team titles from The Yukon Lumberjacks: Eric and Pierre managed by Captain Lou Albano. In the world of the WWWF, Lou managed almost all of the great tag teams. At the time, I was a color commentator for the company, and actually called this match with Vince McMahon, Jr.

As the weeks rolled on, I didn't hear from Larry as often as I used to. At first, I didn't pay too much attention to that since I was immersed in my own affairs. Then some friends told me that Larry was having some serious personal problems.

Larry was reeling from the fallout of a failed marriage, one in which he had fathered a child. I also heard that he was very dissatisfied with the way he was moving up through the ranks of professional wrestling.

In early 1980, right at the time when he faced all the turmoil in his personal life, and knowing that I was leaning towards retirement, Larry had an idea that he should turn on me, his mentor. This would immediately put him in the top spot in the company. I wasn't necessarily in favor of the idea, but I went along with it believing that we could do great business, especially while I was on my way to retirement. So I went to Vince McMahon, Sr. with Larry and laid out the plan for him. We set up the angle over several weeks on TV. Zbyszko ignored me while I was a color commentator attempting to interview him after successful matches. In the 3rd week, Vince McMahon, Jr. went out to interview Zbyszko. This time we had Larry stop and talk. He expressed his displeasure of living in my shadow and wanted the chance to prove himself to the world. He wanted to wrestle me in an exhibition. It was planned that I would initially decline the match, which would lead Zbyszko to announce his retirement unless I reconsidered. Of course, at that point I agreed to the "match" to be held at the television tapings in Allentown, PA.

We had a "scientific match" … just wrestling moves, no kicks or punches, but the way that we worked the match I beat Larry at every move and had him in positions to easily beat him. Then I would release him from the hold which only infuriated him. At one point, Larry had me in a hammerlock. In trying to maneuver my way out of it I ducked down and Larry went outside the ring. The frustration in him was building. I held the ropes open for him to come back in, and when he came in he kicked me in the stomach and then he attacked me. While I was down, he went outside the ring and grabbed a chair. The fans were booing him as he attacked me, smashing me in the head with the chair. At this time, I used the blade and went very deep, so that the blood would flow. The blood was pouring out of my head and the fans were incensed. It was mission accomplished. In the matter of a few minutes Larry became the most hated wrestler in the world.

It was clear that this was going to be a big moneymaker. Larry was happy, but Vince McMahon, Sr. thought that it would only be good for one time around the loop. I could see Larry was incensed, but I motioned for him to be quiet and that I would take care of it. We went in to Madison Square Garden and not only sold out the Garden, but as there was no PPV in those days, only closed circuit, the best that we could do was fill up the small arena connected to Madison Square Garden called the Felt Forum. We set up a closed circuit screen and we sold that out too. It was clear that this angle, if handled properly, could be good for several times around.

In the minds of the fans, Larry Zbyszko was Public Enemy #1, and Larry played it for all it was worth. He was a great heel. He had such a natural arrogance coupled with great ability. He also had he gift of the gab to a point where he didn't need a manager to help build the heat. This was just Larry and me.

The angle was red hot. We sold out everywhere that we went, the fans screaming for Larry's head on a platter. One day we went to Washington in the afternoon, and Baltimore in the evening. We sold out both large arenas even though they were so close to each other.

It was decided that the final match would be held at Shea Stadium inside a steel cage where the crowd was enormous.

In August of 1980, Sammartino and Zbyszko drew 46,000 people to Shea Stadium. We pulled in more than $550,000 in receipts and broke the all-time box office record for a wrestling show.

What made those figures all the more amazing was that on the same night, the Pittsburgh Steelers played an exhibition game against the New York Giants at Giants Stadium, drawing 40,000 football fans. And the New York Yankees were taking on the Baltimore Orioles at Yankee Stadium, hosting 40,000 baseball fans. For wrestling to outdraw both football and baseball in the New York Metro area, this was a major accomplishment.

I believe if it wasn't for the threat of rain that night, always a risk at an outside show, the crowd would have been larger.

Of course, as everyone knows, I won that match. As far as the big clubs were concerned the angle was over. Larry wanted to offer me his hand in friendship after the match, since I had proven that I was the better man. He would accept it and move on. I told him that I had no interest in that whatsoever. I didn't think that the idea made any sense, or that the fans would accept it. Well, if you see a video of that match, you will see that Larry went on with his plan anyway and extended his hand to me in friendship. I punched him twice and walked away.

After that, we took the match to many of the secondary clubs and packed those to capacity and beyond many times. Just getting Zbyszko to the ring in these smaller clubs was difficult at the time. It was a different wrestling business and the fans sincerely wanted to rip him limb from limb.

Leaving the cage, triumphant over Larry Zbyszko

At the same time, since our angle was coming to an end, they wanted to try and start other angles for Zbyszko. They brought back his old tag team partner, Tony Garea, who he attacked. They even put guys in with him like Ivan Putski. Larry expected the same result that we had had, which wasn't to be. The fans' reaction wasn't the same, and the matches didn't draw as well as Larry had hoped.

At the time, I believed that Larry should have taken the many offers that were flooding in from promoters all over the country and moved, but he chose not to do that. He had so much publicity he could have gone to another territory, especially Charlotte where Jim Crockett, Sr. wanted him to wrestle the local heroes there like Ricky Steamboat, Ric Flair, and others. His natural arrogance in the South would have probably drawn turn away crowds.

I was looking to retire but I had made a promise that I would open the new arena being built in New Jersey, The Brendan Byrne Arena (The Meadowlands). It was behind schedule but we made the official announcement that the match in The Meadowlands would be my last in the States. So I waited to retire until it opened on October 4th 1981. On that date I faced one of my old opponents, George "The Animal" Steele. The match lasted about 15 minutes and I thanked the fans for all the support over the years. The next day I left for a 10-day-tour of Japan, and than I would be officially retired.

I had gotten a request from Giant Baba when he heard that I was going to retire to come to Japan on more time. I wasn't looking to wrestle anymore, but I couldn't refuse Giant Baba. He had been a man of honor all the years that I went to Japan for him. I never even had a guarantee of any kind when I went to Japan. I just had faith that Giant Baba would treat me fairly, and he always did. When I arrived much to my surprise—after all these years of being a heel in Japan and wrestling Giant Baba all the time—I was to team up with Giant Baba during the tour. In all the cities that we went to, the fans were told through an interpreter that it would be the last time I would be wrestling in that city. I was retiring.

Over the years, Larry went to other territories like the NWA and AWA, and certainly had his share of success. At the time of the passing of Vince McMahon, Sr. sometime after he sold the company to his son, the invisible boundaries that all promoters respected were erased by Vince McMahon, Jr. The NWA had started bringing events to NJ and they weren't doing very well at all. I was told that Larry would constantly be on television claiming that he had been the one to retire not only me, but Nick Bockwinkel (former AWA World Champion) as well. Any time that the NWA attempted to run shows on the East Coast, even though it had been years since my matches with Zbyszko, and no matter how low or high on the card Larry might have been that night, the fans still called out "Bruno Bruno Bruno." In Larry's mind it was a perfect chance for him to capitalize on the situation, so he talked to me about coming out of retirement to wrestle him again. While I really didn't want to wrestle anymore, I believed that if I was given four weeks on television, Larry and I would sell out The Meadowlands. I sent the message to the NWA that I would take the match under those conditions for $30,000.00. The message was delivered back to me that the financial terms weren't acceptable, so because I had such a belief that Larry and I could sell out The Meadowlands, I agreed to do it for 4% of the gate. The NWA had only been drawing a few thousand people in an arena that held a close to 20,000. What did they have to lose? One can only imagine in a business like pro wrestling, which many times is driven by ego, that they would have been more concerned with what would happen next. Even if I agreed to one more go around the loop with Zbyszko, if asked, I wouldn't be coming back as a regular talent.

Of course, Larry wasn't happy but it was pretty much the last thought that I gave to coming back and having any matches. I assure you to this day, Larry and I would have sold that building out. Still to this day, wrestling fans that were around then, still remember the intensity of that angle and consider Zbyszko my greatest opponent. In this day and age, all of the video that is available has let fans, not even born at that time, be aware of the Sammartino/Zbyszko feud.

By this time, Vince McMahon, Jr. had purchased the company from his father, Phil Zacko, Arnold Skaaland, and Gorilla Monsoon. At the time, Zacko was ready to retire and the latter two men went to work for the company for life.

In my mind I was done with the wrestling business. I had given it all I had. Now I just wanted to spend my life with my wife Carol and the rest of my family. I thought that I could start a normal life away from the spotlight, but the rest of the world had a different idea. I eventually heard from Vince McMahon, Jr. about coming back to the company as a color commentator. This seemed like a simple thing with very limited travel. I would also work as an agent in Pittsburgh at the Civic Arena.

In time, it became clear that Vince McMahon, Jr. had other ideas in mind. He felt like some of the clubs weren't performing well, and he felt that if I put the tights back on again to wrestle, the fans would turn out. While I had no interest in ever wrestling again, for various reasons, I got myself involved in angles with "Rowdy" Roddy Piper and "Macho Man" Randy Savage. McMahon thought we did great business, but always in the back of my mind, I remembered my promise to not be like Gorgeous George and Primo Carnera. I never wanted to feel that I was cheating the fans while they still supported me.

I finally announced I would be retiring on the Championship Wrestling TV show

When I flew back home to Pittsburgh on October 15, 1981, I was officially retired.

FAREWELL TO
BRUNO
FINAL WRESTLING MATCH
OF THE LIVING LEGEND
BRUNO SAMMARTINO
TONIGHT IN THE
BRENDAN BYRNE
MEADOWLANDS
ARENA
OFFICIAL SOUVENIR PROGRAM
SUNDAY, OCTOBER 4th, 1981

THE AUTOBIOGRAPHY OF WRESTLING'S LIVING LEGEND

BRUNO SAMMARTINO

THE AUTOBIOGRAPHY OF WRESTLING'S LIVING LEGEND

With Giant Baba in Japan

1981: Jumbo Tsuruta, Mil Mascaras, Haku, Terry Funk, Dory Funk Jr. Bruno Sammartino, Genishiro Tenryu, Giant Baba

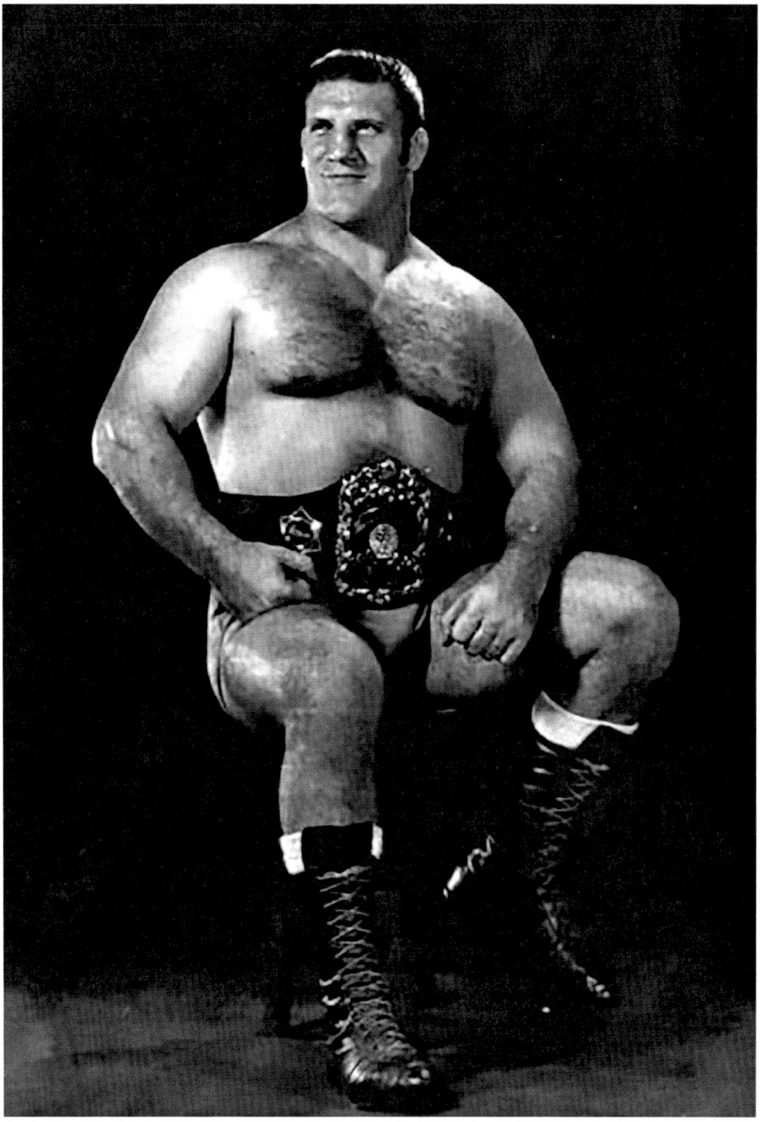

Life After Wrestling

When our first-born David was about five-years-old, I remember asking him, "David, what are you going to be when you grow up?" Without hesitation David said, "I want to be a wrestler." We all laughed because we thought it was natural for a kid to want to be just what his daddy is. When David

From a very early age, David wanted to be a wrestler

reached the age of 10, we'd ask the same question and still get the same answer, "A wrestler." And when he got to be 12, he'd say, "A professional wrestler." To tell you the truth, I started getting worried. I didn't want him to be involved with the business in any way, shape, or form. I know that people will tell you that parents shouldn't interfere with their children's interests, but I had the experience to know what professional wrestling was all about.

Don't get me wrong, I'm very grateful for what wrestling has done for me. The opportunities that presented themselves, especially given my early circumstances as a child in Italy, enabled me to create a fantastic life in America.

However, there were problems along the way that were not so pleasant. I've told you about being on the road all the time, the serious injuries, not seeing my family for weeks. I've always admitted to myself that these aspects of the business did have significant downsides. Believe me, it has been an extremely difficult lifestyle at times.

I thought that if David followed through with this dream that he had since he was five years old, undoubtedly he would have to go through a lot of the same miseries that I went through. Naturally, as loving parents, Carol and I wanted all our sons to have the best chance for success in their own lives that they could possibly achieve ... certainly better than what I had gone through. Because of wrestling's rewards, I could now offer my children an education and that was really the gift that I had wanted to give them.

Early on, I started to get very concerned with David's constant talk about wrestling. Actually, he began wrestling in grade school and continued into junior high. At that point, Carol and I thought that maybe if David went to a private school, perhaps he could be steered more toward academics. We had to face facts. Because of his passion for wrestling, his grades were not very high.

As he reached high school age, we took David to a school near Pittsburgh called Kiski High. This was a place that we believed would provide him with a solid foundation in scholastics. My old friend, Bill Cardille, the television announcer for the old Channel 11 studio wrestling shows, had told me that his son was attending Kiski

David and I in the backyard of our home

High. Both Bill and his son spoke very highly of the school.

After our visit to Kiski and taking some time to think about it, David consented, saying that he would like to go to the school. We were thrilled with his decision.

Since he hadn't done all that well with his grades in junior high, he had to attend summer classes prior to his acceptance and bring his grades up to Kiski standards. This in itself was a good test for our son.

And David did well that summer. He really is the kind of guy who succeeds if he puts his mind to it. His grades ended up earning him a place at Kiski High.

Once he was enrolled, David immediately joined the wrestling team at Kiski and bingo—the grades started sliding down again. After two years at Kiski, just as David should have been promoted to a junior, we were advised that he would not be asked back for his last two years of high school. For the remainder of his schooling, David went back to public education at North Hills High School.

The Sammartino version of "My Three Sons"

There he continued to train hard, working out with the weights and learning as much about wrestling as he could. He grew to be a very powerful young man. And no matter what I did to try to discourage him from wrestling, it was futile. He told us after graduation that he did not want to go on to college.

That's when I refused to continue helping him train. Both his mother and I were very disappointed in this decision. My refusal to coach him made no difference to David. He found other coaches to help him hone his skills.

Then when David reached the age of 19, he announced to us the following, "Mom, Dad … I've been working out for a long time and now I think I'm ready to take my shot. I'm going to work for a local promoter down in Texas that I've gotten hooked up with. He's willing to let me wrestle for him down there."

What could we do? Nothing. David was a very determined young man. He left home and went to the Lone Star State to wrestle professionally.

When we'd talk to him on the phone, it always seemed like the wrestling wasn't going very well. I would shrug my shoulders and say to my wife, "Maybe that's okay. He's still young. If things continue the way they're going, maybe he'll say the heck with this and come back and go to college."

Then the promoters sent me down to Texas for a couple of matches, which gave me an opportunity to see him work. He said his promoters had suggested it to him, so I agreed, not for the promoters' sake but just to see David.

The scenario was all too familiar to me. The wrestlers traveled by car 300 or 400 miles each way, going from places like Amarillo to places like Lubbock. They'd put on their show then jump in the car and travel another 400 miles.

And what do you know, the money that they were paying David wasn't enough for him to stay in any place other than a cheap little room. Since he couldn't afford restaurants, he would go to the local grocery in whatever town they stayed for the night, buy bread and ham, a gallon of milk and go to his room to eat.

That kind of life was quite different than the one David knew growing up in our home, but it certainly was very familiar to me—too familiar. In fact, it crushed me to see him going through it.

A long time ago I had made a promise to myself. After what I had experienced during the war and then coming to America, after the rough tough days of my early wrestling career, I said I never want to see any member of my family go through hardships like that—never.

Yet here was my own son, right in front of my eyes, enduring the same stuff. I wasn't comparing what he was going through to what I had lived, at least not blow-by-blow, but here it was. The life I had tried to give him at home had turned into a cheap little hotel room where you ate ham sandwiches on the bed.

David strikes a pose

I tried to talk to him. I said, "David, now that you're getting a taste of what pro wrestling is like, how do you feel? Do you really want to put up with this nonsense? Why not come home and go back to school? Later, if you still want to become a professional wrestler, then try again. I just think it's very important that you get that degree."

He fired right back at me, "Dad, of course I don't like what's happening. I don't like these long trips and I hate having to eat in my room, but I love wrestling. It's going to be my life and that's it! Okay?"

That trip to Texas showed me that no matter how difficult his situation might be, he was not going to be discouraged. Wrestling was in his blood, the way it has been in mine and nothing was going to make him quit.

Eventually, he moved from Texas to Puerto Rico where he wrestled for about six months, and then he came back to the States.

When my twin boys, Danny and Darryl, were born in January of 1968, I had promised myself that I was going to spend more time at home with them than I had with David. It wasn't until I lost the title in 1971 that I truly started slowing down. By taking only matches here and there, I was able to be at home much more, changing diapers, feeding the babies, helping my wife, and just being around the house as much as possible. That's what I really liked.

My wife was very happy when I was at home. You know, I had been on the road for so many years that it was almost like starting all over again. I started to feel like I was a part of my own family again.

As the twins grew, they both became little leaguers. I used to get the biggest kick out of watching them play baseball. Both Danny and Darryl were pitchers. Both were very good and both developed elbow problems. Darryl's was especially bad. His coaches had seen that he had a strong arm for such a young kid and they started to teach him how to throw curveballs. He was fine for a couple of years then all of a sudden, Darryl started to have pain in his pitching arm.

I took him to the hospital to see Doc Steele, the Pirates physician. Doc Steele examined him and said within a couple of minutes, "Did they teach you how to throw curveballs?"

Darryl nodded and the doc frowned, "That's what I was afraid of."

He explained to us how extensive the damage can be to a

Carol and I enjoy time together at home

youngster who's encouraged to perform at levels that are way beyond the child's physical limitations. What happens is that calcium deposits form as the result of the pitching action and these deposits interfere with the normal growth of bone and tissue. The doc ordered Darryl to quit pitching for a full year in the hopes that the problem would correct itself. After the year layoff, Darryl picked up the horsehide and tried to regain his pitching form, but it was no use. The damage had been done. The pain came back and he had to give up baseball. This was a big blow for the young guy, because even at an early age, Darryl had aspirations to become a professional baseball player.

Danny, on the other hand, had little or no interest in baseball. He had abandoned that gentlemen's game in high school for track events like throwing the shot and hurling the javelin.

Then a funny thing happened. Darryl, now out of baseball, showed up one day at Danny's track practice. He picked up his brother's javelin and tossed it a couple of times. Darryl quickly learned that the motion required for throwing the javelin was completely different than what was needed to throw a baseball. Throwing the javelin didn't hurt his elbow at all. He also discovered that he was pretty darn good at it.

Darryl joined the track team at North Hills High School, threw the javelin, and very quickly broke the school record for that event,

The twins turn four    *What a tag team!*

a mark that had stood for quite a few years. Also, in his first year on the team, Darryl went to the state finals. Later during his first year at Slippery Rock College, he made it to the national finals in javelin, then had a return showing at the nationals the next year. Not bad for an ex-pitcher.

As it so happened, Danny had to quit throwing the javelin because … you guessed it … it bothered his arm. However, Danny went into weightlifting and at the age of 20, was bench-pressing more than 400 pounds. He continues to train to this day and is now 215 pounds of big, husky, young man.

Both Danny and Darryl loved sports.

I am also extremely proud to report that David, Danny, and Darryl are clean from steroids. I've always been straight with them about drugs and the terrible dangers that are involved with their use. All of my sons have trained the honest way—with sweat and hard work.

Yes, it is so very true that I'm proud of my boys. I've really had a great time watching the twins grow up, something that I missed with David. I know that being with the twins helped me learn a lot about myself and I think it was good for them to have Dad around.

Unfortunately with David, because I was on the road so much and because he was an only child until he was nearly eight, my oldest

Danny and Darryl pose with their grandmothers

son experienced a lot of tough times in school. When he was very small, he told me kids would pick on him, saying, "Oh, so your dad's a wrestler, is he? Well, just how tough are you, shrimp?"

David would push right back, but as is the way with bullies, there would be more than one kid on him at a time and they would be bigger, older kids than he was. With regularity, David dragged himself home, sporting a bloody nose.

On the other hand, the twins were always together, protecting each other. As a result, neither one went through the bullies' rituals that David did.

In 1981, when I flew back from Japan, now officially retired, one fortunate thing was that I still had both of my parents around. Throughout my career, particularly in the later years, as I traveled around the world, I began to worry more and more about my parents. I always had this nagging fear that something might happen while

Danny and Darryl in the '90s

I was in Korea or Japan, Australia or Singapore, and no one in the family would be able to reach me.

The years were piling up for them. My dad was born on February 7, 1891 and my mom was born on August 3, 1898. By the time October 1981 rolled around, Dad was approaching his 91st year and my mom had just celebrated her 83rd birthday. After I retired, I was so grateful that I could spend time with both of them then.

Unhappily, my dad's health had begun to fail him as he moved into his 10th decade. Since Mom was in her 80s, it was becoming increasingly difficult for her to do all the things she had been accustomed to do and to help Dad.

Well if there's one thing you can say about the Sammartino family, it is that we are close-knit. Because we are so close, none of us wanted to hear one minute about the possibility of putting Dad into a nursing home. I'm not saying that there's anything wrong with doing something like that, but for us that wasn't a solution. My mom sure didn't want any part of it, and I know it would have been the end of Dad had he been put out to pasture in one of those places.

My sister Mary, without question one of the greatest people I've known in my life, was ready to volunteer to quit her job at the bank in order to help out at our parents' home. I told Mary not to worry. I said, "Look, you should keep your job. I've got plenty of time now

Dad's age was beginning to catch up with him

that I can spend with Mom and Dad. Let me help out."

And that's what we did. Every day, I'd get up early and do my road work. Even though retired, I was still dedicated to physical fitness. After finishing my training for the morning, I'd drive over to Mom and Dad's and be there around 9:30 a.m., about the time Dad usually got up. Mom would have the coffee already brewing and would follow along behind Dad as he made his way to the breakfast table.

Even at his advanced age, there were certain things that Dad refused to let me help him with. For instance, although it might sound funny, he would only let Mom dress and undress him. At her age that was difficult for her, but she was willing to do it for Dad.

Throughout his life, Dad had been a strong, proud man. He spent some nine years fighting for Italy in the cavalry and had been decorated twice for his service during World War I. After the war, he worked as a blacksmith in the Old Country. Later, he traveled to America, working hard in the mines, in construction, and even used his blacksmith skills repairing tools for a time. Then, for the latter part of his working career, he labored in the steel mills, quitting only when he was forced to retire in his early 70s.

He always was a robust and rugged person. His tremendous pride in his own abilities made it tough for him to face the final years of his life when he needed so much help.

I would always be there every single morning, urging him to use his walker. The doctor had said that if he didn't exercise every day, he might reach the point where he couldn't move at all. So I'd say, "Come on, Pop, we have to walk now."

And we'd walk all around their house. Sometimes we'd make it to the front porch where we'd sit for a while. Then I'd stay with him and my Mom until they ate their main meal, which would be around 2 o'clock in the afternoon. We Italians always like to eat this meal early in the day.

After dinner, my parents would take their naps. I would help Dad down into his favorite sofa chair. By the time their nap was over, Mary would be home from work and she would look in on them.

Although saddened as I was to witness my dad's deteriorating condition, I was thankful that I could be there for him now in my own retirement. I hoped that it made up a little for all those years that I was on the road and couldn't be with him and my mom.

During this time, I enjoyed many private moments with my dad. I could still talk with him, sitting and reminiscing about the Old Country. As the months wore on, he started slipping and I noticed that he wasn't able to remember certain people or events. Despite that, Dad always knew who was with him in his own house. He never lost complete control by any means, although eventually he did begin to have flights of fancy.

For almost four years, I was there with Dad every day, and although we went through the same routine daily, I was so very, very happy to have had that time with him.

Sadly, my dad passed away in 1985, at the age of 94. I remember some people said to me, "Well, he lived a long life and 94 years is a long, long time for someone to be around."

That sort of comfort always bothered me, although I understand that those people meant well. When you love your parents or when you love anybody and they die, it doesn't ease the pain you feel at their passing to be told that they lived such a long, long life. Whether they were 50 or 70 or 90, does your love for this person diminish because of their age? Not for me.

We buried our beloved father and my mother's husband. Now my brother, sister and I spent as much time as we could with Mom.

We have always been a very close family. That's my brother Paul on my right and my sister Mary holding my hand. Mom and Pop are in front

BRUNO SAMMARTINO

*My family was always the most
important thing in my life*

THE AUTOBIOGRAPHY OF WRESTLING'S LIVING LEGEND

Primo Carnera poses in our home with my dad and me in June of 1961

*Bruno proudly poses with his son Danny
during his final private signing.
Unfortunately, on November 6th, 2018 Danny
passed away. He was 50 years old.
Rest in Peace Daniel Sammartino*

Bruno never stayed away from a workout

*In my dressing room with
Vince McMahon, Sr.*

The Winds of Change

Back in 1981, I had just returned home from a Far East tour to hear the news that Vince McMahon, Sr. had gone into a Florida hospital. Right away, I called his home down there and talked to his wife Juanita, who didn't volunteer much information about Vince's condition. Instead, she gave me the hospital number and suggested I call her husband myself.

I phoned Vince immediately and asked him what was going on. He joked a little bit and said that it wasn't pretty. Vince told me that he was passing blood in his urine. He said one of the doctors had told him that he had a bladder tumor and that they had to operate as soon as possible. That's what they did. The surgeon removed what they could of the tumor and then after he sewed Vince back up, warned him that a second operation would probably be necessary sometime down the road. Well, his wife didn't like that diagnosis and wanted Vince to get another opinion.

When McMahon got his second opinion, this doctor drew him a completely different picture. The second doctor said that the first doctor was all wet and that Vince didn't need follow up surgery. As a matter of fact, Doctor No. 2 merely prescribed medication and told Vince that if he simply took this medication, then he'd be fine in no time.

When Vince heard this news, he got very angry with Doctor No. 1 and religiously followed Doctor No. 2's advice up until the time he died in 1984. It's true that Vince took the medication and was okay for quite some time ... nearly two-and-a-half-years. But in early 1984, Vince started to pass blood again. He ignored it for a while, then when he reported it to Doctor No. 2, he was put on yet another kind of medication. By the time everybody figured out that the medications weren't doing the job, it was too late.

When they finally got Vince back in the hospital, they found out that Doctor No. 1 had been right all along. The bladder tumor had come back and had spread throughout his entire body. And that's what killed him. He died in May of 1984.

After Vince passed on, his son Vince McMahon, Jr. came charging to the forefront and took over his late father's wrestling business. Actually, Vince Jr. had been running the show for quite some time while his father had been getting progressively worse.

I returned to the broadcast booth to work with the new owner, Vince McMahon, Jr.

Toward the middle of that summer, Vince Jr. called me and posed a question to me. How would I like to come back to wrestling as a television color commentator? That's exactly what I'd done for his father back in 1978 and I had really enjoyed it at the time. His offer caught my interest.

Then Vince Jr. added the kicker. He said that he would be willing to give my son David a break and bring him into the WWF. That would mark a real beginning for David because even though he'd been at it for several years, he still wasn't wrestling for any big organization.

I considered the arrangement and said yes to it. First, it would be an important step forward for David to hook up with Vince Jr. and second, I could sit back and comment on the action instead of being right in the middle of it. The other added benefit was that the shows were taped only every three weeks so I wouldn't have to hit the road that often. It sounded great.

After David started with the WWF and I had begun my commentator's role, McMahon approached David with an idea. He said, "Your dad is still in better shape than most of the guys out there today. He's still lifting. He's running seven and eight miles every day. Even though his weight's down, he could put back 10 pounds and not be flabby. What I'm saying is why don't you and he team up for tag team matches? It'd be one of a kind. You know, father and son."

Well, even though I wasn't thrilled with the idea I didn't want to be the reason for David not getting ahead in professional wrestling, so I accepted his idea. In March 1985, David and I joined up as a tag team for the first time. We wrestled together in Philadelphia and the place sold out. I remember getting goose bumps from the crowd's cheers. Though I hadn't been there in four years, the fans gave me a standing ovation when we entered. It was something that touched me, and energized me.

When I went into the ring, I wanted to be the Bruno Sammartino that everyone remembered. Of course, I'm not going to claim that suddenly I was transformed into the old Bruno, but I went in there with my old spirit and did the best I could under the circumstances. It turned out to be a good match and David did very well for himself.

David and I played Philadelphia a couple more times and we worked Pittsburgh, New York, and Boston that year. After that short swing through those cities, I decided again that I had had enough and took off the tights once more.

Well, when I did this, David had a peculiar reaction. He started to act out, saying that now he felt he had been used. He said to me, "Dad, you know it's true. The only time I'm a headliner is when I wrestle with you. With the tag team dissolved, I'm just back to being a preliminary boy. It's making me mad."

David got depressed about all this and began to behave quite unreasonably. He got to be very confused about it all. One day he would quit wrestling and the next day he would want to come back. He told me once, "I know what my role is here. The promoters just want me around so that anytime they want you to put the tights back on, they call me. But really they just use me to get you back into the ring. Then when the match is over, I stop being Bruno's son. I'm back to being David Nobody when we aren't wrestling together."

I tried to tell him that because the game had changed since my day, we had to face facts. "Look, David, the WWF is now the only act in town. In my day, the country was divided up into territories and different promoters had the Northeast, the Midwest, the South and the North. Now Vince Jr. holds the keys to success. You have to play ball with him or you're out."

Ever since the death of his father, McMahon, Jr. had become a very aggressive promoter. He had expanded to the point where he was gobbling up everybody's territory all across the country. If you wanted to wrestle in the big leagues, you had to deal with Vince Jr.

David's other option was the National Wrestling Alliance, still active but certainly not as big as the WWF. Frankly, I don't think the NWA really considered putting David on its roster simply because I was still with the WWF.

When McMahon, Jr. asked me to start accepting matches yet another time, I found myself in a strange position. Even though I despised the circumstances, I felt I had to go along with Vince Jr. for David's sake. If I cooperated with him and then if David wanted to come back professionally, I would be able to say to Vince Jr., "I realize that David's made a few mistakes in judgment. He'd like to make amends and give it another shot. How about another chance for him?"

I reasoned that McMahon, Jr. would take David back into the fold because certainly if he expected me to go along with his requests, then Vince Jr. would have to respect my wishes. We played this tune several times. And each time, David would climb back in the ring, wrestle for a while, get extremely frustrated for the same catalog of reasons and then would quit again. It wasn't a real comfortable situation for anyone.

Another reason that I hated getting back in the ring was what I perceived was happening with professional wrestling. I just did not like what I was seeing in the sport as the '80s wore on. Professional wrestling was changing in a drastic and, for me, unacceptable way. Wrestling no longer resembled anything I had known and the changes weren't for the good, believe me.

I despised what Vince McMahon, Jr. had done to professional wrestling. It had become a complete, total cartoon. Even though gimmicks existed in my day, and there were things that I fought promoters about back then, I never thought that the game would become as bizarre as it had gotten by the end of the 1980s.

Finally, I wanted nothing to do with it.

There was a whole list of incidents that turned my stomach.

For example, in 1985 I did a "Piper's Pit" interview in Madison Square Garden with Roddy Piper. The Piper's Pit segment was going to be used to set up a series of matches with Piper and myself. During the interview Piper called me a "Stupid W.O.P." It was right then that I attacked him. I had no idea that Piper was going to do that, but that was considered a great insult to me so I went after him. I asked Roddy later if someone told him to do that and he indicated yes, that they had. I left it at that.

I even wrestled for a while as a substitute. McMahon, Jr. would pull me in at the last minute to sub for guys who were either hurt or couldn't pass their drug test.

Of course, I felt abused. Here I was, Bruno Sammartino, the man known for 20 years as the "Living Legend," the man who sold out arena after arena, and now I was reduced to filling in for kids who suffered injuries because they weren't in shape, or replacing youngsters who couldn't stay off drugs long enough to earn a living.

This was a sport filled with tremendous opportunities an all this really affected me deep in my guts.

Finally, I leveled with David. I told him, "Son, it doesn't make any sense for me to wrestle anymore. You're going to have to make or break it on your own without me there to twist Vince Jr.'s arm on your behalf. Either accept things the way they are, or quit and find some other way to make a living."

After that one last talk, David tried one more come back. But when he found out that the WWF intended to keep booking him into the smallest arenas that was enough for him … again. Once more he left the WWF totally disillusioned.

Where that left me was clear—now I wanted no part of climbing through the ropes and into the ring again. I decided to tell Vince Jr. that I was out for good.

I tried to contact McMahon, Jr. three or four times but he never returned any of my calls. I wanted to let him know that I had an offer outside his organization and that I wanted to take it. Finally, in an effort to contact him indirectly, I spoke with a fellow who worked under Vince Jr. and explained to this person what was on my mind and why I wanted to speak with McMahon, Jr. Although I still heard nothing directly from the young promoter, I found out that he apparently had gotten the word.

It was McMahon, Jr.'s wife Linda who called and asked me why I had been calling.

I told her I had a job offer from elsewhere which was much more attractive than staying with the WWF.

THE MAGAZINE FOR MAT FANS

A CHAMPION SPORTS PUBLICATION

WAS ZYBYSKO THE GREATEST?

Wrestling Revue

AUGUST/67 — 50¢

IS BOXING READY FOR BRUNO?

MEET THE COUSIN COUSINS

SPECIAL FEATURE
BLASSIE—
THE VILLAINS' VILLAIN

Also:
VERN BOTTOMS—LES WELCH
LUIS MARTINEZ—THE FUNKS

1983: Hall of Famers Hockey's Phil Esposito, Wrestling's Bruno Sammartino, Baseball's Willie Mays, and Basketball's Walt "Clyde" Frazier

Looking Back

I guess when you've been in one business for a long time you're bound to get philosophical when you finally leave that enterprise. I'm no exception. I'll always think back on professional wrestling with memories of both the good and the bad. That's just the way life is. Nothing's perfect … it's one way or the other. Sometimes you get the bear and sometimes the bear gets you. Then sometimes the bear turns out to be a skunk in a bearskin rug. One issue that really bothered me throughout my career was what newspaper writers would say about wrestling. The ink never varied, be it in Pittsburgh, New York, Boston, or San Francisco. The sports scribes would tell their readers that all wrestling matches are rehearsed. They'd write that wrestlers spend the time before their bouts in the dressing rooms, practicing what moves they're going to use on each other.

If those wordsmiths had ever been backstage and had seen this preparation going on for themselves, that would be a different thing. I'd shrug and say, "Well, guys looks like I've been wrong all these years. Even though I've never rehearsed a match in my life, I guess everybody else was doing it and I never noticed. You saw it with your own eyes so I suppose so you have every right to report the story."

Nowadays the practice of rehearsing a match happens often, especially as wrestling became more of a TV show than an arena event, but back then of course, the reports were ridiculous. Let me give you some details of the backstage mechanics that were involved in a wrestling exhibition. Let's take the Civic Arena in Pittsburgh, for example. In this facility, you have one dugout where all of the wrestlers emerge from their dressing rooms. That doesn't mean that the wrestlers are all waiting in one large room. The dugout contains a dozen of these dressing rooms and opponents are never assigned to the same room. That means you don't come face to face with the man you're wrestling until the moment you get into the ring. Another example would be Madison Square Garden. There the dressing rooms are removed from one another.

There is a wrestling term insiders use: Kayfabe. This word described the cloak of secrecy surrounding the world of professional wrestling. If you were a wrestler earning a living in the business you protected the business, even from State Athletic Commissions, hence the reason for suspensions. These commissioners treated the wrestling business like a real competition. Even if we were in proximity to each other, due to the practice of Kayfabe, there was only a limited amount of contact with your opponent. Many times a finish was either called in the ring, or a referee or office personnel could pass a message along, but the idea of rehearsing matches never happened. Matches were called in the ring as you went along. It was a different time and the business was presented in a different way. On top of that, the constant acrobatics that are injected in today's matches call for a certain amount of precision, and rehearsals are needed.

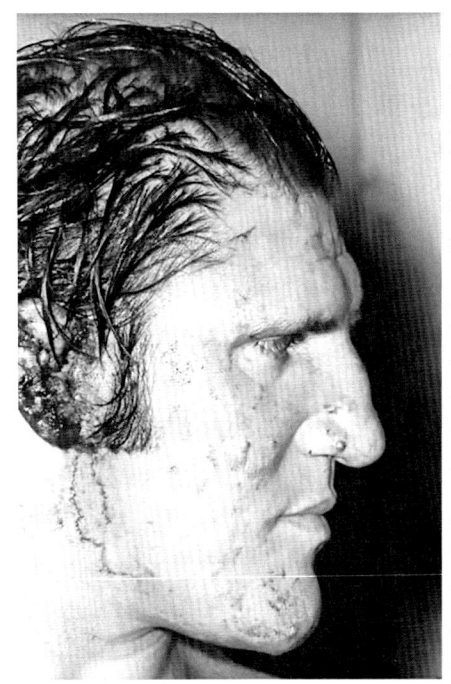

Another issue that the media people brought up and, one that really bugged me too, is whether or not wrestlers use blood capsules. We've talked about that earlier, but let me just say a few more words about it.

I remember one time when I was wrestling Ivan Koloff, the man who would eventually take over from me as champion first time around in 1971. It was a typical Koloff match … tough, gutsy, full of action. Just after he came off the ropes one time, I dealt him a powerful blow and split him open right above the eye. Blood poured out of that wound.

Later when Doc Civitarese was sewing up Koloff's injury, one of the officials from the state athletic commission went up to a sports reporter from a Pittsburgh newspaper. The official asked the reporter if he would like to come back to the dressing room and see for himself how badly Koloff had been cut.

The reporter refused, yet the next day he wrote an article suggesting that Koloff had used chicken blood in a capsule to fake his injury. The reporter wrote this garbage after having refused to go and see for himself how severely Koloff had been hurt. He was one writer who always tended to spew out derogatory stories about wrestling. Naturally, he would refuse to go back to the dressing room. He would have seen the reality of the situation and that would have killed his nice, neat story.

Reporters never let the truth get in the way of their stories

All too often when media people were feeling feisty, when they wanted to puff themselves up by tearing others down, when they had nothing better to do than make up false stories, they would hike over to the wrestling arenas and proceed to rip apart the wrestlers by writing half-truths and innuendos. Very seldom would they feature wrestlers who had gone to the Olympics as representatives of the United States. Hardly ever would they churn out a positive story about the National AAU champion wrestlers who were in our business. Nor would they say kind things about pros who had achieved greatness in other sports like weightlifting or football.

These dirty-collared columnists only wanted to write the bad rap, the mean-spirited angle, the sly lie. Many fans were insulted by this bilge simply because they were there and saw the matches. Then after reading about it in the newspaper the next day, came away wondering, what in the world had the reporter seen? I do admit, however, that there were fans who did believe the trash they read, because unfortunately some people believe anything.

I remember when I broke my neck in that match with Stan Hansen. A reporter made the suggestion that it was all hype, done to maximize the gate for a return bout. Okay, Mister Reporter … did you go to Doctor Civitarese or any of the other doctors who attended to me in the hospital? Did you hear what they had to say? Did you examine the X-rays that were taken and determine that they were falsified?

Ridiculous! A hospital isn't going to involve itself in a conspiracy to increase box office revenues for the wrestling profession. But then again, why should reporters actually investigate their allegations? Why shouldn't they just write what they want to? After all, investigation might turn up the facts and that would ruin a good lie. Like they say, nothing spoils an exciting news story more than a good eyewitness.

I believe that the promoters should bear a lot of the burden for the media's lack of respect for the wrestling profession. Ever since the gimmicks and the show business razzle-dazzle took over, our sport has suffered in the eyes of its critics.

The wrestlers are the ones who've paid for it all. On the one hand, we go into the ring and absorb the blows, suffer the injuries, and at times, face their crippling consequences. Then after we endure the pains for the sport we love best, the media people tell the public that it's all make-believe.

To me, this has been the most frustrating aspect of my sports career. You train all your life to prepare for professional wrestling, then you go into the ring and give it everything you've got, only to have some writer or sports analyst question your very integrity. It's heart-breaking.

Once I remember confronting one of my media critics and saying to him, "Look, my friend, since you suggest that I'm a no-talent fake, just an actor in trunks, then get me somebody you regard as a real athlete. Bring me a tough guy from any sport. I don't care who. Just bring this man around and then put him in the ring with me. Let's see what will happen." Of course, my challenge was never met. Most athletes wouldn't dare to fool with a wrestler. The truth is most athletes fear and respect professional wrestlers. Maybe my challenge was foolish in and of itself, but sometimes out of pure frustration, you want to show these media assassins just where they're wrong.

Another aspect of professional wrestling that took its toll on all of us was, and still is, the loneliness of it all. Because wrestling is not a team sport like professional baseball or football, a wrestler often turns into a loner. That's just the facts of life. Wrestlers are always traveling to different arenas every day of the week. In fact in my era, you constantly wrestled for different promoters around the country ... around the world.

One night, you might run into 16 different guys at the Civic Arena. Then the next night, you're off in one direction and the 16 other guys are off to Detroit or New York or Baltimore. That tends to turn you into a loner real fast. You had your schedule and everybody else had theirs.

I really had very few close friends who came out of professional wrestling. One exception was Dominic DeNucci. He was born and raised not too far from my hometown in Italy. Believe it or not, we never met until we both were touring Australia in 1966. He's just a super guy, a great wrestler and we've remained good friends to this day. But aside from Dominic, there have been few others from the world of wrestling whom I would call a close friend. I've talked a bit now about some of the more negative aspects of my career. Of course, there were many other experiences that I've had that pulled the balance way back into the positive. Actually, all through my stint as a professional wrestler, I've been like a small kid in many ways. No matter what fame I may have achieved, whenever I met top professional sports or show business figures I was always in awe.

One fellow whom I call truly a friend is Jilly Rizzo, who was Frank Sinatra's right hand man for many years. Jilly also owned one of the best nightclub/restaurants in New York City. We got to be great friends and he was always very nice to me. In fact, Jilly introduced me to New York you might say, showing me where all the great restaurants were and who had the best entertainment, places like the Latin Quarter and the Copacabana.

Hobnobbing with the late Liberace

Basically, I was the kind of guy who wrestled, grabbed a bite to eat, and went straight to bed. I wanted to get up early the next morning and go to the gym for my workout. But Jilly made me stray from that routine a few times. He would always come to the Garden to see me, and then he'd invite me over to his establishment. That was where I got a chance to meet a lot of celebrities who also enjoyed Jilly's company, his menu, and his shows. I met people like Frank Sinatra, Sammy Davis Jr. Peter Lawford, Richard Conte, and even Liberace.

The "Schnoz" Jimmy Durante was really down to earth

But of all the entertainers I ever met, I think the nicest, most down-to-earth guy was Jimmy Durante. I met him in Philadelphia at a dinner to honor me for winning the championship. When Durante performed, we all fell in love with him. He was a true star.

Other names I could mention include Jimmy Rosselli, a man with a fantastic singing voice. Then there was Enzo Stuarti and Sergio Franchi. I don't want to forget comic Pat Cooper, otherwise known as Pasquale Caputo, who I knew years before he became a headliner. But that's the way it was in my business. It gave me a chance to meet lots of people who I would never have had the chance to meet otherwise.

Now I'm going to let you in on a little secret. With most of these stars that I met, I was terribly disappointed. I didn't find them to

Jilly Rizzo and me on a magazine cover

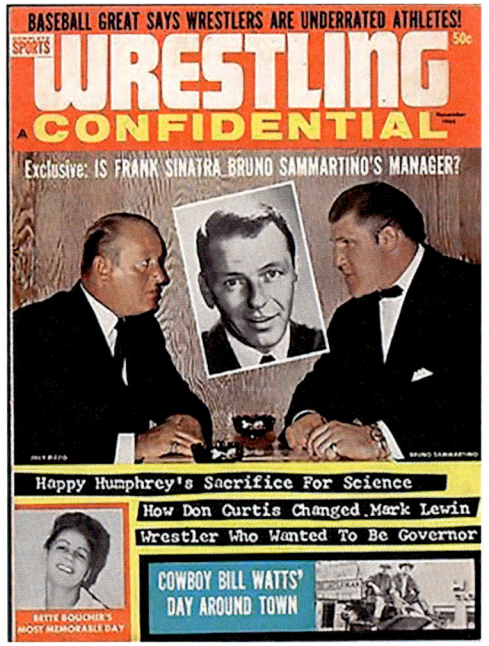

be the genuine people that I had imagined them to be. Although they were usually nice to me, I watched each one and saw what he or she did when a fan came around. I saw a lot of them quickly turn around and become very unfriendly to that fan, getting temperamental and putting on this great show of arrogance. After a while, I reached a point where I just didn't want to meet any more of these show business celebrities. Who needed their bad attitudes?

I've always admired people who have achieved greatness in whatever they've set out to do, and then have remained "of the people." Those celebrities who put themselves above everyone else, like they're something special are the ones that I lose complete respect for.

As great a talent as Frank Sinatra might have been for so many, many years, I found him to be extremely temperamental. In fact, one time in Pittsburgh, Sinatra embarrassed me terribly.

It was in the late 1960s and Sinatra was scheduled to perform at the Civic Arena. Channel 11 was the local television station that carried wrestling programs and the one that I had been closely involved with. One of 11's people who knew that I was an acquaintance of Sinatra's, asked me if I could arrange for an interview with him. And they asked me to do the interview.

Now I had been told that Sinatra wasn't very cooperative when it came to doing such things, but I went ahead and called Jilly Rizzo and asked Jilly if he could check it out for me. In a short while, Jilly called back, said Sinatra had been in a good mood and had agreed to the interview. Great so far.

When the day came we got a whole group together ... the general manager of Channel 11 and his wife; the program director and his wife; my good friend Bill Cardille and his wife; my family; some of my wife's family; and a priest who was a friend of mine, Father Gino Rivey. We gathered all these people together, adding the film crew and their truck.

We all went to the location where the interview had been slated and we were setting up for it when I saw Jilly walking toward me. He definitely had an upset face on. I said, "Jilly, what's the matter? What's going on?" Jilly shook his head. "Frank's in a bad mood."

I said, "Boy, I hope that doesn't mean he won't do this interview. I got everybody here for it—all the big shots from Channel 11, my family, Father Gino ..."

When Jilly didn't say anything, I knew we were in trouble. Not only had Sinatra refused to do the interview, he wouldn't even come out of his room and speak with us.

I was incredibly embarrassed. I thought that if I tell all the people who are waiting to see Sinatra that he's in a bad mood now and won't budge from his suite, that they'd consider me crazy for dragging them over there. Maybe they'd think I had just been trying to be a big shot.

Finally, I faced everybody, apologized and said that the whole thing was off. Sinatra was in a bad mood and wouldn't see anyone right now. When my guests heard that, I was surprised at their reaction. Nobody got particularly upset although they were all disappointed. Most everyone said that big stars like that always have a bad temperament. Everybody understood and believed what I'd said.

As a matter of fact, before this incident happened, I had often been invited to join Sinatra at his special table at Jilly's. This table was Sinatra's and nobody but nobody would sit there unless Frank was in town and he invited you to sit down. When I had joined him and his other guests on those occasions, I had often witnessed his outbursts of temper. That should have been my warning I suppose.

After that, I guess I don't have to tell you what my feelings were toward "Ol' Blue Eyes." Although I met him several more times, I chose not to be in his company for long. I decided I didn't want to be associated with people like that.

In contrast to all these celebrities, big shots, little shots and other self-important people that I've known, let me tell you about one little boy from Pittsburgh, whose name was Frankie too.

In 1968, I got a telephone call from Channel 11 sportscaster Red Donley. Red told me, "Bruno, I have a big favor to ask of you. There's a little boy, maybe 10 or 11 at the most, and he's very sick in the hospital, Allegheny General. He's a big fan of yours and if you could pay him a visit I'm sure it would really give him a lift."

I said sure. When I went to see little Frankie, that was his name as I found out, it really tore at me. He was so sick that I wasn't certain that he even knew I was there. I just sat at his bedside with his mother beside me, and his father standing on the opposite side of the bed, near the window.

With tears in her eyes, his mother told me, "Just talk to him, Bruno. He adores you and he can hear everything we say."

So I said to him, "Frankie, I hear you're a big wrestling fan. I'm so very happy to meet someone like you and I'd like to see you get better real soon. I want you to come to the Civic Arena as my guest and watch me wrestle, okay?"

When I saw tears in the eyes of little Frankie's mom and dad, I got choked up myself. What was really heartbreaking was what his dad told me out in the hall as I was about to leave. He said that Frankie had leukemia.

After my visit, when I got home I called up Red Donley and asked him to follow what happens with Frankie while I was out of town. I wanted to make good on my promise about taking him to the Civic Arena to watch me wrestle. I wanted to know if Frankie was going to bounce back.

In a few weeks, lo and behold, I got the wonderful news from Red that little Frankie had indeed made a comeback. He'd been given numerous blood transfusions along with other medical wonders. He had seemingly taken a few faltering steps back to health.

And you know he had heard everything that I had told him during my visit. Now he excitedly told his mom that he wanted to come to the arena for the wrestling matches and especially to see Bruno.

I was so delighted to hear that Frankie had bounced back. I asked Red to find out just who Frankie wanted to bring with him. Once I knew that, I would make all the arrangements.

I remember that we had decided to meet backstage at the arena before the matches began. When I came out of the dressing room area and saw Frankie with his two friends, his eyes just gleamed. I handed him his ticket and brought him in to meet some of the other wrestlers.

We spent a little time together just talking. I told Frankie to stay well and do everything the doctors wanted him to do, and to listen to his mom and dad. Then the kids went inside to their front row seats and had a great time.

Later I discovered that Frankie's family was very, very poor. His parents were decent people who had a lot of bad luck and had ended up with nothing. How sad it was to know that the boy had so many needs, so many problems, and everything couldn't be done that needed to be done for him.

Some months later, my wife Carol had to go into Allegheny General Hospital for disc surgery. Having been out of town on tour, I went straight to the hospital to visit my wife. All of a sudden, we heard a little commotion going on in the hallway outside our room. It sounded like somebody was having an argument with a child. I stepped out into the hallway to find little Frankie pleading his case to a nurse. A policeman stood by, ready to escort Frankie out of the building. His back was to me so he didn't see me right away. He said, "I have to get in and see Mrs. Sammartino. Bruno's my friend. They're both my friends." I spoke up. "Frankie, what are you doing here?"

He spun around and was shocked to see me. "Bruno, I thought you'd be wrestling someplace. It's great to see you!"

"Frankie, why don't you wait right here and I'll straighten this whole thing out in a minute." Then I pulled the nurse and the police officer aside, out of Frankie's earshot and told them all about Frankie, his illness, his love for wrestling, and what a big fan he was of me and my family. The two understood and said, "Okay."

I brought Frankie into my wife's room and announced, "Dear, here's a good friend of mine I want you to meet. His name is Frankie." Frankie was so happy that he could visit with Carol. We sat and talked for 10 minutes or so, then Frankie sneaked a look at my wrist watch. He stood up and said, "I guess I better get going. It's a long walk home." Just for conversation I asked him how far away he lived from the hospital. He replied, "It's about an hour and a half walk."

I said, "My gosh, Frankie! You mean you walked an hour and a half to visit my wife?"

He nodded and probably wondered what the big deal was.

"Frankie, there's no way you're going to walk back." I pulled out my wallet and gave him $15. "Here's what I want you to do, Frankie. I can't leave my wife right now to give you a ride. I want to spend some more time with her and then after my visit is over, I have to go straight from here to the airport. So you take this money."

As I handed him the money, he looked like I was making a big mistake. He gulped and said, "Bruno, do you know how much money you're giving me?"

I said, "Frankie, it's alright. You take this money. I want you to buy a milkshake for yourself first. Then you jump on a bus for home and you can keep the change for whenever you have to visit someone else."

He couldn't believe his good fortune. Before he left, he paused in the doorway and gave us a big smile and wave. He was so happy at that moment. A short time after Frankie visited Carol in the hospital, Frankie's parents sent me a short letter telling me how grateful they were that I was Frankie's friend. They said that the friendship meant so much to him. Later that month, I went on an overseas tour. I would think about little Frankie every so often. I made a promise to give him a call when I got back. After I returned to Pittsburgh, I got Frankie's number from Red Donley and telephoned to check up on him. Frankie's mother answered and when I told her who I was, she started crying on the phone. Through her tears, she told me that little Frankie had been buried five days earlier. The whole thing touched me so very deeply that I began crying, too. Frankie's death made me very, very sad for a long, long time.

So we can talk about big shots and we can talk about people who really mean something. There was another young man who I met who I can never forget. His name was Johnny and he lived in New York, but he spent most of his time in Roosevelt Hospital because he had cancer.

I remember that Johnny's mother called me up at the station where I was doing a live interview. She caught me just after we went off the air. She had a simple request. Could I please come and visit her son in the hospital? She told me all about Johnny's problem.

Of course I agreed.

When I arrived at the hospital and went to Johnny's room to visit him, I found out that the entire floor where he was staying was filled with cancer patients, and they were all children. Some of them looked healthy, ordinary kids out in the hallways bouncing balls and playing.

Then I stepped into Johnny's room and he was in a plastic tent, laboring for every breath he took. When he caught sight of me, his spirits rose. Johnny was elated to have me as a visitor. I gave him some pictures and a magazine. He accepted them gratefully, not really believing I was there in the same room with him.

Before I left, I told him that on Saturday I was going to be on television wrestling and that when I was interviewed, I would look right at him and say "Hi." He said he'd be watching.

To be honest, the way that poor Johnny looked under that plastic tent, I never could have believed he would be around on Saturday. I was visiting him on Wednesday. Saturday was almost four whole days away.

In the hallway, his mother spoke to me very quietly. She said, "Johnny's doctors have told us that he has very little time left. Thank you for telling him that you'll say hi to him on television but Saturday is a very long way away off for him."

I'm awaiting my interview during a live TV telecast

Saturday rolled around and I told Ray Morgan, the host of the wrestling show, and the guy who was going to interview me that I had a special request. During his questions, I wanted to have just 10 seconds to say hello to a little boy in the hospital.

Ray said sure.

That Saturday evening, I went on the air and I interrupted Ray a few seconds into the interview and said to the camera, "I just want to say hello to a young man in Roosevelt Hospital who's a very dear friend of mine. Hello, Johnny. I want you to know that I'm thinking about you. I want you to take care of yourself and I'll see you real soon."

About a week later, I was appearing in New Jersey. While I was in my dressing room, waiting for the call, two policemen came to the door and knocked. They told me that there was a couple down the hall who wanted to see me because I knew their son.

When I came out, I walked over to find Johnny's mother and father waiting for me. We shook hands and then before I could ask how Johnny was, his mother spoke.

She said, "After you left the hospital that day, Johnny was so very happy. But then he got real sick all the rest of that week. The doctors couldn't understand how he hung on. Finally, Saturday was here and Johnny waited all day for the wrestling show. When you came on and greeted him, he had such a wonderful smile on his face." With this, she stopped short, unable to speak any further. Johnny's father finished the story for her. He said, "Well, Bruno, Johnny died about 30 minutes after he saw you on TV. He stuck around just to see you."

I think by now with what I have told you about myself that you know me to be a man who can endure pain. You can break my arm and I will keep on going. Break my leg and I will withstand it. I broke my neck and I refused to take pain killers. I don't need those kinds of drugs because I can take the pain.

But when terrible things happen to folks like Johnny and little Frankie, I become the weakest man in the world. I can't control my tears and I feel like a weakling. This is what goes to the heart and stays there. This is what's real.

Big shots? Who are they? I hope I am never mistaken for one.

I remember once I received a request to go to the veterans hospital in New Haven, Connecticut. The man who phoned me sounded like he was in a panic. He told me the date he had in mind and it was a day I couldn't do it. We talked a bit and agreed to shoot for the next day after that which was okay with him.

Then he asked me a strange question. "And what will your fee be, Bruno?" I was surprised. "Don't be silly. Why would there be a fee to visit sick people?"

He made a big fuss about that and hung up, saying "God bless you, Bruno. God bless you."

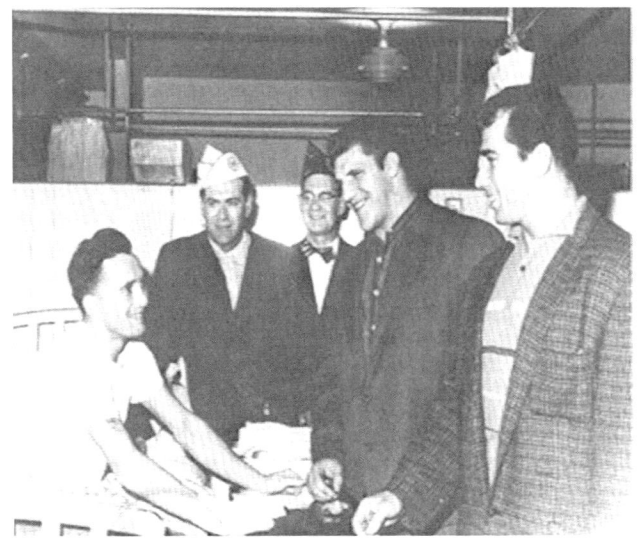

I was more than happy to be able to bring some joy into the lives of our Veterans

I went to the hospital and visited with the patients and it went well. Then I took the guy aside that I'd talked to on the phone and told him, "Hey, you know you kind of insulted me the other day, asking about a fee for coming up here."

He apologized and said, "Well, you wouldn't know this, but we originally had four baseball players scheduled and they held us up at the last minute. They each wanted quite a bit of money to show up or else they told us to forget it. We certainly didn't have the kind of money they wanted so that was that with the baseball players."

"We had already told the patients that we were going to be

getting some important guests and when the baseball players pulled this, we didn't want to let our people down. We knew that a lot of them watched wrestling and when we mentioned the name of Bruno Sammartino, they all seemed to be your fans. We thought that if we could contact you, it would save the day. And it certainly did."

When he told me about what had happened, I got very angry. I thought to myself whether it's me the wrestler or some other athlete in football, baseball, basketball, hockey … you name the sport … here we are, healthy, doing what we enjoy the most in life and getting paid very well for it. So how can anyone with a scrap of decency in them demand to be paid to visit patients at a veterans hospital? This I cannot understand. Never in a million years.

Even though I've been telling you about what mixed feelings that I might have for certain athletes and entertainers that I've met, let me also mention that there have been times when I've lost respect for the fans. Not all of them of course, but for the lunatics that hang out on the fringe of fandom.

Often, people have asked me which opponent I feared the most in the ring. In all seriousness, I have never come up against any opponent who has ever struck fear in my heart as much as what I've seen some fans try to pull. One time I was wrestling Big Bill Miller, who was, if you remember, 6'7" tall and weighed 320 pounds. Well, we were going at it one evening, and all of a sudden we both heard a fracas commence just three or four rows back from the ring. We saw police running in from every direction and fans were hollering and grabbing at one guy in particular. Turned out he had a gun inside a hollowed-out book and he had come to kill Bill Miller. His hate for Miller as a wrestler had tipped his mental balance into the crazy zone.

Just as he was pulling out his pistol to fire, a man next to him saw it and grabbed his wrist, then started screaming for help. He held on to the gunman for dear life until the police could come and haul this nut away.

Another time, I was wrestling Waldo Von Erich at the Boston Gardens, an arena that has a strange shape to it with sections of seats rising nearly straight up into the ceiling. As we were circling around the ring, I felt something whiz by my head. It crashed to the mat with

Entering the ring was a new experience each time. You just never knew if there might be a crazed fan in the crowd

a horrible sound.

We stopped and looked and saw the object was a huge padlock. Considering the distance it had traveled, the lock had generated enough momentum to have killed either me or Von Erich instantly. Luckily, the irate fan's aim was off that night.

I've also witnessed matches where a fan has stormed the ring, waving a knife in the air, overcome with anger to such an extent that the only thing on his mind is to maim and kill. In Oklahoma City, Angelo Savoldi was wrestling Danny Hodge, a former Olympian. Angelo was getting the best of Danny, when Danny's father got carried away and jumped into the ring to defend his son's honor. The frustrated father sliced Angelo's back with a knife, slitting the skin from Angelo's shoulders down below his waist. Savoldi survived somehow, ending up with more than 200 stitches and one of the nastiest scars you'll ever want to see.

Blackjack Mulligan faced a fan in Boston who charged into the ring with a hunting knife. As Mulligan tried to get away, the fan slashed him in the thigh, then continued to drag the knife along the complete length of his upper leg.

Sonny Myers had a fan open him up by sticking a knife into his stomach. Sonny had to hold onto his own guts as they were falling out and run to the dressing room to get away from this jerk. A doctor rushed in right away, and 270 stitches later saved Sonny's life.

A wrestler can also find himself endangered simply from the fans' enthusiasm for you. When I won the title from Buddy Rogers, the crowd's reaction had me literally fighting for my life. Although the fans meant well, they didn't realize that 20,000 people pushing, shoving, grabbing, and moving in the same direction can be deadly. I'll tell you, I've never felt so helpless during circumstances like that, and there's nothing you can do because the mob is so huge. In the heat of the moment, the fans don't realize that their behavior is not only dangerous to the person they are cheering, but also dangerous to themselves.

We have even had fans keel over from heart attacks, scared to death by being caught in the middle of this kind of demonstration. Granted, most of the fans are well behaved, but there are always some who get carried away in the excitement. As a wrestler, when you see incidents like these happen again and again, you really do get jumpy ... and more than a little leery. Whenever I stepped into the ring, I always tried to block those memories out in order to concentrate on the match. But there were always those nagging thoughts.

One wrestler who never failed to draw the ire of the fans was Fred Blassie. Whenever Blassie and I would hold a match, attendance always soared.

Blassie was the rule-breaker, tough as nails with a reputation for ferocious behavior. He was mean, rugged, and a winner.

When you wrestled Blassie, you could expect anything. If he could hurt you, he would. If the match was going badly for Blassie, he'd go for an eye or sneak in a low blow to stop you. And to him, everybody was a "pencil-necked geek." He didn't care who he was talking to, if you got in his way you were a "pencil-necked geek." Blassie even went so far as to record a song called "Pencil-Necked Geek" which you can still find on those compilation albums of "worst ever" music that D.J. Doctor Demento puts out.

I wrestled Blassie in arenas all over the country, and in fact, we sold out Madison Square Garden several times. The one match that I remember most vividly took place at an outdoor baseball park in New Jersey. That night we set an attendance record. That was because the fans were there in full force with nothing on their minds but letting Blassie know how much they hated him.

Toward the end of our match that night, I was handling Blassie well and Freddie knew he was coming up short. He reached back and walloped his fist into me, way below the belt. I fell to my knees from the pain and tried to clear my head. That's when pandemonium broke out.

The fans were outraged by Blassie's illegal shot. Within seconds, chairs started flying into the ring, all aimed at Blassie's head. Then the crowd pressed around the ring and started shaking the posts, whipping the ropes back and forth wildly. Blassie stood in the center, clenching his fists and shouting that he was ready to take on anybody.

The police charged in and attempted to break up the melee with no immediate success. They called for reinforcements and even requested that some of the other wrestlers help them get Blassie out of danger. But no matter what the police tried, for a while, the fans held Blassie hostage. Chairs rained in from every direction and I remember hugging the mat, trying to keep from being hit. Eventually, police and wrestlers formed a human circle around Blassie and escorted him out of the park.

Earlier I mentioned that Ivan Koloff was managed by a man named Captain Lou Albano. In reality, Lou was my longtime friend and even if you aren't a wrestling fan you could potentially recognize him from the Cyndi Lauper video *Girls Just Want to Have Fun* where he played her father, *Super Mario Brothers*, he played Mario the Plumber or any number of films and television appearances.

Lou was born in Rome, but was brought to the United States when he was only three months old. His father became a well-known New York City physician and his mother was a concert pianist.

What most folks don't remember about Lou, is what a great, all-around athlete he was. In college, he made his mark in football, receiving a full scholarship to play for Tennessee.

One unfortunate side to Lou's early career was his temper. He ended up attending quite a few more universities after Tennessee. His off-the-field behavior drew him into lots of street and bar fights, which led to his dismissal from Tennessee and other colleges along the way. Since he was such a talented football player, different schools would pick him up until he got into trouble again. Then Lou would just pack his bags and move on. Finally, even Lou got tired of the vagabond life and he dropped out of school for good.

Lou started wrestling professionally two or three years before I did. I remember him as a guy who loved to hang out in the bars you wouldn't want to be caught dead in.

If somebody would say the wrong thing to him, which was easy enough to do, he'd become an absolute maniac and clear the place out. Lou was a tough customer, the type of guy who'd have to be knocked unconscious before he'd stop fighting.

As a wrestler, he was past of a semi-successful tag team called The Sicilians with his partner Tony Altomare. What most fans would be surprised to find out was that I was responsible for Lou being given an opportunity as a manager. It was clear Lou wasn't going to get much further as a wrestler, and while Tony Altomare always spoke for the team, being around Lou quite a bit I knew that he had the gift of gab. I asked him what he thought about becoming a manager. He was all for it, so now I had to convince Vince McMahon, Sr. to give him a chance.

When it was all said and done there was nothing for Vince to lose. Lou was given a chance managing Crusher Verdu. He wasn't a great talker himself so it made sense to see what Lou could do with him. It worked out great. The people hated Lou, especially since he was an Italian that was constantly trying to "end the career" of another Italian. One of my favorite Lou Albano moments was when he was being interviewed. He said that he was so ashamed to be an Italian because of the way that I embarrassed the Italian people he was going to change his name to Lou Alban. It only incensed the people more which was Lou's job. He became a great manager, and ultimately part of a trio of managers in the WWWF, along with Classy Freddie Blassie and The Grand Wizard. When you look at those three managers, two were former wrestlers and one was 160lbs soaking wet. Freddie had embraced the "Hollywood Fashion Plate" look, always dressed well, hair combed, and looking "Classy." At one time, Lou Albano was a very good looking man, but as the years went on he put on a lot of weight and dressed like a slob. As I mentioned, Lou wasn't a great wrestler but he still didn't quite belong as a manager. He was still

Lou Albano with "Classy" Freddie Blassie

young enough to get in the ring, so from time to time we would put Lou in to the ring. Of course, managers didn't make that much, so Lou sometimes would push me to get him some opportunities as well. I would go to Vince McMahon. He knew what I was doing, just trying to help Lou, but he went along with anything so as not to refuse me. When it was all said and done, the people wanted me to rip Albano's head off. In the long run, Lou eventually became a go to guy for the WWWF/WWF. Whenever the houses were down they could ask Lou to put on the tights and start a program with someone ... or even just wrestle someone with no angle involved. He even had matches against Andre the Giant. No one believed that Lou could win, but no one care. They just wanted to watch Andre beat Lou up.

Now Lou was a wild guy with a reputation for drinking (especially if he was planning to do a blade job), and for pushing the envelope, but he was great at playing the nemesis. The fans truly despised him, and he was my friend. In my day, wrestling was made up of real heroes and villains, not like today. One night we were at Madison Square Garden ready for the matches. Gorilla Monsoon, who I also had brought to the WWWF and was now a part of the company, went searching through his bag while Lou was out of the room. He found a bottle of Vodka. Gorilla went straight to Vince,

Sr. who told Gorilla to fire Lou on the spot. Lou was incensed and insisted that he wasn't drinking, but regardless, I didn't like the idea that Gorilla went looking in Lou's bag. I stood up for Lou and told Gorilla to tell Vince that Lou was not fired, and if he insisted that Lou was fired that I would be leaving with him. Gorilla tried to tell me then that he couldn't locate Vince. I told Gorilla, well then when there was no main event that night he could explain to Vince that I left with Lou. Well, Gorilla quickly "found" Vince who told him to advise Lou that he was not fired. I told Gorilla that I would be staying also, and that was the end of that.

    As with most talent within wrestling, very few stay a hero or a villain for their entire career. The only one that I'm told did was Ricky "The Dragon" Steamboat. While I was always a hero in the United States there were times overseas where I was not, especially in Japan where I almost always wrestled their hero The Giant Baba. He was also the promoter. So, eventually it would be time for Lou to change. When I was no longer around, Lou got involved with those mainstream projects that I had mentioned previously. He also brought Cyndi Lauper to the WWF and along with that, Vince McMahon, Jr. got tied into MTV, and wrestling changed. While Lou Albano became a more mainstream talent he was eventually turned babyface by the heel-of-the-day, Roddy Piper. When a large opportunity came Lou's way to do a movie— he was offered the part of Frankie the Fixer in "The Wise Guys." This was to co-star him with Danny DeVito and Joe Piscopo. It was a great break. However, Vince, Jr. didn't want Lou to make the movie unless Lou asked the permission of the WWF. If he did this, Vince would give his blessing and everything would be rosy. Lou's attitude was, "Hey, look, I do what I'm supposed to do for the WWF. I don't need anybody's permission for anything. How I spend my own free time is my business"

That didn't sit too well with Vince, Jr. Eventually the WWF gave Lou the ultimatum that if he did this movie without the company's permission, then he was through with them for good. To his credit, Lou didn't blink an eye the way most guys might have. He broke with the WWF and went ahead to make "The Wise Guys."

The Wise Guys: Dan Hedaya, Danny DeVito, Joe Piscopo, and Lou Albano

The success of that film led to many other roles including a movie called, "Body Slam," appearances in different TV series like "Miami Vice" and as I mentioned earlier, with the "Super Mario Brothers."

After Lou left, he got involved with the Multiple Sclerosis Foundation, and since I was no longer with the WWF, that gave me the opportunity to do events with Lou as well.

THE TRUTH ABOUT THE YABLONSKI MURDERS

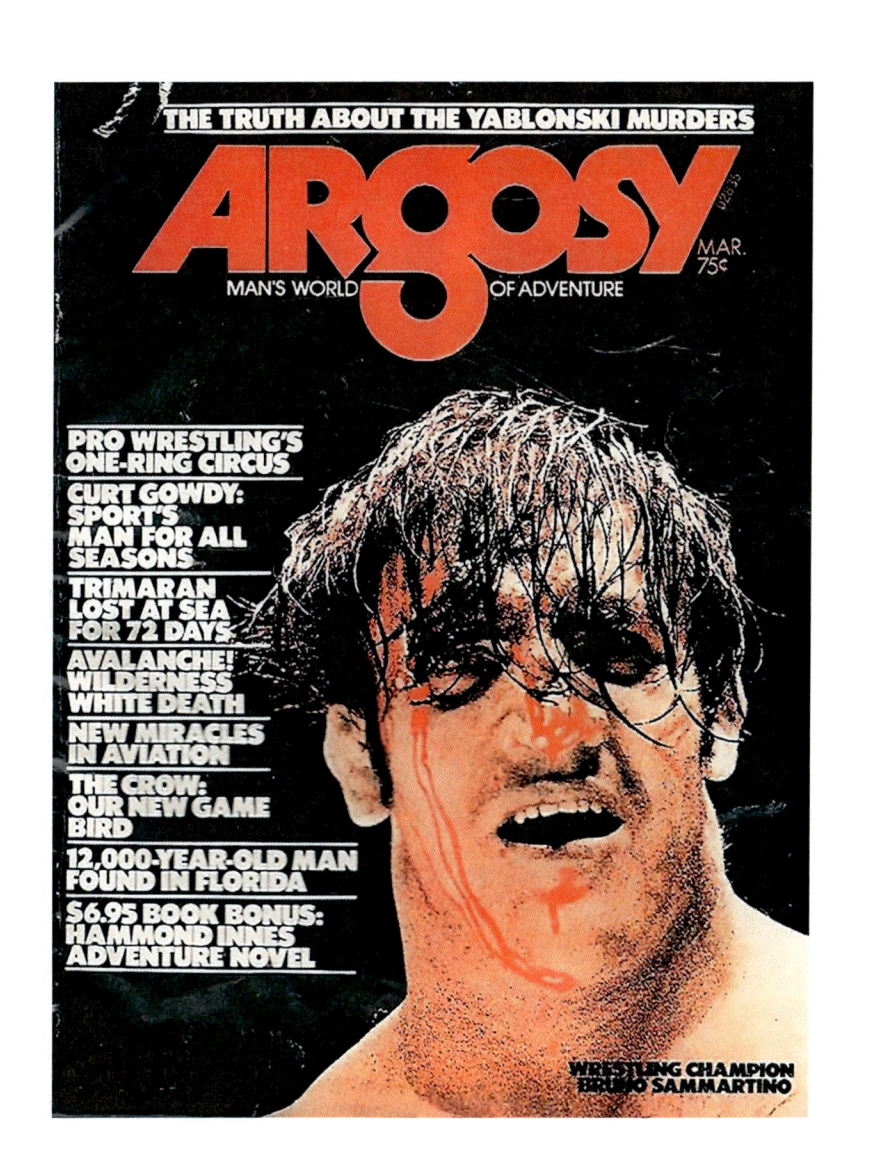

ARGOSY

MAN'S WORLD OF ADVENTURE

MAR. 75¢

- PRO WRESTLING'S ONE-RING CIRCUS
- CURT GOWDY: SPORT'S MAN FOR ALL SEASONS
- TRIMARAN LOST AT SEA FOR 72 DAYS
- AVALANCHE! WILDERNESS WHITE DEATH
- NEW MIRACLES IN AVIATION
- THE CROW: OUR NEW GAME BIRD
- 12,000-YEAR-OLD MAN FOUND IN FLORIDA
- $6.95 BOOK BONUS: HAMMOND INNES ADVENTURE NOVEL

WRESTLING CHAMPION BRUNO SAMMARTINO

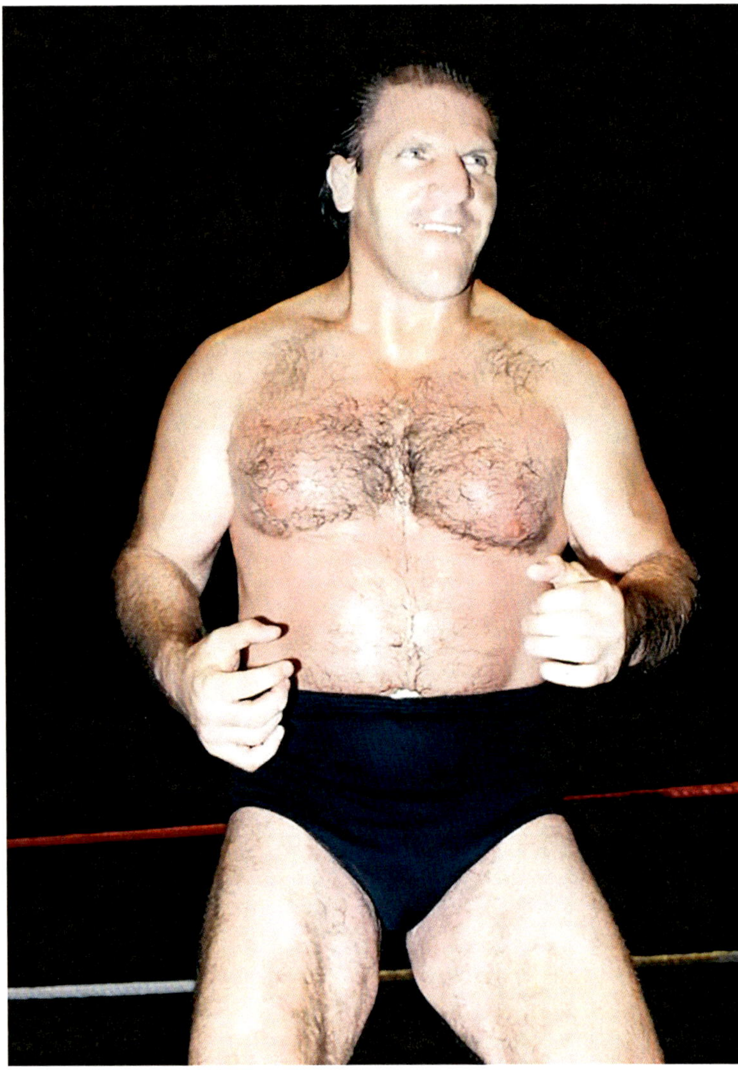

Final Thoughts, Final Shots

During my career, I've known what it is like to be in the spotlight. Yet sometimes that spotlight gives off such a glare that you can't see clearly. The trick is to be able to stand up under the unblinking beam of fame and still walk away a winner. That's the ultimate challenge. Two groups of winners that I've admired for their graciousness under fire have been boxers, and believe it or not, operatic stars.

Let's talk about opera first. Opera people have long owned the reputation for being temperamental, but of all the people I've met in show business, opera stars have impressed me the most, despite their volatile personalities.

I've maintained a life-long love for opera. Whenever I met and chatted with opera stars, each one was always very open with me. Of course, I never had the chance to see them with their public so I can't judge them in that sense. But in their contact with me, these stars displayed none of the bad manners that gossip columnists write about in the tabloids.

Two names come to mind as being particularly thoughtful and kind. The first is Renata Tebaldi. Renata was actually a big wrestling fan and when we met and she acted like I was the big star instead of her. The second was Giovanni Avila, a gentleman who had actually been Caruso's pianist. Ever since I met Avila on one of my tours of Australia, I would seek him out whenever I returned. During my visits, we would sit and discuss Caruso and his life. Avila would share unpublished and rare photographs of Caruso and himself in appearances all over the world.

The one man who had opened the door for me to this world of opera was not only a boxing and wrestling promoter, but also an opera impresario Orelio Tabbiani. Orelio and I took a great liking for each other. Since we were both native Italians, we spoke the mother tongue all the time we were together.

Through Orelio, I met greats like Mario Del Monaco, one of the most highly regarded dramatic tenors of all time; and Giuseppe Di Stefano, one of the greatest lyrical tenors who ever appeared on stage. Of course, I don't want to forget Franco Corelli, a singer with whom I got to be close friends.

Corelli absolutely used to blow my mind when he sang. When he hit a high "C," his power and breath control were phenomenal. His range was just incredible. Franco was a spindo, which meant that he could sing dramatic as well as lyrical roles. Whenever you spelled out his name on the marquee at the New York Met for example, the program would be sold out immediately.

Some years ago the Lincoln Center was about to introduce a new French opera, and Rudolph Bing, the center's director, and others there believed that only Corelli should introduce this new work to New York City. Bing realized that Corelli, who was at this point the greatest opera star in the world, was the one star who could unfold the music's magic for the audience.

Well, politics run deep even in the world of opera. Nicolai Gedda, a Russian tenor, had already made a recording of the work, and Gedda had his core of admirers inside the Met who wanted him and not Corelli to perform in the New York debut. The in-fighting got so ugly that Gedda's supporters let it be known that if Corelli showed up for opening night, he would have his legs broken for his trouble.

Corelli, even speaking no English, picked right up on the seriousness of the threats and panicked, saying he wasn't going to risk life and limb for a French opera. Corelli was assured that extra policemen would be hired to protect him.

He responded by saying that he was fearful his attackers would dress like a policeman to get at him.

Then one of Corelli's people remembered that Bruno Sammartino was a big Corelli fan. With Corelli's permission, his people called me and explained the situation. I readily agreed to stand guard over Corelli throughout the first performance. He was my favorite opera singer. How could I turn down such genius.

Not even singing lessons from the great Corelli could help me

As back up, I contacted two wrestling friends of mine, Tony Marino and Willie Farkus. Together the three of us would serve as Corelli's first line of defense.

The day of the scheduled opening, I flew to New York and went directly to Corelli's apartment on 57th Street. After promising him that everything was going to be taken care of, I escorted the trembling tenor to Lincoln Center and walked him down the long hallway to his dressing room. While makeup artists transformed the Italian superstar into a Frenchman for the night, I hovered around the building, checking the halls and doorways, making sure that no unsavory characters lurked about. Then I followed at his side, step-by-step, until he reached the wings. Before he went on, I pointed out Marino and Farkus seated in the first row, who were in effect securing the safety of the front of the stage.

I told Corelli to sing freely. He had nothing to worry about. I would be backstage and my two friends would be right up front in

I assured Corelli he had nothing to worry about. The show must go on

case anyone stormed the performance. Corelli took a deep breath and thanked me. When he went on, his singing was so phenomenal that at times he made me forget why I was backstage in the first place.

At any rate, nothing happened. No opera terrorists charging the stage. No broken legs. It was just pure unadulterated opera.

After the program, I stayed with him in his dressing room while he climbed out of makeup and changed back into his street clothes. Then I rode back with him to his apartment and turned him over to the security guards that he had hired to watch him through the rest of the night. The very next day he was flying to Milan to appear in an opera there, so once out of New York, he would be safe. As I shook his hand and got ready to leave, his thanks poured out. Corelli had become the happiest man alive just then. Thanks to Bruno and friends, his legs had stayed intact.

Another group that I enjoyed being around might at first seem far removed from the world of opera. For me, the connecting rod between the two was their dedication to excellence. I'm talking about boxers, men who trained hard, worked hard, took punishment, and gave it out ... mostly just for the love of the sport.

My appreciation of boxing, like my enthusiasm for opera, started early in life. When I was wrestling as an amateur, I would either be at the Pitt Field House with the college men or over at the Y where a ring was maintained. The Y was home to a super, super guy named Al Quale, a great boxer in his own right, who had retired from pugilism and become a policeman. Al still kept his hand in the fight game by teaching kids how to box. Some of his charges became Golden Gloves champions and a few even turned pro right out of the Oakland Y. I remember Quale as a great light heavyweight, second only to the legendary Billy Conn.

Al always used to pester me, saying, "Bruno, what are you doing with that wrestling? Boxing ... that's where it's at. You should be a fighter and make all the money."

One time just to please Al, because really I had no interest in actually turning into a boxer, I started to shadow box around the ring. In a short time, Al had moved me over to the bag and I hit that for a while, and then before long, Al had me sparring with different partners.

My heart was in wrestling and not in boxing, but in order to please Al, I kept working out as a boxer for some time. Of course, when he'd leave the building, back I'd go to wrestling.

Finally, Al thought I had progressed in my boxing skills to the extent where he insisted on taking me to Stillman's Gym in New York City. There he introduced me to some real giants in the world of boxing promotion. Guys like Vic Marsell, Whitey Beepsting, and Ernie Barracha. They took a close look at me as a boxing prospect because Al had put out the good word on me. As I waltzed around the ring in Stillman's Gym, sparring with one or two of the local boys, I kept thinking to myself, "What in the world am I doing? This isn't me."

Believe me, the guys they gave me to spar with were the real deal ... heavyweights who knew what they were doing. It didn't take long for me to get the worst of it. One thing in my favor though ... nobody ever put me down. I could take a whale of a punch. Now, at the time I didn't know if that was good or bad for a boxer, but I took some incredible blows. Afterward, the guys told me it wasn't a good idea. It's great to be able to absorb punishment, but one main principle in boxing is to give and then duck, not to give and take.

Everybody was supportive, and the suggestion was made that I get a job at the New York docks and come to Stillman's on a daily basis to continue my boxing training. At that point, I had to call a halt. I confessed that wrestling was the sport that had the number one spot in my heart. I thanked everyone for their interest in me, then told them that I had to fly back to Pittsburgh to return to my true passion ... wrestling.

Even though I passed on a shot at professional boxing, I've kept a fan's lifelong interest in the sport. Thanks to my role as a professional wrestler, I've had the chance to talk with many of the boxing greats. Every boxing champion that I met seemed down to earth, and very considerate to friends and fans alike. To me, boxers are a wonderful breed.

Bruno had no interest in becoming a pro boxer

In the late 1950s and early 1960s, boxing's middleweight division was at its peak, heralding the toughest competition in history. Names like Gil Turner, Bobby Boyd, Willie Troy, and Rory Calhoun may not ring a bell today, but back then these guys were all championship caliber.

One boxer who fought them all and eventually won the crown was Joey Giardello. I met Joey right after he won the middleweight championship and I was very impressed with his level-headed nature. Joey was one of the very best. As proof of this, I only have to remember the whipping that he laid on "Sugar" Ray Robinson. Then there was

Tony DeMarco, a man they called the Little Rocky Marciano. Tony was known as THE knockout artist and I used to love to watch him go to work. Two of the greatest fights I've ever seen in my life were his bout and rematch with Carmine Basilio.

Of course, I couldn't forget Smokin' Joe Frazier, a tremendous champion in the heavyweight class. Yet if you talk to Joe about the fight game and who was the best in his opinion, he'd always point to Joe Louis and Rocky Marciano as his picks for greatness. Joe was a humble man who never boasted about who he could beat or who he could smash to a pulp.

Tough Guys ... Sammartino and Frazier clown for the camera

I met Muhammad Ali a couple of times, and I wish I could say that I held him in the same regard as I do the other boxers I've mentioned. Without question, he was an accomplished fighter, yet he had this need to put himself above everyone else. Maybe a lot of what he babbled on about was just a put on. But for me, the bottom line was this: there's just no way he would have beaten Joe Louis or Rocky Marciano in their prime.

I got to be friends with Jake LaMotta, the man whose story was told in the movie "Raging Bull." Jake was one of the toughest middleweights to ever walk the streets, yet if you talk with him, he's one of the funniest guys you'll ever meet. In fact, he once made a nice living appearing in night clubs as a comedian. His wisecracks and jokes would bring tears to your eyes.

Rocky Graziano, another middleweight champion, recorded some of the most memorable fights in boxing history, taking on the likes of the great Tony Zale. Out of the ring Graziano, too, was one of the nicest guys you'll ever meet.

Hey, who's leading anyway?

Two other boxers who I got to know personally were Willie Pep and Jersey Joe Walcott. Willie worked with the State Athletic Commission in Connecticut. When I'd see him, I'd ask him to tell me about his fights. He loved to tell the stories and was always very thoughtful when a fan like me would ask questions about certain fights.

I got to know Jersey Joe because he refereed many of my matches. Jersey Joe is unquestionably one of the sweetest human beings on the face of the earth.

One time in Madison Square Garden a promoter came up to me just before my match was to begin and said, "Bruno, everybody knows you're a big fan of boxing. We got this kid, Nino Benvenuti, coming in from Italy. He's going to be training in the Catskills and what he'd like most is to meet you. I guess he read all about you in the Italian papers and magazines."

I said, "Sure, I'd love to meet him. As a matter of fact, I've been reading all about him, too!"

A week or so later, I flew into New York early one morning and drove out to the Catskills, to Nino's training camp. Since my match wasn't until later that evening, I had plenty of time to get there and spend a few hours with the young challenger.

When I shook hands with Benvenuti, he seemed in awe of my physique. He said he couldn't believe how big and muscled I was in person. I guess at that time I weighed in around 275 pounds.

The publicity man had me take off my shirt and they took a couple of pictures of Nino and me doing road work. Later, we even sparred a couple of rounds in the ring. Nino complimented me, saying that I had good, quick hands.

Nino introduced me to all of his family that he had brought with him to the training camp. Everything in the camp was aimed at making him feel right at home. He said he really missed his parents.

Then I watched him train for a while. He seemed to go into a trance as he worked. His concentration was so intense. He wanted to be champion so very much.

Later, Nino expressed curiosity about me and my training. He wanted to know how I could weigh 275 pounds and still be in the shape that I was in. He was puzzled by my stamina and speed. When we were running or sparring in the ring, Nino expected my arms to drop off since my biceps, triceps and forearms were so well developed. Instead, he saw that I kept up at a good speed and didn't tire out.

I explained to him that wrestling was a fantastic conditioner. I told him that when you wrestle daily and with some of the matches lasting an hour or more, you ended up in great shape. That boggled his mind. Then he wanted to know how after a wrestler gets body slammed or thrown from the ring, can we jump up and keep going … without pads or protection of any kind. He wanted to know if there was a trick to it.

I said, "Nino, how can there be a trick to somebody picking you up, taking you over their head and then smashing you to the mat? You boxers use the same ring that we use. You know there's no trick to being a good boxer. You've just got to be in the best possible condition that you can."

Nino appreciated that argument. I went on to say, "As a fighter, how many body shots can you take? You know that depends on your conditioning. The average fan out there can't really relate to a body shot. They see the head shots and see the head jerk back and know that the fighter has gotten hurt. But as professional athletes, we both know that body shots can be even more devastating if you aren't in shape."

The longer Nino and I talked, the more I felt like I was being interviewed by a newspaperman. He was so open ... curious about

Nino and Bruno enjoy sharing an Italian newspaper

so many things. What I remember best though about Nino was his professional dedication and his pride in all things Italian. Whenever Nino saw an Italian succeeding in any sport, he would always make an effort to acknowledge that person. He never lost his love of his country.

In 1967, he beat Emile Griffith for the middleweight titles, only to lose them back to him 5 months later. A third match between the pair took place at MSG in March 1968, and he bounced right back to regain the title by unanimous decision.

Nino held the crown for quite some time until he was defeated by the Argentinian Carlos Monzón in 1970.

One name that I certainly don't want to forget is Rocky Marciano, someone who I considered a very good friend. His real name was Rocco Marciano and his family came from the same province in Italy that I did. Shortly before Rocky was killed in a plane crash in Iowa, I met with him to talk about a South African tour that I was to be making that year. Rocky wanted to join us as a guest referee, a role that he had filled in some of my earlier bouts. His death was a tragic waste.

But you know sports figures, entertainers, all those people who must travel, run that extra risk. Although they say each time you board a plane, your risk of dying in a crash is less overall than if you were riding in a car. However, the more miles you log in the air, the closer the odds come together.

Traveling was always one of the most frustrating things for me. When I first won the title, I had an incredibly hectic schedule. I wrestled six days one week, took a day off and then wrestled seven days the next week. Then I'd start the 14 day cycle again … one day off every two weeks. The reason I had to spend the second Sunday of this cycle wrestling was because of the promise I had made to Frank Tunney in Toronto. There was no way I was going to back out on my agreement with Frank to come to Toronto every two weeks. He had been very decent to me, giving me a chance to earn a living when I'd been suspended in the United States.

The problem that this created for me though was formidable. I could only make it back to Pittsburgh to see my family every two weeks. And you'd be surprised how many times that I'd be flying in from New York and the airport would be closed because of the bad winter weather. Then we'd have to fly on to Chicago or Omaha and land there. By the time Pittsburgh airport would reopen, I'd have to catch a plane to head toward my Monday wrestling engagement. I'd spend a whole day running between planes and airports and I'd never make it home.

Bill Cardille was the host of WIIC-TV's Studio Wrestling in Pittsburgh. That's him on the left with the great Baseball Hall of Famer Pie Traynor in the center

Besides keeping my commitment to Frank Tunney, I had to make myself available for live television interviews on Channel 11 in Pittsburgh. These live shots were very important tools for the promoters and they insisted that I appear on air on a regular basis to talk about upcoming bouts at the Civic Arena.

Talk about scrambling. Here might be a typical scenario for my

TV appearances. The promoters would book me for an interview late in the afternoon and, at the same time, commit me to wrestle later that night in Philadelphia. Since the TV spot would air live, I couldn't pre-tape it and duck out to the airport, so I had to hang in there until they were ready for me, and then, more often than not, it would be so late that there would be no commercial flights left to Philly.

That meant the promoters would have to charter a single-engine Cessna for me. I'd finish my interview, head for the airport, climb into this lawn mower with wings ... it'd be me and the pilot buzzing across Pennsylvania in an attempt to reach Philadelphia in time for my late night wrestling match.

Those planes were no bargain, let me tell you. Once I was flying to Philly in weather so bad that with every lurch of the plane, I was thinking, "Oh, my God. This is it!"

Ray the pilot had such an intense look on his face that I was far from reassured about my safety. When we finally reached the outskirts of Philadelphia after what seemed like an eternity, the tower told us that the airport was closed. Ray pleaded with them that he had to make an emergency landing, and so with that sense of urgency conveyed, the tower gave him permission to try one.

All I can say about that landing was that we both walked away from it. The plane hit the runway terrifically hard, spun and flipped over onto its side. The force of this broke the wing clean away.

I had a similar experience flying from Windsor, Ontario to Indianapolis. After a television interview in Windsor, I headed to my next wrestling engagement in Indiana. Again, this was a charter flight with just me and the pilot stuffed into what appeared to be a flying phone booth. As we approached the Indianapolis airport, we found that bad weather had shut down all of their runways. I listened to the pilot discuss our situation with the tower.

It seemed that we couldn't fly on to the next available airport because we were running out of fuel.

The tower finally declared that we were an emergency and told the pilot to try and put the plane down on Runway 4. The weather had now blocked everything in to the extent that it seemed as if the windshield had a layer of cotton gauze over it. You could see nothing but rain and fog and clouds.

We descended for the longest time and then, suddenly, trees appeared right below the wheels. I swear we touched the tops of them. Then all at once we saw the end of the runway ... very close. The plane slammed so hard into the concrete that we shot up into the air again. The pilot circled and made a second attempt at a landing.

Again a downdraft hammered us and the plane bounced up, but this time instead of circling for a third try, the pilot persisted. He aimed us right at the middle of the runway and brought the wheels back to earth once more. The aircraft pogo-sticked up and down two more times, now we were running out of real estate.

At the last second, to avoid diving off the end of the runway and plunging down a steep embankment, the pilot swerved the plane to his extreme right into a grassy field. As soon as the wheels left concrete and hit dirt, the plane up-ended itself and flipped over several times. Again, both the pilot and I climbed out of the wreckage unhurt.

After that one, I told the promoters NO MORE LITTLE PLANES! I told them to schedule my interviews well in advance of my matches. I refused to risk my neck just for some five-minute interview. And that was that.

The truth of the matter is that I've had some close calls on the big birds, too. But you cannot be a champion wrestler and not fly. In the old days, wrestlers took the train. Why not? If you only had one or two matches a week, why not take your time in getting there? The modern era brought in the match-a-night pace. There was no other way to handle it than by flying.

Once I remember flying out of Boston in a four-engine prop driven plane. We were on our way back to Pittsburgh. I was sitting about halfway back, next to Father Rocco whom I had bumped into at the airport. I had met him some years ago at an opera. He was a wrestling fan and as we both shared a love for opera, we had become friends. Since he spoke little or no English, he was pleased to find out that we were booked on the same flight. Now he had someone to talk to.

After we took off, Father Rocco turned to his Bible and began reading. I respected his wish for quiet reflection and I began to reflect myself ... only I started to become aware that something was wrong with the plane. The aircraft seemed to be struggling, waddling through the sky. I glanced out into the night but couldn't make out anything. Then I realized that the engines weren't making as much noise as usual. I quietly excused myself and headed for the back where I recognized one of the stewardesses. I flew so much in those days that I was a familiar figure in the air so she knew me right away, too. I whispered to her, "You know I've been flying too long not to know that something's up. Can you tell me what's going on?"

She told me as quietly as possible, "Well, Bruno, we're not supposed to say anything, but three engines have conked out". I said out loud, "Three!" then quickly lowered my voice again, "Three?"

"Yes, but we don't want to make a big deal out of it. We've already turned around and are headed back to Boston. We can still make it on one engine with no trouble," she reassured me.

I thanked her and returned to my seat. Father Rocco was still reading his Bible. He looked up at me and smiled and I smiled back, thinking, "Please, keep reading that Bible of yours! Don't stop reading for anything!"

Well, we made it back to Boston okay and Father Rocco and the rest of the passengers never knew what had happened. The pilot just announced that they were having some difficulties and had to return to Boston to transfer us to another aircraft. Everybody moaned and groaned, but I thanked our lucky stars for that one good engine ... and Father Rocco's Bible.

I remember one time in the early 1970s that I nearly went to Boston on a connecting flight from Montreal to Philadelphia and it was only the luck of the draw that kept me off that plane. Because of bad weather throughout the Northeast, flights were being canceled and rerouted all night long. So when I reached the Montreal airport, my direct flight to Philadelphia had been canceled.

The ticket attendant who greeted me with this news scanned his screen and said, "Bruno, here's the best I can do. I can fly you from Montreal to Boston then change you over there on a flight to Philadelphia. It's a little round a bout, but better than spending the night sleeping in a chair here, right?"

I shrugged and said, "Okay. Let's do that."

He arranged my ticket, handed me my new flight envelope and wished me well. I got on the phone and called Vince McMahon at the Philadelphia Arena and told him that I was probably going to be late for my match because my original flight had been canceled. Then I told him the airline had booked me into Boston where I'd have to catch a connecting flight into Philly. With the weather the way it was, I told him I couldn't predict when I'd arrive. In his usual style, Vince told me to get there the best way I could and he'd see me at the arena.

I hung up the phone, then just as I was walking away to get to the right gate, the attendant called out, "Bruno! Bruno, come on back!"

I hurried over to see what he wanted. He told me a flight that was headed for Philadelphia has landed briefly at the Montreal airport. It had been rerouted through Montreal because of the lousy weather all up and down the Lakes. And there was one seat left on it. "Did you want to take it?" he asked.

Of course I said yes. I'll take a direct flight any day. So we changed my ticket one more time. I was scratched off the flight to Boston and penciled in on the straight shot to Philly. I rushed to claim my seat on that flight. Of course, I didn't have enough time to call McMahon back to tell him of my second change of plans.

When I walked into the arena in Philadelphia, Phil Zacko, who was one of McMahon's partners, took one look at me and I thought he was going to faint. It was like he had just seen a ghost.

I said, "Phil, what's the matter?"

He squinted and said, "Bruno, it's really you!"

"Sure it's me, Phil. What's wrong with you?" I thought maybe Phil had temporarily lost his mind.

Phil stammered, "My God, Bruno. We just heard on the news that the flight you told us you were on … you know, the one from Montreal to Boston. It crashed trying to land in the storm … exploded on impact … burned to ashes. No survivors. Nobody."

I couldn't believe it. "Crashed?"

Phil grabbed my arm and twisted it, making sure that I really was there. "But what happened? Vince said you called him. Told him you had to take that Boston flight to get to Philly."

I explained that last minute switch to Phil. All I could think was, "My God … all those poor people."

Let me tell you one more airplane story and I'll get off this. Once I was touring Australia. On this particular day I wrestled in Brisbane, then returned to my hotel room knowing that I had to get up early the next morning to catch a 7:45 a.m. flight to Sydney. The promoter had booked me on the earliest available plane because I had to do a TV interview at 11 a.m.

No matter where I've traveled around the world, I've always brought my own little alarm clock as a backup for the hotel's wake up call. Too many times the front desk has failed to call me on time, if at all. When you wake up in the morning, and already you're an hour behind schedule, that makes the whole day pretty traumatic.

Anyway, just as I was about to crawl into bed, I set my own alarm for 6 a.m., called the front desk and asked them for a wake up call for the same time and went to sleep. Actually, I seem to have my own built-in alarm clock and I usually wake up on my own, just a few minutes before the alarm is set to go off.

Well, the next morning nothing happened. The alarm didn't go off. The front desk didn't call. And I didn't wake up until 8 a.m. I was furious and I called downstairs, asking that they get me a cab right away. Maybe my flight had been delayed, and I still could make it. I got dressed, didn't even brush my teeth, checked out and jumped into a cab. We careened out to the airport and I found out that the flight I had been booked on had indeed taken off on time. The plane had crashed on takeoff, plunged into the earth and blew up in a monstrous explosion.

Everyone died.

People have asked me, "Do you think you have a Guardian Angel hanging over your shoulder?"

I suppose I've thought about that as I've gotten older. I stop to remember the close calls and sometimes it does give me the chills for an instant. But I still got on that next plane to Sydney. You have to keep going. You have to fulfill your obligations. That's what it is to be a professional, no matter what you do.

This match might never have taken place if I hadn't switched flights

Of course, I think about those people who didn't make it. Did they have Guardian Angels, too? If so, was it just their time to pass over?

Or maybe it was just the luck of the draw. I don't know. I have a hard time defining luck.

Was I lucky to have survived the hazards of World War II? If I had been lucky, maybe I would have been born in another time, and in another place. Was it luck that when I broke my neck, I wasn't completely paralyzed? If I was truly lucky, I wouldn't have broken my neck in the first place.

I remember once, after we had come to America and had settled in, my mother said to my father, "Could you imagine how life would have been different if we had gone to the United States before the war started? How much heartache and suffering we would have avoided."

I thought about this and said to my mother, "I have absolutely no regrets, Mom. It happened the way it was supposed to happen."

What I meant was that because of the war, I learned how courageous my mother was. I experienced what it's like to be hungry and to be without warm clothing in the cold. These were things that were necessary to know.

Relaxing at home with my grandchild

My family drew close together because we all came so close to dying on that mountain top. Today, we all love each other so very much and that love flows from the well of our hardships back then.

I remember what it was like to have nothing but scraps to eat ... sometimes not even that. I remember what it was like to watch my mother vanish down the mountain side and not know if I'd see her again. And I remember the joy of her return, her striding up the trails, moving as fast as she could manage, to bring food back for her children. I remember her smile. It was a smile you could see for miles.

That's what life is all about—courage and family, honesty, and commitment.

I must have been on more magazine covers than Elvis

Let me leave you with one last story. Because of the many times that I had headlined at Madison Square Garden, I was invited to go visit the New York World's Fair as a special guest of the city. While I was there, the fair's officials wanted to have me leave the imprints

THE AUTOBIOGRAPHY OF WRESTLING'S LIVING LEGEND

At the New York World's Fair

of my hands in cement for posterity. So I agreed and stuck my hands into the wet cement, pulling up the sleeves of my suit coat so it wouldn't get dirty.

As I wiped my hands on a towel, one of the photographers from a newspaper came up with a bright idea. He suggested that I lift up two barrels of beer that were sitting behind us and hold them in the air while everybody took a picture.

I didn't realize just how heavy these barrels were, especially with beer inside them. With the help of a few men, first one barrel was hoisted onto my left shoulder and then the other was shunted up onto my right shoulder. Because of the barrel's size and shape, I couldn't simply rest them on my shoulders. I had to wrap my arms around each one and just muscle them up. As I would adjust my position, the beer would slosh back and forth, nearly knocking me over with each swoosh.

The photographers and TV crews went wild. They loved the image ... this big guy in a suit and tie, holding two giant beer barrels on his shoulders. They took picture after picture and rolled film for what seemed like an hour.

Everybody thought that since I was so strong, I could hold the barrels up forever. Smile, they told me. Well, I ended up in so much pain, I thought my arms were going to fall off, but I wasn't going to complain. I was determined to endure it.

Finally, everybody had enough pictures and some guys helped me get the barrels of beer back down. People came up and wanted to shake my hand and I remember I could barely lift my arm to do it.

When I got back to the hotel, I gingerly slipped off my jacket and saw that the weight of the barrels had cut into my shoulders.

Blood had soaked through and stained my shirt. As I unbuttoned my shirt to attend to my wounds, I thought how great a day it had been over at the World's Fair. Everywhere I had gone, a crowd had followed. The fans had made me feel like a real celebrity.

Bruno Sammartino somewhere between 1988-1990

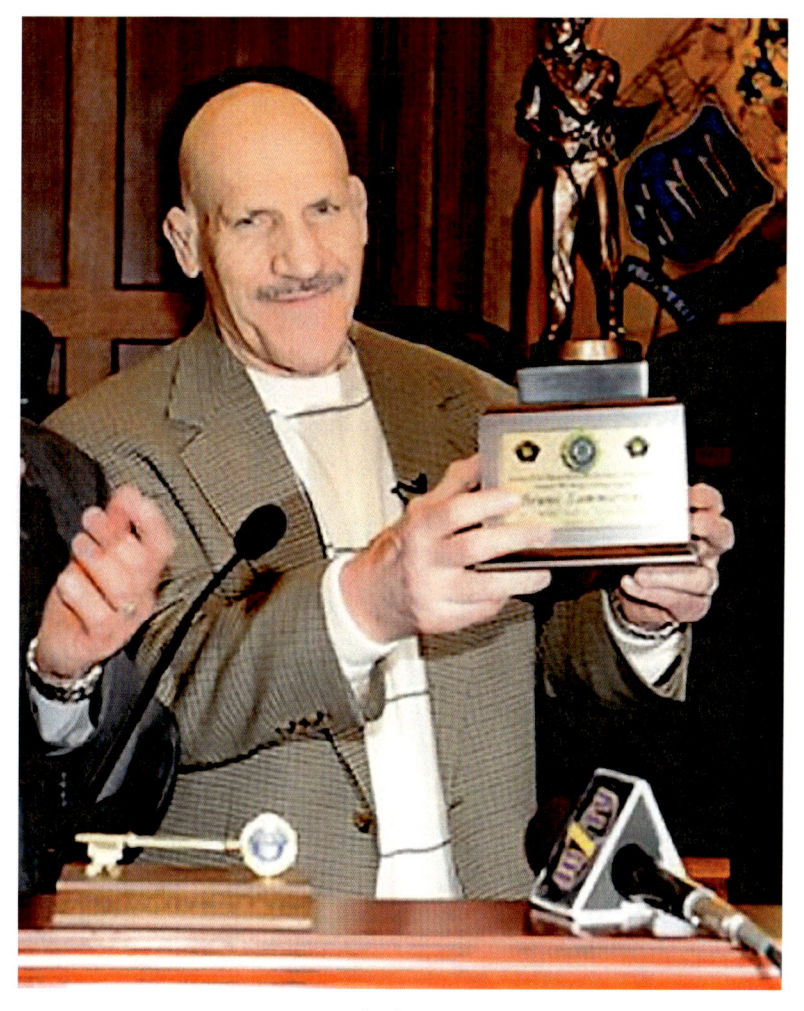

I was given the keys to Jersey City

Introducing the tape recorder that won't say "uncle."

CYCOLAC

MARBON
BORG WARNER

Photo Gallery

Pizzoferrato: Where it all began

Me and my dear friend and Fan Club president Georgiann Makropoulos

Dom and I seeing the sights in Japan

THE AUTOBIOGRAPHY OF WRESTLING'S LIVING LEGEND

A favorite portrait of Carol and me attending a banquet

After a bout, back in my dressing room with visitor Miguel Perez

THE AUTOBIOGRAPHY OF WRESTLING'S LIVING LEGEND

1965 with Monsignor Fusco, Father Rivi and John Ricchuito

*Receiving an award from Pennsylvania State
Athletic Commissioner Paul G. Sullivan*

Talking with baseball legend Roy Campanella

Yet another award. This time it's presented by commissioner and promoter Pete "Figo" Carvella as Blackie Gennaro looks on

THE AUTOBIOGRAPHY OF WRESTLING'S LIVING LEGEND

In the 70s I thought I'd try dropping a few pounds and growing a mustache

In Monsignor Fusco's study from left to right are Stan Marsico, John Ricchuito, me, Msr. Fusco, Henry Bellini and Fr. Rivi

John Ricchuito, me and Father Rivi

THE AUTOBIOGRAPHY OF WRESTLING'S LIVING LEGEND

Enjoying some rare time at home with my son David

Celebrating a birthday with my twins Darryl and Danny and my wife Carol. David was off wrestling somewhere

THE AUTOBIOGRAPHY OF WRESTLING'S LIVING LEGEND

Being congratulated after another match

BRUNO SAMMARTINO

THE AUTOBIOGRAPHY OF WRESTLING'S LIVING LEGEND

I made several successful trips to Japan

David poses with the twins Danny and Darryl

Carol and I enjoy a night on the town

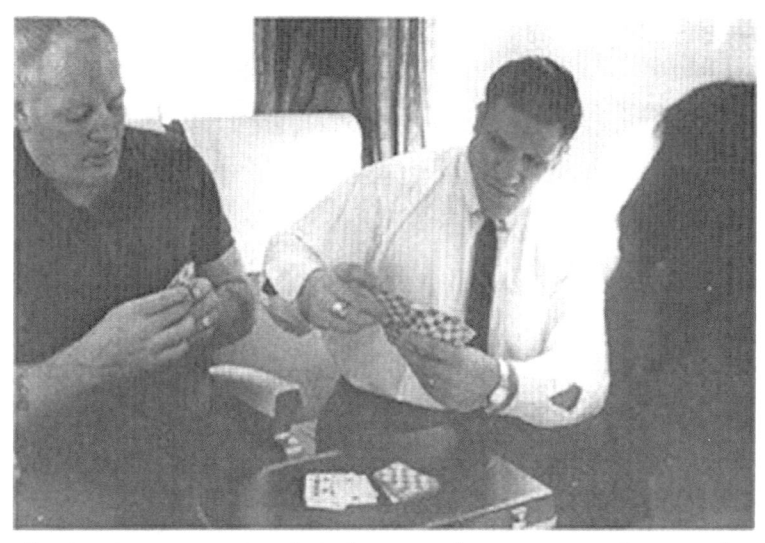

Passing time on a train trip in Japan on the way to one of my matches

A photo from one of the many hospitals that I visited throughout my career

*Posing with an Australian horse right before I
left for one of my Australian tours*

THE AUTOBIOGRAPHY OF WRESTLING'S LIVING LEGEND

Sports legends get together at Bally's Casino. From left to right are Phil Esposito, Johnny Unitas, me, Walt Frazier, VP of Bally's Richard Knight, Berl Rotfeld (Producer Greatest Sports Legends), Bobby Riggs, Brooks Robinson, and Willie Mays

With opera legend Franco Corelli

BRUNO SAMMARTINO

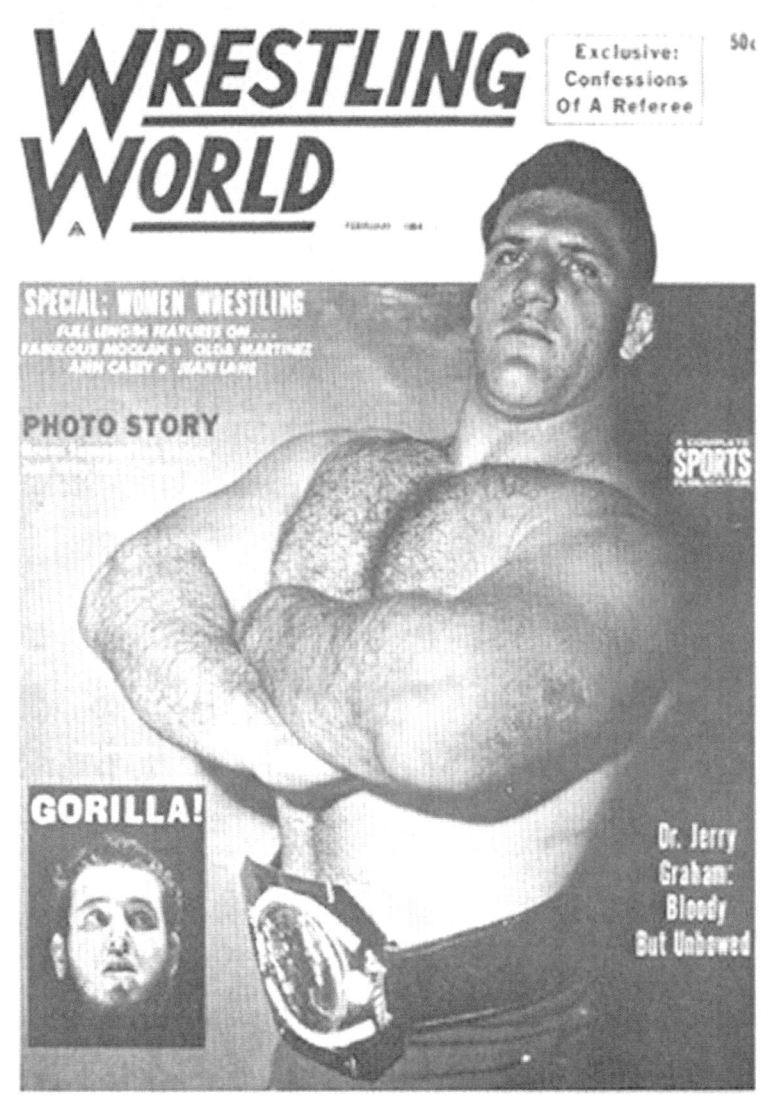

One of the many magazine covers that I appeared on during my career

THE AUTOBIOGRAPHY OF WRESTLING'S LIVING LEGEND

Madison Square Garden Souvenir Program

Practicing my backflip in mid-air! A match in 1968 with Waldo Von Erich

Arm wrestling with singer/composer Mel Torme

THE AUTOBIOGRAPHY OF WRESTLING'S LIVING LEGEND

Come and get it

Carol and I pose with Danny and Darryl. This photo was taken not too long after I had broken my neck

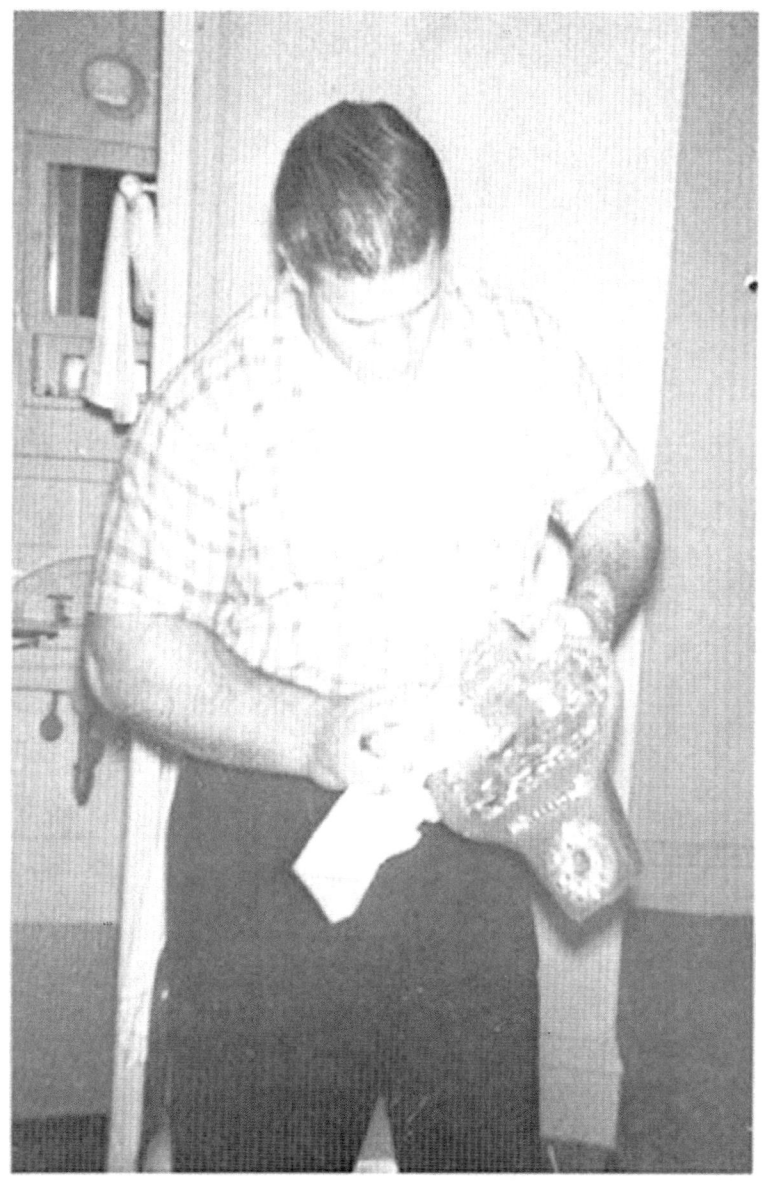

THE AUTOBIOGRAPHY OF WRESTLING'S LIVING LEGEND

Polishing the belt I was so proud to have

BRUNO SAMMARTINO

One of my matches against Don Leo Jonathan

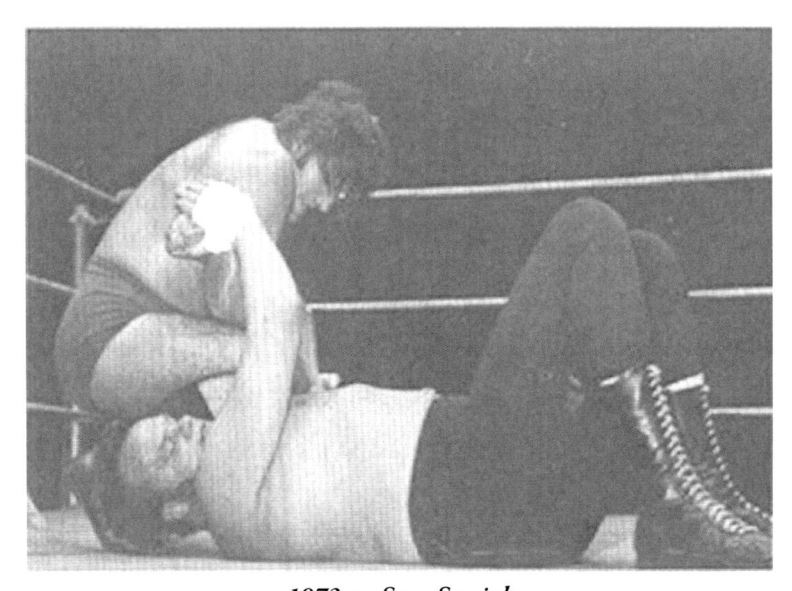

1973 vs. Stan Stasiak

THE AUTOBIOGRAPHY OF WRESTLING'S LIVING LEGEND

*December 10, 1973 after regaining the belt with
Vince McMahon, Sr. and Willie Gilzenberg*

In 1974, I wrestled a "masked" Killer Kowalski

Putting the squeeze on Billy Graham

THE AUTOBIOGRAPHY OF WRESTLING'S LIVING LEGEND

Here I am ready for action

Here I am posing with then champion Pedro Morales

A frequent opponent, former NFL star Ernie Ladd

Interesting reading

Bruno reading the original version of this book

At home at my desk still answering fan mail

THE AUTOBIOGRAPHY OF WRESTLING'S LIVING LEGEND

★★ SAMMARTINO VS. KOWALSKI ★★

FENWAY PARK, BOSTON JUNE 1969

The Giant Baba has the uppper hand on Bruno

Some clippings that appeared in the papers

Bruno, Giant Win Matches

Bruno Sammartino pinned Baron Von Raschke in 14:11 and 7-4 giant Jean Andre Ferre stopped Killer Kowalski in 17:21 in feature wrestling bouts last night at the Civic Arena.

Ogre Cantwell, Tony Parisi and Johnny Defazio won over Baron Schickne, Joe Crofonera and Cowboy Parker, 15:33; Luis Martinez and Pete Sanchez won over Frank Monte and Frank Durso, 13:36; Larry Zbyszko won over Frank Monte, 8:12; Arena Holtz won over Mike Loren, 10:26.

Bruno Team Wins Match

Bruno Sammartino and Dick the Bruiser defeated Baron Von Raschke and Ricky Cortez in 13:04 of the pro wrestling co-feature last night at the Civic Arena.

Pedro Morales pinned Erik the Red at 11:03 in the other main event.

Geo DeMucci and Tony Parisi won over Jimmy Valiant and John J. Sullivan, 15:43; Luis Martinez pinned Bruce Swayze, 9:44; Johnny DeFazio and the Executioner, no decision, a double knock-out; Frank Holtz won over Al Monte, 6:55; and Frank Durso beat Dino Ferra, 7:12.

Wrestlers Cut, Match Halted

Bruno Sammartino's match with Joe LeDuc last night at the Civic Arena was halted after 14:15 because both wrestlers were bleeding from cuts over the eyes.

Ivan Koloff won over Carlos Montoya, 4:12; Baron Schickne pinned Mike Paradise, 9:14; Dr. Bill Miller pinned Tony Tyrell, 7:12.

Sammartino breaks neck during bout

PITTSBURGH (AP) — World Champion heavyweight wrestler Bruno Sammartino is recuperating from a broken neck suffered during a bout Monday in New York, a local physician said Thursday.

Dr. Louis Civitrese, a longtime friend of the wrestler, said the 6-foot, 265-pound Sammartino suffered a fracture of the sixth cervical vertebra during a match with Stan Houston, a 6-foot-7, 327-pounder. The match was stopped by the referee.

Sammartino, 37, was initially treated at New York's St. Clair Hospital, but returned to Divine Providence Hospital here for treatment, said Dr. Civitrese, head of surgery at Divine Providence.

Civitrese said the wrestler is in traction and will be out of action for at least five weeks and perhaps longer.

"This can be a permanent disability, but not necessarily and I doubt it in this case," the doctor said. "There has been no damage to the spinal cord."

He said Sammartino was ambulatory when he entered the hospital here and has no loss of feeling or movement in his limbs. Sammartino lives in the Pittsburgh's North Hills area.

Leaving the ring heading back to the dugout area in Shea Stadium after my Steel Cage Match with Larry Zbyszko

THE AUTOBIOGRAPHY OF WRESTLING'S LIVING LEGEND

Candid shots of life on the road

BRUNO SAMMARTINO

WRESTLING
CIVIC ARENA — FRI. DEC. 3 — 8:30 P.M.

WORLD CHAMPION

SAMMARTINO
VS
BRUISER BRODY
300 LB. GIANT

WORLD TAG TEAM TITLE BOUT

THE EXECUTIONERS
VS
POLISH POWER IVAN PUTSKI & GORILLA MONSOON

NICOLI VOLKOFF
VS
HOSEA GONZALEZ

PLUS 3 OTHER BIG STAR BOUTS

Ringside $5.00 Res. $4.00 Gen. Adm. $3.00
For Information & Reservation Call 471-9298
Advance Tickets at Arena Gate 1 - Horne's - Kaufmann's
Lauar Ticket Agency, Carlton House

Getting ready to square off against Ivan Koloff

vs. Waldo Von Erich

One of my appearances during the title reign of Pedro Morales

THE AUTOBIOGRAPHY OF WRESTLING'S LIVING LEGEND

Waiting for the tag

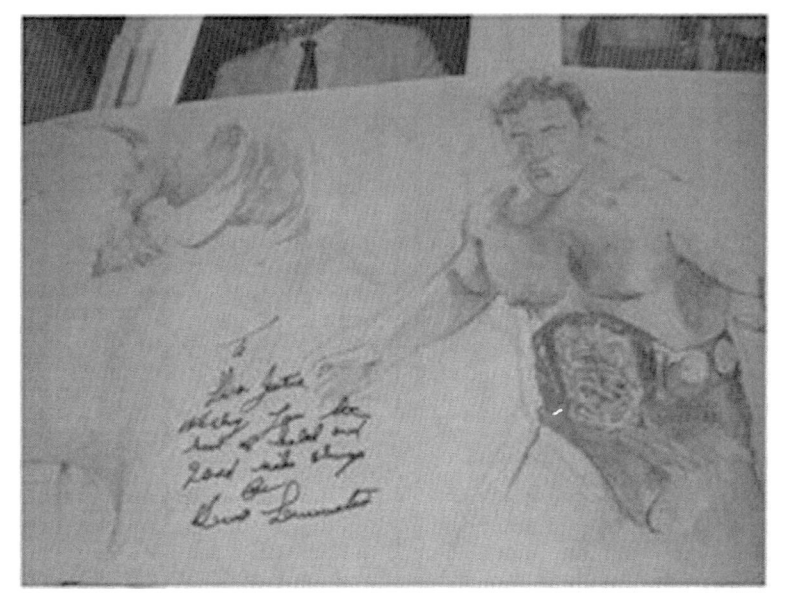

I'm always touched and amazed at the generosity of my fans. This was given to me in Framingham, MA at the Sheraton Hotel. (November 2008)

THE AUTOBIOGRAPHY OF WRESTLING'S LIVING LEGEND

With Giant Baba in Japan

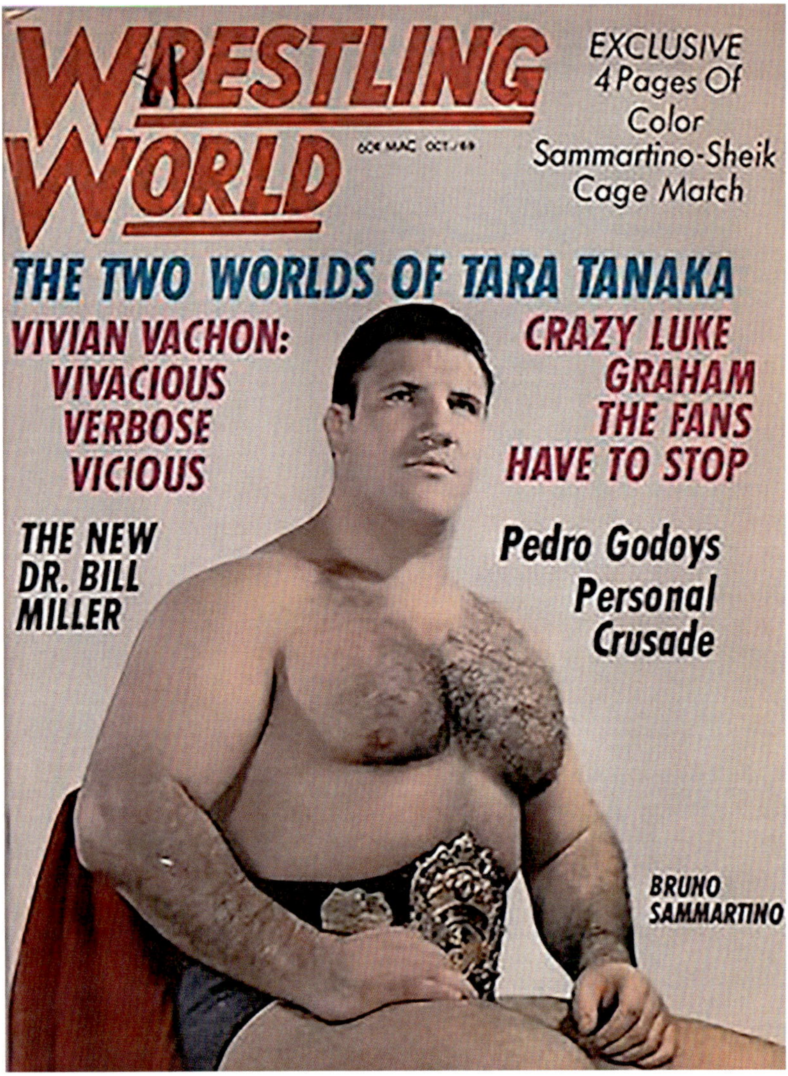
WRESTLING WORLD
EXCLUSIVE 4 Pages Of Color Sammartino-Sheik Cage Match
THE TWO WORLDS OF TARA TANAKA
VIVIAN VACHON: VIVACIOUS VERBOSE VICIOUS
CRAZY LUKE GRAHAM THE FANS HAVE TO STOP
THE NEW DR. BILL MILLER
Pedro Godoys Personal Crusade
BRUNO SAMMARTINO

THE AUTOBIOGRAPHY OF WRESTLING'S LIVING LEGEND

Posing with Dick Murdoch

Visiting Pizzoferrato

BRUNO SAMMARTINO

T.V. WRESTLING
In Color — on
CHANNEL 41
EVERY WEDNESDAY at 7:30 P.M.

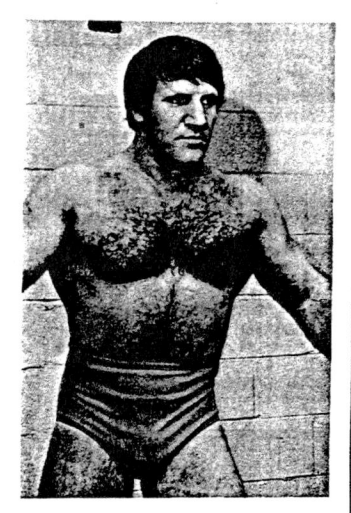

BRUNO SAMMARTINO
WWWF Heavyweight Champion

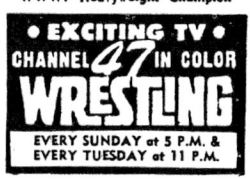

• EXCITING TV •
CHANNEL **47** IN COLOR
WRESTLING
EVERY SUNDAY at 5 P.M. &
EVERY TUESDAY at 11 P.M.

MADISON SQUARE GARDEN
MONDAY, APRIL 26th, 1976

Wrestling Program

MAIN BOUT

WWWF HEAVYWEIGHT CHAMPIONSHIP MATCH
— One Fall to a Finish —

Bruno   **Stan**
SAMMARTINO vs **HANSEN**
Champion - Italy - 260   Challenger - Texas - 312

SPECIAL ATTRACTION — One Fall to a Finish

KING Ernie LADD   vs   ANDRE the GIANT
Houston - 300   France - 7'5" - 444

4 MAN TAG TEAM MATCH — 2 out of 3 Falls

Super-Star Billy GRAHAM   Irish Pat BARRETT
Paradise Valley, Ariz. - 275   Dublin, Ireland - 260
and   vs   and
Ivan KOLOFF   HAYSTACKS Calhoun
Russia - 260   Morgans Cor., Ark. - 600

— Time Limit Matches —

Rocky TAMAYO   vs   Big Bobo BRAZIL
Peru - 245   Benton Harbor, Mich. - 285

Nature Boy Rick FLAIR   vs   Kevin SULLIVAN
Minneapolis - 250   Lexington, Mass. - 235

Louie CYR   vs   Dominick DeNUCCI
Canadian Yukon - 285   Italy - 260

Baron Mikel SCICLUNA   vs   Tony PARISI
Isle of Malta - 275   Italy - 241

Johnny RODZ   vs   Louis CERDAN
Brooklyn - 240   France - 240

FIRST BOUT STARTS AT 8:30 P. M.

Next Garden Mat Show Monday, May 17th

THE AUTOBIOGRAPHY OF WRESTLING'S LIVING LEGEND

BRUNO SAMMARTINO

SOUVENIR WRESTLING PROGRAM

No. 1425

CIVIC ARENA - FRI. DEC. 15, 8:30 P.M.

Promoted by Spectator Sports, Inc.

WHO WILL WEAR THE BELT?

PROFESSOR TANAKA | BRUNO SAMMARTINO

3 LUCKY NUMBERS ON PROGRAMS WIN 2 RINGSIDE TICKETS FOR THE NEXT ALL STAR WRESTLING CARD AT THE CIVIC ARENA SAT. JAN. 13th

Price 25c

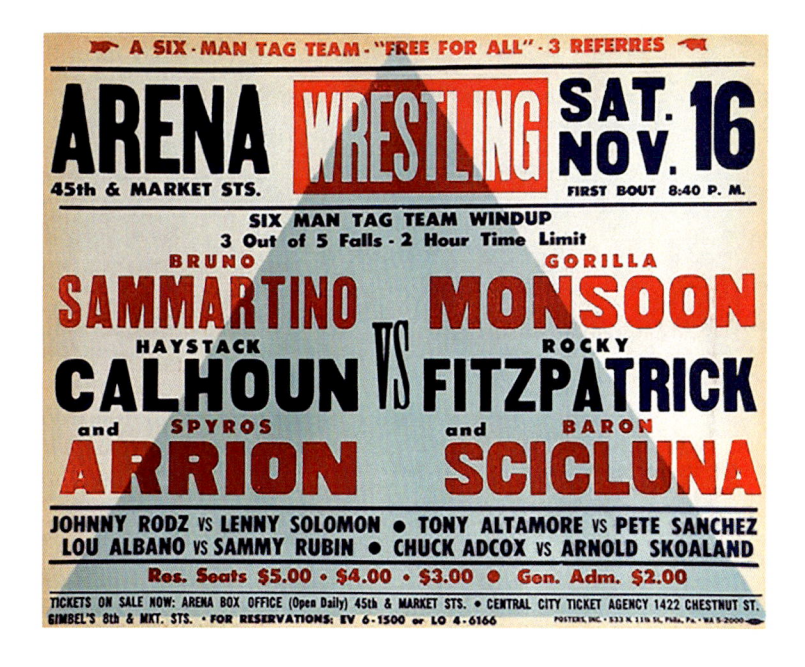

THE AUTOBIOGRAPHY OF WRESTLING'S LIVING LEGEND

BRUNO SAMMARTINO

My statue in Pizzoferrato

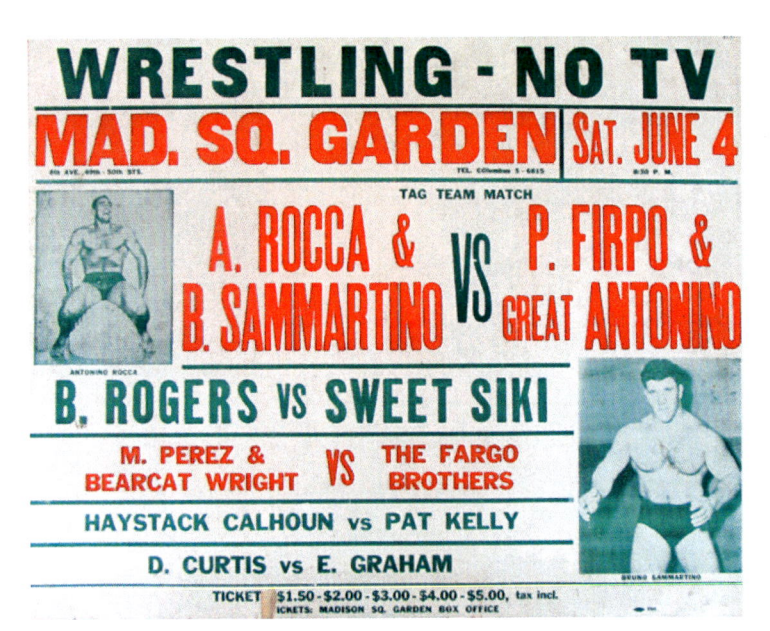

BRUNO SAMMARTINO

THE AUTOBIOGRAPHY OF WRESTLING'S LIVING LEGEND

Slamming Haystacks Calhoun

THE AUTOBIOGRAPHY OF WRESTLING'S LIVING LEGEND

Here I am lifting Mr. Olympia Franco Columbu with one hand

BRUNO SAMMARTINO

THE AUTOBIOGRAPHY OF WRESTLING'S LIVING LEGEND

TRI-STATE WRESTLING

BRUNO SAMMARTINO
World Heavyweight Wrestling Champion

PRICE $1.00

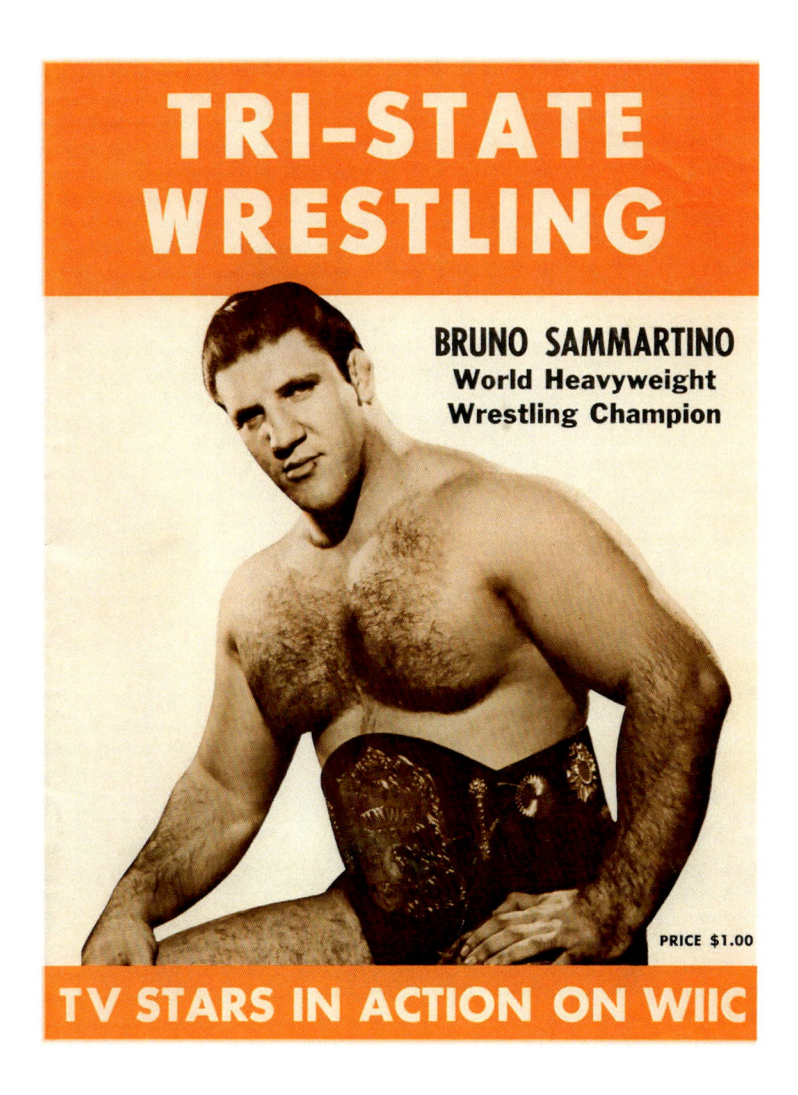

TV STARS IN ACTION ON WIIC

BRUNO SAMMARTINO

WRESTLING'S TOP ATTRACTION!

★

Holder of the World-Wide-Wrestling Federation Belt

★

Born: Abruzzi, Italy
Home: Pittsburgh, Pa.
Age 27; Weight: 265 lbs.

STRONGEST MAN IN THE WORLD!

BRUNO SAMMARTINO — WORLD HEAVYWEIGHT WRESTLING CHAMPION

THE AUTOBIOGRAPHY OF WRESTLING'S LIVING LEGEND

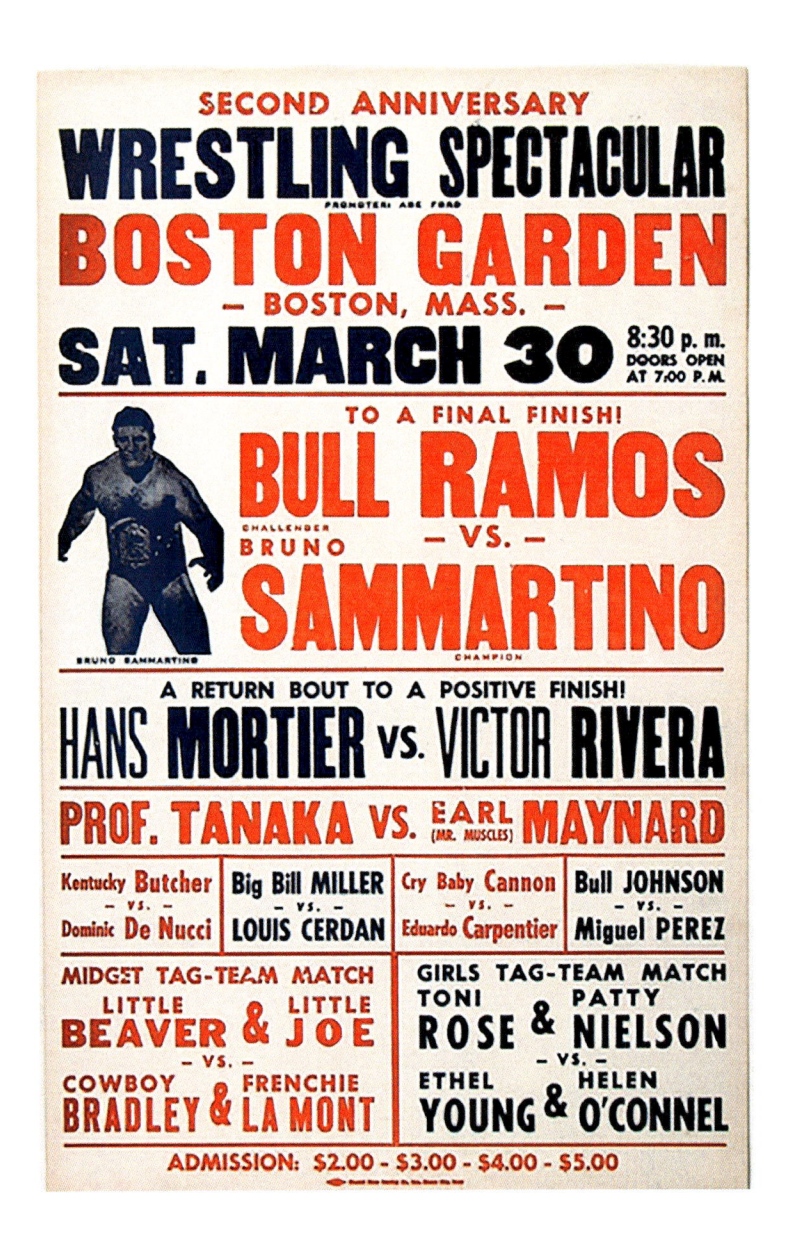

BRUNO SAMMARTINO

THE AUTOBIOGRAPHY OF WRESTLING'S LIVING LEGEND

WrestleReunion 2 Poster from 2005

THE AUTOBIOGRAPHY OF WRESTLING'S LIVING LEGEND

The **BRUNO COURSE** ..of.. **BODYBUILDING** ..by.. **BRUNO SAMMARTINO**

World's Mightiest Developed Man and Strongest Athlete

BRUNO SAMMARTINO

*Meeting another European immigrant, the
WWE's Rusev who is from Bulgaria*

*Marufuji on the left and KENTA on the right who
went on to success in WWE as Hideo Itami*

*With Japanese wrestler Marufuji and a young
Bryan Danielson (Daniel Bryan)*

THE AUTOBIOGRAPHY OF WRESTLING'S LIVING LEGEND

Bruno with fan Ring of Honor fan favorite Bryan Danielson who went on to be Daniel Bryan in WWE

With Noel Neill (Lois Lane) from TV's The Adventures of Superman

BRUNO SAMMARTINO

*Addressing the crowd at Ring of Honor Event
in NYC September 16th, 2006*

At Rico's with Chris Jericho

Bruno is honored by The Italian American Museum

The Feast of San Gennaro 2013 in Little Italy, New York

Met the Great Khali. He is bigger than Shohei Baba

Hanging out in the box before WrestleMania 29

THE AUTOBIOGRAPHY OF WRESTLING'S LIVING LEGEND

At breakfast with Ric Flair

A firm handshake with Steven Regal

As much as Bruno loved wrestling, and his fans, he was always happiest when he was with his wife Carol and his family

THE AUTOBIOGRAPHY OF WRESTLING'S LIVING LEGEND

Bruno blowing out the candles

Bruno with close friend Dominic DeNucci in Japan

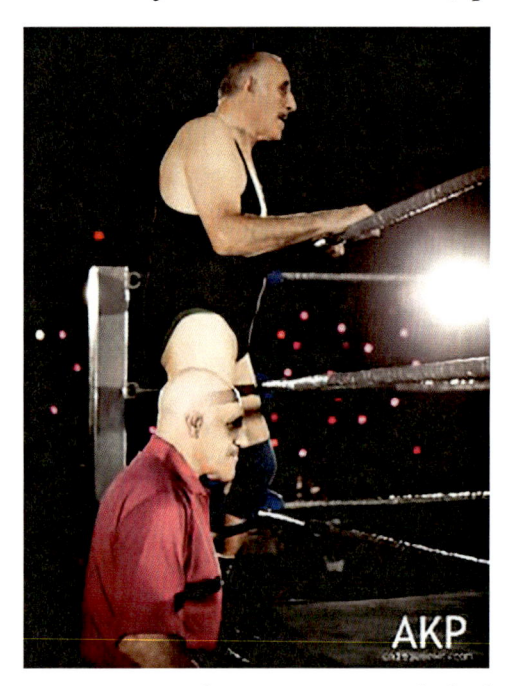

Bruno accompanied Dominic DeNucci for his last match at WrestleReunion Toronto in 2012

Bruno with Davey O'Hannon and Capt. Lou Albano

Bruno with close friend Davey O'Hannon and Dominic DeNucci at the wedding of Dominic's daughter

Bruno and Sal with Nitro Girls (Spice) Melissa Peterson Grill and (AC Jazz) Amy Crawford

THE AUTOBIOGRAPHY OF WRESTLING'S LIVING LEGEND

Bruno with Tony Torre, the General Manager of the New Jersey Cardinals baseball team in the Penn League, at one of his guest referee appearances for IWA Championship Wrestling

*Bruno with former N.W.A. Junior Heavyweight
Champion Gorgeous Gary Royal*

THE AUTOBIOGRAPHY OF WRESTLING'S LIVING LEGEND

*Bruno with Salvatore Corrente after dinner
at Giulio's Restaurant in Yonkers, NY*

BRUNO SAMMARTINO

Bruno and Sal with former WWE Wrestlers Los Boricuas: Miguel Perez, Jr. Jose Estrada, Jr and Jesus "Hurrican" Castillo. Bruno was friends with Miguel Perez, Sr.

Bruno along with Sal Corrente and Salvatore Toscano at a personal appearance

THE AUTOBIOGRAPHY OF WRESTLING'S LIVING LEGEND

Bruno with Gene Ligon aka Thunderfoot #2

*Bruno along with Giulio Notaro and Yonkers Mayor
Mike Spano at Giulio's Restaurant in Yonkers, NY*

THE AUTOBIOGRAPHY OF WRESTLING'S LIVING LEGEND

Bruno holding a copy of his original autobiography

*Bruno doing his final bulk book signing for
Highspots.com at the hotel in Yonkers, NY*

THE AUTOBIOGRAPHY OF WRESTLING'S LIVING LEGEND

*Bruno holding up the signature to be
used for authentication purposes*

Tom Unger and Brian Barth of The Big Event with Bruno and Sal posing with robes that Bruno was asked to sign as part of his last personal appearance outside of Pittsburgh

"Living Legend" the name the fans gave to Bruno, deservedly so

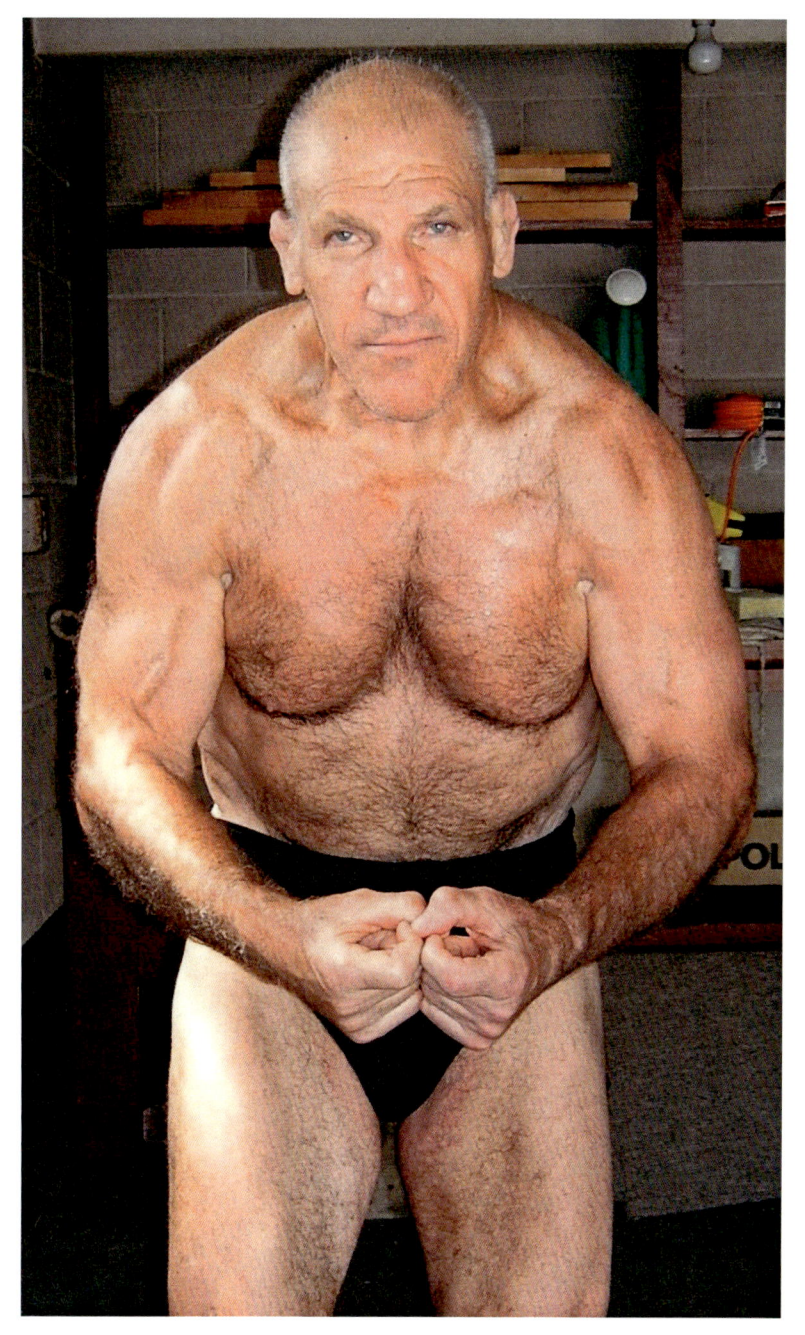

THE AUTOBIOGRAPHY OF WRESTLING'S LIVING LEGEND

Even after I retired I kept myself in great shape

BRUNO SAMMARTINO

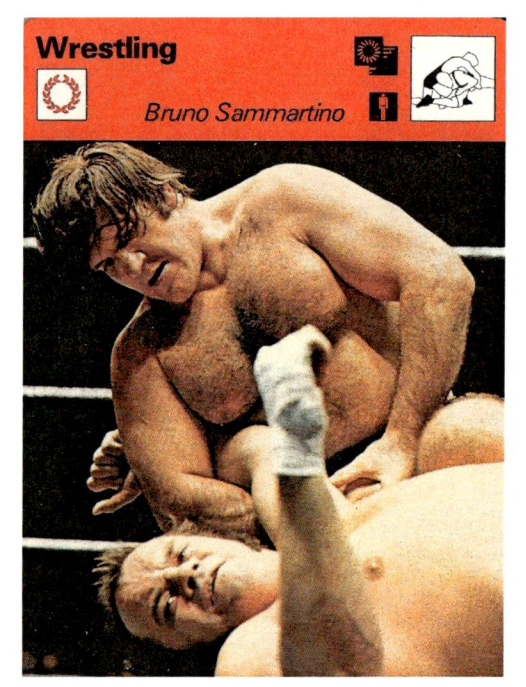

Bruno with an armbar on Stan "The Man" Stasiak

Bruno loved pumping iron

THE AUTOBIOGRAPHY OF WRESTLING'S LIVING LEGEND

Catching up with Ivan Koloff

Deep in conversation with Harley Race

Bruno and his mother Emilia

*Bruno always looked like a Champion
inside and outside the ring*

THE AUTOBIOGRAPHY OF WRESTLING'S LIVING LEGEND

Bruno with Leslie Nielsen in Massachusetts

THE AUTOBIOGRAPHY OF WRESTLING'S LIVING LEGEND

Bruno with one of his fans, Walter Rodriguez

BRUNO SAMMARTINO

THE AUTOBIOGRAPHY OF WRESTLING'S LIVING LEGEND

*Bruno on stage at WrestleReunion addressing
the crowd with Bill Apter moderating*

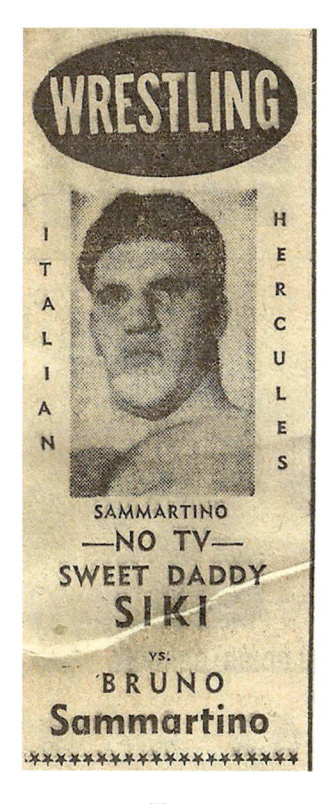

Two newspaper ads from Bruno's career

Stan Hansen, Ron Simmons, Nikolai Volkoff, Bruno, Jerry Brisco.

Afa, Bruno, and Rocky Johnson

THE AUTOBIOGRAPHY OF WRESTLING'S LIVING LEGEND

Bruno was inducted into the International Sports Hall of Fame in March 2013 by Arnold Schwarzenegger. The event is held annually as part of the Arnold Sports Festival in Columbus, OH. Arnold was inducted in 2012

Bruno flanked by International Federation of BodyBuilders co-founder Joe Weider (L) and Sergio "The Myth" Oliva who held the Mr. Olympia title from 1967-1969

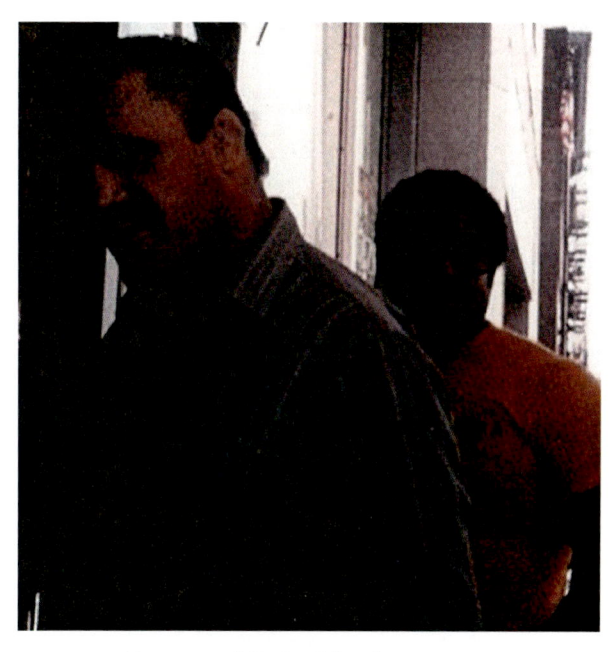

THE AUTOBIOGRAPHY OF WRESTLING'S LIVING LEGEND

*Bruno and Pedro Morales entering
a NY diner during the '70s*

*Another monster crowd gathering for a Bruno
match at Madison Square Garden*

Friends and partners through the years.

Dominic DeNucci, Christopher Cruise, and Bruno

THE AUTOBIOGRAPHY OF WRESTLING'S LIVING LEGEND

Bruno's WWE Hall of Fame ring

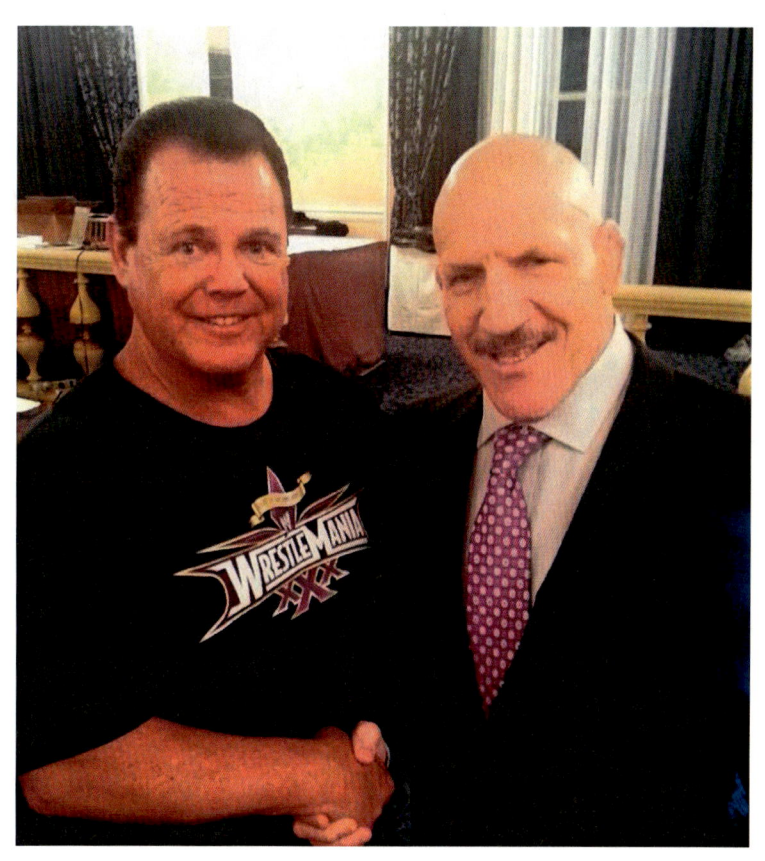

Jerry "The King" Lawler greets "The Living Legend"

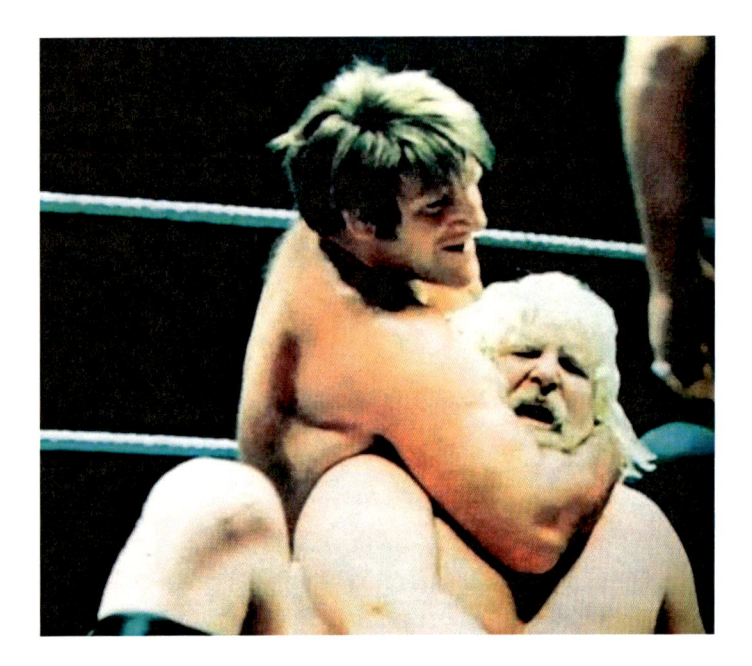

One of Bruno's most famous feuds was against Stan Hansen

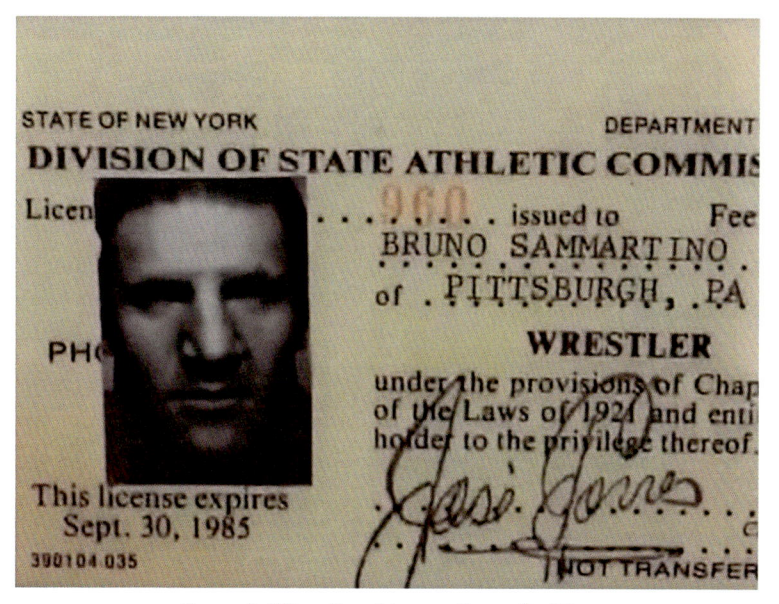

THE AUTOBIOGRAPHY OF WRESTLING'S LIVING LEGEND

Bruno's Wrestling License from the New York State Athletic Commission

Bruno with Rob Russen who was the owner of IWA Championship Wrestling. He also helped Sal Corrente start WrestleReunion

A typical scene from Bruno's life, signing autographs at an airport

George "The Animal" Steele with Bruno

THE AUTOBIOGRAPHY OF WRESTLING'S LIVING LEGEND

Bruno's caricature on the wall of Primanti Brothers in Pittsburgh. Bruno signed it in 1993

Bruno with Scott Schwartz from A Christmas Story (Flick) and The Toy (Eric Bates)

Bruno at Deaf Wrestlefest 2012

Bruno with Bob Cassin at the WrestleReunion autograph signing held in Atlanta during Wrestlemania weekend April 3rd, 2011. Bob traveled from Charlestown, MA for the event

When I retired, I chose Ivan Koloff as the man to pass the championship belt to. Vince McMahon, Sr. then chose Pedro Morales to carry the mantle until I agreed to return to the company. I considered both men my friends

Ted DiBiase, Nikolai Volkoff, Sgt. Slaughter, Bruno, Bob Backlund, Stan Hansen, Jim Duggan, Ricky Steamboat

Sculpting Bruno's WWE Hall of Fame statue

Bruno's workout regimen

Mike Migut with Bruno and Larry

Arnold Schwarzegger, Franco Columbu, Matt Ferrigno, Bruno, and Lou Ferrigno

Whenever he went out, The Champ was always the center of attention

THE AUTOBIOGRAPHY OF WRESTLING'S LIVING LEGEND

Championship belt is displayed by Bruno Sammartino. In 20 years of wrestling his nose has been broken 11 times. "When I bleed, it's my blood," he says.

the voice

The Extraordinary Life of a Pittsburgh Living Legend

JAY BATCH
THE VOICE STAFF

For 4,040 days he was the world heavyweight champion in wrestling – a time that spanned 11 years. This month, he is coming to CCAC.

He was one of the highest paid athletes in the 1960s with the likes of baseball greats Willie Mays, and Mickey Mantle.

Nicknamed the "Living Legend" Bruno Sammartino plans on making a visit to CCAC in April.

Sammartino's illustrious career as a professional wrestler began in Pittsburgh. But before that, in the midst of World War II, Sammartino and his family would be tested like no other.

He was just a young boy in 1937, when Nazis took over his village in Italy.

Bruno Sammartino and his family hid in Valla Rocca, a mountain that sheltered them from the brutalities of the German soldiers.

Unsure of what the future would hold, young Bruno held onto the little hope he had and the courage that would ultimately define his legacy.

In 1950 at the age of 15, with the dangers of World War II behind him, Sammartino and his family immigrated to Pittsburgh, where his father had been living for several years.

Not speaking any English and weighing just 84 pounds Sammartino quickly became a subject to bullying in school. Sammartino attended Schenley High School but trained at Pitt as Schenley did not have a wrestling team.

Sammartino used his altercations with the bullies as motivation to work on his physique. The hard work paid off.

An opportunity in 1956 with the United States Olympic Wrestling Team presented itself for the once feeble Sammartino. But Paul Anderson, who was nearly 70 pounds heavier than Sammartino, would get the nod.

Getting beat out by Anderson did not deter Sammartino, as he would continue to work on his craft.

Showing everyone that not getting on the Olympic team was a mere bump in the road. Sammartino in his first professional match would go into pin his first opponent in 19 seconds.

The boy who once spoke barely any English and weighed just eighty-four pounds was now 265 pounds standing at 5' 10".

Sammartino set a then world record in 1959, by bench pressing 565 pounds is just one of the many accolades in his storied career.

He was inducted into the WWE Hall of Fame on April 6, 2013, by his longtime friend, Arnold Schwarzenegger.

Sammartino is the subject of a two-part class being offered at CCAC North. The Extraordinary Life of Pittsburgh's Living Legend – Bruno Sammartino will be held at CCAC North Campus on April 19 and 26 from 6:30 p.m. to 9:30 p.m.

Students will have an awesome opportunity not only to learn more about Bruno Sammartino, but also the chance to meet him.

THE AUTOBIOGRAPHY OF WRESTLING'S LIVING LEGEND

Bruno was the subject of a college class: The Extraordinary Life of Pittsburgh's Living Legend - Bruno Sammartino taught by Christopher Cruise. Here is Ken "Lord Zoltan" Jugan with Dominic DeNucci and Bruno during his appearance at the Community College of Allegheny County

Bruno's Final Private Signing

Freddy Pampillonia with Bruno, and Jeff Hestnes, both partners in Fan City Sports

There are times in one's life when an opportunity is presented to you. It is what you do with that opportunity that defines you. My name is Neil Castellano and I had the privilege of not only meeting Bruno Sammartino, but experience a private signing with him in his hometown of Pittsburgh, PA.

I was invited with my son Valentine by a company called Fan City Sports—which is run by Jeff Hestnes and Freddy Pampillonia—to attend this event. Bruno's longtime friend Sal, and son Daniel were also there. You see the anticipation of meeting Bruno in a casual setting with good friends and family is a once in a lifetime event. Bruno was and will always be considered a legend. To any fan of wrestling there was nobody of a higher level. I grew up admiring wrestling and the legacy Bruno created.

Bruno arrived in great spirits and spent a nice amount of time with us. Bruno still shook hands with a strong grip, that grip he used numerous times to grapple over the years. He astonished us by

THE AUTOBIOGRAPHY OF WRESTLING'S LIVING LEGEND

Bruno is #1

Some of the unique items that Bruno signed that day included these custom made ring robes

One of Bruno's original championship belts

*Bruno's action figures were always a popular
item for the fans to have signed*

bringing in his original belt and allowing us to take pictures with him and that prestigious award. He spent that time to get to know us and share many stories of his wrestling years.

Freddie who is of Italian descent spoke with Bruno about his heritage and shared their native tongue. Jeff brought in some unique items that Bruno was proud to sign, and even signed one item with his full given birth name. My son Valentine could only sit in awe knowing he was in the presence of a hero to us all. I can't thank Sal and Daniel enough for that special day. I am glad we have plenty of videos and pictures to remember it, but who needs those. This was day that will be indelibly etched in our minds and hearts for the rest of our lives.

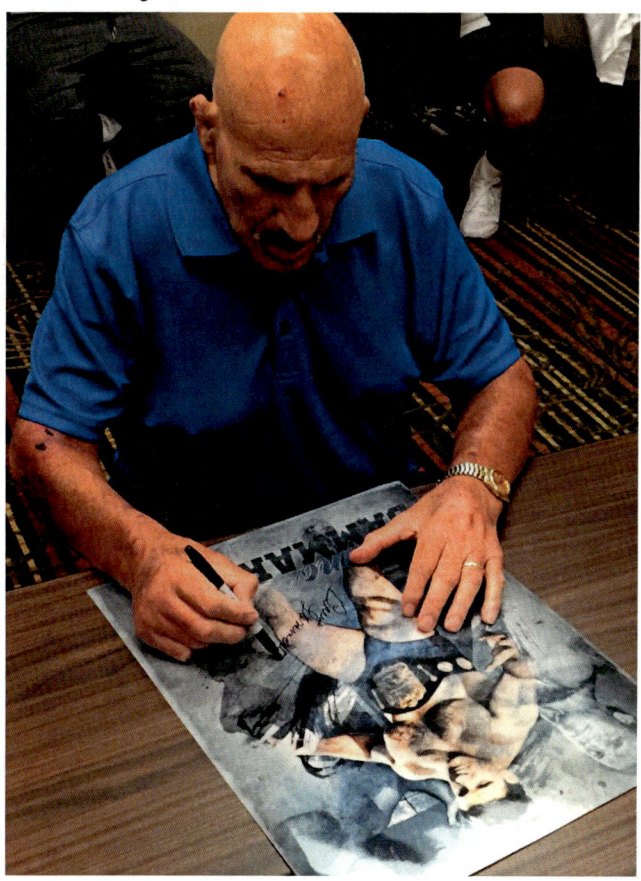

It was an unforgettable day for those who were present

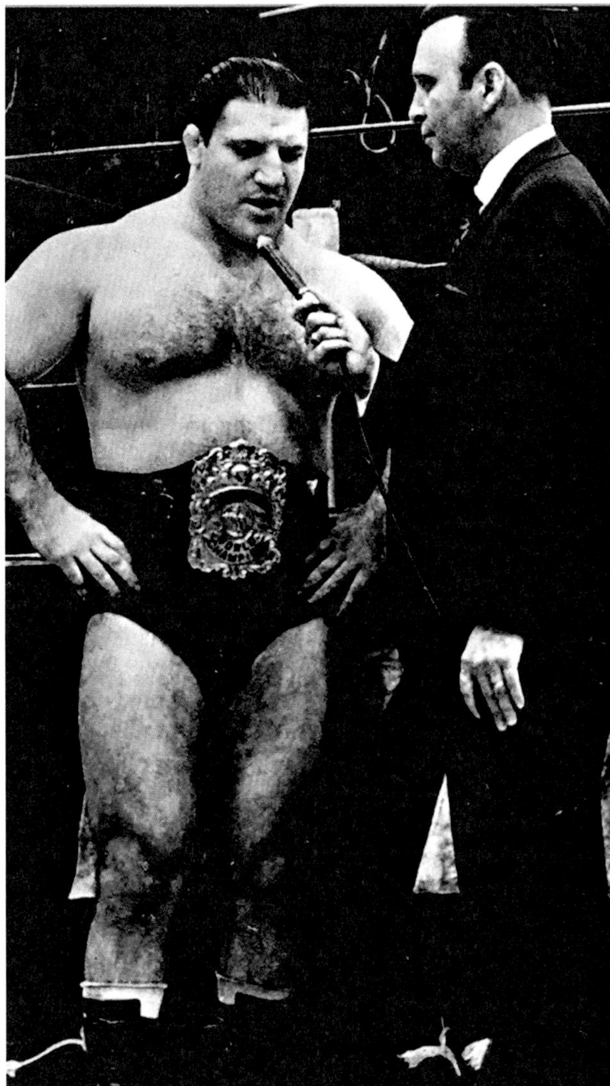

Retirement ... Again

I had always hoped that in my retirement that I could just spend time with my wife Carol, my children, and grandchildren. I had traveled the world for my entire career many times to make appearances whether I wanted to or not. I had my time in the sun and was hoping to just fade away quietly, but that didn't happen. I was constantly, and still until this day, even though I am officially retired from making any appearances outside of the Pittsburgh city limits, having offers presented to me either via personal contact or them contacting my representative Sal Corrente, or other personal friends.

I found myself making many appearances after I had my last match, sometimes at autograph events, and other times at wrestling conventions. I was working for a call-in telephone service that was hosted by Blackjack Brown who ended up introducing me to Sal Corrente. He was a referee who traveled to different areas to work events. At some point Sal was contacted by Joel Goodhart, a promoter that he worked with, to ask if he could convince me to make an appearance at one of his events. While at first I didn't want to do it, I was finally convinced to appear. It would be my first-time meeting Sal face to face. I was asked to be in the corner of my son David as he faced my "archenemy" Larry Zbyszko for the AWA World Championship, who was managed by a young Paul E. Dangerously, better known today by his real name of Paul Heyman.

One of the things that I didn't like about attending live wrestling events was that it was a regular occurrence that at the very least I was asked to hit someone, if not beat them up. I had no interest in that. It wasn't that I didn't want to be cooperative, I just didn't think that it made sense for a retired wrestler in his '60s to be getting the best of young guys that were being competitive in the business today. Somehow the wrestlers or managers felt that getting "hit" by me was something that they just had to do. I did go along with it for a long time, but eventually put a stop to it.

I enjoyed my time at home and went on the road as little as possible, trying to never travel outside of the Pittsburgh area during the wintertime. I didn't want the hassle of traveling in inclement weather that I had to tolerate for so many years. I was lucky to have time, and the financial resources to go back to Italy and take some cruises with Carol.

With WrestleReunion Partner Anthony Attanasio

In mid-2004 Sal Corrente called me about a wrestling event he was going to produce, along with his partner Anthony Attanasio. The event was going to take place in Tampa, Florida and was called WrestleReunion. He wanted me to be a part of it in the January of 2005. While I didn't travel in the winter, I made an exception for Sal because we had become close friends and associates by this time. The event featured 95 wrestlers and had live wrestling matches featuring legends of wrestling, some current stars, and future standouts. There had been wrestling conventions prior to this, but nothing of this magnitude, with the highlight being the live wrestling matches with the legends. I attended the event, and luckily there were no weather issues. I saw many guys that I hadn't seen in several years.

Sometime after this event, Sal called me with an idea for the next WrestleReunion. It was going to be 25 years since my big Shea Stadium match with Larry Zbyszko. He wanted the theme to be a tribute to that day in 1980, with Larry Zbyszko challenging me to a match. Of course, Sal knew that I wouldn't wrestle Zbyszko, but I did agree to participate, and potentially have a physical altercation

At the first WrestleReunion

with Zbyszko at some point. It was suggested that Bob Backlund would step up and take on the Zbyszko challenge since Zbyszko got a victory over Backlund in Madison Square Garden many years ago and he never got a rematch. While I don't know the reason why, and I never mentioned it to Bob myself, I was told that he refused the spot. Sal went to Diamond Dallas Page, who was a fan of mine while growing up. I would be in the corner of Diamond Dallas Page and If Zbyszko won the match he would get "5 minutes" with me. In Zbyszko's corner Sal booked Ivan Koloff the man who took the title from me in Madison Square Garden in 1971. The event was held in Valley Forge, PA and Diamond Dallas Page hit Zbyszko with his finishing move The Diamond Cutter. While Zbyszko was "out in the middle of the ring" Diamond Dallas Page laid down and pulled him on top of him so that I would have my 5 minutes with Zbyszko. It was the first time in years that I participated in an actual altercation in the ring, and while the crowd responded wildly, it only lasted a brief time, and it would be my final in-ring confrontation, beyond a one punch situation.

I was often asked to participate in some sort of in-ring encounter and I did my best to avoid it. I asked Sal Corrente when negotiating an appearance on my behalf, to stress that I didn't have any interest in that. It's not that I didn't want to cooperate with the promoter, it's just that as I got older, and my time was over, I wanted to help elevate

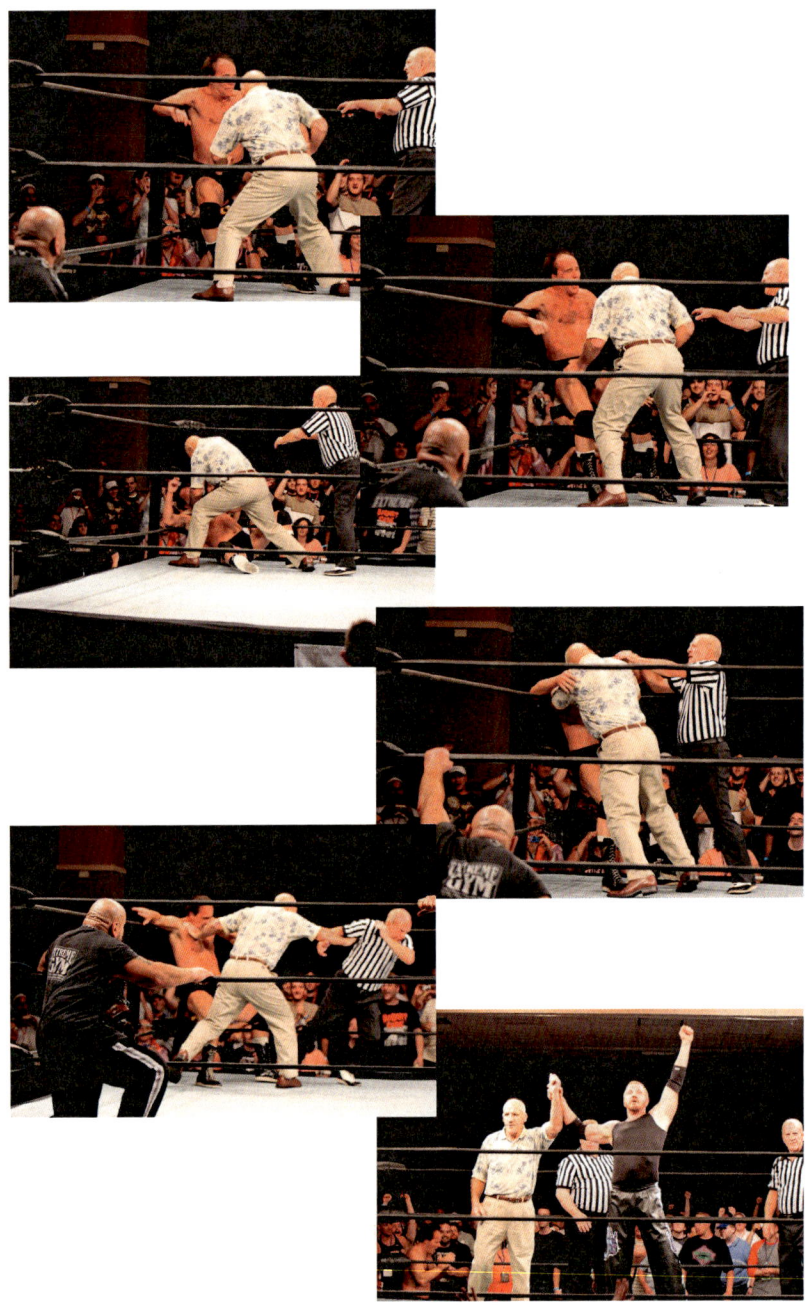

*WrestleReunion 2—DDP vs. Zbyszko got me
5 minutes with Larry in the ring*

the current talent, not have a man like myself, well past his prime knocking guys around. I would even be asked to hit managers and they would take a big bump for me, but I didn't like that. I didn't see how it helped the talent or the promotion.

At some point, a deal was negotiated and agreed to with an independent promotion, for strictly an appearance/autograph signing, but regardless of what was decided ahead of time, I was asked to get in a confrontation with someone. I didn't want to do it, but I went along so I didn't create a problem. At that point, I decided that it was over, and I would no longer allow myself to be talked in to these situations that I didn't believe in. If a promotion wanted me to appear it would be to sign autographs and maybe say a few words to the audience, but other than that I had no interest, and wasn't going to do it.

In 2010, Sal Corrente started WrestleReunion back up again in Los Angeles with the assistance of Michael Bochicchio from Highspots.com. By this time, I had stopped traveling to the West Coast, and certainly didn't travel anywhere in January, but because I had been working with Sal Corrente for so long, and it was so important to him, I decided that I would head to the West Coast one more time for a convention appearance.

In 1990, I was contacted by a man, Herb Abrams, who was going to start a new wrestling company. He told me that he was a huge fan of mine and wanted to bring wrestling back to what it used to be. He asked if I would be a color commentator for his company. Based on what he told me, I agreed. I stayed with the UWF for the better part of two years, but the things that I saw made it clear that what Herb Abrams had originally told me wasn't going to be supported. So when I realized it was the same old thing, and that I wasn't happy with the product of the day, I turned in my notice and went back to staying home, which I greatly enjoyed.

The saddest and most traumatic time of my life was when the end was drawing near for my mother, Emilia Sammartino. The end of her life occurred on May 4th, 1995. Whatever I have achieved in my life, the accolades of the fans, awards, money, and recognition, none of it would have been possible, or even attempted without her heroic efforts, and how she protected me and my siblings during the war. I went to visit my mother every day that she was in town, helping her in any way that she needed, and just visiting with her. By 1995, my father had been gone almost 10 years. I certainly loved my father, but due to all the challenges my family had when I was young, I didn't get to know him until I was about 15 years old. When I would sit and think about all that had happened to me as a young boy, and what my mother went through to fight for my survival I was in awe. While Italy was occupied, she not only worked in the fields from morning until night, but through her heroics, she kept us safe while we had to hide from the Nazis.

My mother never learned to speak English, so when she was in the hospital at the end of her life she felt uncomfortable. I would stay with her as often as possible. I know many of the fans saw me as a strong man who was never afraid of a battle, but the loss of my mother was a battle that I never wanted to face. I was brought to tears, many tears and it was a loss that felt insurmountable to me. When we had the service for my mother, I stayed in the cemetery with the casket alone for a while. I would go to the cemetery on a weekly basis until 2015.

The unveiling ceremony in Pizzoferrato

THE AUTOBIOGRAPHY OF WRESTLING'S LIVING LEGEND

My giant statue in Pizzoferrato

The love, respect, and admiration that I have for my mother will live on in my heart forever, and I am grateful in a way that I can never repay for everything that she did for me, and the never wavering love that she showed me throughout my entire life.

In 2000, I was honored in my hometown. They erected a statue, and built a recreation center for youth sports that bore my name. I was able to return home to Pizzoferrato for the ceremony. At the time, I was very happy to make the trip to Italy. Previously, I had taken many trips to Italy with my wife Carol, but at a certain point, travel became very unappealing to me, and so we had made what we considered one final trip to Italy.

In 2017, I received a call from the Mayor of Pizzoferrato telling me that people who came to see my statue were unhappy because the statue was an abstract piece of art, and the likeness was disappointing to them. He told me that they had commissioned a new statue and would be naming a hospital after my mother. It was very important to the Mayor and the town that I return to Italy for the ceremony. At this point in my life, I would have made the decision not to return to Italy, but because they were naming the hospital for my mother I agreed to return for the ceremony, with my wife, and my son Darryl. It was the last time that I would return to Italy, but I am glad that I made the decision to attend the ceremony, or I would have regretted

I was thrilled to receive the Lifetime Achievement Award from the Dapper Dan Society

it the rest of my life.

It was an incredible honor to be recognized by my childhood home in South Oakland, PA along with Dan Marino and Andy Warhol

    I have had the pleasure of being honored many times over the years, but recently I was honored to be placed on a plaque alongside Hall of Fame Quarterback Dan Marino, and Andy Warhol the famous artist on May 3rd, 2016. We all grew up in the same neighborhood ... South Oakland. I have known Dan Marino his whole life, his father being a friend of mine while we were growing up. It was great seeing him again and being recognized on the plaque with Dan and Andy.
    On March 25th, 2010, I was given the Lifetime Achievement

BRUNO SAMMARTINO

*Headlining the 74th Annual Dapper
Dan Dinner & Sports Auction*

Award by the Dapper Dan Society. It is a very prestigious organization that was founded in 1936. I considered it a great honor to be a part of the organization. They raise money annually for the Boys and Girls Club of Western Pennsylvania. In the past, this award has been given to men like Arnold Palmer, Stan Musial, Dan Marino, and Franco Harris, just to name a few.

One day, Sal Corrente had been contacted by the WWE. I don't remember who it was, but it was likely Mark Carrano. He asked for my number, telling Sal that Paul Levesque, more commonly known as Triple H wanted to talk to me. Of course, Sal didn't give them the number, but called me immediately to deliver the message. I initially told him to find out what they wanted, I wasn't inclined to speak to the WWE. When Sal called back they wouldn't divulge what they wanted other than that it was a business matter. After some discussion with Sal and some thought, I decided that I would talk to Triple H.

Once we got in to a discussion, he let me know that the WWE wanted to induct me in to the Hall of Fame. The ceremony would be in MSG. Now most people in the business know that Triple H was trained by one of my greatest opponents, and longtime friend, Killer Kowalski. He had a tremendous respect for me and for the old school business. Of course, the disagreements that I have had with WWE were pretty much with Vince McMahon, Sr. from the past, and Vince McMahon, Jr. after he took over the company from his father.

Bruno with Westchester County Clerk Leonard Spano and Assemblyman Mike Spano (Current Yonkers Mayor) at Giulio's Restaurant in Yonkers NY in the late 1990's

In speaking with Triple H, he was committed to the task of

407

getting me to agree to the induction into the Hall of Fame. There was so much to consider, and my feelings about the company and its direction had to be addressed. In explaining to me the direction of the company, I listened to Triple H explain the more PG rated direction that the company had taken. I also consulted with my friend Dr. Joseph Maroon, who has been a physician of mine for many years. He is the main physician for the WWE, and has a good understanding of where the company was these days. He supported the things that Paul Levesque had told me. I truly believe that when Vince McMahon started the Hall of Fame, and the fact that we had no relationship, that he felt he could have the inductions without me, and it would look bad for me. However, it never worked out that way. The WWE was constantly asked how there could be a Hall of Fame without Bruno Sammartino in it. I was asked as well, but all I could say was I was never asked. For many years, other former World Champions hadn't been inducted, such as Bob Backlund and Ivan Koloff. At this point, Bob Backlund is in, but Ivan Koloff, the man that beat me for the World Championship is not.

That's bodybuilder turned actor Arnold Schwarzenegger on my left

While I was happy to hear what Paul and my trusted friend Dr. Maroon were saying, along with me watching Monday Night Raw ... which I almost never did, to confirm for myself, there were still many things that had to be discussed. I had many issues over the years where I felt that I hadn't been treated fairly, that deals made hadn't been honored. I wanted to be sure to tell my side of the story to Paul Levesque, since some of these things happened before he was born, or he would have been a young child. He hadn't had his first match before I had my last match. I'm sure that Paul would have rather not had to go through all of that, but these things were important to me.

THE AUTOBIOGRAPHY OF WRESTLING'S LIVING LEGEND

There was a lot of back and forth discussion, this wasn't a quick process, or a simple one, but in time it looked like we were going to be able to come to an agreement. There were things to consider also, such as if I didn't agree to the induction, then one day when I was no longer here the WWE could induct me anyway. I am not sure how the fans would have reacted to a forced induction, but there were just as many fans who wanted me to accept the induction as there were that wanted me to never accept a spot in the Hall of Fame. There was no way to please everyone.

I had something else to consider as well. Since there was no idea whatsoever that WWE would contact me or that I would consider an induction in to the Hall of Fame, I had agreed to make an appearance at WrestleCon for Sal Corrente. When Sal decided to discontinue WrestleReunion, his partner Michael Bochicchio continued with a new name and concept that Sal and he discussed. Instead of running Royal Rumble weekend he ended up doing it Wrestlemania weekend in the same area as Wrestlemania. I explained my situation to Paul Levesque and made sure that he understood my relationship with Sal and that I couldn't leave him stuck, especially since my appearance

Donald Trump, Arnold Schwarzenegger, me, Paul Levesque

had already been announced. I discussed being able to do Sal's event while still being in the Hall of Fame. While this type of thing has happened before, Paul Levesque explained that in my case they had a full schedule for me and couldn't spare the time. What Paul Levesque offered was to work with Sal on a replacement from the company under terms that would be acceptable to Sal. With that situation being addressed, I explained it to Sal, and true to his word Paul

With Lou Ferrigno (The Incredible Hulk) and my best friend and lawyer, Marty Lazzaro

Levesque sent William Regal at Sal's request and everything worked out for everyone.

I was inducted in to the Hall of Fame on April 6th, 2013 at Madison Square Garden, along with Booker T, Bob Backlund, Mick Foley, Trish Stratus, and inducted in to the Celebrity Wing of the Hall of Fame, our now 45th President of the United States, Donald J. Trump. I never thought that the day would come where I would have been inducted in to the WWE Hall of Fame, but if it was going to happen, Madison Square Garden was the place where it should have happened. I won the WWWF Championship in Madison

Square Garden from Buddy Rogers on May 17th, 1963. I lost the championship there to Ivan Koloff on January 18th, 1971, and regained the title there from Stan "The Man" Stasiak on December 10th, 1973. I was also already a member of the Madison Square Garden Walk of Fame since March 24th, 2007. The only other place that would have really been special to me, was my lifetime home of Pittsburgh, PA

I was inducted in to the Hall of Fame by my longtime friend Arnold Schwarzenegger. Once he heard that I was being inducted he requested that he be allowed to induct me, and was very gracious in changing his schedule to accommodate the event.

When I had retired, I really believed that I would walk away from the wrestling business and live a peaceful quiet life with my wife Carol, my parents, and my children. While I certainly got to spend more time with my family than I had previously, I never actually got away from the wrestling business. I never understood how, and why I hadn't been forgotten. Of course, things had changed since my championship reigns. The business had expanded, a Hall of Fame had been created, and there were many video options for people to see me. It all lead to me appearing one more time in Madison Square Garden as a headliner. It was one more sellout, but this time it was for the last time for sure. It was a great evening, and when it was over,

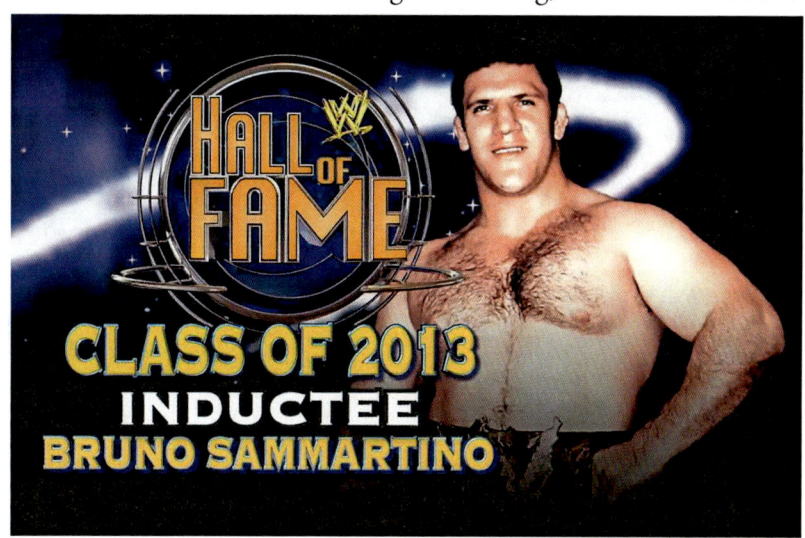

Donald Trump came back to see me to tell me that he would have normally already left, but he wanted to stay for my induction. It was humbling to know that he stayed all night with his children to hear my speech.

I knew my decision to enter the Hall of Fame would be embraced by many, and seen as a cop out by others, but I stayed out of the Hall for reasons of my own, and I accepted the induction when I felt that Paul

My own action figure

Levesque had addressed my concerns. By that point, I was comfortable not only accepting the induction, but once again being associated with the WWE, the company that had evolved from the WWWF. I was very comfortable with the choices that I had made previously,

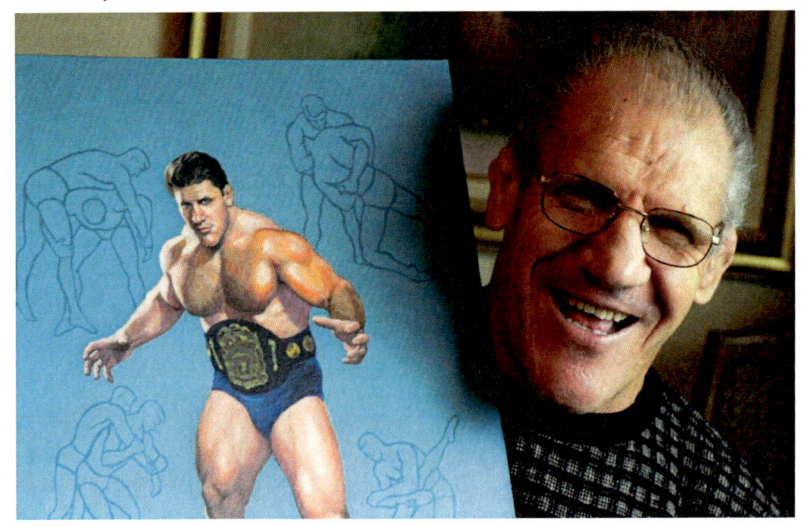

and comfortable that I made the right choice when I accepted the induction.

I had promised Sal that I would do one more appearance wherever he wanted us to do it. While neither of us were in any hurry

THE AUTOBIOGRAPHY OF WRESTLING'S LIVING LEGEND

to do it, we were thinking about doing it with the rewrite of the book. We had a few offers and opportunities but we never did it. At some point, Sal was contacted several times by Tom Unger. He runs a convention called The Big Event that runs out of Queens, NY twice a year, we did it one other time previously but Sal still turned it down.

After a few more calls Sal accepted and we decided that it would be my last appearance on November 16th 2016 outside of Pittsburgh. I went to NY for the weekend with my son Darryl. I was pleased that we had a great turnout and that closed out my appearances outside of my home area. I did agree to consider Wrestlemania every year for the WWE, and I was happy to make the appearances and fulfill the schedule they had for me there. I didn't like the travel, but the WWE treated me right, and made it comfortable for me to travel.

At some point during all this, Sal approached me about rewriting my autobiography. He had gotten feedback from fans many times that he felt should be addressed. It had been originally put together in the very late '80s and at that time I took the same approach with the book as I had in my career, to completely protect the veil of secrecy that had always covered the wrestling business. At a certain point, I realize that any attempt I was making to "protect the business" was strictly an exercise in futility.

I finally agreed that it was time to let Sal rewrite the book with more of the reality behind the stories, and not treat professional wrestling as an actual competition. In reality, my match with Buddy Rogers could have been considered a competition because no matter what Rogers thought going in to the ring, when we met in the middle I told him to do his best because I would be doing my best. I don't know if he thought that I was serious at the time or not, but when I told him to give up or I would break his back he gave up.

Most of the stories had been told to Sal so many times over the years he could dictate them from memory. I had heard the feedback over the years that the book wasn't written from an honest perspective, and that people wanted to hear the real backstage stories. I hope that people feel they are getting that now.

Well, that's my story. I did get to live the American Dream and found out, that just as I imagined as a kid, the streets in America really are paved in gold.

Donald Trump stayed for my induction

BRUNO SAMMARTINO
"WRESTLING'S LIVING LEGEND"

Bruno Sammartino

October 6, 1938 to April 18, 2018

Tributes

Bill Apter, former Senior Editor of The Wrestler, Inside Wrestling, and Pro Wrestling Illustrated, fondly known to the fans as "The Apter Mags"

Man. Icon. Legend. Friend.

"Bruno Sammartino did not just die. An entire era perished along with him." ~ ***Bill Apter*** April 18, 2018.

On the morning of April 18th 2018 I received a telephone call from my dear friend Sal Corrente. His words changed my life forever. He told me that my dear friend and the most iconic wrestler of all time—Bruno Sammartino had died. The shock of that day will never wear off."

The echoes of 22,000 fans chanting "Bruno, Bruno, Bruno!" I can still hear them flowing through my mind as I write this tribute just a few days after I was told that the iconic Bruno Sammartino had died. It just could not be. Bruno was always going to be here forever.

I have written so much about him through the years. I've taken thousands of images as well. My early career chronicled so much of his career in magazines as well as on my radio show. We were tied together that way. He did—and I wrote and shot pictures of what he did.

A few first time ever written disjointed thoughts ...

The first time I met him face-to-face in the late '60s I did a radio show out of New York City and had gotten a press pass to see him in a small arena in Queens, New York—Sunnyside Garden. Armed with a camera and a cassette tape recorder (Google it kids) I interviewed him for 10 minutes. The show I was doing was called "Billy's Place" and I did celebrity interviews. I had a few wrestling questions to hit him with as I was a follower but toward the end of the chat I became brave and said, "I've seen you against many opponents. You beat them all. I think I can take you!" He paused for a moment and snapped, "You can take me where—to the movies, or dinner?" Great answer. Then I asked him that taboo question every reporter from that era asked, "Is wrestling fixed?" (I had no idea that would be the title of a book I would pen ages later) He said, "If it is I wish someone would tell me!" He then went onto show me all the parts of his anatomy that were broken, cracked, sewn up, and convinced me beyond a doubt what he was doing in that ring was not "fixed."

My telephone rings very late one night. Bruno had gotten a copy of one of the stories written about him by editor/writer David Rosenbaum.

"Who is this guy," he wanted to know. He was upset because there were comments attributed to coming out of his mouth yet he says he never told anyone those words. I asked him to give a few minutes and I'd call him back. I got my copy of the story and the quotes flowed well with the context of the story about a feud Bruno was involved with some bad guy wrestler. I called Bruno back and said I thought he would have said what was written.

"Sure it goes along with my feud with this guy but I never said what is written," he emphasized. Let me explain here that most wrestlers gave us license to do that as long as the quotes stayed in character and were true to the story. Not Bruno.

"I always appreciated the reporter who would call me and ask the questions and let me answer," he pointed out. From that day on in the magazines the rule was "no Bruno quotes unless he is talked to about what we need and then let him say it." He was the only wrestler who we made this special rule for.

So many more stories. I could fill every page in this book five times over with Bruno stories. Those few have not been written about before and this is the right place for them to be documented.

We know by now Bruno Sammartino was a gentleman, an excellent wrestler, and was the "Babe Ruth" of professional wrestling.

More than that he did something for me personally. He endorsed me to the other wrestlers in the WWWF. Without that endorsement my career could have had a very short span. Bruno trusted me and I never broke his trust which is why we remained so close—even without speaking or seeing each other over the past year.

Bruno Sammartino will be a part of my life forever. He still lives. He is "The Living Legend"—there is no one else who will ever occupy that space.

Bill Apter

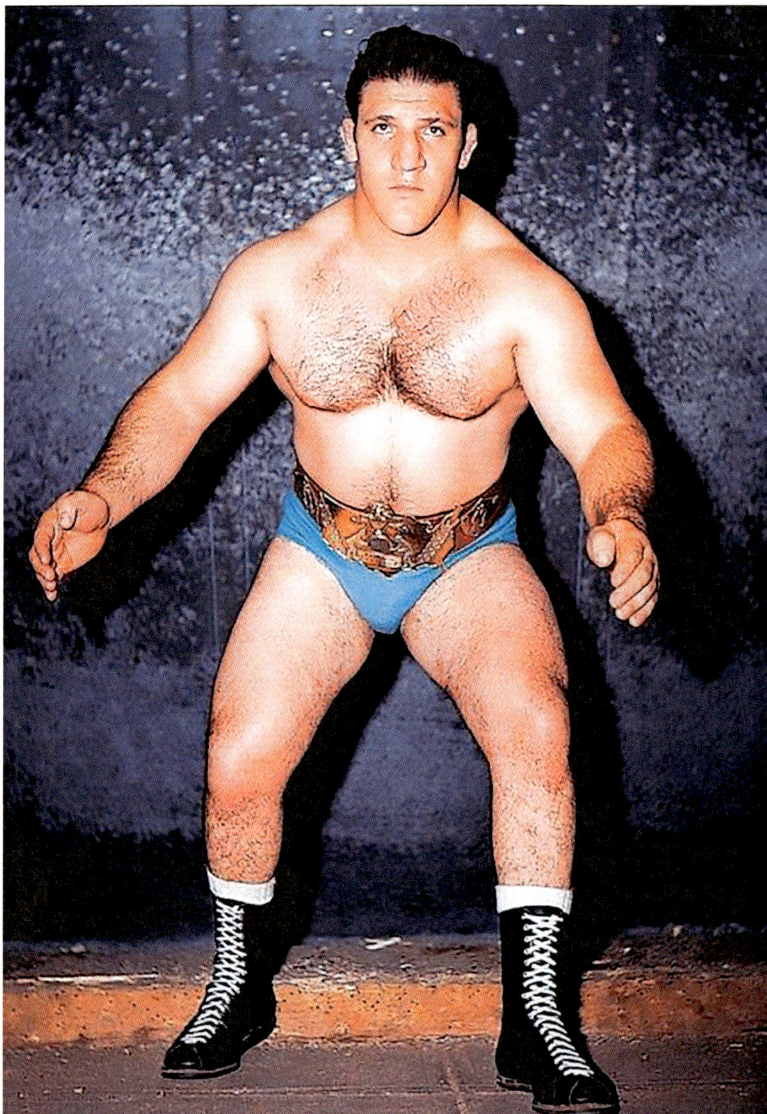

Sal Corrente

On the morning of April 18th 2018 I was out getting coffee and making a business call. I was working out of Yonkers, NY when I saw a call come in from Blackjack Brown, the man that is responsible for starting my relationship with Bruno. At some point we lost contact and a gentleman that promoted wrestling for many years on the Indy circuit got me back in touch with Bruno, his name was Bob Raskin out of New Jersey. I hear from Blackjack Brown via phone rarely and it was an odd time for him to be calling, so I switched over to inquire if he had something urgent or could I call him back. He said "Is it true?" I said "is what true?" He said "Did Bruno die?" I said "I don't know, but if he heard that, it was likely true and that I would verify." I texted Bruno's son Darryl who confirmed that his dad had passed away a little while ago. At that point I was being told something that I hadn't considered an option, the man was gone. Bruno Sammartino, who to many including myself, seemed invincible, after almost 83 years had finally lost a battle. The rheumatic fever he overcame as a child was ultimately the cause of his death.

I immediately called Bill Apter and told him. He was as stunned as I was. I didn't have many answers for him other than Bruno was gone. I next called long time Bruno friend James Morrison known to the world as J.J. Dillon, the leader of The Four Horsemen. He was as stunned as Bill and I. He was going to call Davey O'Hannon a wrestler who had worked many of the territories over a 20-plus year career. He had also become very close to Bruno. I sent a text to David Isley who communicated regularly with Stan Hansen and told him to let Stan know that Bruno was gone. I also spoke to Paul Schaller who happened to text me and had gotten to meet Bruno in 2005, he of course couldn't believe it either.

I did receive a call from Mike Johnson with PWInsider, of course I knew why he was calling. I did confirm for him that Bruno had passed away. Of course, at that point, just like Mike and Bill, all wrestling journalists would have to get writing.

It was later in the day that I heard from Stan Hansen by phone and J.J. Dillon and I started to plan our trip to Pittsburgh with Davey O'Hannon. I can tell you that neither J.J. nor I like attending wakes or funerals, but there was no way that we wouldn't make this trip to Pittsburgh, to pay our respects to a man that had meant so much to all three of us.

When J.J. Dillon started in the business he was a referee and he had gotten help in his career from Bruno Sammartino who obviously recognized the talent and commitment of J.J. to our business. It was many years before I realized that likely the opportunities given to me by J.J. Dillon, were in some ways him paying back the kindness that Bruno had shown to him in his early days.

On Friday April 20th 2018, I started out on the road to the hotel where I would meet Davey and J.J. and I would spend the night there. We would head to Pittsburgh in the morning. It was agreed that Davey would drive. It was ironic that I really didn't know Davey, but he was one of the wrestlers on the card for the first real show that I was to referee. The previous show barely counted and I only did one match. In a real stroke of irony, Larry Zbyszko was the main event that night. Three of us in that building, two of us already had a strong relationship with Bruno Sammartino and my future still unknown to me. It was a long drive, but there were so many stories to tell that time passed quickly as we shared our memories of Bruno, our individual relationships with him, and what he meant to us and our industry.

We arrived in town and went over to the wake. When we arrived we saw Dominic DeNucci former tag team partner and longtime friend of Bruno Sammartino outside the funeral home doing an interview with the local CBS affiliate. We went inside and waited in line to say our goodbyes to Bruno. The room had friends, family, and fans waiting to pay their respects. We saw Mike "Virgil "Jones who lives in Pittsburgh, also Johnny DeFazio who wrestled for many years in the WWWF and was a part of the Studio Wrestling company that Bruno owned for about six years. It was a surreal moment for me since I had never considered a world without Bruno Sammartino in it. I know that it was hard for J.J and Davey as well to see Bruno there, but although he had been ill for a few months, he looked just as I had seen him the last time. We spoke to his wife Carol and his sons Danny and Darryl. It was Danny who shared how things had been at the end. He said that the last good meal that his dad had, Danny had made turkey legs and they each had a turkey leg and glass of beer. That was on Easter Sunday April 1st 2018.

J.J. Dillon, Davey O'Hannon and Sal Corrente at Bruno's favorite Restaurant Rico's having a tribute dinner to our friend and co worker The Living Legend Bruno Sammartino

I had told Davey that I wanted us to go eat at Rico's, a restaurant Bruno and his wife Carol would frequent. We would return to the funeral home after dinner. I had been there with Bruno once before I ordered gluten free pasta, but Bruno had wanted me to have a steak or pork chops. He mentioned it so many times that night, I felt like I owed it to him to go back at some point and have that steak. We got to the restaurant where I immediately saw the maître d' who had seated Bruno and I, and reminded him who I was. He showed us to the table that was set up as a tribute to Bruno. We sat down and had dinner. In between Rico came out from the kitchen to meet Bruno's friends. He had one of Bruno's favorite dishes, figs and prosciutto sent out for us. When it came time to order I showed them the picture of Bruno with his meal in front of him from our previous visit I told them that I wanted that steak, J.J. Dillon had the

Bruno at Rico's with Sal Corrente the night before a private signing they were doing the next morning in Pittsburgh

same thing. It was a great meal any day of the week but this day it was special and symbolic. If you are a wrestling fan and you ever find your way to Pittsburgh, go eat at Rico's and tell them Bruno sent you.

Bruno Mars meeting his namesake Bruno Sammartino

The night that Bruno and I were at Rico's was the week that Bruno Sammartino had met Bruno Mars, which broke out all over social media. As many know, Bruno Mars' name came from his father's love for Bruno Sammartino. So many people came up to the table to say they heard about it and saw mention of it on the news. I remember asking Bruno if Bruno Mars' whole name came from Bruno Sammartino, or just the Bruno part? He said that he didn't know. I later found out that the Mars part came from many girls thinking that he was out of this world. It was years earlier, that Bruno Mars had stated on television that he was named after a big fat wrestler. Well, when this opportunity came along he brought pictures of him in his prime to show Bruno Mars. It was a funny moment between the two as it was told to me, while Bruno Sammartino really had no ego, he did work hard all his life to stay in condition and look good. I believe he was glad he got the opportunity to set the record straight. He had nothing but positive things to say about meeting Bruno Mars. I am very glad that Bruno Mars for just a little bit got a chance to know the man that meant so much to me and also that Bruno Sammartino got a chance to interact with a man that carries his name and is known the world over. If nothing else, Bruno Sammartino got an understanding how popular Bruno Mars was from this long overdue meeting of legends.

Bruno with two of his greatest opponents Larry Zbyszko and Stan "The Lariat" Hansen, along with Nick Bockwinkel. Four former World Champions

    We returned to the wake to pay our final respects to our hero, a man we knew as the man who stood up for the little guy, who had earned everything that he had gotten. He overcame odds that seemed insurmountable, from a skinny weakling beaten up because he couldn't speak English, to one of the strongest men in the world. The greatest single attraction in the history of the worlds most renowned sports arena. We also came across the son of Baron Mikel Scicluna who Davey had known when he was a young boy. He was the son of Tony Marino who was The Battman for the Studio Wrestling Group
    Before we said our final goodbyes Carol asked me what was

going on with the book. "I told her that I had stopped working on it since I didn't know what the future held. She said "I think Bruno would want you to finish it don't you"? I said "Yes I do." So I find myself here writing the end of a story that I never considered ever having an ending.

We returned home the next morning and while we didn't attend the actual funeral, Vince McMahon and Stephanie McMahon did along with some other local wrestlers such a Ken "Zoltan the Great" Jugan, Johnny DeFazio, Shane Douglas, and Dominic DeNucci.

It was an honor—that I still don't understand—to represent Bruno Sammartino in some aspects of his career for the last twenty years or so. It was a privilege to have him appear on my events. I never thought when we agreed that this book would be rewritten that this would be the ending. The thing that Bruno loved the most was his wife Carol and his sons. He had comfort knowing that his sons had good careers and that his wife Carol would be looked after as needed. They had THE marriage that we should all strive for. After 50 years, not only were they still deeply in love, but they still liked each other. In life, Carol shared Bruno with the world but Bruno's heart was only for Carol. He appreciated everything the fans did for him and his family, and all the support that they gave him over the years. A champion inside the ring and around the world, but first and foremost in his home.

I wanted to share a couple of previously untold Bruno stories with you. I was in Malibu, California one day during the time that Tony Danza had his talk show. I had heard that Tony was a fan of Bruno Sammartino's. Well, out of pure coincidence I happened to be at Cross Creek Shopping Center when Tony Danza comes driving by in a convertible. After he got out of the convertible, I told him who I was. He was aware of my attempts to get Bruno to promote WrestleReunion on his show. I called Bruno so that Tony could speak to him but he wasn't at home at the time. He did call back but by that time Tony was gone.

It was several years later after some opportunities to meet Henry Winkler I accidentally bumped in to him. His agent Bob Belenchia is a friend of mine that I met on the autograph circuit ironically Bob grew up in Yonkers as well. I introduced myself to Henry and asked him where he grew up he said "New York City". I asked him if he knew who Bruno Sammartino was he said "of course I used to watch him on television growing up". Of course Bruno has met so many famous people through his career and while knowing me he basically would only talk to me about how the person conducted themselves many times he admitted to me that he had no idea who they were it was other people that told him later how famous that particular person was.

I called Bruno and gave the phone to Henry but didn't tell Bruno who he would be speaking to. When Henry took the phone he said "Hi Bruno, my name is Henry Winker and I would like to, that's right Henry Winkler. After that I didn't listen but I had a good laugh out of it from the surprise that must have taken over Bruno.

When I talked to Bruno later it was clear that he enjoyed talk to Henry and told me that when his wife Carol got home that he said "Honey, I was talking to Fonzie". I have worked with Henry at some autograph shows and most people of course identify with his iconic character Arthur Fonzarelli from Happy Days but some of the younger generation know him from many of his other works.

It was sometime after that Henry was booked to come to Pittsburgh for an autograph convention that happens there a few times a year. I asked Bob to see if Henry wanted all of us to go to dinner Henry accepted the invitation. I told Bruno about it and of course he wanted to go I told him to bring Carol along as well. He said "Sal, my wife would have no interest in something like that at all. I said "OK as long as she knows that she is welcome to attend. When I talked to Bruno again he said "Sal, I need to correct something Carol let me know that she absolutely wanted to attend the dinner with Henry Winkler. So we were all set but sadly something forced Bruno to have to cancel the dinner and we were never able to get schedule in sync again. It was clearly a compliment to Henry that Carol wanted to attend the dinner when Bruno was so convinced that she wouldn't want to. I was really looking forward to The Living Legend having a conversation with the television icon. I always regretted that never happened it would have been a great night at Rico's in Pittsburgh

THE AUTOBIOGRAPHY OF WRESTLING'S LIVING LEGEND

which is where we were going to go.

My final thought of Bruno the Wrestler. The most amazing thing to consider about his career was the longevity of his title runs. He was never asked to give up the title, as a matter of fact he was pressured to keep it much longer than he wanted it. The grueling schedule and hard rings of the early days, took its toll on Bruno's body. While an easier schedule and time to heal would have likely been in the long term interest of the WWWF and Bruno, it didn't work out that way. His secret to his lengthy success was his ability to adapt his style to his opponents. He knew he would have to return to the same arena monthly, or more, and so not wanting to get stale he would work highspot matches with certain opponents, wrestling matches with others, and occasionally strongman stuff. With that approach, the fans never lost their desire to watch Bruno perform.

As a man, his word was his bond, he stood up for those that couldn't help themselves and he tried to give back to those that helped him. He didn't judge you by your standing in the world, he

Sal Corrente in the ring with Bruno Sammartino. Bruno would be in the corner of the other two men in the ring Dory Funk, Jr. and Mike Graham at the 6:05 Reunion PPV in Orlando, Florida. Ironically it was the first time Bruno had ever been to, or appeared in Orlando

judged you based on who you were as a person. It was hard not to be in awe of him, but at the same he made you feel you were his equal at all times.

I am grateful for all the time that I had with Bruno, it's not quite been a month since he has been gone, but he has been on my mind every day and he likely will be for as long as I am able to remember.

Live in Eternal Peace Bruno, as you will live in the memories of all those that saw you, and participated or heard the chants of Bruno ... Bruno ... Bruno!

J.J. Dillon, Sal Corrente, Sweet Daddy Siki, Bruno

Richie Giannantoni with his hero "The Living Legend" Bruno Sammartino. When Richie was a young boy he met Bruno at his Yonkers, NY home in the '60s. A mutual friend of Richie's family asked Bruno to visit Richie's home and he did with another wrestler, Tony Marino. The picture Richie is holding actually shows Bruno holding him up as a young boy. It was a big night for Richie when almost 50 years later he got a chance to meet Bruno again.

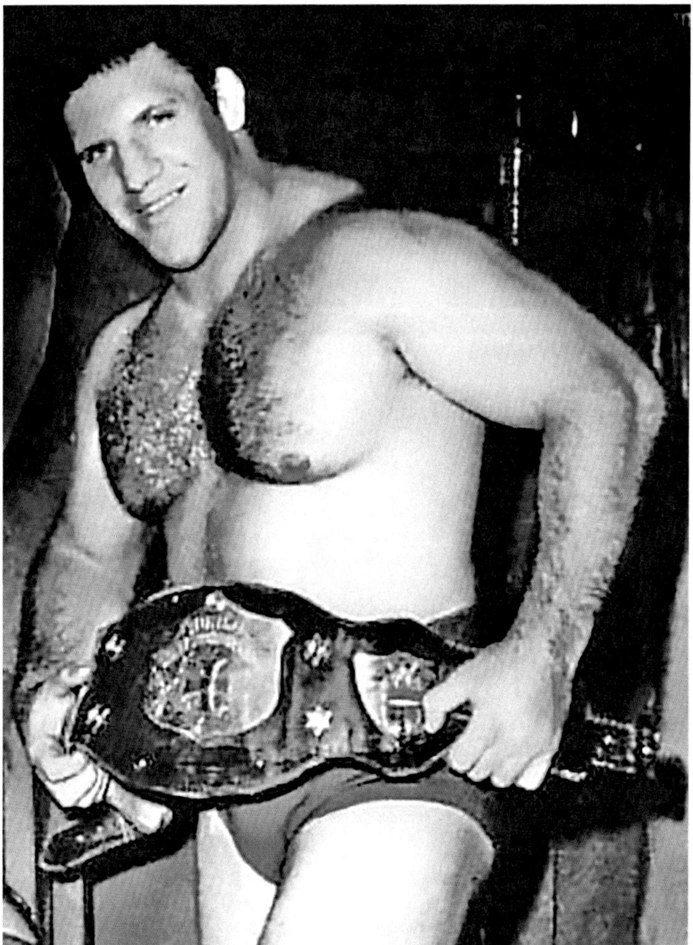

Davey O'Hannon

Bruno was a constant in my life since I was 11 years old. Like many in our business, I started out being a fan. I was at Madison Square Garden on May 17, 1963 to see Bruno win the belt, and I was hooked! Years later to be able to be in the business and call Bruno my friend is what dreams are made of.

We all know about Bruno the wrestling legend. I would say to him, "You are the face of pro wrestling." He would always come back with, "Couldn't you find a prettier face?" Bruno didn't live his gimmick because he didn't have one. He was always just Bruno. He stood up for people who were sometimes not in a position to stand up for themselves. Bruno never acted like, "Hey, I'm the Champ," but he represented our profession better than anyone ever has.

Bruno made it easy to say "I'm a professional wrestler," with a great sense of pride. What you saw was genuine. A no-frills guy who was honest, respectful, and who really cared about people. He lived life right, and that's why people identified with him, and loved him.

That was Bruno the wrestler.

Pictured is Don Runco, longtime maître d' at Rico's, Bruno's favorite restaurant. The table that he shared with his wife Carol was set up in his memory upon Rico's hearing of his passing

Bruno the friend was loyal, engaging, and a pleasure to be around. We almost never talked about wrestling when we traveled, sat in a hotel, or killed time at an arena. Bruno was always talking about Carol and his kids, and asking about yours. He wanted to know how your wife and kids were doing. It wasn't a show, he was really interested.

I'll miss our phone calls, holiday greetings, and singing Dean Martin songs on long car trips. When Dean sang in Italian, Bruno would scold me ... "Your Mom is a Caruso and you can't get the words right!" I'd glance over and he would be laughing and shaking his head.

Bruno had a lasting influence on this young fan, and was a tremendous role model for this young professional. 55 years later, it doesn't feel like I should be writing this. I always thought Bruno would be here forever. I'm sad, but so proud to say he was my friend.

THE AUTOBIOGRAPHY OF WRESTLING'S LIVING LEGEND

As we say in the business ... "See you up the road, Pal!"
He will be with me forever.

*Davey O'Hannon and Larry Zbyszko.
Two men that were booed most of their careers
but were very close to Bruno Sammartino, a man
who heard mainly cheers his whole career*

Larry and Bruno

Larry Zbyszko

The first time I met Bruno I was 14 years old. My parents dragged me off to Sunday mass at a small church in the suburbs of Pittsburgh, Saint Sebastian. As I sat down in the pew and looked next to me I went into shock! I was sitting next to my hero Bruno Sammartino! After mass, I chased him down and got his autograph on the Sunday bulletin. Little did I know it was only the beginning

Two years later, I was driving by his house and caught a glimpse of him standing by his pool. After crawling through the hedges I introduced myself and asked him if he would help me become a wrestler like my hero, him. I would soon find out he did, and with

nothing in it for him, gave me the break of a lifetime!

Bruno had a totally unselfish nature, which he constantly shared with his family, friends, and fans. Integrity was Bruno's middle name! His word was his contract. Several times he was carried into an arena, was worked on by therapists, just so he could walk out to the ring and have a match that would not let the fans down, then he would collapse in the dressing room afterward.

Knowing Bruno was to understand what truth, honor, integrity, and a loving nature really are! At Bruno's funeral, Heaven itself showed me a sign that his legacy would live forever. The very last time I would be with him was at Saint Sebastian, the same church in the suburbs of Pittsburgh, I met him for the first time over half a century earlier.

Bruno Sammartino. My Hero. My Mentor. My Friend.
THE GREATEST LEGEND OF THEM ALL!
I miss him!

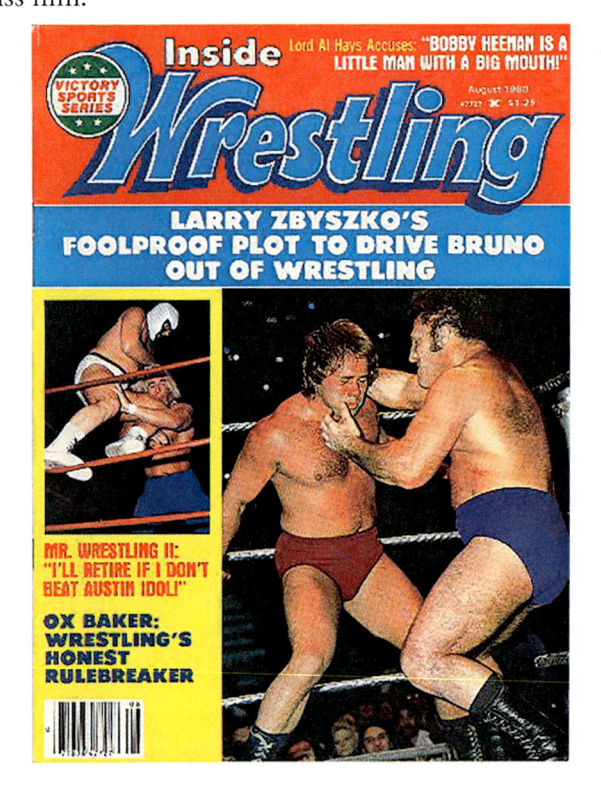

THE AUTOBIOGRAPHY OF WRESTLING'S LIVING LEGEND

*Bruno and Larry posing in the dressing room during
WrestleReunion 2 on August 27th, 2005 in Valley Forge, PA.
Later that night they would have their final in-ring altercation.
Once again it made the cover of a wrestling magazine*

THE AUTOBIOGRAPHY OF WRESTLING'S LIVING LEGEND

BRUNO SAMMARTINO BATTLES LARRY ZBYSZKO IN A STEEL CAGE MATCH

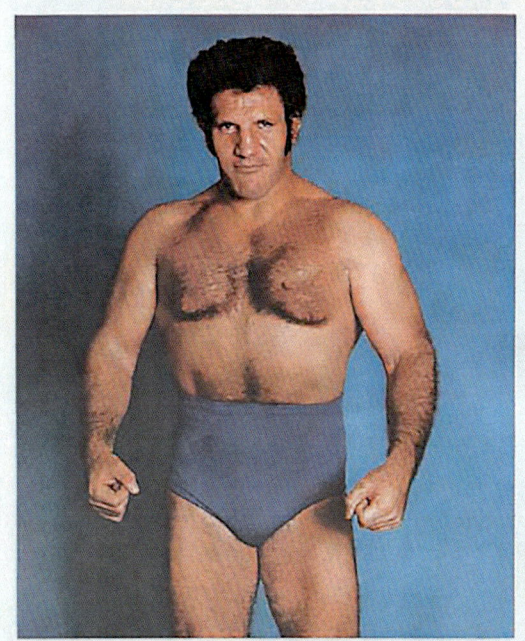

Tonight's match between Bruno Sammartino and Larry Zbyszko has been called by many ring experts the grudge match of the century.

Before they step foot in the squared circle to do battle, there will be a steel cage constructed around the entire ring.

Cage matches are among the most brutal type of matches held in professional wrestling, and in fact are frowned upon by the officials. There is always a great chance that a wrestler will become permanently injured after repeatedly being thrown into the steel cage.

There will only be one winner of tonight's contest. That will be the man who can leave the ring first! He can climb out over the top, or somehow either go through the ring or the fence, but of course that is nearly impossible!

Tonight's Sammartino-Zbyszko contest is a rubber match. In their first meeting in Madison Square Garden Bruno was disqualified when he got completely out of control and wouldn't stop choking his rival.

In their return bout "The living legend of wrestling" won on a count out when Larry left the ring and headed for his dressing room. Tonight they will battle to the finish, neither man will be able to escape the cage until he has completely conquered the other!

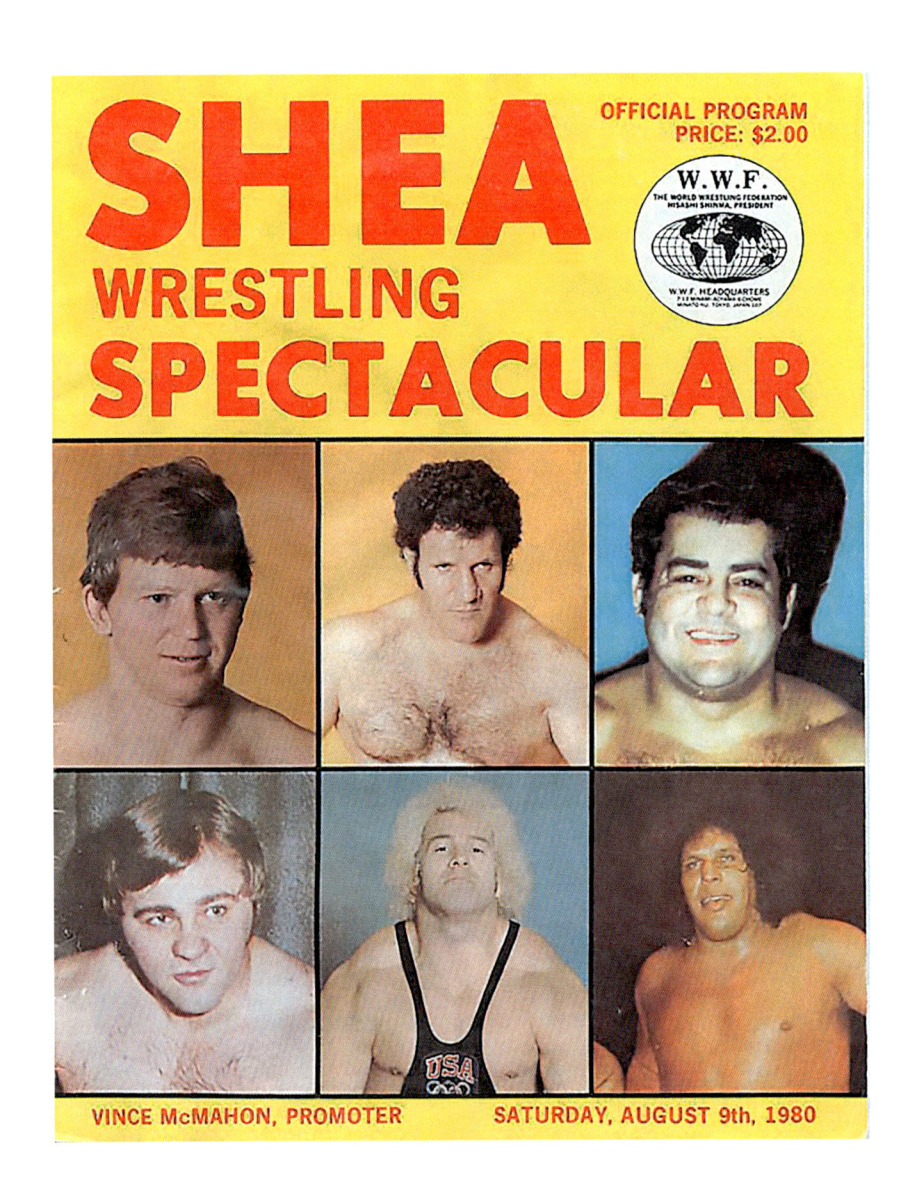

BRUNO SAMMARTINO

THE AUTOBIOGRAPHY OF WRESTLING'S LIVING LEGEND

SHEA STADIUM   **SATURDAY, AUGUST 9th, 1980**

TONIGHT'S OFFICIAL LINE-UP

****

The Main Event - Steel Cage Match

BRUNO SAMMARTINO	vs.	**LARRY ZBYSZKO**
Abruzzi, Italy		Pittsburgh, Pennsylvania

****

Battle Of The Super-Heavyweights

THE FABULOUS HULK HOGAN	vs.	**ANDRE THE GIANT**
Venice Beach, California		Paris, France

****

Inter-Continental Heavyweight Championship

KEN PATERA	vs.	**TONY ATLAS**
Portland, Oregon		Roanoke, Virginia
"Champion"		"Challenger"

****

World Wrestling Federation Tag Team Championship

THE SAMOAN #1		**PEDRO MORALES**
Samoa		Puerto Rico
and	vs.	and
THE SAMOAN #2		**BOB BACKLUND**
Samoa		Princeton, Minnesota
"Champions"		"Challengers"

****

National Wrestling Federation Heavyweight Championship

LARRY SHARPE	vs.	**ANTONIO INOKI**
Paulsboro, New Jersey		Tokyo, Japan
"Challenger"		"Champion"

****

World Wrestling Federation Junior Heavyweight Championship

CHAVO GUERRERO	vs.	**TATSUMI "DRAGON" FUJINAMI**
Mexico		Japan
"Challenger"		"Champion"

****

TOR KAMATA	vs.	**PAT PATTERSON**
Japan		San Francisco, California

****

GREG GAGNE	vs.	**RICK McGRAW**
Mound, Minnesota		Charlotte, North Carolina

****

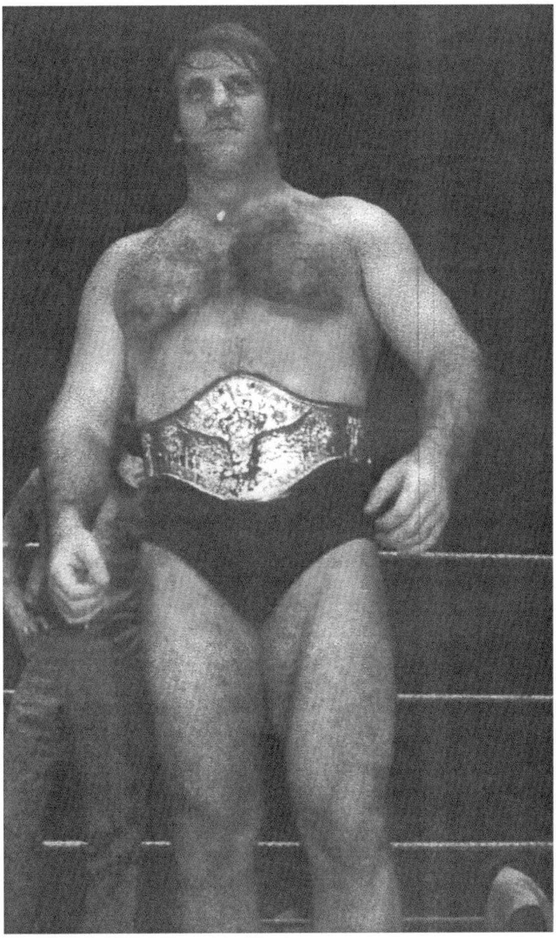

Tito Santana

I had a great experience with Bruno when I first came to New York in 1979. I was very young in the biggest markets of wrestling. I was still wet behind the ears. Vince Senior was my boss, and he was very classy and I felt he was hard to approach. I remember having questions about where my career was heading, but did not know how to approach Vince. I decided to ask Bruno for advice. I can't tell you how much he was willing to help me. He went out of his way to direct my approach. He told me not to approach Vince until the second day of TV taping. He told me that on our first day of taping he took care of all the big business he had to do as far as TV goes. He would always talk to top guys early during the second day of taping. He would always come out where we were doing interviews and I would see him talking to everyone for a little while at a time. That is when I asked Vince if he had a couple minutes to talk to him. Bruno told me what I should ask. I can't remember what I asked, but that was the beginning of me feeling confident about my career.

When I found out I would be teaming up with Bruno, I knew I was on my way. He was very unselfish as my partner, but I learned so much by being in the ring with him.

He did have his last match as my partner in MSG, but we actually wrestled in all the big markets in the WWF. I will forever be in debt to Bruno for all his help and advice. He was a great man, and recognized that I was sincere when I approached him for help. I would always be grateful to Bruno for his help my first time in the WWF.

Tito and Bruno after winning a cage match

Bruno addresses the audience at his Dapper Dan induction

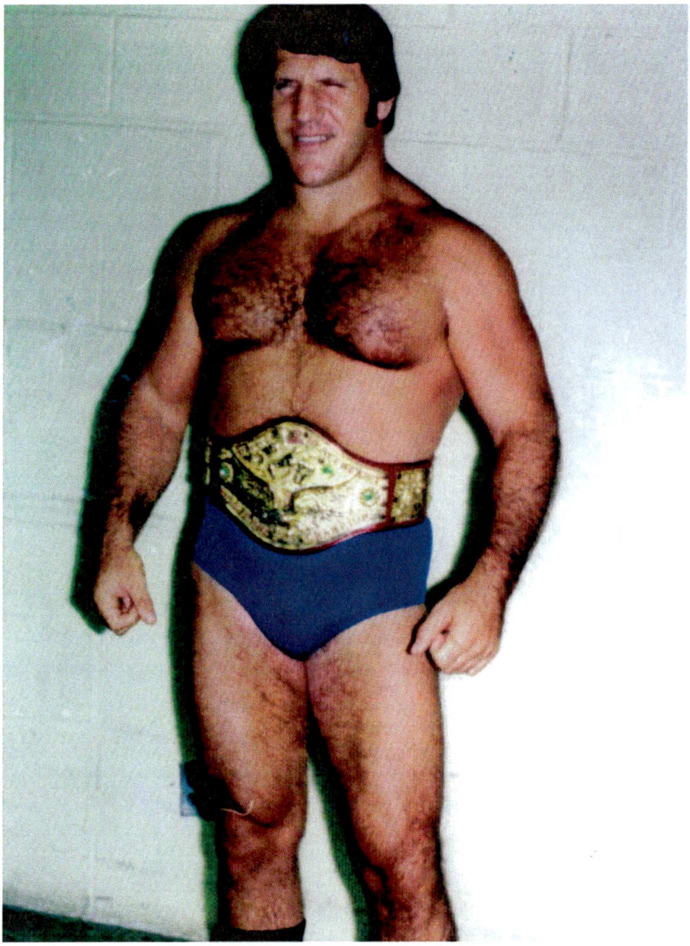

Honky Tonk Man

I had been given the Intercontinental Championship in the WWF all that was required of me when the decision was made was to get out there on the road and defend the belt. The opponent that I was supposed to face wasn't going to be available so the office asked The Living Legend Bruno Sammartino to step in with me at some big clubs in the North East and other places. We only had a few weeks to throw something together which was nothing. At the time they ran something across the bottom of the screen that Bruno Sammartino would be facing The Honky Tonk Man. We sold out everywhere that we went.

The Honky Tonk Man and Bruno Sammartino in one of their series of matches

I only knew Bruno Sammartino from the magazines growing up. I had no real understanding of what he meant to the fans until I had this series of matches with him. I am very grateful I got the opportunity to have this series of matches with Bruno. I feel like we both gained an admiration for each other as well as having some great matches. I really feel like those matches were a jump start to making The Honky Tonk Man the greatest Intercontinental Champion of all Time. Bruno will grace all our memories and live eternally in the minds of wrestlers and fans around the world.

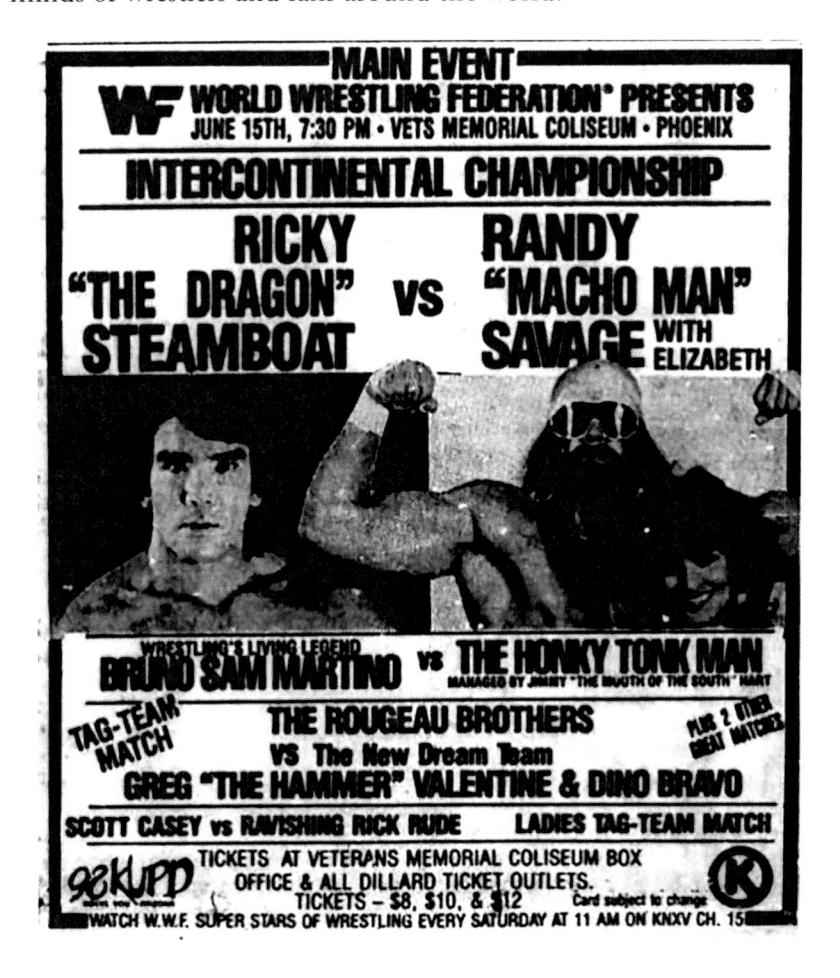

*Bruno with B. Brian Blair and Tom Prichard at
Giordano's Restaurant in Tampa, Florida*

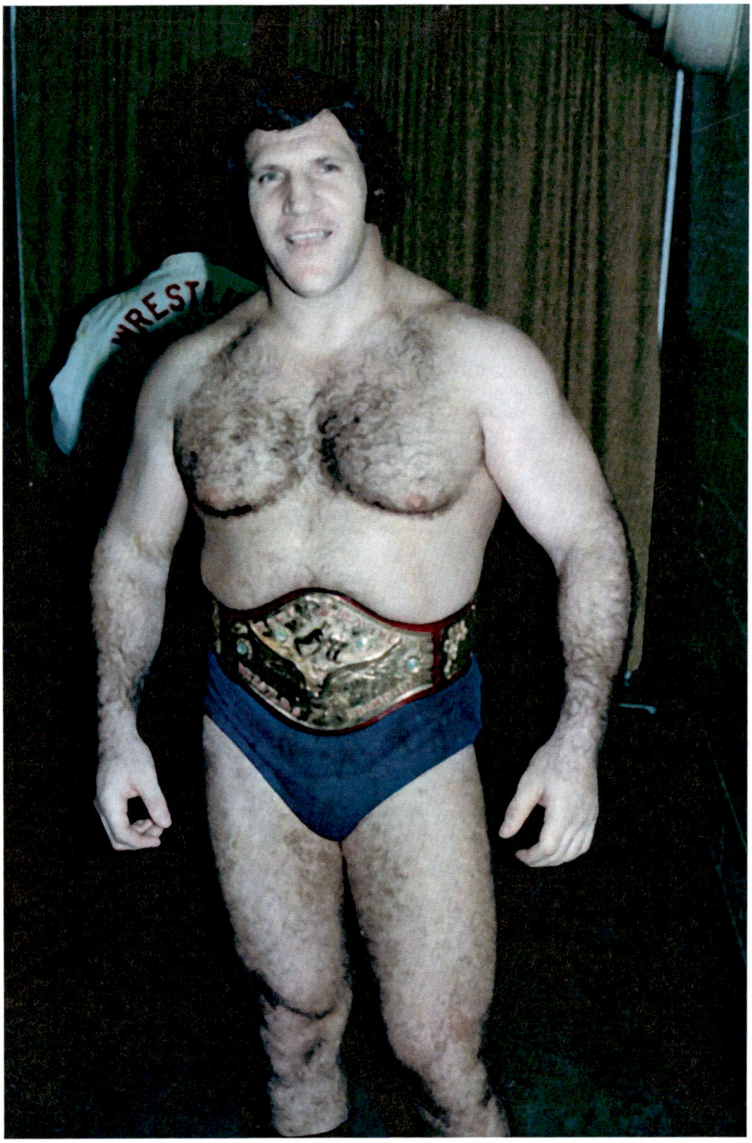

Mick Foley

BRUNO SAMMARTINO: A LEGEND NEVER DIES

I can hear Bruno's voice in my head like it was yesterday. I was introducing the legendary WWWF champion at an awards dinner during WrestleReunion 2 on August 26th 2005 in Valley Forge, PA, it was a tribute weekend to the legendary Sammartino and Zbyszko Steel Cage match at Shea Stadium I had closed my remarks by mentioning how honored I was that Bruno actually liked me. Bruno stepped to the microphone, and his very first words were "I do you like you! I don't understand why you do some of the crazy things you do — but I like you. I do!"

I had the great privilege of being around Bruno Sammartino quite a bit, simply because his best friend was my trainer, Dominic DeNucci. But in all those years I was around him—over thirty—I never took his presence for granted; I never once forgot that he was one of the all-time greats in our business. He sold out Madison Square Garden more times than any performer, in any line of business.

I would listen to Paul Heyman on late night road trips, explaining why the knock on Bruno's promos weren't fair; how they were exactly what they needed to be to draw money, and create interest, week in and week out, month after month, year after year.

Whenever I'm asked how a legend of one era would have fared against the best of a newer generation, I always say that the great ones would have found a way to adapt. Bruno Sammartino would have been great in any generation. I looked at a photo of Bruno in a Pittsburgh neurosurgeon's office, and I almost laughed. It was as if the head of a 70 year old man had been photoshopped onto the body of a bodybuilder in his 30's. Bruno transformed himself over the years from a thick, barrel-chested power-lifter into a lean, mean bodybuilding machine. I have no doubt he would have done whatever was needed to excel in any era, in any style.

Maybe I'm biased, but I will always feel that my WWE Hall of Fame induction class of 2013 was the finest of them all. With Bruno and Bob Backlund making their long awaited, and richly deserved entrance into the hall, along with Booker, Trish Stratus and myself, I was so proud to be part of that historic night. And I'm proud that Bruno liked me!

If you attend any of my event's and meet me by all means let me know if you have a favorite Bruno moment.

Bruno and Mick Foley chatting at WrestleReunion in Tampa, FL

Bruno, Bill Cardille, and Dominic DeNucci

Former ECW and WWE Commentator Joey Styles with one of his idols, Bruno Sammartino at WrestleReunion in Tampa

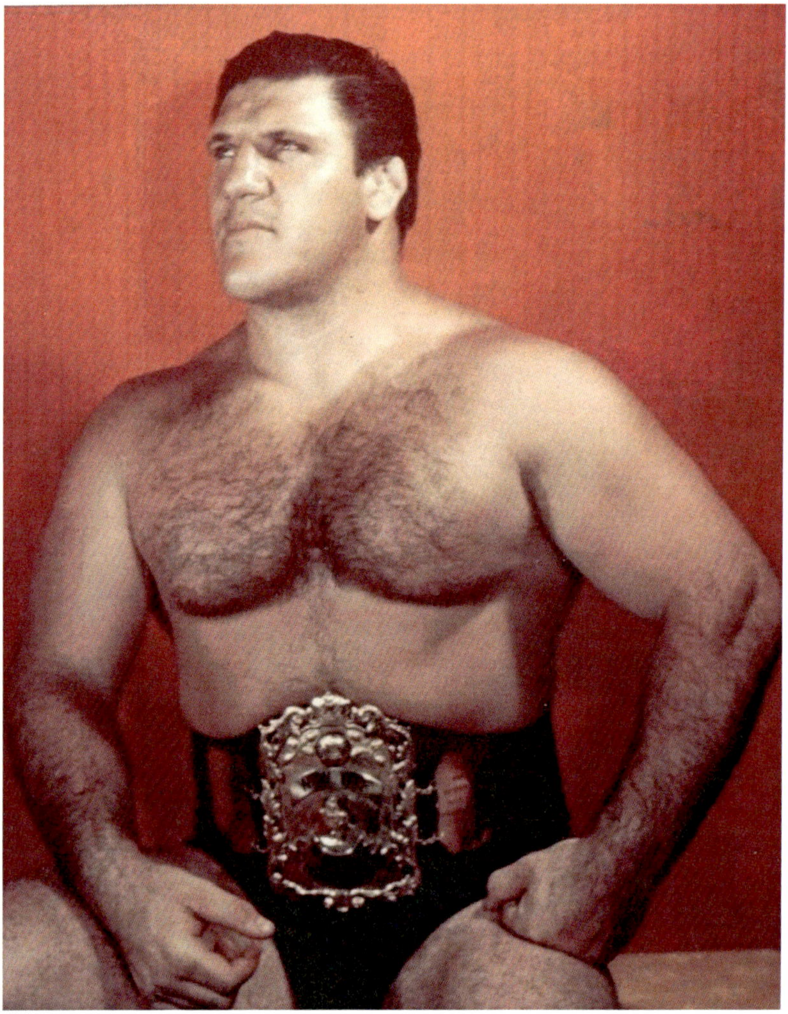

Jimmy Hart

I was on the road with The Honky Tonk Man on a West Coast loop when our opponent couldn't wrestle for a while. The WWF asked Bruno Sammartino to replace him. As I grew up in Memphis where "The Fabulous" Jackie Fargo was our version of Bruno Sammartino, I didn't have the historical reference to know what Bruno meant to fans across the globe.

We worked the match in the style of the day which was different than what Bruno had in mind, and while he thought that things went OK, he also thought that they could be better. Bruno came to our hotel room door to discuss the match and asked if we wouldn't mind trying it his way the next night. We said "Sure." While Bruno felt that things could go better, he was also generous enough to say "If my way doesn't work then we can go back to how you guys want to do things." Things went very well, the people loved it, and I have had the ultimate respect for Bruno since that day.

He was an individual who in his day was by far the biggest drawing card in the industry, both here and worldwide, and long after his retirement he still had the respect of fans worldwide.

He will be missed, but not forgotten for his contribution to the wrestling business, and his conduct inside and out of the ring.

Jimmy Hart, Sal Corrente, Bruno, with Yvonne Craig—TV's Batgirl

Bruno with Paul Heyman, also known as Paul E. Dangerously

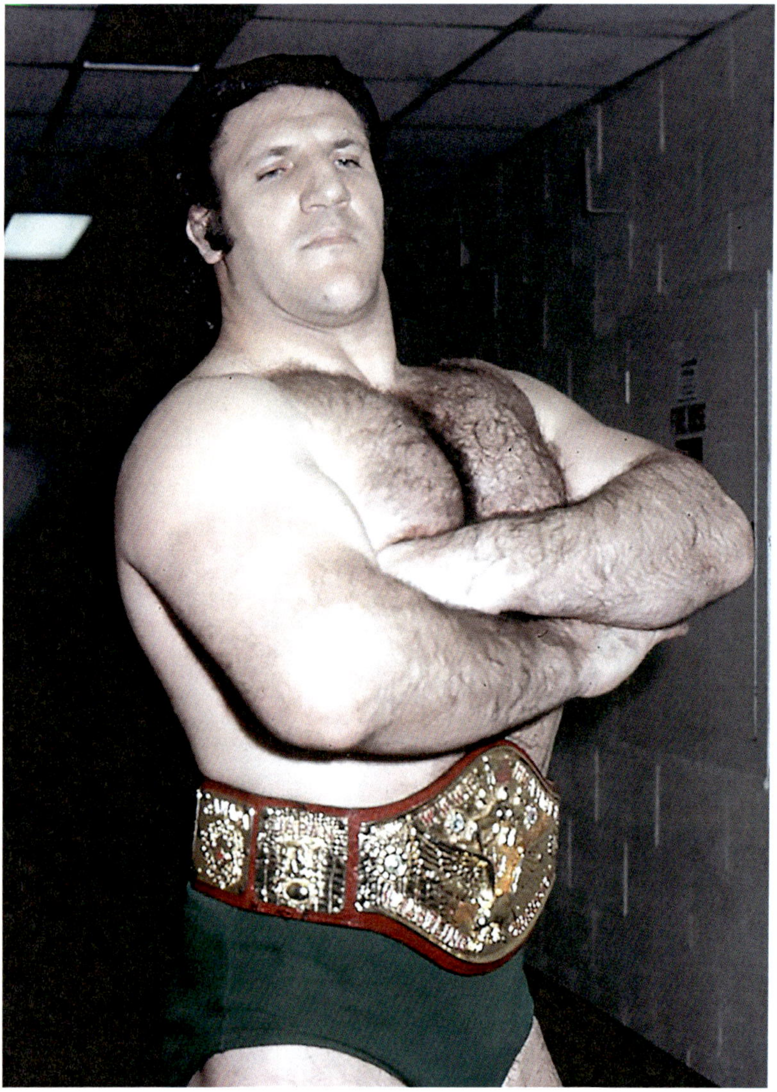

Larry Richert

Salute to Bruno April 23rd 2018

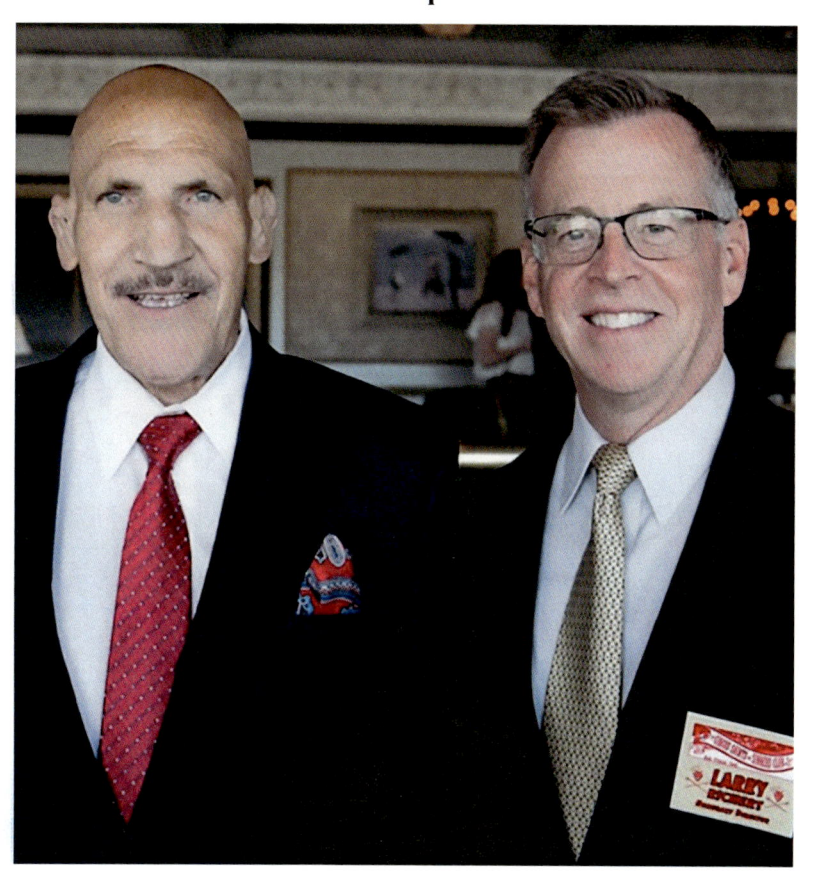

My name is Larry Richert, a childhood friend of Bruno's, sort of ... like millions of children around the world I felt like he was my friend especially every Saturday night. Growing up in Pittsburgh it was the thing to do ... watch Studio Wrestling with the Champion of the World ... Bruno Leopoldo Francesca Sammartino, who made Pittsburgh proud in every corner of the world at a time when our city "didn't look so good."

With three brothers ... my mom would call out to us in the backyard, "It's time! Bruno's almost on ..." and we would race inside and get our ration of potato chips, B&L French Onion Dip and a 7oz Coca-Cola. Everything was right with the world. Afterwards, broken furniture may, or may not have ensued after a few dives off the couch.

Bruno with Pittsburgh Pirates Hall of Famer Roberto Clemente

The fact is every guy I knew in the neighborhood wanted to be like Bruno. He was as big to us as anybody, including the Pirates' Roberto Clemente or Steelers' Franco Harris, right up there with the best of the best. In fact, Bruno was the first person I remember outside of my own parents that I looked up to. My Lord, to see him LIVE at the Civic Arena would almost be too much to take.

Flash ahead to a time when I was a young broadcaster on

KDKA-TV. Nearly 30 years ago, my producer told me that he had booked Bruno Sammartino for my morning television show. WOW — Bruno — this would be great. I told my late father-in-law, Dan Marino, Sr. about it and he informed me that he went to Schenley High School with Bruno, and that they were neighbors and classmates, and he supplied pictures to prove it. He added, that his father and grandfather came from the same little town as Bruno in Italy ... Pizzoferrato.

When Bruno came in to do the show I was starstruck. After explaining my family connection he was unbelievably engaged, warm and kind. Then LIVE on TV he started to reveal another side of his life. Long before he became a wrestling champion. One that very few people knew. He told me about a horrific time in his childhood that his sister Mary and brother Paul, endured with their mother Emilia

Bruno, Larry Richert and Rocky Bleier
from the Pittsburgh Steelers

while his father Alphonso was working here in Pittsburgh and was cut off because of the war.

At age 8 in 1943, his Uncle pounded on the door, "We must get out now, the Nazi SS are coming." With little but the clothes on their back they left, and eventually made it to another mountain summit called Valla Rocca. That would be their home for the next 14 months while the Germans occupied Pizzoferrato. With nothing to eat, Bruno's mother, at the age of 48, would journey back usually

Darryl Sammartino, Bruno, Arnold, and me

once a week, a full days walk to the edge of their town and she would wait. Under the cloak of darkness she would sneak into their village and gather what food she could find, even under the noses of the SS sleeping upstairs in her own home. Potatoes and beans. Dangerous duty. One time she was captured and she escaped by jumping off a stake bed truck though barbed wire so determined was she to make it back to her children. Even though she was shot though the shoulder, she still somehow made her back way up that mountain.

Bruno went on ... he told me how Mary, Paul, and he would wait for her return, sitting on a rock ... and hours seemed like days and days weeks. He recalled with detail the feeling of seeing Mom come back.

He told our audience how they were once discovered, near the end of their isolation in hiding, by a small German patrol and they were to be executed. Bruno said his mom gathered her three children close to her and said "Don't worry, we will never be hungry or cold

Bruno with Joe DiMaggio

Photo Courtesy of George Napolitano

again, we will be together in paradise with Jesus." They were saved at the last possible second by the resistance fighters. I was stunned.

Bruno explained that shortly after that a tremendous bombing took place in and around their town as the Allies moved in. Bruno had developed rheumatic fever and was carried off the mountain. Near death, his mother old him, "I have lost two children I will not lose another" ... Bruno was so sickly, it took the family three years for him to pass a physical to come to America. 13 years old now and weighing only 75 pounds.

His arrival in America was not as smooth as they thought it might be, the streets were not paved with gold and he was bullied for not knowing the language, frequently on the wrong end of punches. A young Jewish man took Bruno under his wing to the old Jewish Y to lift weights. Bruno said that it was like a light switch went off ... he knew this was for him.

I was stunned at this story and had no idea that our Champion had suffered such horrors with his family. "Why doesn't anybody know about this?"

Year later, at an awards dinner, Bruno received another of his countless honors. He was gracious in his acceptance and sat down. As

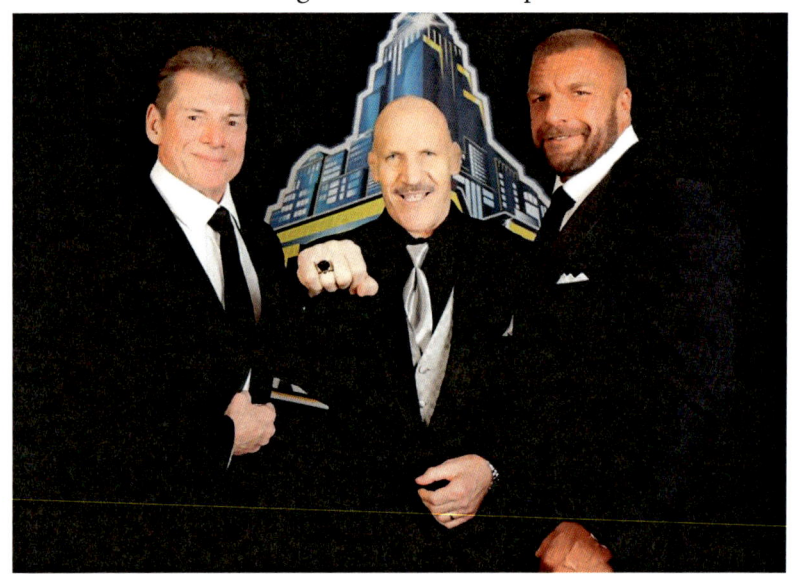

Bruno with Vince McMahon, Jr. (L) and Paul "Triple H" Levesque

the emcee, I went back up and said that was only part of Bruno's story and shared the rest. In the audience that night was our late friend Marty Lazarro. He was so emotionally moved by the revelations and was determined to meet Bruno. Through Dr Frank Costa, he finally met the Champ. They became fast friends and traveled back to Italy a number of times. Marty was going to make sure that the story was told.

During the times we were together, I often wondered, "How is it possible for a man with such humble beginnings to achieve such greatness?"

How is it that Bruno became literally the strongest man in the World?

How did he sellout Madison Square Garden 188 times as a headliner?

How did he become the Champion of the World and hold the title for nearly 12 years?

He was the celebrities' celebrity, they wanted their picture taken with him. You name them and they loved him. Frank Sinatra, Willie Mays, Micky Mantle, Mike Tyson, Phil Esposito …

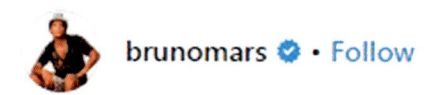

brunomars • Follow

brunomars I was nicknamed after this professional wrestler Bruno Sammartino. Tonight in Pittsburgh I had the honor of meeting him! 🤟 #OG #24kmagicworldtour

Arnold Schwarzenegger looked up to him and recently agreed to record a foreword for our documentary. He told me, "I saw Bruno Sammartino in a Madison Square Garden packed to the rafters, he was the best of the best. He was the greatest professional wrestling Champion ever," and went on to say, "His is one of the greatest immigration stories of all time … Bruno Sammartino".

He once turned down a role on the HBO show *The Sopranos*

Bruno with the love of his life, his wife Carol

because he wouldn't swear. "But Bruno, it's just a character the producer begged." "Well my fans don't know that and I would not use that language."

Music superstar Bruno Mars was named after him. This past summer thanks to Steelers GM Kevin Colbert, and Jimmy Sacco who runs Heinz Field, we took Bruno to meet Bruno. He said, "Mr. Sammartino, when I told my dad I was going to meet you he was over the moon. He grabbed his phone and read a text that his dad sent, "Please tell Bruno that he's the Muhammad Ali of wrestling."

Bruno , so gracious handed Mars a replica of his championship belt to give his father ... he lit up like a Christmas tree. The picture of Bruno meeting Bruno went viral the next day and was the number one trending photo in the world. I told Bruno you went viral. He said, "What?" I told him, "That's a good thing ... you're back on top, Champ."

So how is all of this possible?

I concluded that it must be a Mother's love. There is no greater force on Earth than a Mother's love. Bruno said many times that his mother had the heart of a lion and what she faced was inhuman. He took the commandment, "Honor Thy Mother and Father" to a new level. He never wanted to disappoint her and wanted the Sammartino name to be associated with respect and goodness. He never disappointed her and never disappointed his fans.

Then he met the love of his life, Carol. Carol is the woman who rocked Bruno's world for nearly sixty years. They found a way to make it work. Carol will tell you in the beginning things weren't easy. She sacrificed immensely with Bruno traveling the world. Bruno would tell you that it's a tough life on the road too, that sacrifices family time, he wanted to be home. Carol wanted to be with him and that went on for a long time.

It's no surprise why Bruno had such tremendous respect for women.

Bruno promised Carol that when he was off the circuit he would go wherever she wanted to go, and they went everywhere together and were inseparable right up to his passing.

I especially miss his warm sense of humor, one of Bruno's favorite things was to have dinner with friends and family.

Like the time we were in New York for the WWE Hall of Fame weekend in 2013. Dr. Frank Costa, a close family friend took us for lunch at the Yale Club in Manhattan. There were a dozen of us in this very regal setting. The staff were not permitted to ask for autographs or pictures of the guests. However, as Bruno began telling the story of wrestling a "monkey" the waitstaff lined the wall next to our table and began to lean in, riveted to his tale.

Bruno went on ... "I was a carpenter's apprentice making $2 an hour. There was an exhibition in town and this man was offering $150 if you could stay in the cage for 5 minutes with a monkey. My buddies said you can do this. I saw a little monkey on TV and thought this isn't fair, I'm so big! So off we went and when I got there the cage was covered with canvas and it was rattling. I thought what the heck? When they pulled back the tarp and opening the door I saw a giant orangutan. I couldn't back out now ... as soon as I went in that beast leaped up and grabbed the bars on the top while his feet came at me like pistons ... pummeling me ... boom, boom, boom. He was beating the hell out me. It knocked me around the cage. This went on for almost fifteen minutes. He scratched my chest and I was bleeding everywhere. Finally it had me in a headlock, I saw his belly coming in and out breathing heavy so I took my shot. I punched him as hard as I could and he dropped. The owner came in screaming, you hurt my monkey! He never did pay me either. Can you imagine going home to your wife and when she asks what happened and you tell her I was beaten up by an orangutan?"

Bruno's story had all of us in stitches, guests and staff. Just then one of the workers politely asked for Bruno's autograph and picture. Bruno said "Sure!"

As they gathered around him the maître d' came running over. I was thinking he was going to give them hell for bothering Mr. Sammartino. Instead he stuck his head in to make sure he got in the picture too.

Then on the way out the doorman was so excited to see him, "Mr Sammartino, I didn't know you went to Yale."

Bruno smiled and said, "I didn't."

"Well you're welcome here any time. You were the best ever."

Bruno Sammartino was a simple man of principle. He worked hard, was disciplined, had the highest ethics — never wavered and was genuinely humble in everything he did. He was most appreciative of his fans ... he knew that they were the working people who spent their hard earned money to buy a ticket to see him put on a show and he never wanted to let them down, so many times staying hours after a show to sign their autographs.

But I would argue that Bruno's strongest muscle was his heart.

As I was leaving the hospital a week ago today, the last thing Bruno said to me as he extended his hand was, "Thank you pal for coming to see me," as if it was a burden on me. It was an honor.

THE AUTOBIOGRAPHY OF WRESTLING'S LIVING LEGEND

What I would have liked to say to Bruno was ... "No, thank you pal. On behalf of millions of people on every continent who you entertained for decades, gave hope, showed kindness and humility, taught respect, especially for women, we thank you, for showing us a way to live and we marvel at the impact you have had. This is a better world because you were in it."

Champ, you're on a mountain so high ... but you're not alone, there's a woman named Emilia who is there to greet you with her million dollar smile and those rough warm gentle hands. She will touch your cheeks and say, "Welcome home son ... you made me so proud."

Salute ... Bravo Bruno, grazie mille!

Stephanie McMahon with Bruno

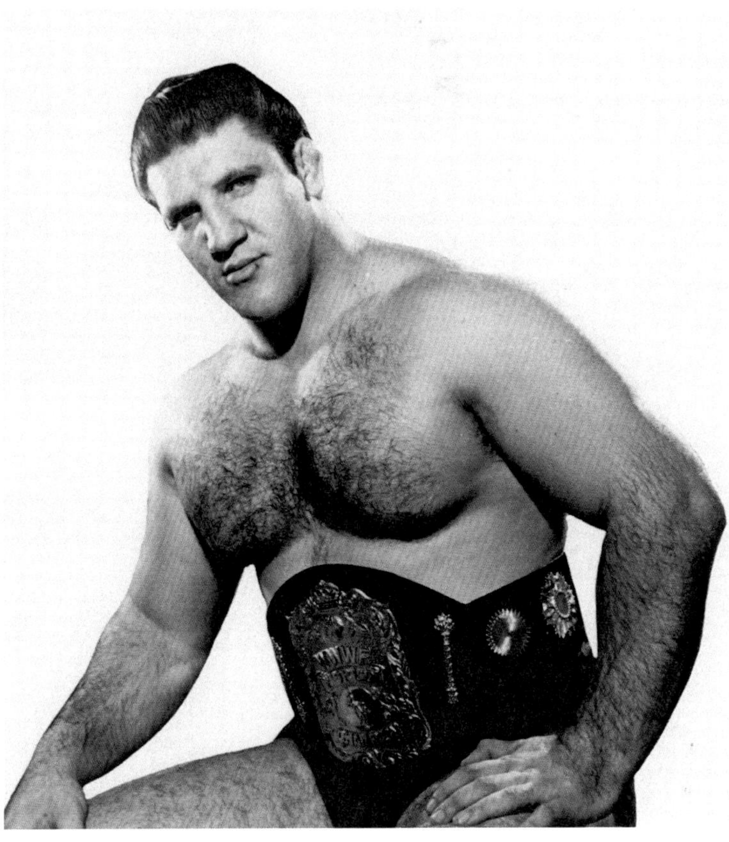

James J. Dillon

I have read and reread the foreword that I sent while Bruno was still with us. It so expresses how I have always felt about Bruno that I don't know that I would add anything or change one word.

I am a very private person and don't call my closest friends on any kind of a regular basis. However, I always called Bruno on his birthday and during the holiday season. Each call would usually last about an hour as we would talk about anything and everything.

I too was shocked when I received the news about the passing of Bruno. I cried when my father passed and I cried when my mother passed and yes ... I cried when I was informed that Bruno had passed. I don't do well with viewings and funerals and prefer to focus on my memories of time spent with special people I knew and spent time with during their life. Bruno was at the top of my list of those "special people."

However, I had to go to Pittsburgh to see Bruno one last time at the funeral home. Davey O'Hannon was also close to Bruno and when I called Davey he too felt a need to see Bruno and pay final respects. I drove to Davey's home in South New Jersey and we met up with you Sal for the drive to Pittsburgh. It was a six to seven hour drive and we shared our individual Bruno stories with each other. We went directly to the funeral home arriving ahead of the first formal viewing. Bruno looked just like the Bruno I had last seen almost a year before. He looked at peace. It was dinner hour as we left the funeral home and we went to Rico's which was Bruno's favorite place to dine We were told by Rico that Bruno and Carol would dine there at least three times a week. Bruno and Carol had a special table which had been covered with a black tablecloth. There was a photo of Bruno on the table along with wine glasses with the names of Carol and Bruno engraved on them. Bruno would always have dates and prosciutto which were not on the regular Rico's menu. Rico was kind enough to prepare a special plate of dates and prosciutto for Davey, Sal and myself in honor of Bruno. After dinner we drove past Bruno's home only a few blocks from Rico's. Bruno and Carol lived in what I would consider a very modest neighborhood home considering all the fame, notoriety, and financial rewards that Bruno had earned during his wrestling career.

After dinner, Davey, Sal and I went back to the funeral home where I met Carol in person for the first time. Law enforcement personnel from all over the Pittsburgh area came by the funeral home and many local media had video crews present as Bruno was a true icon in the area. We also saw Dominic DeNucci and the son of Mike Scicluna and his wife and one of Bruno's brothers among many others.

We spent the night in Pittsburgh thanks to Sal and we were up early for the journey back home. The next day we were told that so many people came to pay their last respects to Bruno that it was elbow to elbow. Apparently we were among the first to see Bruno and I am glad we had the quiet time we had to pay our respects to Bruno. Bruno my friend ... God Bless You ... and may you forever RIP.

J.J. and Davey O'Hannon with Rico Lorenzini of Rico's Restaurant

J.J. Mike Scicluna, Dick Woerhle, and Davey O'Hannon

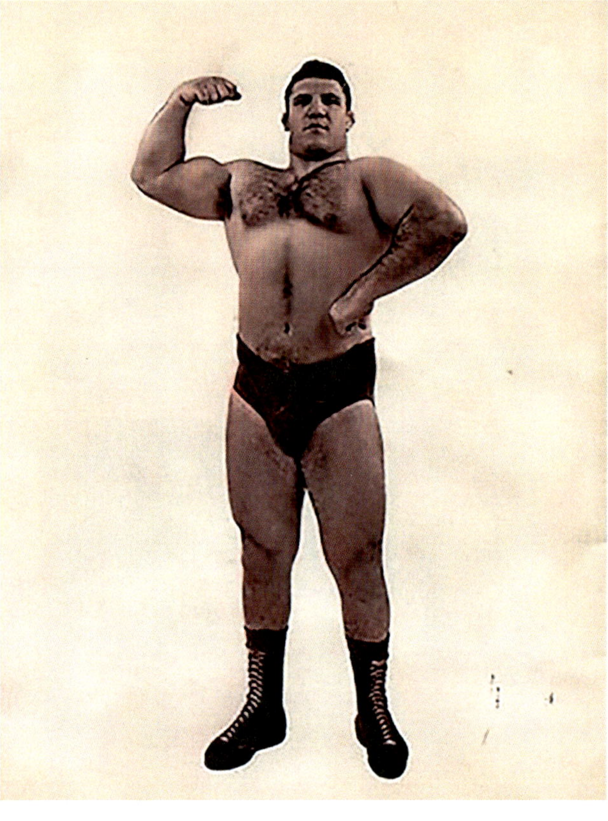

Michael Bochicchio

The old adage says you shouldn't meet your heroes. Most of my heroes were wrestlers from the 70s and 80s, and unfortunately, that phrase often rang true. My company Highspots.com got into a working relationship with WrestleReunion a company that had a very strong working relationship with "The Living Legend" Bruno Sammartino. In my years running my company I have dealt with many Legends in the world of Professional Wrestling. I had never had the opportunity to work with Bruno before, but I quickly came to realize that Bruno was the greatest ambassador for wrestling of any era, and without a doubt, the most professional Legend I've ever had the pleasure to meet. He made you feel important with every interaction, and his connection to his fans was an authentic bond. My company had various deals with him beginning in 2010 and you could always count on Bruno personally and professionally. As a promoter and a businessman you felt confident entering in to any agreement with Bruno based on a handshake.

My first interaction with wrestling was at the age of 4 in 1977. My great grandmother was a first generation full blooded Italian and spoke no English while living in New York. Like so many Italians that came to America, Bruno Sammartino was her hero. One of my earliest childhood memories was sitting with my great grandmother in front of a TV watching wrestling. I visited New York annually and professional wrestling was always our connection, despite not even speaking the same language as each other. Its quite possible I would have followed wrestling my entire life without her, but undoubtedly it was the beginning of my fandom, and in turn, my own profession.

As a vendor and promoter of wrestling for over 20 years, I've had the opportunity to meet wrestling fans from our all over the country. Certainly every fan has his/her favorites. Bruno certainly has his large share of those fans. However, I've also met so many people that were not wrestling fans per se, but they always had a wrestling story. For anybody living above the Mason Dixon line, that "famous wrestler" story always was about Bruno and was always a positive encounter. He clearly was a star bigger than wrestling itself.

Without question, he was among the greatest wrestlers of all times and literally carried the McMahon family business on his back for nearly 20 years. More importantly, he was a role model for all—kids, adults, and literally for the entire Italian heritage.

Bruno was a role model for all

Bruno with Claudio "Super Mario" Montrosse and the late Claudio Montrosse, Jr. It was quite a thrill for them to meet the Italian Superman when we were on the way to an Indy Show in Ohio

Bruno in discussion with his friend Paul Sarachelli (Left) and Ronnie "Snoopy" Lapinsky of The Regents and The Runarounds at Giulio's Restaurant in Yonkers, NY

*WWWF World Champion Bruno Sammartino and
NWA World Champion Dory Funk, Jr.*

Blackjack Brown

Bruno and The Big Cheese have often thanked me for introducing them. I was glad to do it and even happier to see such a long standing personal and business relationship grow from the introduction.

Bruno loved the wrestling business and protected it — even while participating in the Gabb Line on a weekly basis — the best that he could, and did a great job with it. Bruno had great reservations for many years of letting the WWE induct him in to the Hall of Fame. In my opinion, I felt that the WWE made the right changes to convince Bruno to rejoin the WWE Family for his family, friends, and fans. It was definitely an honor to meet, to know, to work with, and watch Pro Wrestling with The Living Legend of Pro Wrestling Mr. Bruno Sammartino.

If "The Living Legend" Bruno Sammartino trusted you and liked you there isn't anything that he wouldn't do for you. He was a great family man, and a truly great man. When Bruno was no longer happy with the wrestling business in the early '90s we ran the wrestling Gabb Line along with Capt. Lou Albano. The system was built around 12 paid caller lines and 4 lines for guests. It was the first of its kind. Once the fans knew that Bruno was a part of it, many in the wrestling community jumped on board. Some of the guests that appeared on the line were The Wild Samoans, Shane Douglas, Rob Van Dam, Terry Funk, Gary Michael Cappetta, The Power Twins: David and Larry Sontag, Johnny Rodz, Gino Caruso, Wild Bill McNulty, Mean Gene Okerlund, Eric Bischoff, Sabu, Justin Roberts, Tommy Dreamer, The Fabulous Moolah, The Hart Family, The McMahons, Bruce Prichard aka Brother Love, Matt Striker, Billy Caputo, Teddy Long, Lenny Dauber, Lord Zoltan Ken Jugan, Kevin Nash, Scott Hall, King Jordan Shulman, Tazz, Capt. Ivan Rothstein, Jerry Vitetta, Lou Thesz, Verne Gagne, The Bushwhackers: Luke and Butch, Bill DeMott, Kokomo Joe Ferrer, Dominic Valente, Anita the Hulkette, The Blackjacks: Mulligan and Lanza, Wrestling Historian Tom Burke, Mr. Stinky, Jeff Mangels, Sheiky Al Greco, Classy Freddie Blassie, George "The Animal" Steele, Sgt. Slaughter, Nikita Koloff, Cactus Jack, Bobo Brazil, Buddy Rogers, Nikolai Volkoff, Sensational Sherri Martel, Professor Elliott Maron, Ken Patera, Greg "The Hammer" Valentine, Pedro Morales, "The Macho Man" Randy Savage, Rowdy Roddy Piper, Bobby "The Brain" Heenan, Vince Russo, George Napolitano, Bill Apter, Killer Kowalski, Paul E. Dangerously, The Dudley Boyz, "Carolina's Own" David Isley, "The Big Cheese" Sal Corrente, Georgiann Makropoulos, Ringside Vladimir Abouzeide, Ringside Charlie Adorno, Mike Johnson from PWInsider, Pitchman Mitch Seinfeld, and of course, Dominic DeNucci, Bruno's very close friend.

I am grateful for being given the chance to share my thoughts of my relationship with Bruno with all of his fans and I am very thankful I went out of my way to stop in and see Bruno and Sal at Bruno's final personal appearance outside of Pittsburgh at The Big Event in Queens, NY on November 16th, 2016. I didn't know that it would be my last time seeing Bruno but I am positive this won't be the last time that I think of him.

Blackjack Brown has covered Professional Wrestling since 1972 as a photo journalist and a writer. His photos and columns have appeared in many of the top wrestling publications including Wrestling All-Stars, Wrestling World, Inside Wrestling, and Wrestling Maniacs.

Blackjack has been a weekly contributor to the NY Daily News. His personal wrestling column has appeared in the Chicago Sun Times since April 1988. Blackjack also provided weekly updates for WPLJ radio in NY City from 1977-1991 and continues to make guest appearances on wrestling programs around the country.

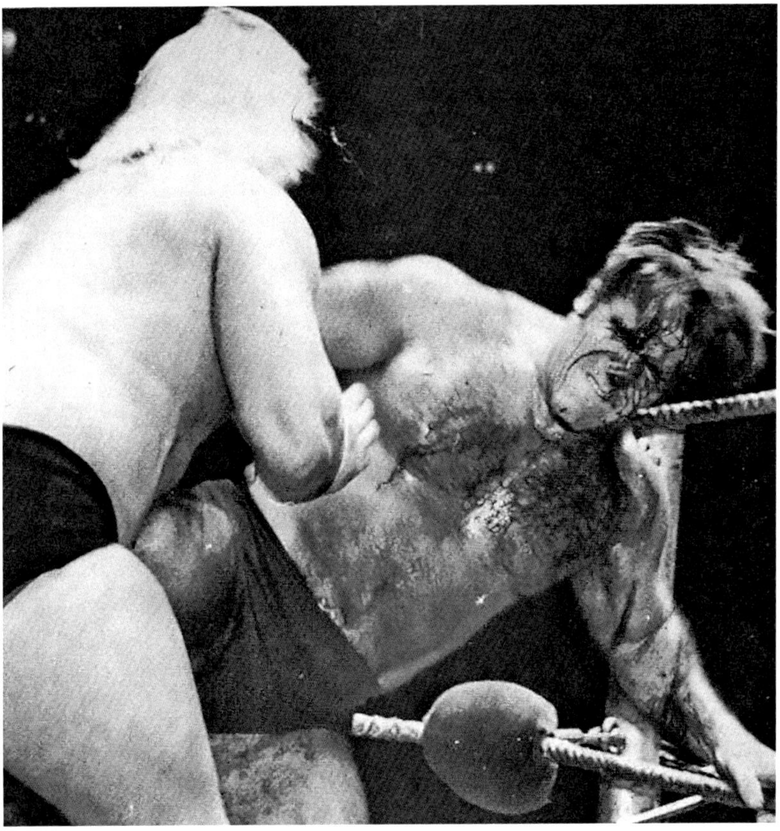

Stan Hansen

CLASS ACT! That is the term that comes to mind as I reflect on Bruno. Of course, the word act is used as an expression because he was surely not an act. He contacted me at the end of 1975 on the recommendation of a good friend of his, Mike Paidoussis, the retired wrestler from Steubenville Ohio. He got me booked to come into the WWWF for Vince McMahon sight unseen. I then proceeded to break his neck in Madison Square Garden in early 1976. It was the biggest opportunity that I had had in the business. This injury was devastating to the WWWF as he was champion and the whole territory was built around Bruno. He never once voiced anger or disappointment in me for hurting him. He came back and continued his stellar career after three or four months off.

Over the years we ran into each other in Japan and again for the WWE in 1981. He always was a gentleman and carried himself as a man of class. He was instrumental in putting me on the right path to my long career. I have over the years called him often and thanked him for him treating me with no ill feeling. In fact, I think that he enjoyed our friendship as much as I did.

There is always newer talent that comes along and becomes big stars, but there was no one that was bigger or more over with the people than Bruno. The reaction he got when he came back after me hurting him in Shea Stadium was something to behold. People were literally crying in happiness as he made his comeback appearance.

There will never be a more natural strong guy that represents the common man, immigrant, and blue-collar fan. He was literally loved by millions of fans in the WWWF territory.

Just a man of class.

*Bruno and Stan "The Lariat" Hansen. Even a broken
neck couldn't destroy this friendship of 40+ years*

THE AUTOBIOGRAPHY OF WRESTLING'S LIVING LEGEND

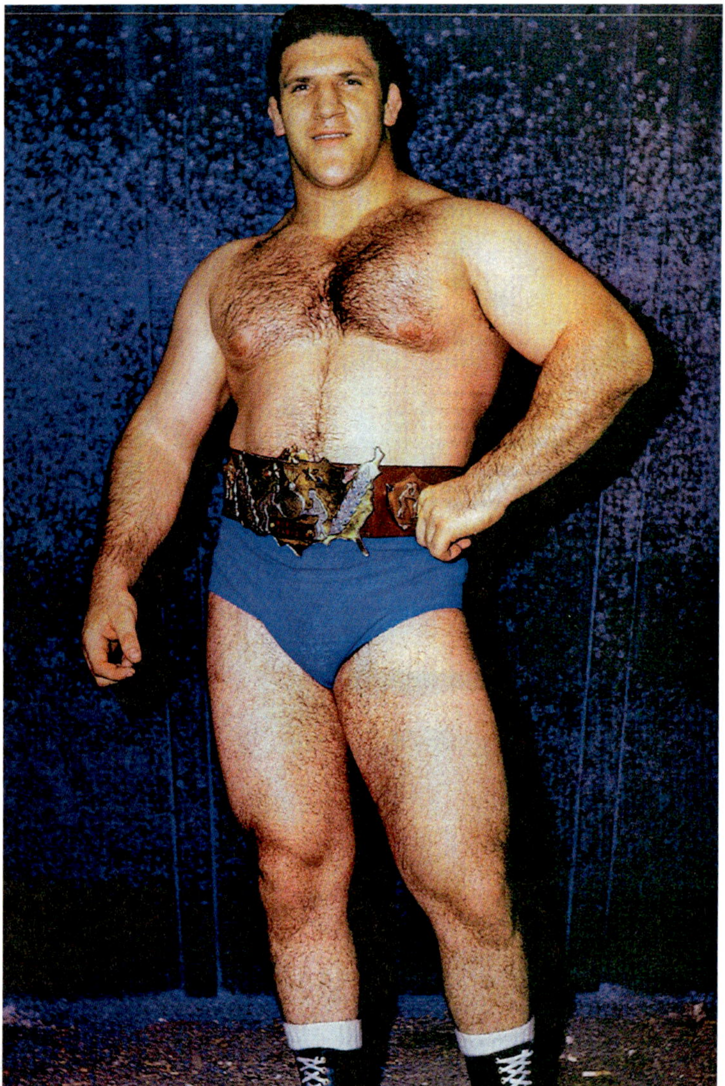

Dominic DeNucci

I first met Bruno in Canada when he came to work for Frank Tunney. We found out that we were born only 40 miles apart in Italy. I came from Frosolone, in the province of Campobasso, of course, Bruno came from Pizzoferrato.

I was working for Jim Barnett in Australia when Bruno came over to wrestle. We were booked in a tag team match while in Australia, and well, we became firm friends quickly during that stint in Australia. After I finished in Australia, and had gone back to San Francisco to get my car which had been in storage for a year, I called him. He asked me where I was going to wrestle next and I told him that I didn't know. He invited me to come to the WWWF. I asked if he didn't have to clear it with Vince McMahon, Sr. and he said that he already had. Based on the friendship we built in Australia, he wanted me to come to NY.

It is my opinion that no man before and no man after would be able to draw fans on a consistent basis to an arena like Bruno Sammartino. It was my pleasure to be his friend and tag team partner.

I saw Bruno six days before he died in the hospital, he was talking for a little while, but it was clear he wanted to sleep. It was very hard for me when I was leaving, I was starting to cry. Between the passing of my wife and the loss of Bruno it has been very hard for me to lose two of the most important people in my life.

Bruno was a very special man, and a loyal friend and business associate. As far as integrity, Bruno was a very honest person who's word was his bond.

I miss him now and I will always miss him until I see him again.

One of my many tours of Japan. Luckily this one included my pal Dominic DeNucci

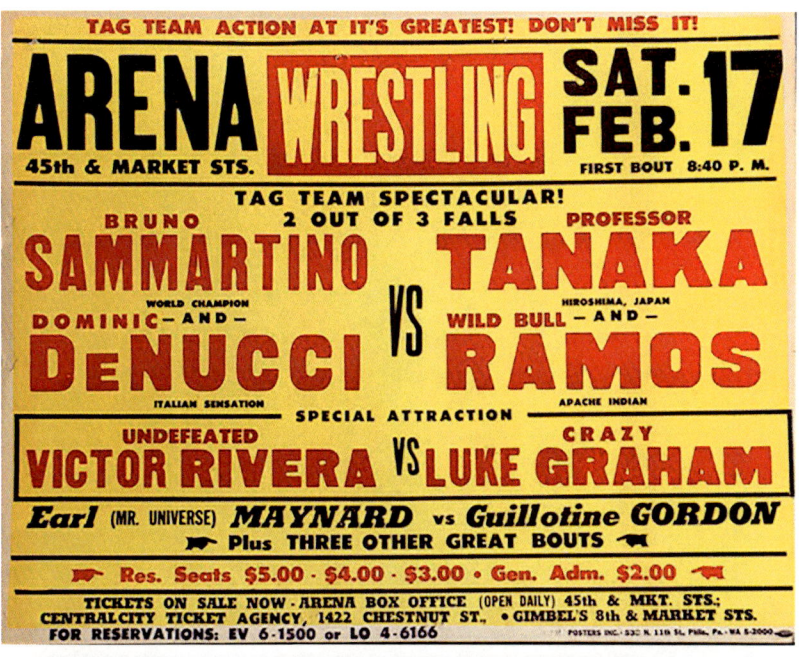

THE AUTOBIOGRAPHY OF WRESTLING'S LIVING LEGEND

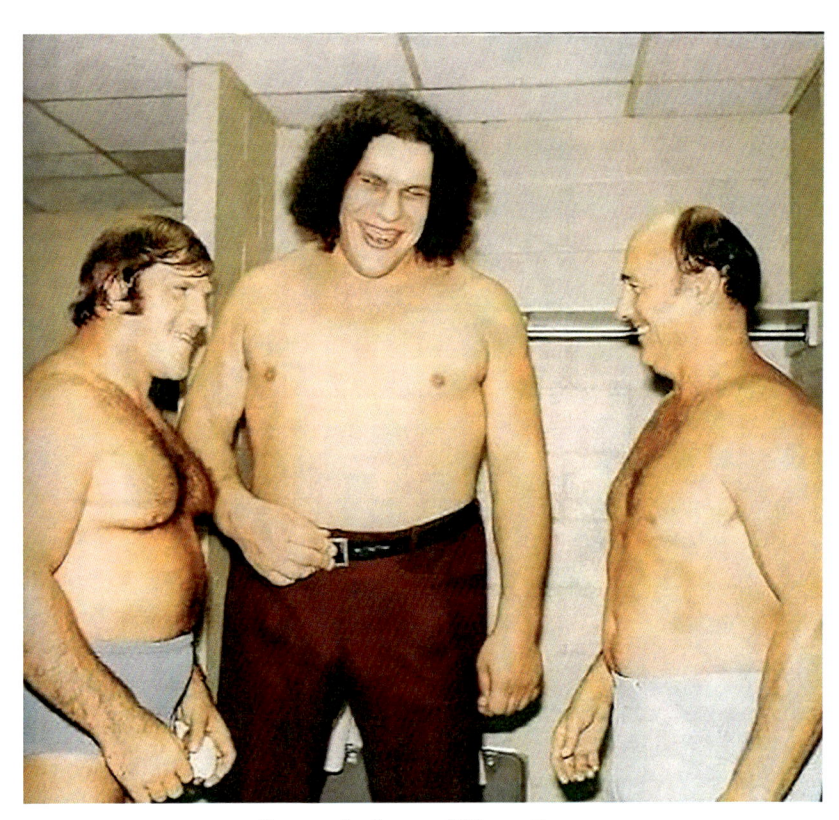

Bruno, Andre, and Verne Gagne

Gary Michael Cappetta

Like many kids of my youth, I became a lifelong wrestling fan because of Bruno Sammartino. He would enter my living room via weekly wrestling programs and spoke directly to me. Bruno likewise connected with millions of his fans with an earnest look and sincere words stressing the highest values of loyalty, family, integrity, and fairness. He spoke to me with respect. He drew me in to his rivalry of the moment and to the venues where he defended his title. Without Sammartino, the WWWF would have been just another wrestling territory. But he made the WWWF. He was The Federation.

Years later, when I began to announce many of Bruno's most memorable matches; I came to know the hero of my childhood, a figure you'd think who certainly could never live up to his mystique. But he did. Bruno would remember our conversations years later. He expressed care and concern. He offered advice during my full-time stint with WCW. And my respect for Bruno grew.

On both a personal and professional level, there will never again be a representative of pro wrestling so admired and deserving as Bruno Sammartino.

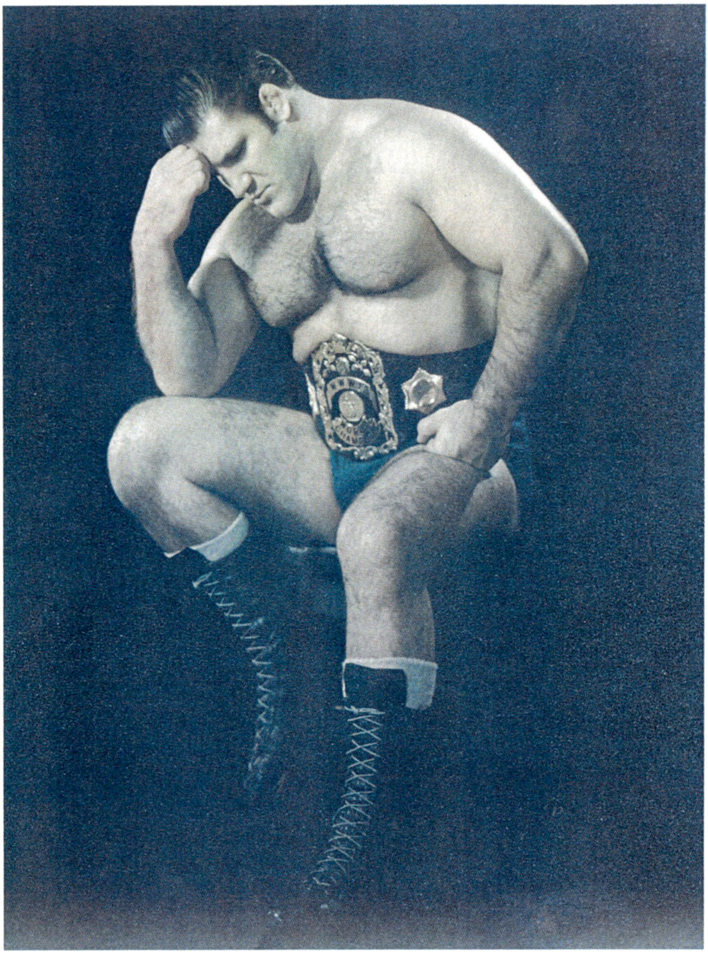

Afa "The Wild Samoan #1" Anoai

I have been in this business for over fifty years. I recognize Bruno Sammartino as a great champion, but most of all he was a great human being, and friend.

The few times my brother Sika and I wrested him and his partners—his son David or Dominic DeNucci—was some of the best experiences that I had in the ring. It was hard at the beginning because of the respect that we had for the man, but as we started to lock up we felt like it was an honor to be in the ring with the greatest Living Legend of all time.

We became close friends through the years and we will all miss Bruno forever. One man stands out when talking about the wrestling business with respect … "The Living Legend" Bruno Sammartino.

Bruno along with friend Davey O'Hannon, Capt. Lou Albano and Afa "The Wild Samoan #1" at an event in upstate New York

Dr. Mike and Bruno in 1989 - "I put this on a tripod to shoot it, well before selfies."

Photo Courtesy of Wrealano@aol.com

Remembering Bruno
by Dr. Mike Lano

"The most ethical man, not just in our industry of wrestling; but in life and important on so many levels. Bruno was loved and beloved because he was so completely genuine, caring and giving, He spoke to everyone the same way, whether it was a global leader or world celebrity to his fans around the world, giving the same amount of attention." ~Mike Lano

NWA Hollywood Wrestling, Los Angeles, CA

Bruno and I had been friends since January 1972, when he came to work the Los Angeles territory (I was one of the main ringside photogs for each program sold at our venues). He was put over in our annual 22 Man Battle Royal. That card was historic because as Bruno would repeatedly say on my national radio show, "It was the only time my friend Mil Mascaras and I ever locked up or were in a ring together." Bruno was to have worked regularly for us and our big boss/promoter Mike LeBell. That fell apart in March 1972. After Killer Kowalski "broke" a then-babyface Freddie Blassie's leg prior to a TV match, Bruno returned to LA to take on Kowalski in a revenge match, but following the terrific 45-minute broadway draw, Bruno became upset that LeBell hadn't even bothered to watch that match. "All he (LeBell) said he did was count the ticket money in the box office which upset me greatly. He didn't seem to care at all about what he was putting out there for the fans, nor did he want to listen to the boys' suggestions. I gave my notice after that match and told Walter how upset I was before I left LeBell for good."

Almost 20 years later Bruno had me host and produce his ***Bruno Legends DVD Interview Series.*** Our eighth, and last 90-minute taped interview was Bruno along with Koloff, Morales, DeNucci,

Billy Graham, Shawn Stasiak—representing his father Stan, and SD Jones debating the state of the biz at that time with a group of young stars including Raven, Missy Hyatt, ECW's Francine, Teddy Hart, Jack Evans, promoter Court Bauer, Chris Daniels, Matt Stryker, the SAT's, and Homicide.

Bruno shakes hands with a young Teddy Hart during the taping of the DVD. Also pictured are Ivan Koloff on the left, Pedro Morales, Dom DeNucci, and Lou Albano's head.

Old Foes ... Better Friends

Bruno and Nikolai in 1991 at a Hall of Fame dinner. Sadly we lost both in 2018.

Nikolai Volkoff returned to Vince McMahon, Sr. and the WWWF in January 1974, this time not as Bepo of the Mongols tag team, but instead as his famous Blassie-managed Soviet heel character. He feuded with Bruno all over the Northeast, including a memorable match in a sold out Madison Square Garden, as well as appearing in the very first wrestling main event ever held at the then-new Nassau Veterans Memorial Coliseum Arena in Long Island, NY.

WrestleMania 32, Arlington, TX

Photo Courtesy of Wrealano@aol.com

In 2016 at the private WrestleMania 32 after-party in Arlington, Bruno congratulated Roman Reigns on his third WWE World Heavyweight Championship

For decades, Bruno called me every Sunday to ask how today's "kids" were doing. How Vince's WWE ratings and PPV buy rates were, as he truly tried to keep up with the way the business was moving forward. "There's one constant about our industry. It's always changing and you have to keep up with it. It's hard for someone like me who is used to doing things the old way, but you can't argue with these gigantic outdoor stadiums they're running in now," he told me on my SiriusXM radio show back in February 2013.

Shea Stadium, New York

Billed as The Match of the Century: Bruno vs. Pedro Morales in 1972

This was the very first Shea Stadium wrestling main event—two others followed: Andre vs. Chuck Wepner that ran underneath Ali/Inoki on Closed-Circuit; then in 1980, Bruno vs. his former protege Larry Zbyszko—a face vs. face gamble by Vince McMahon, Sr., that would've been even more of a success if the weather had cooperated. Bruno told me "I was pleased with my match against Pete, even with the interference stuff involving George Steele. We had a nice babyface match until curfew which was how it was booked."

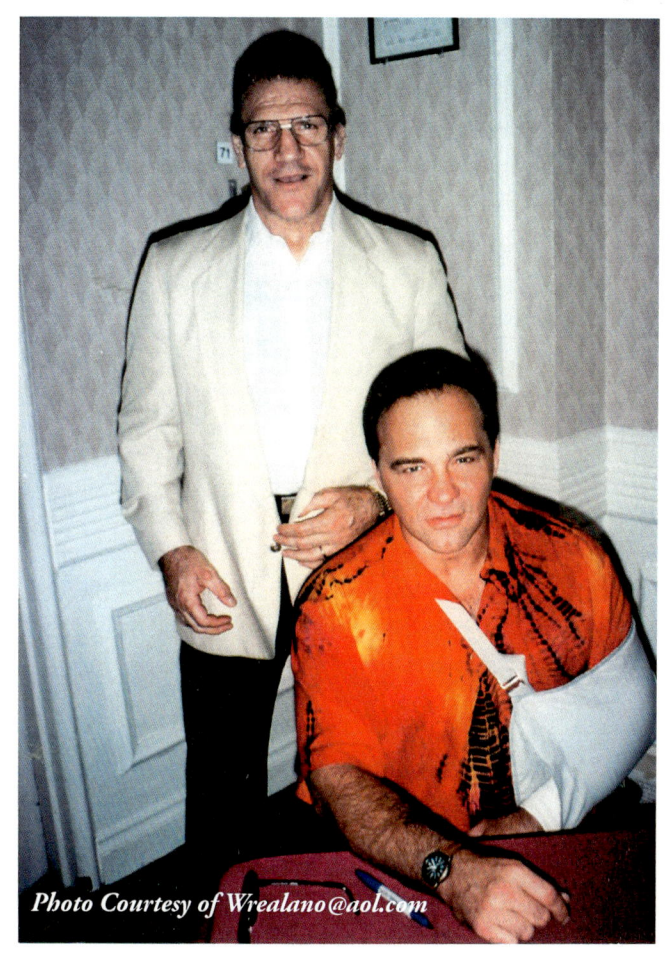

The Greatest Feud of All Time: Bruno vs. Larry

Photo Courtesy of Wrealano@aol.com

The "heat" leading up to their history-making Shea Stadium main event was worked to classic perfection after Larry finally turned on Bruno during a WWF TV show "work out." Later they had some legit heat that Bruno never really spoke to me about. That was the constant with Bruno, if you did something to violate his trust in you, he seldom forgave.

He was happy when he finally made up with Larry, right before I nagged them to pose for this photo.

Pittsburgh Post-Gazette

Pittsburgh warrior: Bruno Sammartino was the essence of the city

The passing of Bruno Sammartino, a legend of the wrestling world known for his immense strength and longevity, marks the loss of a Pittsburgh icon.

He was a pretty good life coach, too.

It may sound funny to some that a professional wrestler could provide meaningful lessons for life, but that was the kind of man Mr. Sammartino was: Loving toward his family, proud of his city and tough as nails in the ring.

Mr. Sammartino, who died at the age of 82 on Wednesday, was born in Italy. In a life marked by fighting, the young Mr. Sammartino had his life threatened by rheumatic fever as the Nazis invaded his community. His mother was able to nurse him back to health using leeches, and Mr. Sammartino cited this moment as one that forever changed his outlook on life.

After immigrating to Pittsburgh with his family, he turned to wrestling as a way to deal with high school bullies, who mocked him for his inability to speak English. Before long, he found himself on the professional circuit, on his way to a streak of dominance the wrestling world had never seen before and has not been equaled since.

Mr. Sammartino's reign as WWE Champion, then known as the WWWF Champion, is still awe-inspiring. His two championship reigns lasted a total of 4,040 days — or more than 11 years. His first, from 1963 to 1971, is still the longest in WWE history.
His toughness was a thing of legend. Mr. Sammartino was never

an easy fight. In fact, he rubbed some wrestling promoters the wrong way because he refused to lose. "If anybody can really beat me, fine," he once said. "But that's the only way I'll go down."

But outside of the ring, Mr. Sammartino proved himself to be a thoughtful and considerate family man. He married his wife, Carol, in 1959, and together they had three children. After his retirement from wrestling in 1988, he dedicated himself to spending more time with his family.

Mr. Sammartino was, in so many ways, a perfect representative for Pittsburgh. Ours is a town that prides itself on toughness and grit, but also on caring for family, friends and neighbors. Few people embodied that culture better than Mr. Sammartino, and few people were prouder to be a Pittsburgher than he was.

In return for his adopted hometown pride, Pittsburgh has loved Mr. Sammartino back. His passing has caused an outpouring of remembrances and tributes from major figures and organizations, including every major sports franchise. Mayor Bill Peduto described Mr. Sammartino "as one of the greatest ambassadors for this region."

But even as the stories stop being told and life moves on, those driving into South Oakland will see the welcome sign highlighting three native sons: Dan Marino, Andy Warhol and Bruno Sammartino.

Mr. Sammartino may have been the greatest of them all

Obituary originally published by *THE EDITORIAL BOARD of the Pittsburgh Post-Gazette*—April 20, 2018

BRUNO SAMMARTINO

Arnold ✓
@Schwarzenegger

Bruno Sammartino was a legend. He was the American Dream personified. From his childhood in Italy hiding from Nazis to selling out Madison Square Garden 188 times as the biggest star of professional wrestling, he was a hero in every stage of his life.

10:06 AM · 18 Apr 2018

THE AUTOBIOGRAPHY OF WRESTLING'S LIVING LEGEND

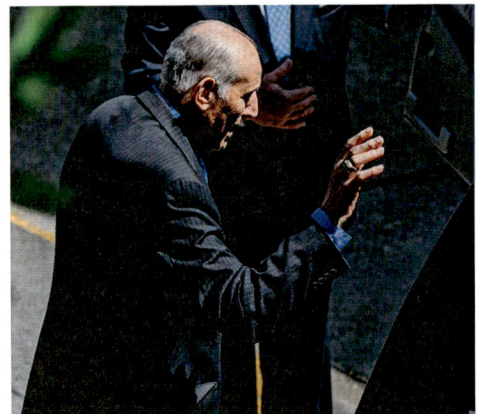

Dominic DeNucci bids a final farewell to his friend Bruno, supported by Shane Douglas

THE AUTOBIOGRAPHY OF WRESTLING'S LIVING LEGEND

Bruno with Smith Hart and Bret Hart

Bret Hart

Forever a champion.
Rest In Peace

Apr 18, 2018

BRUNO SAMMARTINO

THE PITTSBURGH STEELERS ORGANIZATION IS DEEPLY SADDENED BY THE PASSING OF THE GREAT BRUNO SAMMARTINO.

BRUNO WAS TRULY A WORLD-RENOWNED CHAMPION WHO NEVER LOST HIS IDENTITY OF A TRUE PITTSBURGHER, ALWAYS PLACING HIS FAMILY AND FRIENDS AHEAD OF ANY PERSONAL ACCOMPLISHMENTS.

OUR THOUGHTS AND PRAYERS GO OUT TO HIS WIFE, CAROL, AND SONS DAVID, DANNY AND DARRYL.

— GM KEVIN COLBERT

Bruno Mars ✓
@BrunoMars

Sending love and prayers to Bruno Sammartino's family. He was such a gentleman when I met him & really meant a lot to my father & I. RIP 👑

6:32 AM - Apr 19, 2018

THE AUTOBIOGRAPHY OF WRESTLING'S LIVING LEGEND

My hometown hero, Bruno Sammartino has passed. I grew up watching Bruno. He was an amazing performer, who made his Pittsburgh natives proud. He was a champion's champion. I got to know Bruno in his latter years, after he retired from the then WWWF. He carried himself with dignity, and was always courteous to his fans. A true role model and hero. We will miss you Bruno. #itstrue

MSG (@TheGarden)

Today is a sad day for wrestling and sports fans. Simply put, Bruno Sammartino was one of the biggest stars in the long and storied history of Madison Square Garden, a legend in every way. Our thoughts and prayers are with his family today and always.

The marquee at Madison Square Garden pays tribute to the Living Legend

THE AUTOBIOGRAPHY OF WRESTLING'S LIVING LEGEND

Dan Marino (@DanMarino)

I'm saddened to hear about the passing of Pittsburgh & @WWE legend and my father's classmate Bruno Sammartino. My thoughts and prayers are with the entire Sammartino family. #PittsburghFamily #LoveBruno

Dan Marino's dad as pictured in Bruno's school yearbook

Dominic, Mike Migut, and Bruno at Christmas

From childhood hero to great friend. This is the final photo of Mike and Bruno

Away from the Spotlight
by Mike Migut

Have you ever heard the old adage, you should never meet your childhood hero because you will be disappointed? In my case that turned out to be 100 percent false. I got to meet my childhood hero Bruno Sammartino some years back with the help of Sal Corrente, and little did I know that first lunch with Bruno would turn into an incredible friendship with not only him, but both of our families.

My first meeting with Bruno was a lunch scheduled at Bruno's favorite restaurant, Rico's in Pittsburgh. I went with my brother Jeff, and our friend Dana who works for the Pittsburgh Penguins hockey team, and just happened to have a day off. During lunch, the three of us were very quiet and respectful of Bruno, we did ask some questions, but not all the questions we had written down on a cheat sheet. During the lunch, we had a group photo taken, and I asked Bruno if I could send the photo to him to get it autographed. He said certainly, and he gave me his address. When we left Rico's that day, we were just amazed that we had gotten the opportunity to have lunch with Wrestling's Living Legend. When I got the photo made, I sent it to Bruno. My family and I own Valley Printing in Johnstown, PA so I

Bruno's 82nd birthday

also printed Bruno some 8 x 10 photos for him to keep, and some he could sign for his fans. I never thought I would hear from Bruno again, but one Saturday afternoon during my lunch break at work my mom comes to me with the phone and she says Bruno is on the phone. I couldn't believe it. I said, "Hello," and the voice on the other end said, "Hello Mike, this is Bruno, Bruno Sammartino," like there is any other Bruno than The Living Legend. Bruno called to thank me for all the 8x10 photos we had sent him, and he wanted to know how much he owed me. I told him it ad been an honor to meet him and have lunch, the photos were a thank you. He said, "Mike can I be perfectly honest,"—and getting to know Bruno these years after this phone call one thing I can say is, what you saw was what you got with Bruno, he was a very honest person—"you guys at lunch were so quiet." I said, "Bruno we were nervous and star-struck, getting to have lunch with you." Then in typical Bruno fashion, he says, "I'm no different than anyone else." I told him that we had notes written down with questions that we didn't get to ask him, so he told us that the next time we were in Pittsburgh to call him for another lunch and we can ask him all our question's. He gave me his number and said, "I know Johnstown is over an hour's drive, but please call me."

As it happens, I travel to Pittsburgh a lot because we did some printing for the Pittsburgh Penguins, so the next time I was heading down, a few weeks later, we met again—not as nervous. At this lunch Bruno told me about his mother and what she did to keep her family alive during the war. I just couldn't believe the sacrifices his mother made, and as he was telling me the story, he had tears

Carol with Mike's mom Margie

in his eyes remembering his mother and the hardships they endured. My mother raised me and my two brothers as a single mother in the projects, so I also am also very close with my mom. I asked Bruno if the next time I came down if I could bring my mom to meet him Bruno looked me straight in the eyes and said, "Is your mother your best friend?" I replied "Yes, she is," and Bruno told me that so was his mother and that he would love to meet my mom.

Bruno loved meeting people

  I drove back to Johnstown and told my mom that we were going to have lunch with Bruno. Surprisingly my mom said flat out that she wasn't interested, I pushed her some more, she still said: "I'm not interested". You watched that wrestling as a kid and I was never a fan." This was true, she only let us watch it if our school grades were good, if we got bad grade's we weren't allowed to watch the Saturday wrestling show. Even though she was convinced that she knew nothing about wrestling and therefore would have nothing to talk to Bruno about, I eventually convinced her to come. I had already told Bruno that I was bringing my mom to Rico's to meet him, and the one thing I learned about Bruno from the very start, was that Bruno was a man of his word. Once he told you something, or once you told him something, you kept your word. He respected those who kept their word. Honesty and loyalty were important to Bruno, so it was important to me to convince my mom to come to lunch

  The day arrived we all sat down to lunch. I was anxious for my mom to see that Bruno was such a classy, humble person. He wanted to know about my mom, how she was raised on a farm with a large family, and Bruno tells my mom about how he helped his mom on their land in Italy. Honest to God the entire lunch was my mom and Bruno talking, I couldn't get a word in at all. So that is how Bruno Sammartino, the greatest wrestling champion that ever lived, became my good friend.

In the beginning, I would only talk to Bruno about wrestling, but as we became better friends through phone calls, lunches, and dinners, I would call him for advice and we would talk about everything from family to politics to food. One Saturday I called him to get his recipe for his garlic and spaghetti dish. He would make it with mussels, so I'm on the phone while he explained to me how to cut the garlic, prepare the dish, and don't eat the mussels that don't open. He finished by telling me to call back and let him know how it turned out. Later, I called him back and jokingly said, Bruno, I'm not a good cook, I burnt the water, he laughed hard and out loud. Now when I prepare that mean for dinner, I call it Bruno's Spaghetti in memory of my friend, and I smile, because I remember during our dinners at Rico's, I would order mussels and Bruno would joke with me and say, "It's funny that you always order the mussels, because you don't have any muscles."

Bruno had a wonderful sense of humor

Bruno had a great sense of humor. I will never forget him and how humble he was. Once I became friends with Bruno, I was able to take friends to Rico's to meet him. I wanted them to see not the pro wrestler Bruno Sammartino, but the person Bruno Sammartino. Every year, our families always had a big annual Christmas party at Rico's. Through our dinners, we got to know Bruno's wife Carol, and she is such a wonderful person. My mom and her connected the first time they met because my mom raised 3 boys by herself, and Carol mostly raised her boys alone, as Bruno was on the road so many days

Mike's greatest claim to fame: "Beating" Bruno at a charity arm-wrestlingg event

as WWWF Champion. Carol is such a special person, just like Bruno as, and if you saw them together over the years you could see that they had so much love for each other, it was a truly great marriage.

We attended Madison Square Garden for his WWE Hall of Fame induction, I flew with Bruno and his son Darryl to New York for Bruno's last ever public signing and I went to Wrestlemania in New Orleans when the WWE unveiled his statue. When the news came up that they were going to dedicate a statue of Bruno in his hometown of Pizzoferrato, Italy, there was no way we could miss it. That to me was truly a trip of a lifetime. I had an awesome time two summers before that when Bruno came to Johnstown with his friend Dominic DeNucci to arm wrestle me for charity to raise money for our local police department. It was an honor having Bruno at our place, and "kayfabe" lives on from that day, because The Living Legend, the Champ let me beat him in arm wrestling, although I did use two hands. One thing I can remember about Bruno from that day was it

That first drink in Pizzoferrato with Bruno, Mike, the Mayor, and Bruno's cousin

was hot and humid. I picked him and Dominic up at his house and Bruno was in his recliner, but he looked tired and somewhat uncomfortable. I asked him if he was ok and he said he was having trouble with his shoulder and didn't get much sleep, so I told him if this isn't going to work, if you're not feeling good, we can cancel the event.

"Absolutely not. You have a lot of people coming today and I will be OK." Always the man of his word.

Another story I love to tell, was just after we landed in Rome and then had to get on a bus for 3 hours to get to Bruno's hometown of Pizzoferrato. My mom and I are sitting behind Bruno and Carol on the bus, and while Bruno is telling stories about his town, the bus keeps going up and up and up. These were very steep hills. The bus slowed down, and everyone asks why we were going so slow. Bruno tells everyone to look to their right so that they could see Pizzoferrato, off in the distance you could see his town perched up in those mountains. We arrived at the town square Bruno asked the bus driver to pull over at his cousin's cafe. He wanted to see him immediately, and Bruno looked back at me and tells me to come in with him. I did, and when we got inside Bruno said to me, "Mike, the next few days here they have me doing all kinds of interviews and appearances so I might not have much time to see you, but I wanted you to have your first beer in Italy with me and Darryl." So, his son Darryl, Bruno, Bruno's cousin, the Mayor of Pizzoferrato and I had a beer together before we had even got to the hotel it was a special moment I will never forget. Bruno was a true friend. Later that night, Darryl said Bruno wanted to go back into town to see some family. The hotel we stayed at was way further up the mountains and I remembered talking to Bruno before this trip telling him I

The rematch: Mike "wins" again

couldn't wait to see your city, and he would laugh and say it's no city it's a village. It was such an awesome town. The people were all so welcoming thrilled to host their hometown hero.

After dinner, I followed Bruno and Darryl outside to where there was a car waiting to make the drive back down the mountain. It appeared that there was no room for me, so just as I was about to tell Darryl that I will stay, a guy gets out of the car speaking Italian and gives his seat to me so that I can to join Bruno, Carol, and Darryl. About an hour later we are at Bruno's cousin's cafe, and here comes this guy all soaked in sweat from the long walk down the mountain in that heat. I felt so damn bad he walked all that way down the mountain so I could join Bruno. I don't speak Italian, so I asked Bruno to tell him thanks and I wanted to buy him a beer. He told me, through Bruno, it was no problem. That I was Bruno's friend and he respected the fact that I was friends with Bruno. They were such great people. Bruno yells over to me if I have any photos on my phone of when we arm-wrestled for charity. He wanted to show his cousin, so I showed them the photo and his cousin is laughing

BRUNO SAMMARTINO

Mike found this framed poster of Bruno and Emilia in a municipal building. It's am advert for The Body Shop in French. It translates as: "Especially for Mom. Extraordinary gifts for an exceptional woman."

while they are speaking in Italian. I asked Bruno what his cousin was saying, and Bruno says, "You really want to know? There is no way in hell that you could ever beat me in arm-wrestling." I laughed and reminded him that it's in the books. Bruno laughed and set up a rematch "here on my turf." Of course, Bruno let me beat him again in his hometown. His sense of humor was great, and when we had dinner for his birthday, back in Pittsburgh, Bruno told the whole dinner group how a printer from Johnstown embarrassed him in Pizzoferrato and beat him in arm-wrestling, and that he was so embarrassed he had to flee his hometown in shame never to return again.

These are my stories and they will always be a part of me but what I didn't know until Carol told me after Bruno passed away, the extent of Bruno's health issues during that trip to Italy. I had known he wasn't well, but I didn't know to what extent, and after Carol told me I just cried. Here was Bruno not feeling good, he did not want to be on this trip—he told me before this, that he and Carol did their farewell tour of Italy a few years ago, and he was only here because they were dedicating part of the new hospital wing in memory of his mother—that's the only reason he came back to Italy. But as bad as Bruno was feeling, he still thought of me and jokingly let me beat him in Pizzoferrato so I could have this story to always treasure.

I sure do miss my friend as I am typing these memories. The years that I knew Bruno, I did some great stuff with him. Like I said, WrestleMania in New Orleans to see his statue, his last autograph signing

Mike and Bruno at a charity picnic

Celebrating Mike's 50th birthday

in New York at The Big Event, his WWE induction in Madison Square Garden. Going to New York for his last signing there was a mix up with the airline tickets, so I bought a first-class ticket, but Bruno and Darryl had coach. I gave my first-class ticket to Bruno to use and I sat with Darryl which was great. We had a few beers on the flight and I got to know Darryl and hear his stories about Bruno. Darryl is just like Bruno, a class act. On the return flight there was a drunk kid giving the attendants a hard time, and while we were on the runway Darryl unlocks his seatbelt and helps restrain this kid. The next thing you know, the New York Police Department comes on to the plane and removes him kid from the plane. Once the flight gets in the air, the attendant brings a note from the airline captain thanking Darryl and tells him there is one seat available in first class if he wanted to sit there. Darryl, humble like his father, says no and tells her that I gave my first-class seat to Bruno to sit there. The person sitting in the row across from Darryl asks if that is Bruno Sammartino and Darryl says yes, he's my dad. Well, the attendant says her son is a fan and that she is going to say hi. Darryl says he has a better idea, go up to him and say, "How is your flight, Mr. Migut?" She comes back, and she said Bruno had told her the flight was good and he just wants to get home. Darryl asked if she had asked him his name and she said she couldn't as he was so sweet. Darryl says please, let's tease him. So, she goes back to Bruno and says, "Mr. Migut, I never knew you were a World Champion Wrestler." Bruno looked at her laughed and said I'm busted, aren't I?

THE AUTOBIOGRAPHY OF WRESTLING'S LIVING LEGEND

Mike had this tie made for the trip to Italy. It is the huge painting from Bruno's trophy room. He had always seen the photo in wrestling magazines growing up and thought it would be a great tie to wear to Italy. Bruno loved it.

*Bruno with Mike's family—his mother Margie,
and his brothers, Kirk and Jeff*

We laughed about that when we landed, and Bruno said: "Hey Mike, thanks again." I said, "Are you kidding. Now I can say that Bruno Sammartino pretended to be Mike Migut on a flight back to Pittsburgh."

I have so many great memories and stories but to be honest what I will remember and really miss the most about Bruno is just talking to him on Saturdays. I would call, he would have his opera music playing but he would turn it down, and we would talk, sometimes for a half-an-hour, and other times for over an hour-and-a-half. When my mom got diagnosed with breast cancer, the first person I called for support was Bruno and I cried like a baby. I apologized on the phone for crying and he said are you kidding me, what kind of man would you be if you didn't cry while you are worried about your mom. I told him thanks and later that night he called me back to see how I was doing, and all through my mom's treatments and surgery he always called, always asked about her, always with caring and reassuring words to stay positive. He was so happy that I was taking my mom on the trip to Italy and that her health was great, the surgery had gone well. When I got back from Italy—the tour was around 11 days and Bruno had left after the Pizzoferrato part of

Mike, Margie, and Bruno at Mike's 50th birthday party

the trip—I called him and told him all about the trip and the sights we had seen. He had been so worried about the group, hoping that everyone had a great time, and I assured him the group had a once in a lifetime trip.

This past Christmas, I invited some of the Italy group to join us at the annual party, and we all went around the table telling Bruno how much that trip meant to us. We sang Christmas carols with Bruno and Carol, but I never ever thought that would be the last time I would ever see Bruno. I knew he was sick, but I always looked at Bruno like I when I was that 8-year-old fan with stars in my eyes. Bruno was the champ, nothing could keep him down or beat him.

BRUNO SAMMARTINO

Mike, his brother Kirk, and Margie, with Bruno and Carol, celebrating Bruno's birthday at Rico's

So, my first-time meeting Bruno was at Rico's and it was also my last time seeing my friend. When we went to Rico's after Bruno's funeral it was tough because of all the get-togethers we had there over the years. It just felt empty without the champ. I cried when we went in as I passed the first table where we had that lunch. That first lunch. I honestly don't know how it happened, why it happened, but my childhood hero became my best friend. A lunch at Rico's and there we were after the funeral having a meal at Rico's, that was tough. I didn't know Bruno a lifetime like some of his friends who also miss him dearly, but I was blessed to have known him for a few years. It's tough typing this with tears streaming down my face, remembering Bruno. He was a great friend, but he was also a huge part of my childhood, and at Rico's after the funeral, it was like saying goodbye to the best part of my childhood. I could say so much more about Bruno, but I will close with this. Thank you, Bruno, it was truly my honor to call you my friend and I will never forget you.

Your friend,

Mike

THE AUTOBIOGRAPHY OF WRESTLING'S LIVING LEGEND

Bruno with his brother Paul, Mike, and Margie during the trip to Pizzoferrato

The whole village attended the ceremony

Bruno Sammartino
Living Legend

Per aver rappresentato in tutto il mondo con il suo carisma e la sua forte personalità, tutta la comunità di Pizzoferrato

The plaque in front of the statue

THE AUTOBIOGRAPHY OF WRESTLING'S LIVING LEGEND

Mike and Bruno in front of the statue. Bruno signed this when they returned from the trip

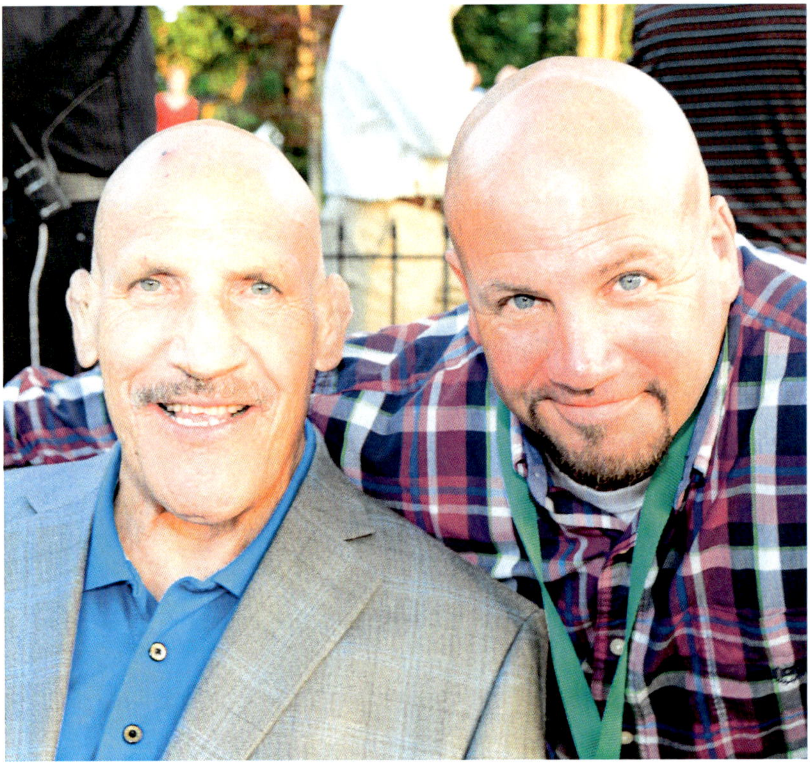

Darryl Sammartino

How many people can say they have witnessed thousands of fans chanting their dad's name in arenas across the world? I am fortunate enough to say I have, and no words can come close to describing what it feels like.

Traveling the world with my dad over many years afforded me the opportunity to see fans, celebrities, professional athletes, politicians and even a future president share their memories and appreciation of not only my dad's career but more so his professionalism and integrity.

Time and time again people expressed how important my dad made them feel; what they may not realize is they all were important to him. He loved his fans, he appreciated his fans, without his fans he would not have been able to provide his family the lifestyle he desired.

My favorite trip with my dad was WrestleMania 33 in Orlando, Florida in April 2017. We took my son with us. My dad could not have been more proud to introduce his grandson, Bruno Leopoldo Sammartino II to everyone.

At that time we didn't know it would be our last WrestleMania together—but what a finale!

I am so grateful for all the experiences I had with my dad but more than anything, I am grateful and lucky to call him "DAD".

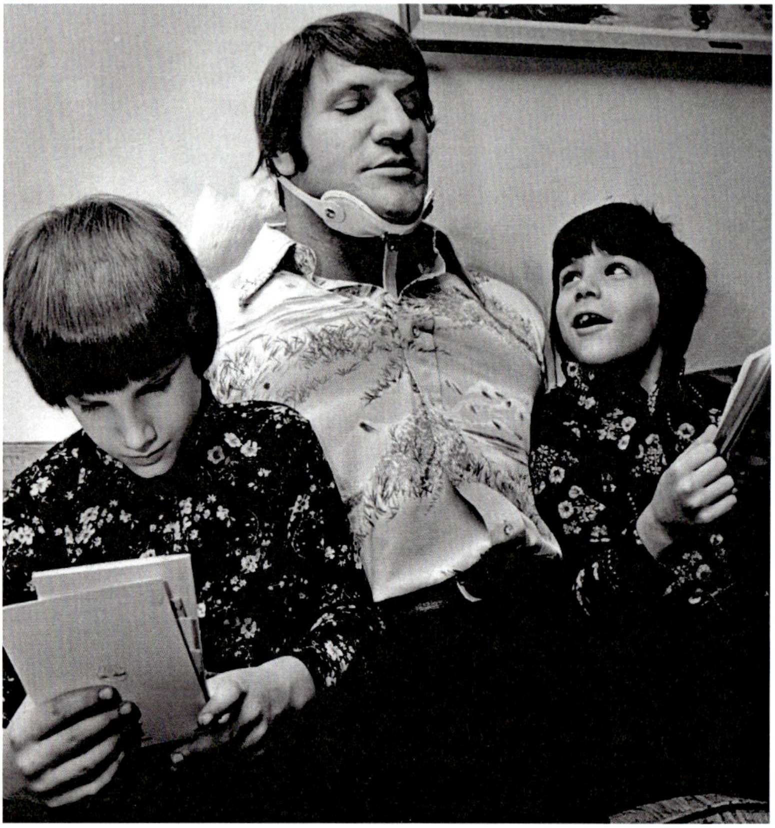

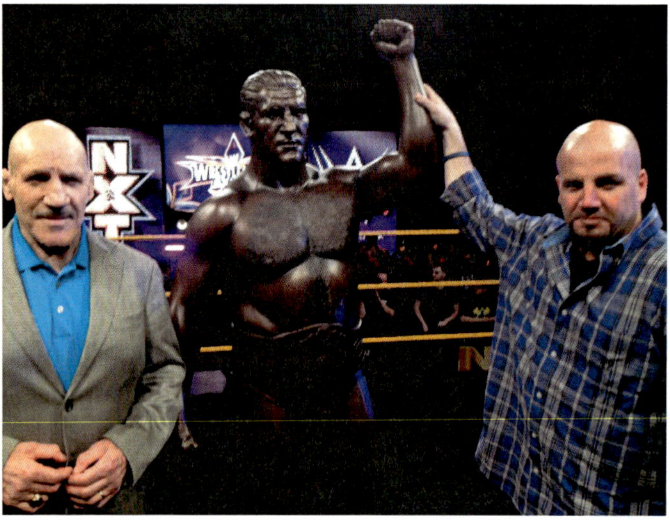

THE AUTOBIOGRAPHY OF WRESTLING'S LIVING LEGEND

Bruno Leopoldo Sammartino II with his Granddad Bruno

BRUNO SAMMARTINO

BRUNO AND CAROL SAMMARTINO FOUNDATION

BRUNOSAMMARTINOFOUNDATION.COM

FIND US ON FACEBOOK
@SAMMARTINOFDN

FOLLOW US ON TWITTER
@SAMMARTINOFDN

Mission Statement

The mission of the Bruno and Carol Sammartino Foundation (BACS) is to help provide those we serve with food, shelter, and services to ease their burdens of life's basic necessities.

Vision Statement

The Bruno and Carol Sammartino Foundation will strive to provide quality programs and services that will establish the foundation as an integral member of the community. The services provided by the BACS Foundation will help to provide/assist those living in Western Pennsylvania who might otherwise go without the basic necessities of life.

Values

One core value of the Bruno and Carol Sammartino Foundation is that value and assistance can only be achieved if our actions are forthright and integrate our strengths and integrity. The BACS Foundation will provide services to the poor and less fortunate.

Alfonso and Emilia Sammartino

THE AUTOBIOGRAPHY OF WRESTLING'S LIVING LEGEND

Integrity. Humility. Fairness. Kindness. These are things that made my husband the best of the best.
Carol Sammartino

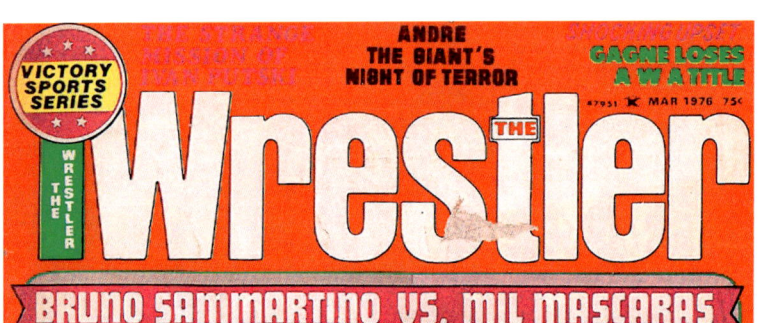

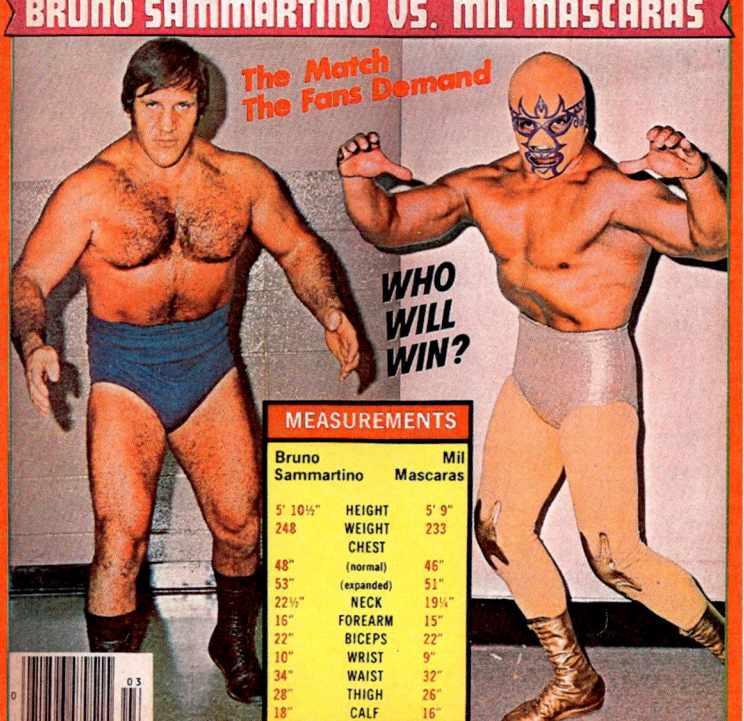

VICTORY SPORTS SERIES

ANDRE THE GIANT'S NIGHT OF TERROR

GAGNE LOSES A W A TITLE

MAR 1976 75¢

THE WRESTLER

BRUNO SAMMARTINO VS. MIL MASCARAS

The Match The Fans Demand

WHO WILL WIN?

MEASUREMENTS

Bruno Sammartino		Mil Mascaras
5' 10½"	HEIGHT	5' 9"
248	WEIGHT	233
	CHEST	
48"	(normal)	46"
53"	(expanded)	51"
22½"	NECK	19¼"
16"	FOREARM	15"
22"	BICEPS	22"
10"	WRIST	9"
34"	WAIST	32"
28"	THIGH	26"
18"	CALF	16"

BRUNO! BRUNO! BRUNO!

His Career in Covers

Throughout his career, Bruno was regularly featured on the front cover of wrestling magazines across the world.
On the following pages you will find the selection that were ranked the greatest courtesy of the
Kappa Publishing Group

BRUNO SAMMARTINO

June 1965

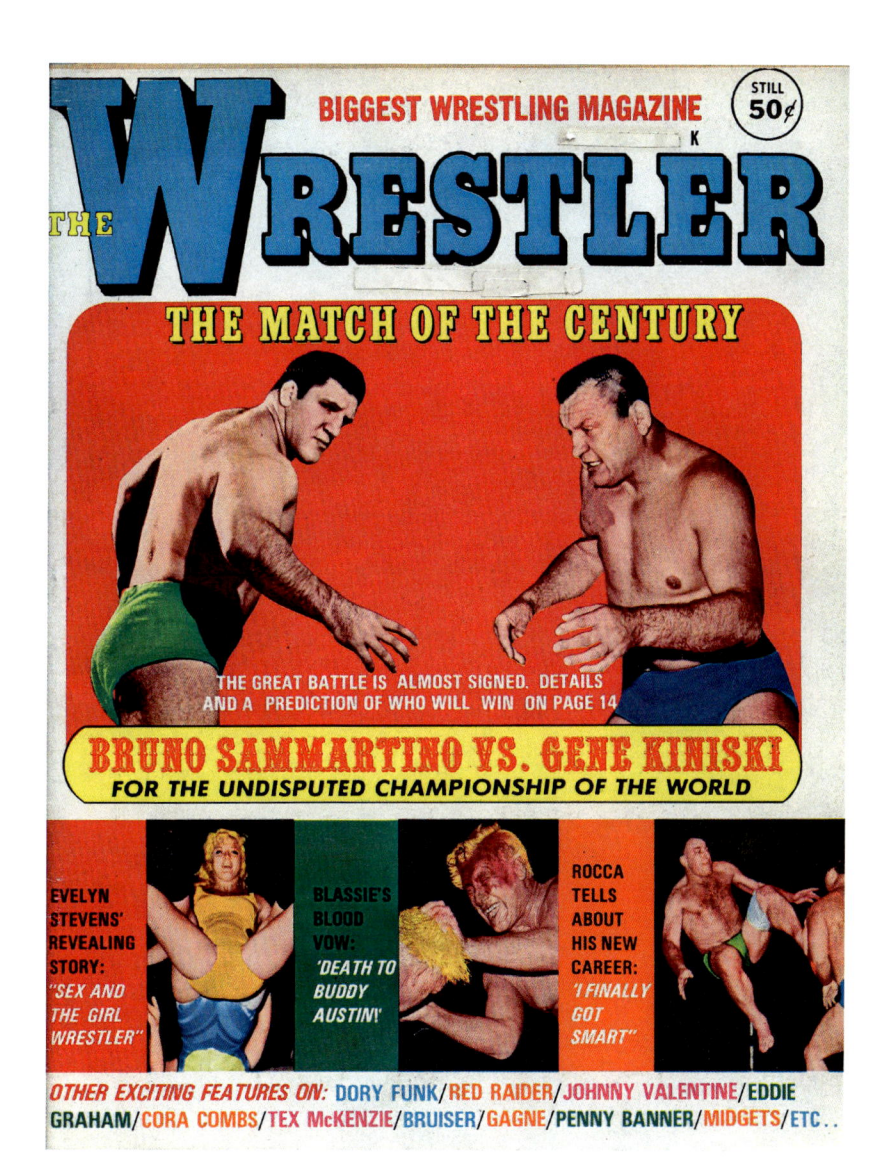

THE AUTOBIOGRAPHY OF WRESTLING'S LIVING LEGEND

April 1969

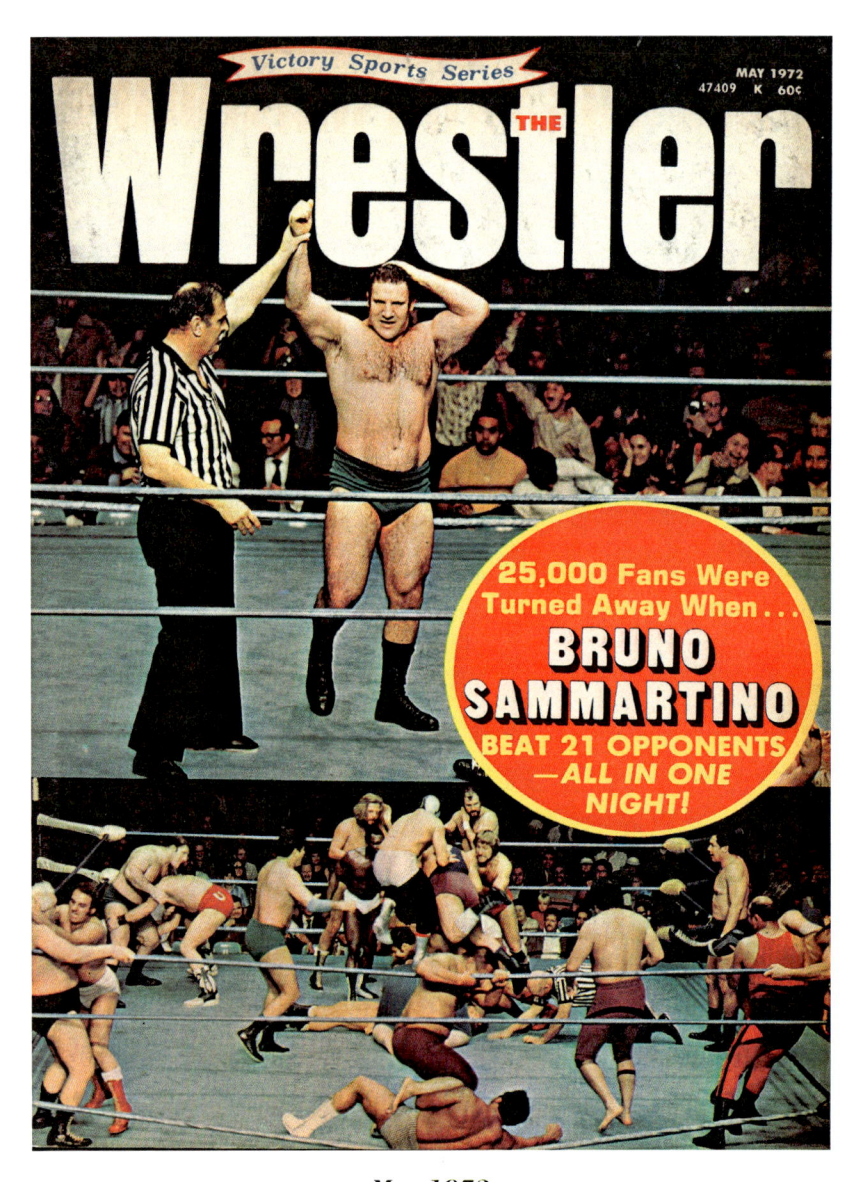

May 1972

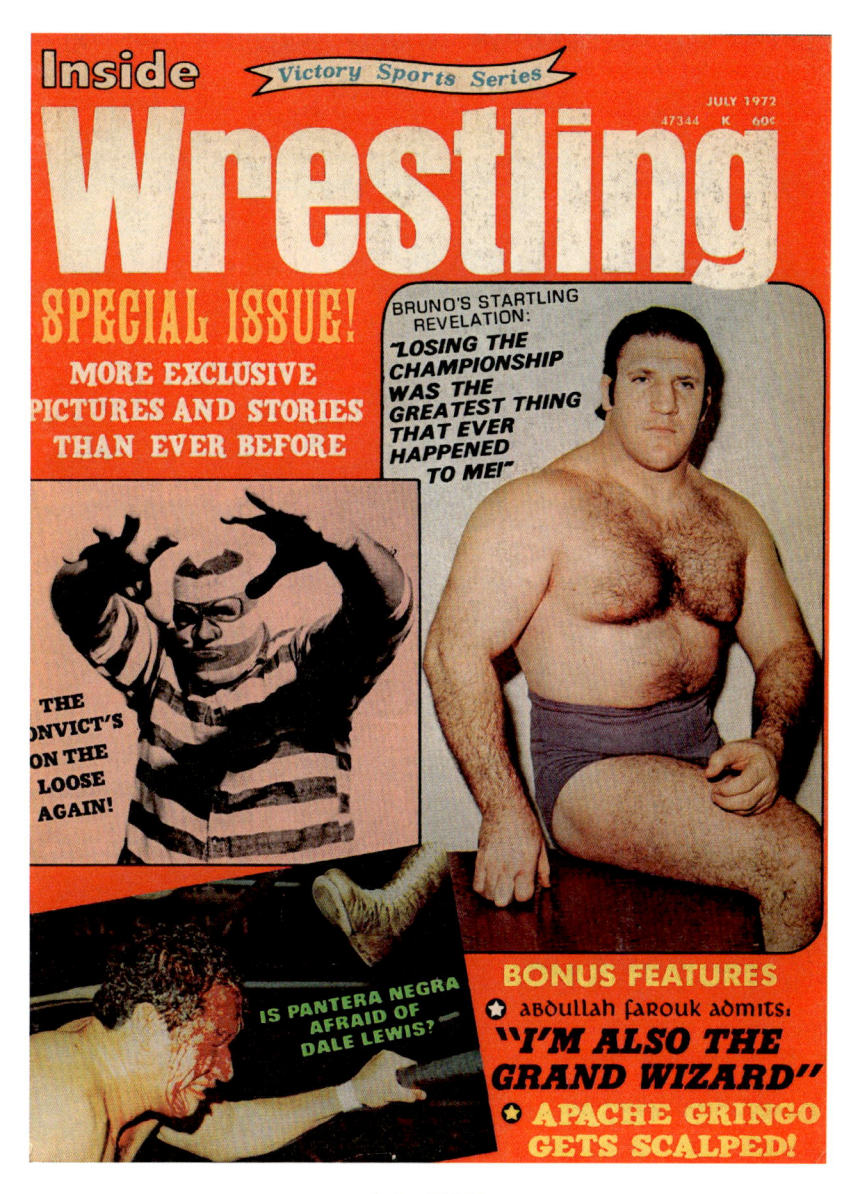

THE AUTOBIOGRAPHY OF WRESTLING'S LIVING LEGEND

July 1972

BRUNO SAMMARTINO

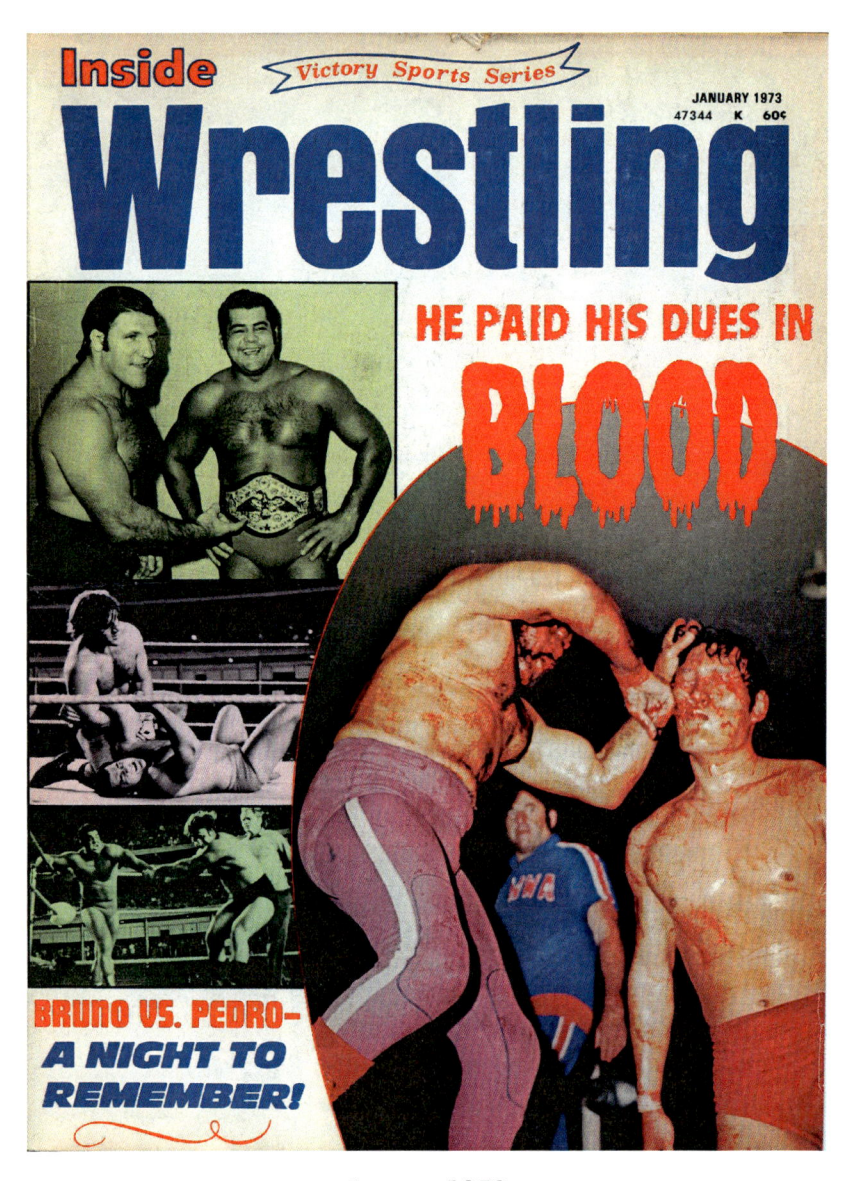

January 1973

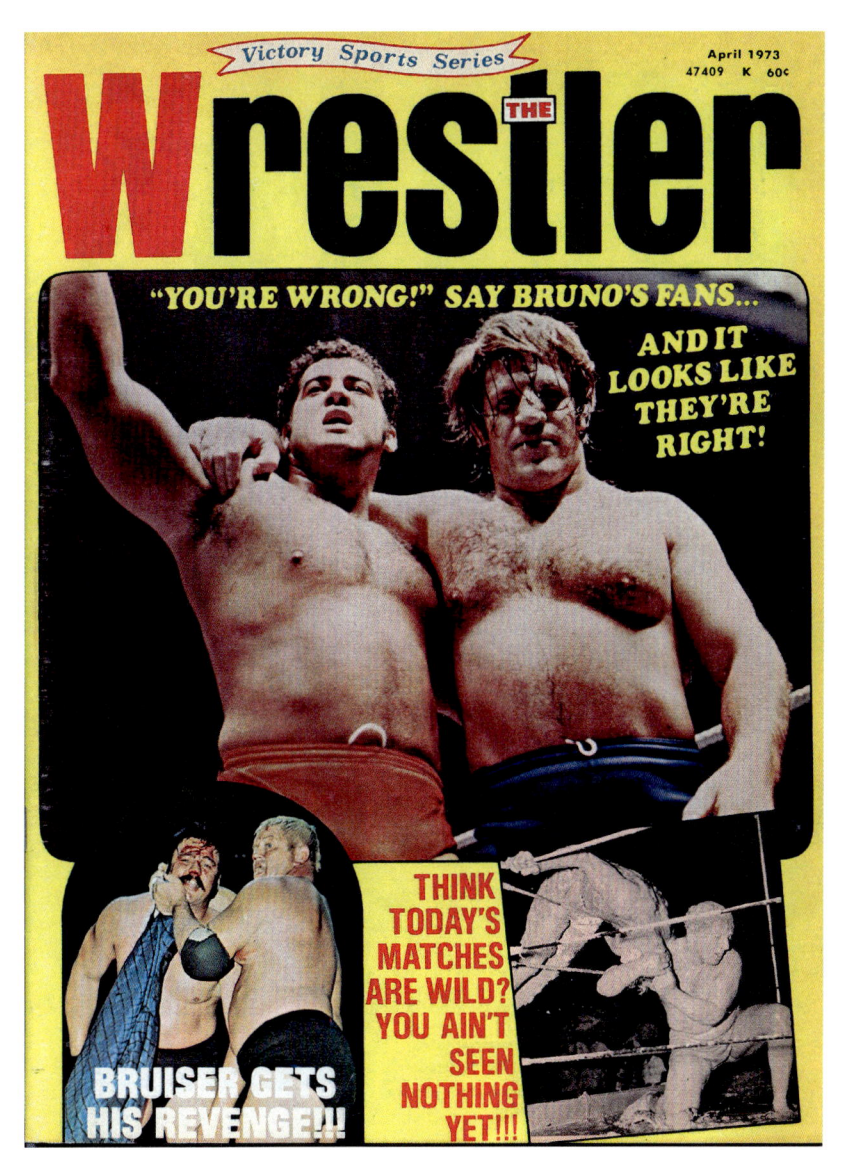

THE AUTOBIOGRAPHY OF WRESTLING'S LIVING LEGEND

June 1973

September 1973

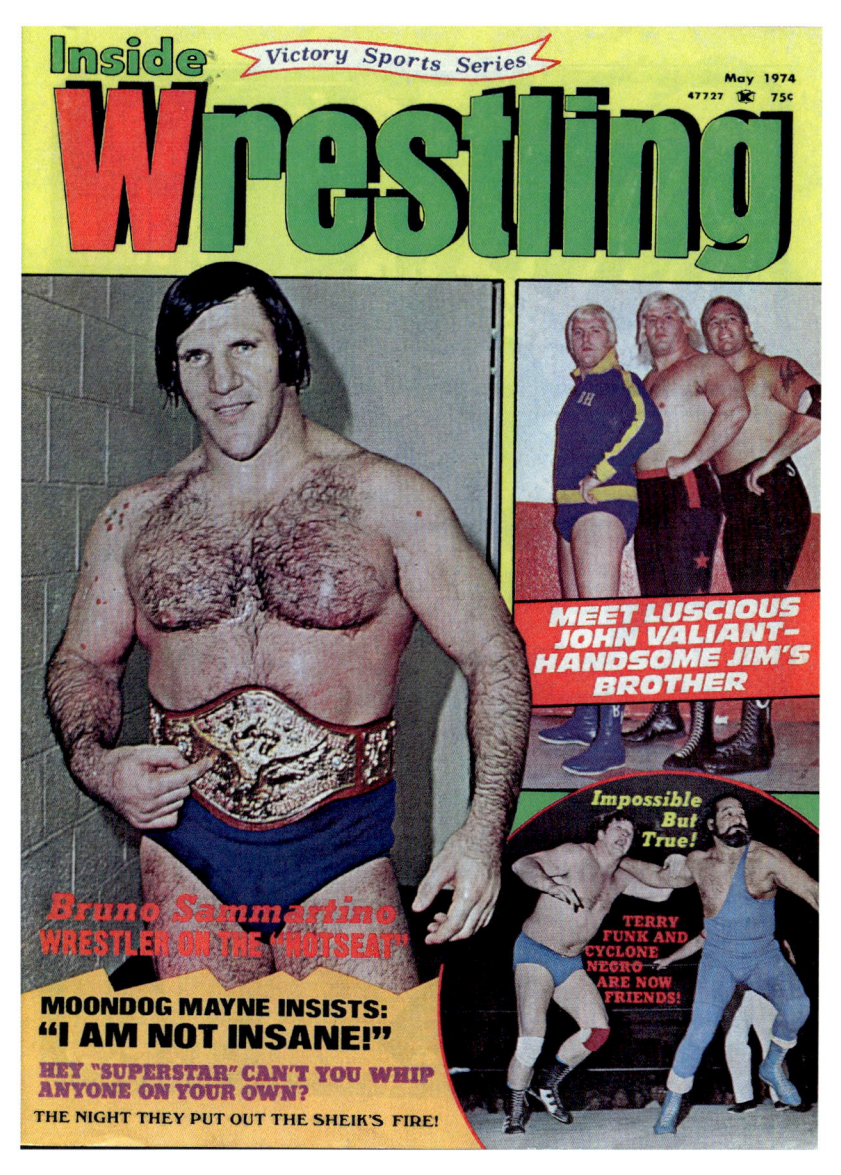

THE AUTOBIOGRAPHY OF WRESTLING'S LIVING LEGEND

May 1974

BRUNO SAMMARTINO

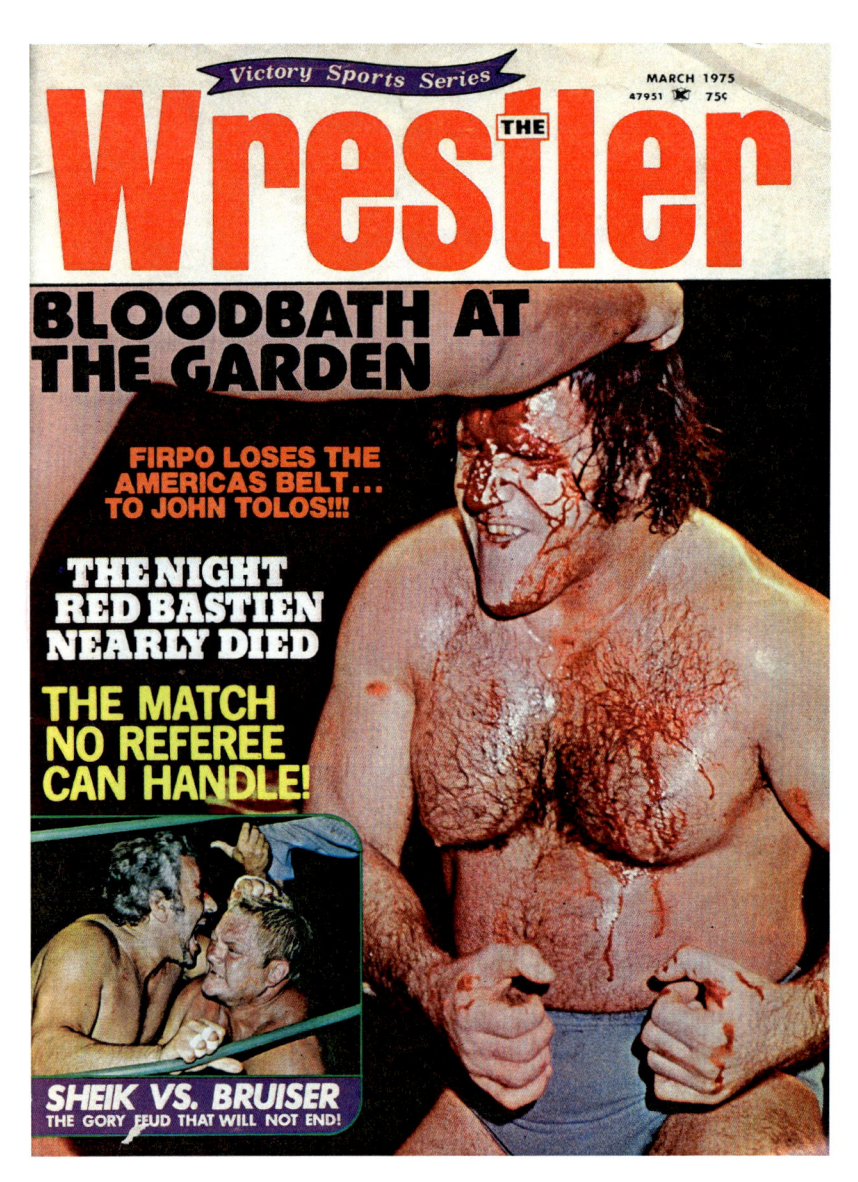

March 1975

THE AUTOBIOGRAPHY OF WRESTLING'S LIVING LEGEND

August 1975

BRUNO SAMMARTINO

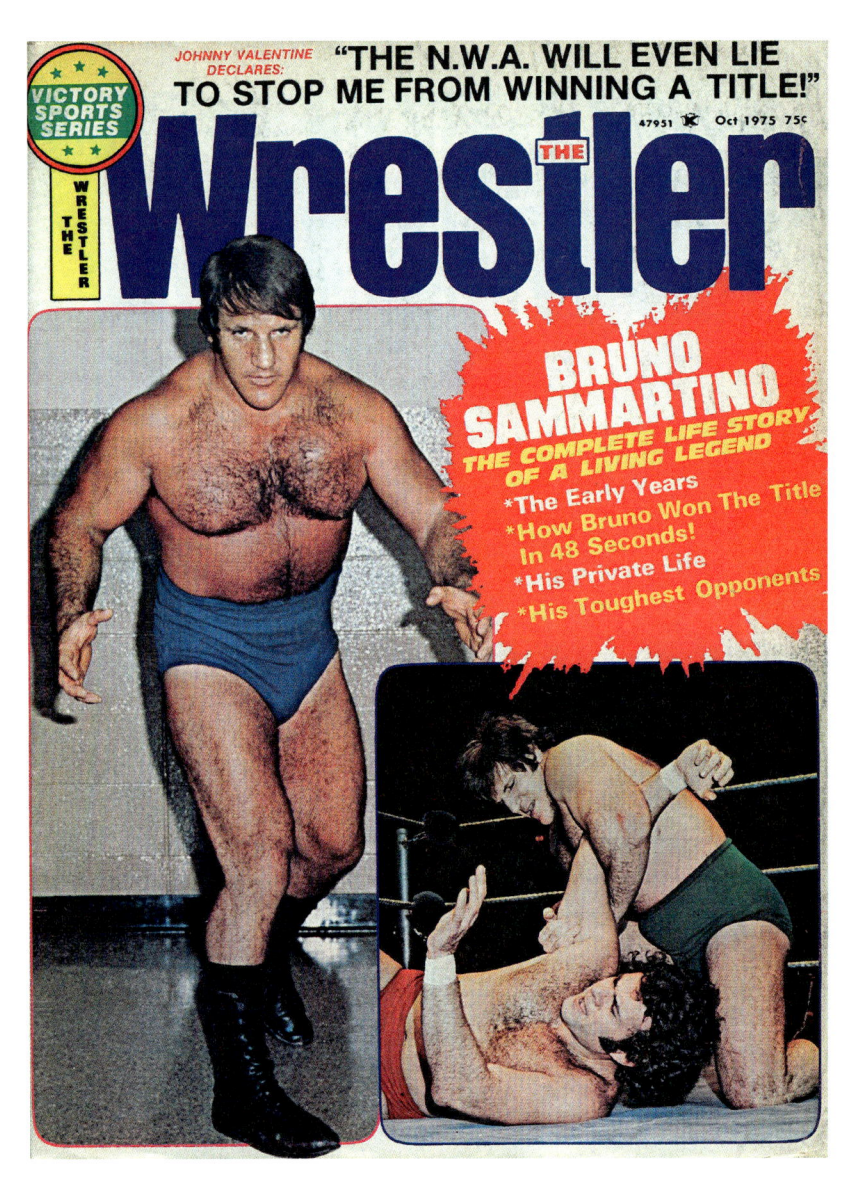

October 1975

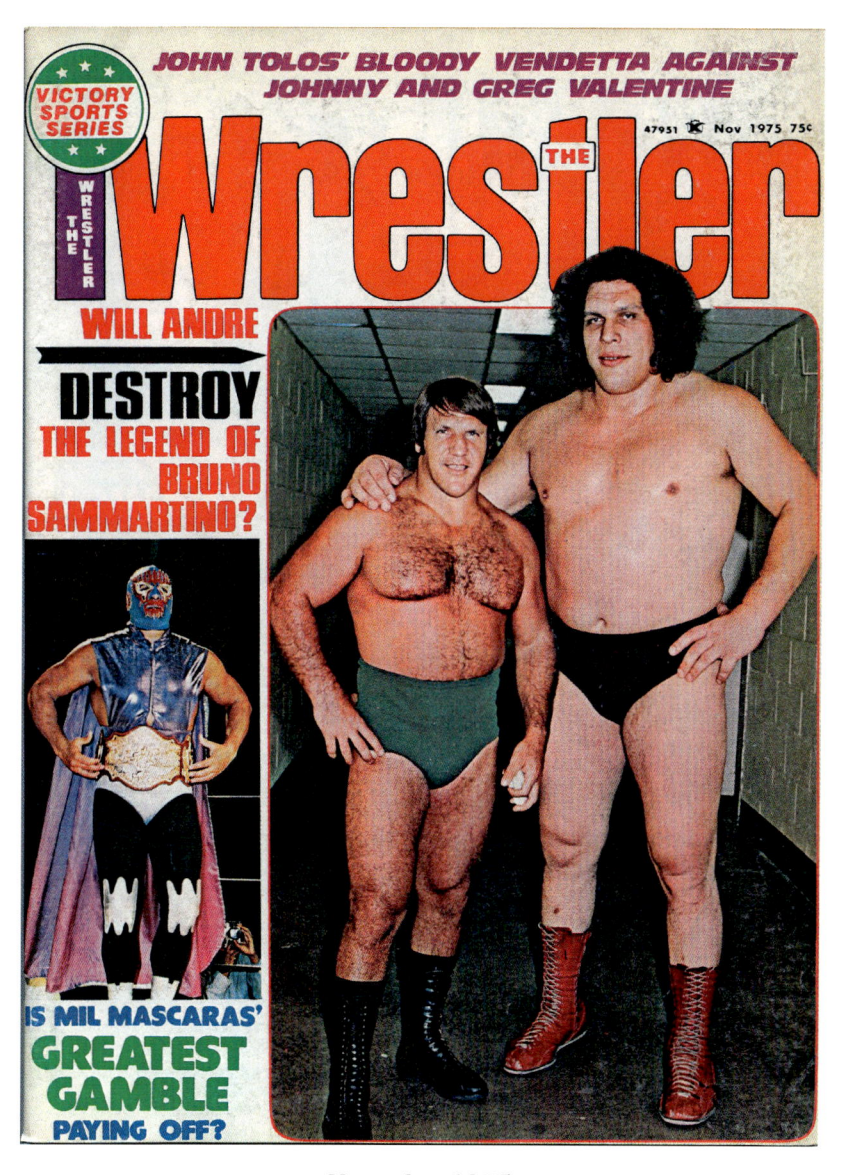

THE AUTOBIOGRAPHY OF WRESTLING'S LIVING LEGEND

November 1975

BRUNO SAMMARTINO

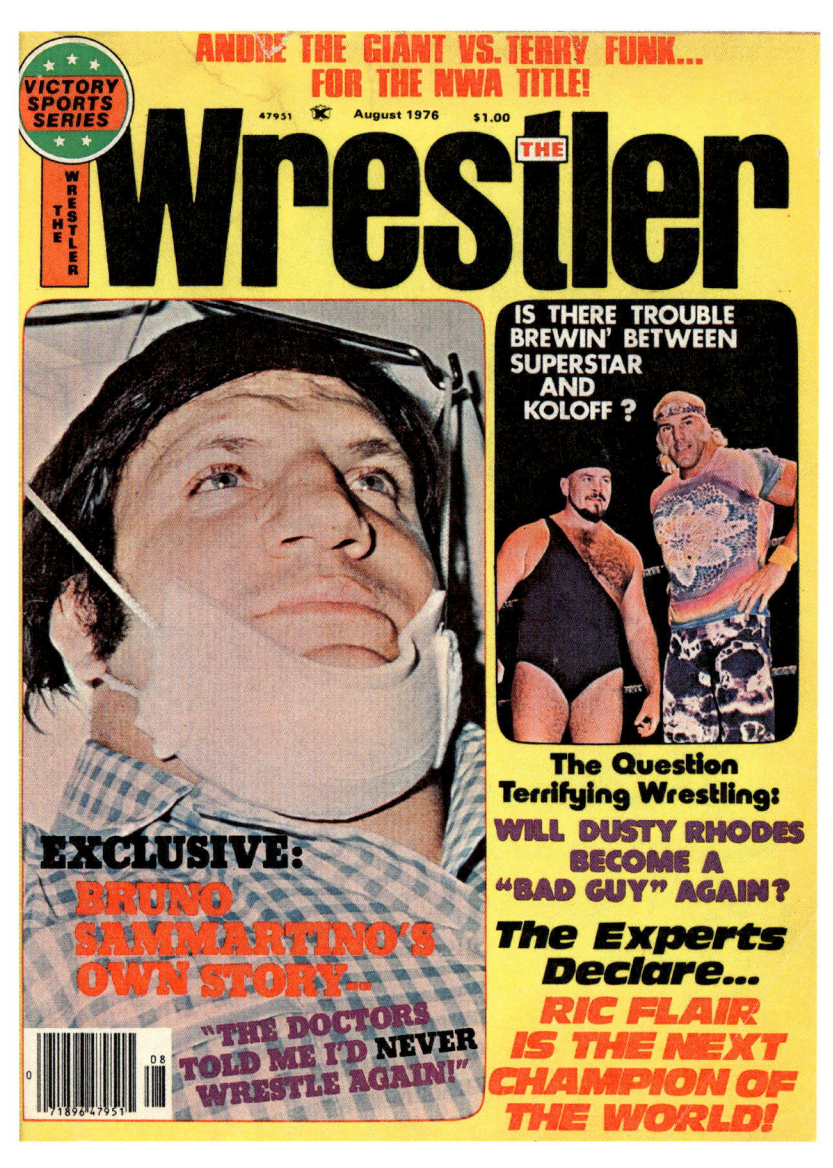

August 1976

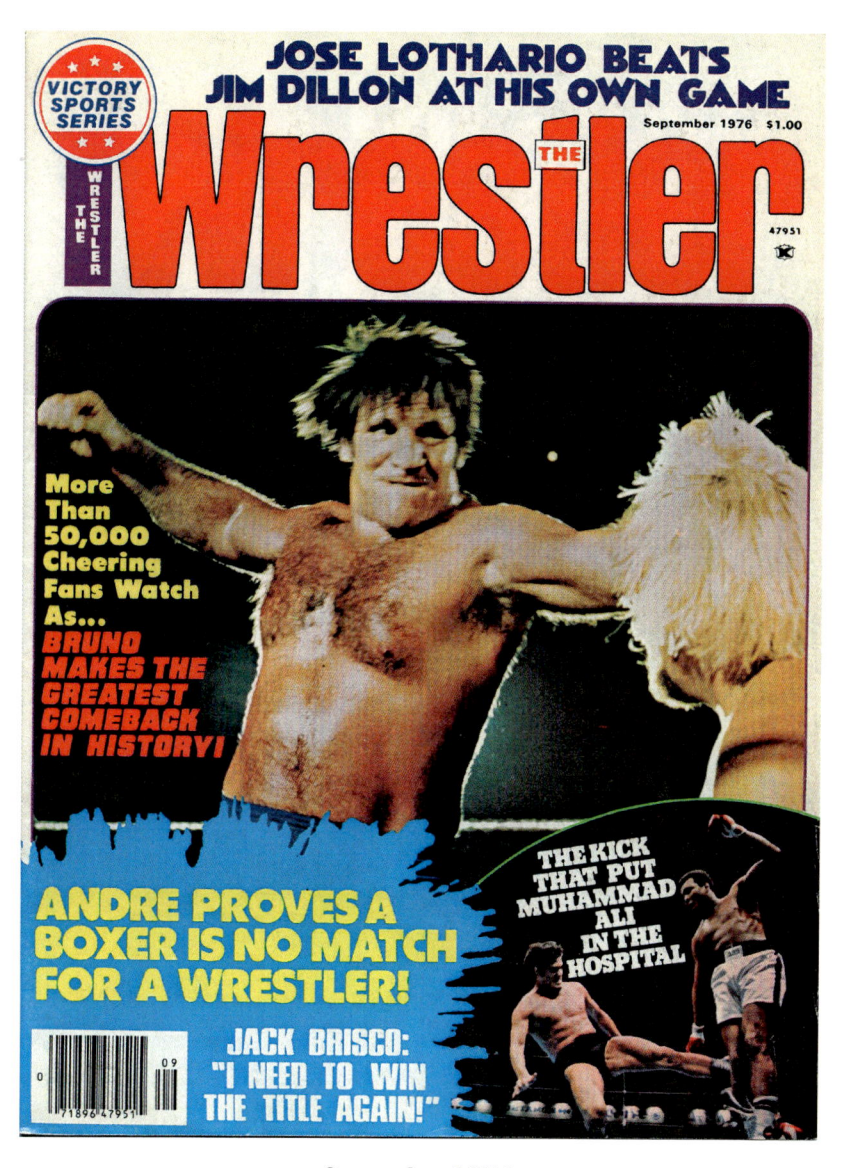

THE AUTOBIOGRAPHY OF WRESTLING'S LIVING LEGEND

September 1976

BRUNO SAMMARTINO

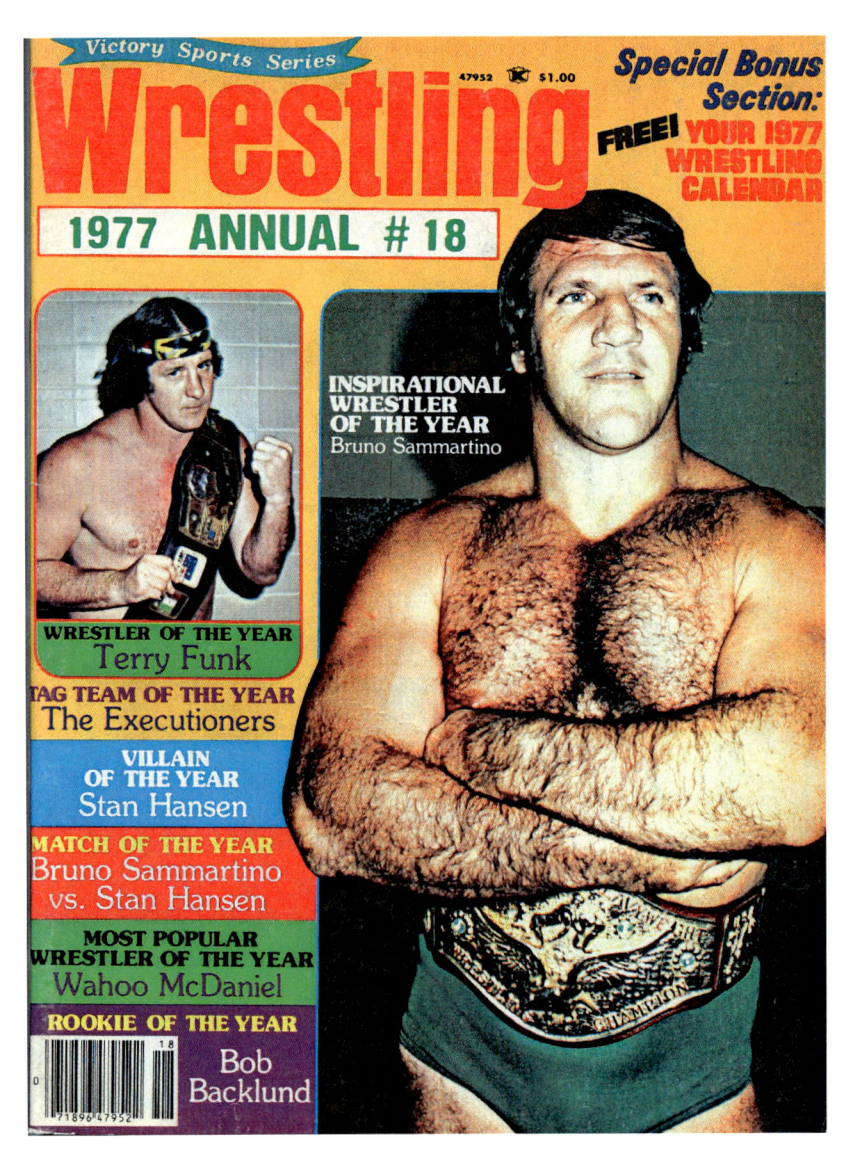

Annual 1977

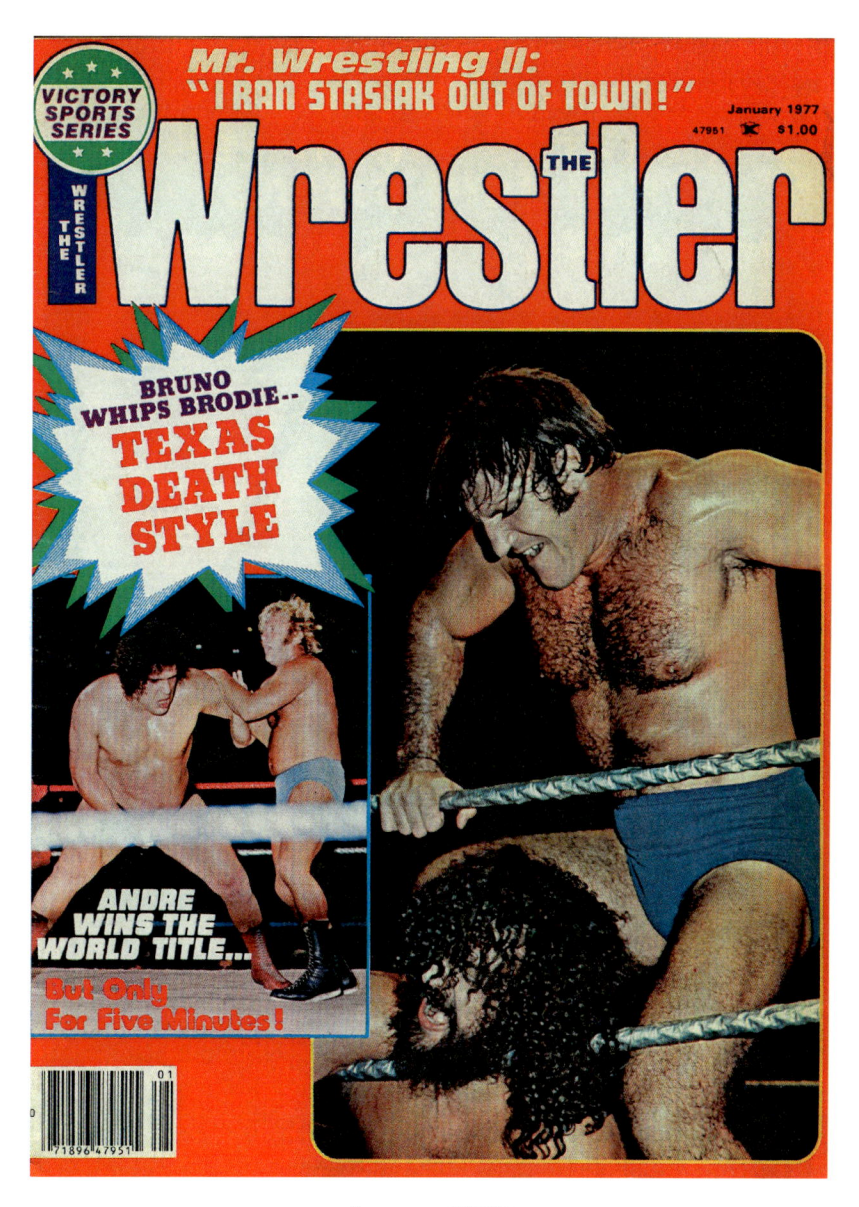

THE AUTOBIOGRAPHY OF WRESTLING'S LIVING LEGEND

January 1977

BRUNO SAMMARTINO

July 1977

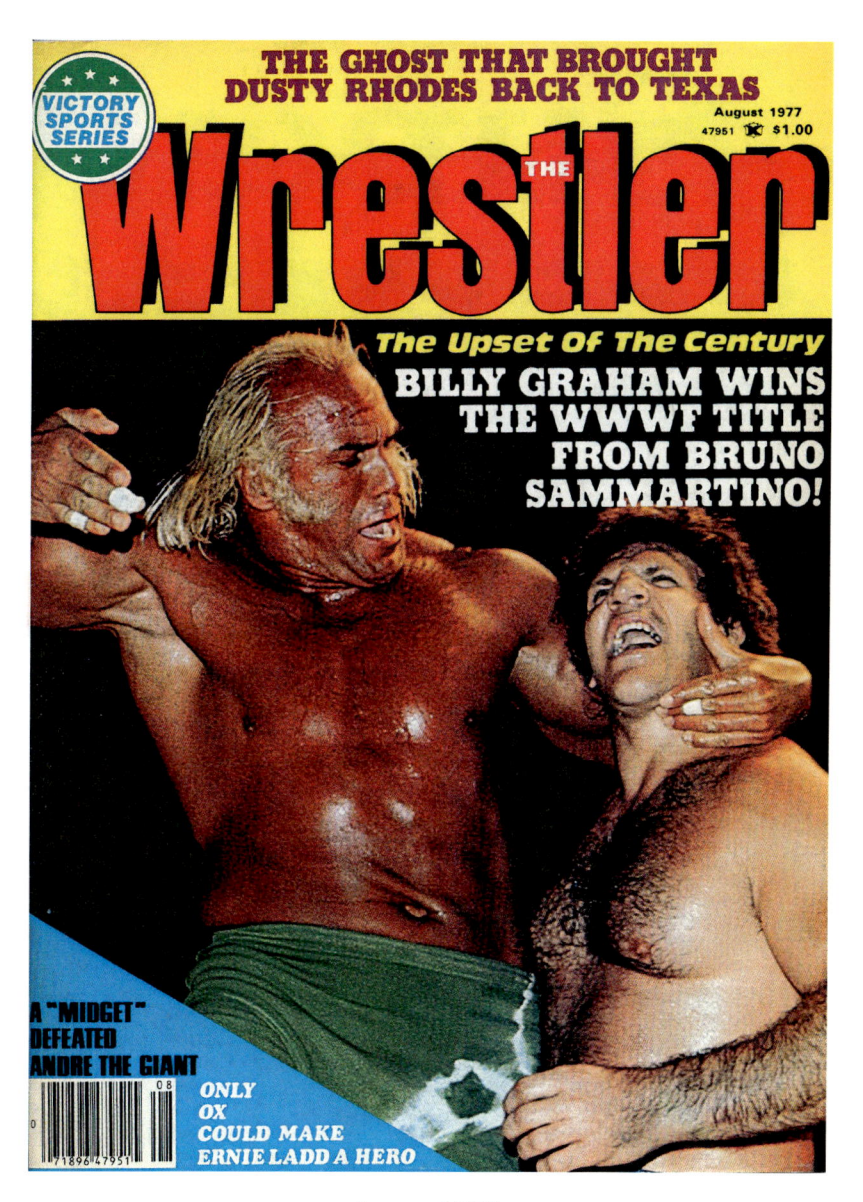

THE AUTOBIOGRAPHY OF WRESTLING'S LIVING LEGEND

August 1977

BRUNO SAMMARTINO

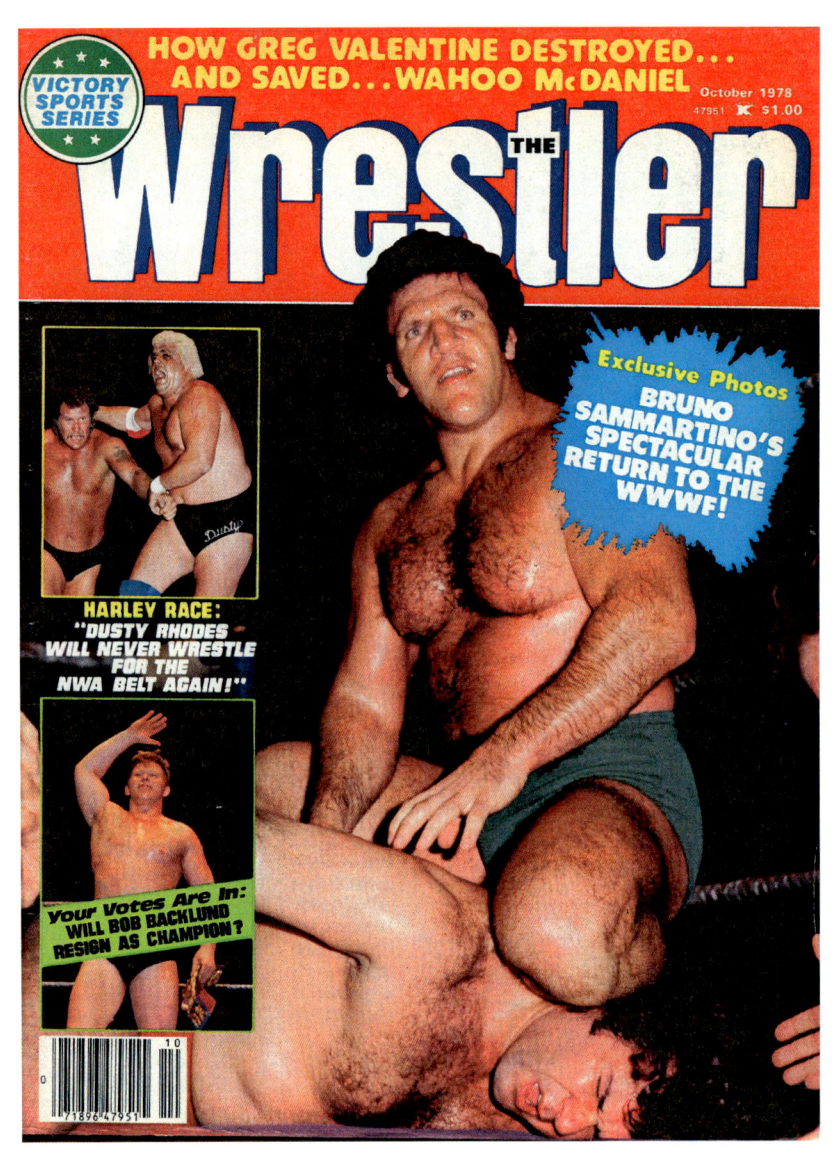

October 1978

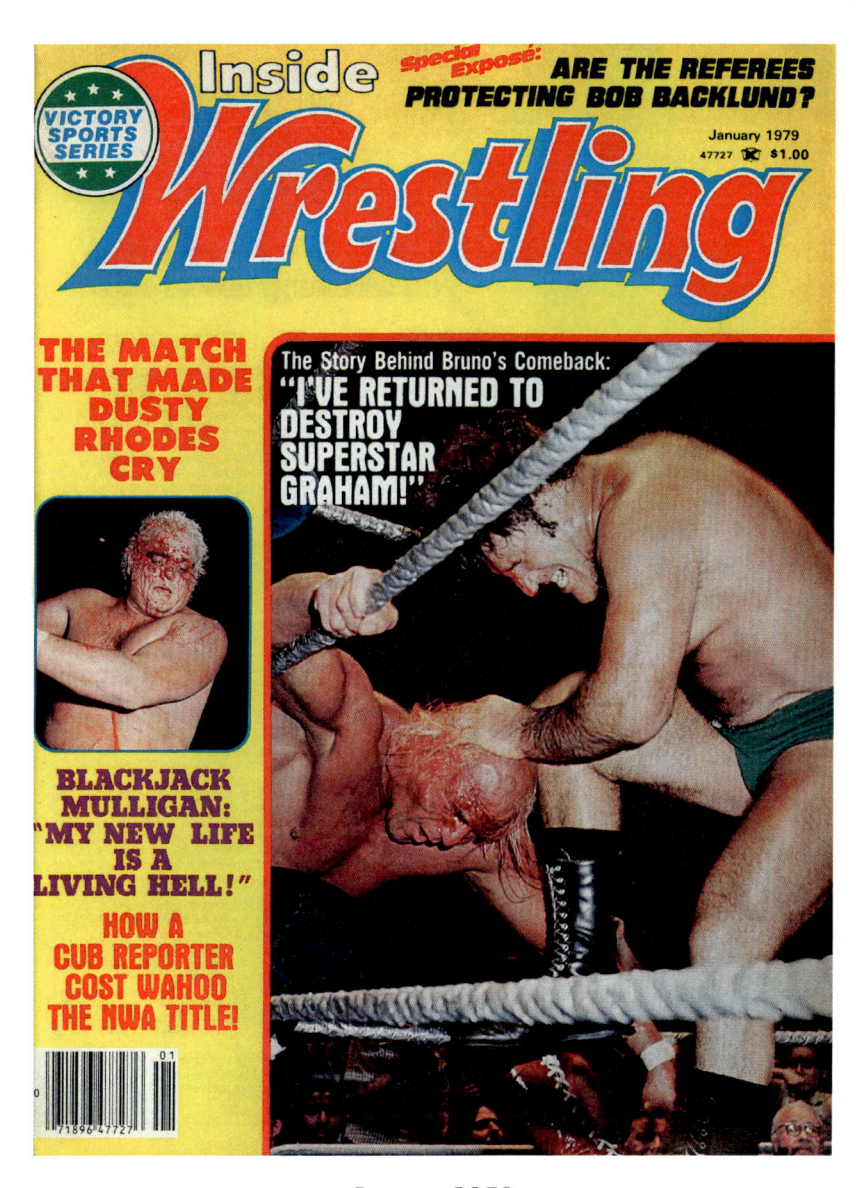

THE AUTOBIOGRAPHY OF WRESTLING'S LIVING LEGEND

January 1979

BRUNO SAMMARTINO

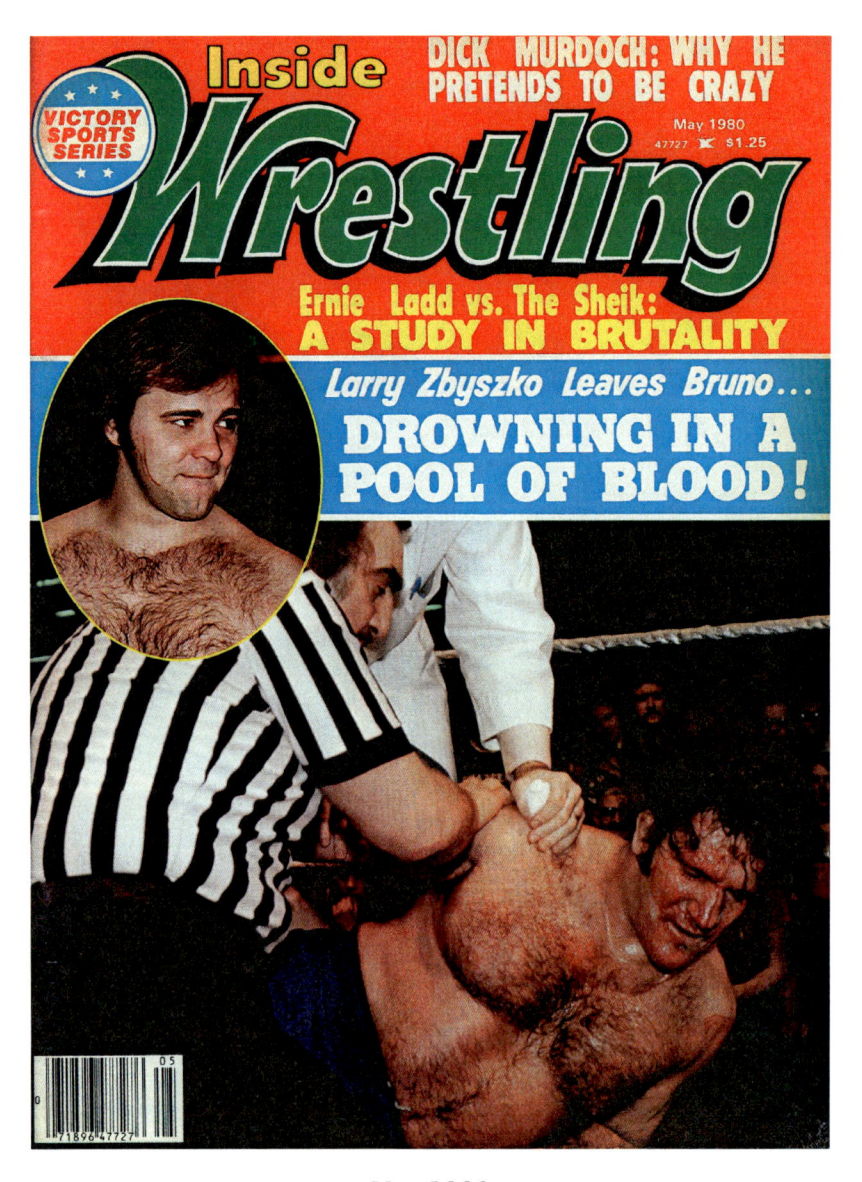

May 1980

THE AUTOBIOGRAPHY OF WRESTLING'S LIVING LEGEND

August 1980

BRUNO SAMMARTINO

Fall 1980

THE AUTOBIOGRAPHY OF WRESTLING'S LIVING LEGEND

September 1983

BRUNO SAMMARTINO

Spring 1998

THE AUTOBIOGRAPHY OF WRESTLING'S LIVING LEGEND

The Ten-Bell Salute

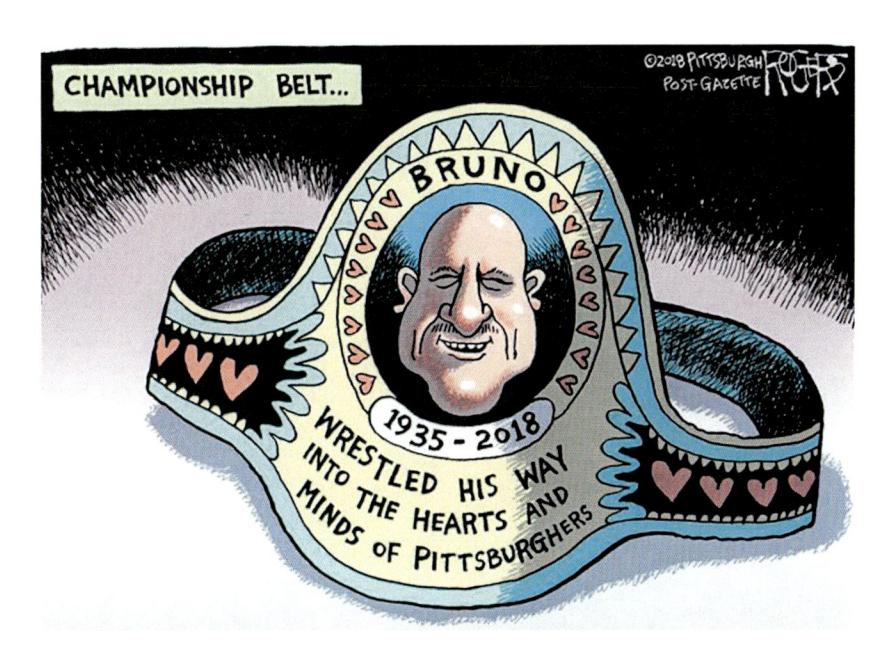

Made in United States
North Haven, CT
12 May 2023

36512041R00316